FEMINIST MESSAGES

Publications of the American Folklore Society
NEW SERIES
General Editor, Patrick B. Mullen

FEMINIST MESSAGES

CODING IN WOMEN'S FOLK CULTURE

Edited by
JOAN NEWLON RADNER

University of Illinois Press
Urbana and Chicago

FIRST PAPERBACK EDITION, 1993

© 1993 by the Board of Trustees of the University of Illinois

Susan Gordon's version of "The Handless Maiden"
© 1988 by Susan Gordon.
Manufactured in the United States of America
P 8 7 6 5 4

This book is printed on acid-free paper.

Library of Congress Cataloging-in-Publication Data
Feminist messages : coding in women's folk culture / edited by Joan Newlon
  Radner.
      p. cm.—(Publications of the American Folklore Society. New series)
  Includes bibliographical references.
  ISBN 0-252-06267-1 (pbk. : alk. paper)
  ISBN 978-0-252-06267-4 (pbk. : alk. paper)
  1. Women—Folklore. 2. Feminism. I. Radner, Joan Newlon.
II. Series: Publications of the American Folklore Society. New series
(Unnumbered)
GR470.F46 1993   92-15701
398'.082—dc20   CIP

CONTENTS

Preface   vii

Acknowledgments   xv

Strategies of Coding in Women's Cultures   1
Joan N. Radner and Susan S. Lanser

PART 1: Women in the Patriarchal Household   31

Burning Dinners: Feminist Subversions
of Domesticity   *Susan S. Lanser*   36

Wishful Willful Wily Women: Verbal
Strategies for Female Success in
the Child Ballads   *Polly Stewart*   54

PART 2: Women Together   75

Mothers' Double Talk
Janet L. Langlois   80

"She Really Wanted to Be Her Own
Woman": Scandalous Sunbonnet Sue
Linda Pershing   98

"Awful Real": Dolls and Development
in Rangeley, Maine
Margaret R. Yocom   126

PART 3: Women in the Larger Community   155

More in Anger than in Sorrow: Irish
Women's Lament Poetry
Angela Bourke   160

"How They Knew": Women's Talk about
Healing on Kodiak Island, Alaska
Joanne B. Mulcahy   183

"We're More than a Novelty, Boys":
Strategies of Female Rappers in the Rap
Music Tradition   *Cheryl L. Keyes*   203

"At Home, No Womens Are Storytellers":
Potteries, Stories, and Politics in
Cochiti Pueblo   *Barbara A. Babcock*   221

PART 4: Women Interpreting the Stories They Tell   249

The Powers of the Handless Maiden
Susan Gordon   252

Burning Brightly: New Light from an
Old Tale   *Kay F. Stone*   289

Notes on the Contributors   307

PREFACE

In the resistance movement in Chile, poor women adapt their traditional needlework skills to produce *arpilleras,* appliqué and patchwork pictures representing the lives of working-class Chileans since the military coup of 1973. Sold internationally to raise money, the *arpilleras* depict not only traditional rural life but also urban shanty-towns and soup kitchens, military brutality, and the anguish of the families of the disappeared. The women have used protective codes in their handiwork, representing the members of the junta as vultures among doves or as clowns in a sinister circus, or portraying the Andes in the background as "the symbol of grandeur and promise against which to measure the cramped, grinding existence imposed by the present-day social system."[1] This documentation of injustice would be dangerous if the military authorities knew how to read the symbols of folk needlework, but they have not been trained to attend to the lives or arts of women: "The women of the shanty-towns do not measure up to their idea of artist, nor do the little 'landscapes,' 'street scenes' and 'interiors' excite their Pavlovian response to the clichés of left agitation."[2]

Such acts of coding—covert expressions of disturbing or subversive ideas—are a common phenomenon in the lives of women, who have so often been dominated, silenced, and marginalized by men. Like the *arpilleristas,* women of many cultures have encoded messages crucial to them under the cover of female traditions that receive little male scrutiny. The essays in this book argue that the "texts" of women's folklore—the texts of their oral performances, of their material creations, and of the routines of their daily lives—may communicate a variety of messages to different segments of their audiences. Some of the coding that enables this selective communication may be deliberate and conscious; some is unconscious. The essential ambiguity of coded acts protects women from potentially dangerous responses from those who might find their statements disturbing.

The process of coding is not limited to folklore, of course. The introductory essay, "Strategies of Coding in Women's Cultures," proposes an interpretive tool for all women's expressive culture, beyond the boundaries of genre and medium, from folk expressions to literature to "fine" arts. The fields of women's studies and folklore have not yet paid enough attention to each other, and this book, in representing a fairly broad range of folk groups[3] and folklore genres, contributes to the dialogue between the disciplines.

Folklorists study and interpret the expressive creations—stories, games, songs, crafts, foodways, rituals—that people make in and of their everyday lives. They thus attend to the aesthetic choices people make, their ways of bringing beauty and entertainment into their daily occupations and of ritualizing their identities. They focus on the art *in* the everyday: the saving games that make the repetitious drudgery of house or factory work bearable; the clever stories that buffer with laughter pent-up anger at the boss or husband; the expertise of stitchery or step dance or carpentry that evoke sustaining admiration and empathy from those in the know. The concerns of folklorists span the range of creative traditions, across boundaries of class, race, and age, from birth to death, in the home, in the community, on the job. Emphasizing field interviews and observation, folklorists often make audible the voices of those not otherwise heard or publicized beyond their own communities.

Feminist folklorists, therefore, have much to offer feminist scholars in other fields. Folklore study, concerned with a broad range of traditional artistic creation including even the most domestic, private, and ephemeral cultural expressions of women, augments with humanistic insights the more usual sociological analyses of women's daily lives. In recent years, the study of women's folk aesthetics has significantly intensified, and female genres that have in the past been undervalued, such as personal narratives, fabric arts, and cooking, have come to new prominence.[4] The emphasis in contemporary folkloristics is broadly cultural: folklorists study not "texts" in isolation but creations rooted in specific cultural contexts and in the needs, values, and dynamics of individual close groups.[5] Much analysis focuses on performance and process. Barbara A. Babcock proposes that "the ephemerality of much women's art, which facilitates its being both trivialized and ignored," bespeaks the existence of a distinctive, "process-centered female aesthetic."[6] Susan Kalčik has suggested that women in the American mainstream are more likely than men to collaborate as a group in the telling of stories, rather than to take turns in solo narratives.[7] Studying the performance of gender identity in festival, Beverly J. Stoeltje has traced the transformations over time of local gender roles, represented in the changing functions of women as "hostess" and "cowgirl sponsors" in the Cowboy Reunion, a Texas regional celebration.[8]

In its rooted aversion to essentialism, the study of folklore also has much to offer feminist theory across the disciplines. Folklorists are trained to see groups from the inside, to honor their individual and particular worldviews, creative styles, and coping strategies; folklore methodology urges impartial observation and stresses description and analysis of the systems within a folk group, respecting the way the group sees and understands itself. But this cultivated attentiveness to the small group as a functioning, creative organism can divert field researchers from the need for theory that stands outside the system and evaluates it; dialogue with feminist theorists across the disciplines thus maintains a useful tension for folklorists, offering them models of understanding social relations as (gendered) relationships of power, constructed both within the folk group and also—crucially—in the larger surrounding culture.

Although women researchers have been prominent in the field of folklore since its beginnings,[9] the discipline has shared the patriarchal and nationalist biases of the related fields of anthropology and literary study, also founded in the eighteenth and nineteenth centuries.[10] The development of feminist folklore studies in recent decades has proceeded in characteristic stages, from the recuperation of women's traditions, to their political interpretation, to the development of theory—as is clear from some of the major landmarks in the field. Claire R. Farrer, editor of the groundbreaking 1975 *Journal of American Folklore* symposium issue on "Women and Folklore," sought to distinguish and foreground women's images and genres and felt the need to legitimize this study, to "convince even the most skeptical that the art [of women] is not only alive and well but also that it has a history as well as a future."[11] A decade later Rosan A. Jordan and Susan J. Kalčik, the editors of *Women's Folklore, Women's Culture,* still perceived a "lopsided orientation in folklore scholarship" and extended the goal in a more explicitly political direction, stressing in that collection women's "power" and "control . . . despite male dominance of one sort or another" and calling on folklorists to move beyond their historical pattern of "describ[ing] women as men see (or don't see) them."[12]

As late as 1986, Rosan A. Jordan and F. A. de Caro could comment that "there has been little folkloristic work directly addressing feminist theoretical issues."[13] Recently, however, this lack has begun to be corrected. We owe the enthusiastic reception of the Folklore and Feminism Day, which was incorporated into the American Folklore Society's annual meeting in Baltimore in October 1986, to the labors of many feminist folklorists who have changed the profession's perception of its own scope, resources, and responsibilities. To date, two published collections of papers from that day have appeared, and at least one other is in process.[14] The call for papers for the 1986 event announced a "Feminist Retrospective on Folklore and Folkloristics," asking for "scholarship produced with new paradigms," aiming "to introduce feminist theory and criticism into the scholarly study of folklore and to bring folklore scholarship to bear on feminist theory."[15]

The present volume's introductory essay, "Strategies of Coding in Women's Cultures," was first conceived as a joint paper in response to that call for disciplinary reciprocity. Susan Lanser and I discussed the meeting places between our respective fields of literature and folklore; settling on coding as our topic, we aimed to evolve theory that would cross cultures and span the forms, media, and arenas of women's artistic creations, from folksongs to novels, quilts to oils, homes to business offices. Our essay explores the nature of coded acts and the complexity of their interpretation and proposes a provisional typology of coding strategies that seem common in various women's cultures. Several of the other essays in this collection had their beginnings in presentations at the 1987 annual meeting of the American Folklore Society in Albuquerque, principally in two related panels entitled "Feminist Messages" that were designed to extend the investigation of women's coding into specific areas of oral and material folk culture. All the studies in this book—though they do not necessarily derive their methods or approaches from the lead essay—are concerned with the interpretation of strategic communication in women's folklore. These essays cover a broad range of subjects, representing contemporary feminist folklore scholarship on women's creations of the past as well as the present and on various (but chiefly North American, heterosexual) women's communities. Although some individual pieces in the collection make reference to lesbian communities and cultures, folklore research has yet to produce studies focused on coding among lesbians.

The first section, "Women in the Patriarchal Household," is concerned primarily with women's domestic culture. Essays about the politics of incompetence and about the Anglo-American ballad-singing tradition illustrate that because women's freedom in their homes—their traditional domain—is usually hedged by the intimate proximity of men and by the obligation to serve them, women's home folklore is very likely to encode messages of protest. The essays in the second section, "Women Together," highlight the safety and comfort (but sometimes self-protective limitation) of communication in women's groups, whose folk creations encode many of the ideas that women friends share. Women issue practical cautions, but imply deeper dilemmas, as they tell legends about inept mothers who cause the deaths of their children. Quilters who produce a parody quilt "as a joke" also convey their own values and principles; women knitting doll clothes encode in them their protest against both male dominance and economic development in their Maine town.

The third section, "Women in the Larger Community," focuses on some ways in which women use coding to express their points of view outside the relative safety of home and women's groups, while performing ritual roles (lamenting the dead in Ireland), maintaining traditional functions and values despite societal changes (healing on Kodiak Island, Alaska), and choosing to enter territory normally reserved to men (African-American women gaining a foothold in the rap music industry; Pueblo women making and marketing *Storyteller* potteries that represent men's ritual roles). In the final and reflexive section, "Women Interpreting the Stories They Tell," two contemporary storytellers have written about their development and performance of traditional tales and about the messages—feminist and otherwise—they feel they are conveying to audiences. They speak of their creations in relation to their lives and thus join several other authors in the book in the feminist project of integrating the personal and the professional.

It seems appropriate that this collection ends with women's voices unmediated, interpreting their own work. Most of the time, as those of us who are folklorists write about our fieldwork, we are interpreting the statements—and even the lives—of other women.[16] Essential as it is for us to try to understand and honor their creations, their work and its most important meanings are finally their own. Let me close this preface, then, with the words of one of the *arpilleristas:*

There's one *arpillera* I'll never forget. I made it at the end of 1975.

"El Gordo" [her husband] had lung trouble, in fact he had cancer and he had to go to hospital. I was left with the kids. My boy, who was about ten then, asked for something to eat and we just had nothing to give him.

It was such a big problem for me, I felt impotent, I didn't know what to do. I decided to vent my feelings by making an *arpillera*. I made a road which went up into the mountains and had no end, then I made a sun which I gazed at and it gave me strength. This sun I made from pure red wool.

When I tried to sell it I couldn't. How could I sell this *arpillera* which was so much "me"? How was I going to do business with my own life?[17]

Notes

1. Guy Brett, *Through Our Own Eyes: Popular Art and Modern History* (Philadelphia: New Society Publishers, 1987), 47.

2. Ibid., 15. For comparison with Hmong refugee textile arts, see Marsha MacDowell, "Textiles of Refugee Women: New Ways with Old Traditions," in *Needlework of New American Women: New Threads in the Fabric of American Culture,* ed. Amy Skillman and Ann Rynearson (St. Louis: International Institute of Metropolitan St. Louis, 1989), 25–28; and MacDowell, *Stories in Thread: Hmong Pictorial Embroidery* (East Lansing: Michigan State University Museum, 1989).

3. For a discussion of the concept of *folk group*—"any group of people who share informal communal contacts that become the basis for expressive, culture-based communications"—see Barre Toelken, *The Dynamics of Folklore* (Boston: Houghton Mifflin, 1979), 49–91.

4. Several helpful bibliographies on women's folklore have recently appeared. Rosan A. Jordan and F. A. de Caro, "Women and the Study of Folklore," *Signs* 11, no. 3 (1986): 500–518, cover primarily verbal art; F. A. de Caro, *Women and Folklore: A Bibliographical Survey* (Westport, Conn.: Greenwood Press, 1983), covers a broader range of material. *Folklore Women's Communication,* a periodical published by the Women's Section of the American Folklore Society, has issued a bibliography of articles relating to women published in the first century (1888–1988) of the *Journal of American Folklore:* "Women: A Selected Bibliography," *Folklore Women's Communication,* no. 44–45 (October 1988): 3–48. Well annotated is Patricia E. Sawin's "Ethnicity and Women's Status: An Exploratory Bibliography," *Folklore Forum* 21, no. 2 (1988): 114–65.

5. For discussion of these basic concepts, see, for instance, Dan Ben-Amos, "Toward a Definition of Folklore in Context," *Journal of American Folklore* 84, no. 331 (1971): 3–15; Richard Bauman, "The Field Study of Folklore in Context," in *The Handbook of American Folklore,* ed. Richard M. Dorson (Bloomington: Indiana University Press, 1983), 362–68; and Toelken, *The Dynamics of Folklore.*

6. "Taking Liberties, Writing from the Margins, and Doing It with a Difference," *Journal of American Folklore* 100, no. 398 (1987): 392.

7. "'... like Ann's gynecologist or the time I was almost raped': Personal

Narratives in Women's Rap Groups," *Journal of American Folklore* 88, no. 347 (1975): 3–11.

8. "Gender Representation in Performance: The Cowgirl and the Hostess," *Journal of Folklore Research* 25, no. 3 (1988): 219–41.

9. The Women's Section of the American Folklore Society is working to recover the histories of women folklorists in the early years of the discipline and is also conducting a contemporary oral history project, Women in Folklore.

10. See Beverly J. Stoeltje's discussion, "Introduction: Feminist Revisions," *Journal of Folklore Research* 25, no. 3 (1988): 141–53.

11. "Women and Folklore: Images and Genres," *Journal of American Folklore* 88, no. 347 (1975): xv. This issue of *JAF*, without the helpful "A Response to the Symposium" by Polly Stewart, was reprinted as *Women and Folklore,* ed. Claire R. Farrer (Austin: University of Texas Press, 1975). Also notable is the important collection of articles on "Women as Verbal Artists," edited by Marta Weigle, *Frontiers* 3, no. 3 (Fall 1978): 1–38.

12. (Philadelphia: University of Pennsylvania Press, 1985), ix, xii, xi.

13. "Women and the Study of Folklore," 502.

14. A selection was printed in the centennial volume of *Journal of American Folklore* 100, no. 398 (1987); and three papers appeared in a special issue on "Feminist Revisions in Folklore Studies," edited by Beverly J. Stoeltje, *Journal of Folklore Research* 25, no. 3 (1988).

15. *American Folklore Society Newsletter* 15, no. 1 (1986): 8.

16. Among recent studies of the political implications of folklore fieldwork, see Debora Kodish, "Absent Gender, Silent Encounter," *Journal of American Folklore* 100, no. 398 (1987): 573–78; and the special issue on "Folklore Fieldwork: Sex, Sexuality, and Gender," *Southern Folklore* 47, no. 1 (1990).

17. Brett, *Through Our Own Eyes,* 32–34.

ACKNOWLEDGMENTS

Many have preceded us in the study of folklore from a feminist perspective; the essays in this book are built on the foundation of other scholars' work. In addition, the writers in *Feminist Messages,* individually and collectively, have been inspired and encouraged in this project by our colleagues in the Women's Section of the American Folklore Society.

Painstaking readers have guided me along the way. Marta Weigle read the manuscript twice and made sound demands; Glynis Carr recommended significant revisions, as did Pat Mullen, reading for the Publications of the American Folklore Society Series. From beginning to end, Judith McCulloh of the University of Illinois Press has been a fountain of encouragement, honest assessment, and practical aid. Numerous colleagues and students have helped shape *Feminist Messages* and its individual essays and have particularly tested the introductory essay, "Strategies of Coding in Women's Cultures."

In conceiving and bringing together this book, however, I have been principally aided by its other authors, many of whom gathered to create the first "Feminist Messages" panels at the 1987 annual meeting of the American Folklore Society in Albuquerque. Throughout this project's long development, the contributors have maintained our goal of creating a focused symposium on women's strategic communication. Busy people all, they have been generous with time, labor, and ideas.

I thank especially Susan S. Lanser, who has collaborated, critiqued, heartened, and kept me sane.

FEMINIST MESSAGES

Strategies of Coding in Women's Cultures

JOAN N. RADNER & SUSAN S. LANSER

In Susan Glaspell's story "A Jury of Her Peers" (1917), two women read the kitchen of a third woman and come to a series of understandings. There has been a murder in a rural North American community: the miserly John Wright has been strangled in his sleep with a rope, and his wife, Minnie, has been arrested. No motive is known, but Minnie's claim that she simply slept through the murder—in the same bed—is hardly convincing.

The story focuses on the sheriff's wife and the wife of a neighbor, who accompany their husbands to the Wright farm to hunt for clues. While the men tramp upstairs, downstairs, and out to the barn searching in vain for traces of a motive, their wives sit in the accused woman's kitchen. They notice chaotic details: a filthy hand towel; dirty dishes under the sink; a bag half-filled with sugar sitting next to the open sugar bucket; an empty bird cage with a broken door. Observing such disorder, the men scoff that Minnie Wright lacks "the home-making instinct," yet the women see in the kitchen evidence not of slipshod habits but of anguish and lonely despair. Their reading of the signs is confirmed when they take up Minnie's sewing to find that she had been skillfully piecing some Log Cabin quilt squares but that the last square she had worked on is grotesquely missewn.

As the women begin to understand the horror of Minnie's life, they focus on the "crazy sewing" of the quilt block, which one of them quickly begins to repair. "Holding the block made her feel queer, as if the distracted thoughts of the woman who had perhaps turned to it to try and quiet herself were communicating themselves to her."[1] By the time the women find the crucial clue—Minnie Wright's canary, dead, its neck wrung by her cruel husband—they have also recognized the oppressiveness of their own married lives and have become allies in protecting Minnie against the masculine world, which dismisses women's concerns as "worrying over trifles." They conceal the damning evidence, and the investigators return to town without the clues they had gone to find. The men are unable to piece into significant patterns the scraps of Minnie Wright's life and laugh at their wives' interest—at such a *serious* moment—in an activity so trivial as quilting.

The events represented in Glaspell's story, and indeed the women's presumed success in saving Minnie Wright from conviction, depend on two phenomena: the existence of what we will call women's cultures and the ability of women within a particular culture to communicate with one another in code. In using the concept *women's cultures,* we do not mean to suggest that women share a universal set of experiences or any essentially "female" understanding or worldview. Rather, we understand gender itself to be constructed through the social relations of particular communities. We assume, therefore, that women's experiences, material circumstances, and understandings— hence women's identities—vary from culture to culture, community to community, and individual to individual. At the same time, we assume that in many, if not most, societies there is a realm of practice that is primarily or exclusively women's domain, through which women may develop a set of common signifying practices (beliefs, understandings, behaviors, rituals—hence a *culture*) whose meanings are not necessarily accessible to men of the same group. The community Glaspell portrays is characterized by a sharp separation between men's and women's spheres of activity, and it is this sexual difference that allows and encourages the women to constitute an interpretive community.

This separation of spheres does not, however, generate parallel male and female cultures, each of which is inaccessible to the other group, for the two usually exist in a relationship not simply of difference but of dominance. While men in a particular community may be able to articulate both solidarity among their sex and opposition to "women's culture"—for example, by ridiculing the women's "kitchen things" and "trivial" concerns—the women's attitudes and understandings cannot always be openly acknowledged because of their social, economic, and emotional dependence on the goodwill of the men. This also means that women are normally more knowledgeable about the "male" world than men are about the "female," because dominated people need this knowledge to survive. Glaspell's women are aware that "a sheriff's wife is married to the law" and that this law would see no "legitimate" motive for Minnie's crime.

While sexual difference provides the foundation for "women's cultures," then, it is sexual dominance that makes women likely to express themselves, and communicate to other women, through *coded* means. We are not using *code* simply to designate the system of language rules through which communication is possible; in this sense any message is "in code." Rather, we mean a set of signals—words, forms, behaviors, signifiers of some kind—that protect the creator from the consequences of openly expressing particular messages. Coding occurs in the context of complex audiences in which some members may be competent and willing to decode the message, but others are not. In other words, coding presumes an audience in which one group of receivers is "monocultural" and thus assumes that its own interpretation of messages is the only one possible, while the second group, living in two cultures, may recognize a double message—which also requires recognizing that some form of coding has taken place. *Coding,* then, is the expression or transmission of messages potentially accessible to a (bicultural) community under the very eyes of a dominant community for whom these same messages are either inaccessible or inadmissible.[2] In "A Jury of Her Peers," the men are unable even to recognize that there is something to be read, while the women can hardly avoid reading what we are calling *feminist messages*—that is, messages critical of some aspect of women's subordination.

Indeed, the very process of deciphering Minnie's coded kitchen is a process of changing consciousness. Mrs. Peters and Mrs. Hale become active readers of messages encoded into their surroundings that change them and allow them to effect change. The reading process is not circular; the two women do not see feminist messages simply because they are looking for them, for they do not begin as conscious feminists. They read the text of Minnie Wright's kitchen because they understand its signs, and in reading, they learn new messages by which they can reinterpret their own lives as well as hers. They can then begin to assert themselves against the men in ways that have consequences not only in their "own" sphere but in the male (public) sphere as well; they are presumably able to save Minnie Wright at least from death, if not from imprisonment. If the production of coded messages is a sign of oppression and censorship, the deciphering of such messages may be the very process through which liberation becomes possible.

It is in the spirit of identifying such covert feminist messages, within and across cultures and in various genres and mediums, that we offer the concept of *coding* in women's cultures and a provisional typology of coding strategies that seem common in those women's cultures that are known to us. The theoretical framework we will be developing here grew literally out of dialogue between us and thus in some sense between our respective disciplines. It builds on the work of many other feminist scholars not only in folklore and literature but also in linguistics, the arts, and the social sciences; the phenomenon of coding has been recognized (though not, to our knowledge, scrutinized) virtually since feminist theory began.[3] Such scholarship, in turn, is largely indebted to African-American scholars who have studied acts of coding used by slave communities as a crucial means of communication and survival.[4] We are thus adding our voices to a general understanding among feminists, African Americanists, and scholars of other oppressed and suppressed peoples when we state as our first premise that in the creations and performances of dominated cultures, one can often find covert expressions of ideas, beliefs, experiences, feelings, and attitudes that the dominant culture—and perhaps even the dominated group—would find disturbing or threatening if expressed in more overt forms. We further suggest that such coded messages may ultimately help to empower a community and hence to effect change, as they did for Mrs. Hale and Mrs. Peters and through them for Minnie Wright. The recognition of coding—that is, the identification of messages whose feminism is not immediately evident—is a crucial aspect of the reinterpretation of women's lives and cultures and hence of feminist critical consciousness.

Nonetheless, the feminist study of coding raises difficult questions of interpretation and intentionality. How do we know when or even whether something is coded? How do we interpret the code? When is an act or a performance "feminist," even in our broad definition of the term, and who has the right to say so? In confronting some of the theoretical and practical complexities of identifying and interpreting particular acts or texts as coded feminist messages, it is helpful to distinguish among various forms of coding and work our way toward the most complicated form, the implicit coding that will be our main focus of inquiry. In this essay, we are looking particularly at acts of coding that (a) are undertaken in situations of risk, (b) are ambiguous in that neither the fact of coding nor the key to the code has been made explicit, and (c) are therefore indeterminate in intentionality. In other words, we are looking at situations in which both the fact that coding has occurred and the nature of what (if anything) has been encoded are uncertain.

By situations of *risk* we mean those occasions when the code has been adopted to provide safety or freedom rather than simply pleasure or play. Coding may be undertaken for a variety of purposes, not all of them involving real or perceived danger to the encoder or the encoding community. Children or teenagers, for example, may delight in devising expressions or disguised languages (such as "Pig-Latin") that adults cannot understand; adults of a particular ethnic group may switch into the "mother tongue" when children or strangers are around; lovers may devise private terms of address. Such cases involve a "bicultural" context but not necessarily an operant context of dominance; there is thus no need to suppress the fact that coding is taking place, and the revelation of what has been coded might be embarrassing or uncomfortable but not of serious consequence. In the forms of coding with which our strategies are concerned, on the other hand, not only the message but the very fact of coding must be concealed because the operant context seems to hold significant risk.

The kinds of coding in which we are particularly interested are implicit rather than complicit or explicit acts. In what we are calling *complicit coding*, a code has been collectively determined ahead of time and can therefore be adopted by an entire community: passwords and code names are examples of such complicity. In American culture, the most vivid examples of complicit coding come from slave history. Frances Harper's novel *Iola Leroy* (1892), for example, records the "phraseology" African-American slaves invented "to convey in the most unsuspecting manner news to each other from the battlefield. . . . If they wished to announce a victory of the Union army, they said the butter was fresh, or that the fish and eggs were in good condition. If defeat befell them, then the butter and other produce were rancid or stale."[5] In this instance the surface meanings of innocuous everyday discourse conceal the existence of coded behavior; the conversation appears to be entirely about butter and eggs, and presumably any white Southerners listening would have no idea that coding was taking place.

In cases of *explicit coding*, on the other hand, the fact of a code is usually apparent even to those who cannot decipher it. A nineteenth-century Yorkshire woman named Anne Lister kept a diary in which she used an invented code to write about her lesbian relationships. Lister probably never intended anyone to understand the code, though indeed it was "cracked" in the 1980s by a social historian.[6] But anyone reading the diary would know that coding had occurred and hence that there was something to conceal. In situations of great risk, explicit coding is dangerous, for it constitutes an announcement that coding is taking place, and opens the possibility that the code will be cracked by the "wrong" audience.

Sometimes a code is not visibly signaled, but the fact of censorship is sufficiently foregrounded that the possibility of a coding practice becomes evident. In 1832 a letter appeared in the Philadelphia periodical *Atkinson's Casket* that claimed to have been written under the censoring eyes of a husband by a newly married woman to her best friend. Beneath its surface discourse of exaggerated happiness—a discourse filled with hyperbole, repetition, double negatives, and stylistic anomalies—is concealed a tale of marital misery that is decoded by reading every other line of the text.[7] For this letter to have passed by the husband-censor, however, it obviously could not reveal openly that it was coded, let alone provide the key. When a receiver suspects that a covert message is present, the search becomes a search not only for the message but also for the strategies that make the message readable.

Both complicit and explicit acts of coding are manifestly deliberate—unambiguously conscious and intentional in that both the concealed message and the adoption of a code are undertaken knowingly and purposefully. In complicit coding, an unwitting receiver has no idea an act of coding is taking place; in explicit coding, any receiver knows the code exists, even if she or he cannot crack it. For the observer-analyst or scholar, however, there is no question that coding has taken place in both cases.

Coding need not be deliberate, though. Minnie Wright probably did not plan to encode her murderous rage and despair into the chaos of her kitchen and her sewing basket, but she nonetheless left an implicit message that the male investigators could not read accurately and that their wives could hardly miss. The *implicit* kinds of coding with which we will be concerned in this essay are precisely those acts whose very codedness is arguable. Such forms of coding thus raise complex questions about the creator's conscious and subconscious intentions and about the interpretations that may be constructed both by the original receiving community and by outside observer-analysts like ourselves.

The question of intentionality, which complicates all interpretation, is particularly intense in the case of coding because when one identifies a "feminist message," one is attributing a conscious or unconscious political stance to an author, performer, or text.[8] We want first to distinguish intentionality from consciousness: as we conceive intentionality, one can unconsciously intend to send a coded message (as perhaps Minnie Wright does in leaving her kitchen and sewing askew). Such an intention may become conscious in retrospect, as it does for Adrienne Rich when (in the essay "When We Dead Awaken: Writing as Re-Vision") she looks back at some of her earlier poems and reads their formal devices as coding strategies.[9]

But even this distinction between intentionality and consciousness is insufficient, because it relies on the performer's acknowledgement, however belatedly, that a desire to encode exists. The broader understanding of intention that we wish to articulate here is compatible with that of Meir Sternberg, who approaches intention not as a "psychological state consciously or unconsciously translated into words [or other signs]" but as "a shorthand for the structure of meaning and effect supported by the conventions that the text appeals to or devises: for the sense that the language makes in terms of the communicative context as a whole."[10] In other words, given the impossibility (especially with respect to coded performances) of any certainty about an individual's desires, intention must be inferred from the contextual knowledge available, and this knowledge includes an understanding of the conventions for aesthetic production in a given cultural circumstance. By locating meaning in the "communicative context," Sternberg shifts the site of intention from the author to the receiving community. Like Sternberg, we acknowledge all interpretation to be uncertain, but we assume that plausible, if provisional, meanings can be inferred through an understanding of the situation in which they have been produced. As we are using *intentionality,* then, we mean assumptions inferable from the performance-in-context, which includes what we know of the performer and her circumstances but does not rely on the performer's own word for its guarantee.

This insistence on intention-as-contextually-realized still leaves us with troubling questions. What conventions are operant in any given performance, and who identifies them? What is the "communicative context as a whole" and for whom does it have to make "sense"? On the basis of complex features of context, a given audience may decide that coding has taken place—which is to say that it is operatively "intentional"—for the detection of coding and the construction of the (de)coded text by an audience obviously depend on a prior conviction that coding has indeed occurred. But does this mean that if we, as feminists ever alert to the possibility of feminist messages, say that something is coded, then coding has occurred? This is the dilemma raised by the acts of implicit coding that concern us in this essay, for in such cases there has been neither the signaling of an intention to code nor any open complicity in a coding system; the performance is meant to pass for an uncoded activity.[11]

Moreover, the surface meanings of texts that may be implicitly coded are not readily dismissed. In complicit and explicit acts of coding, the mechanisms for the code are merely instrumental: Anne Lister's cryptic symbols, the butter and eggs, and the "superfluous" lines in the bride's letter are all fictions meant to be replaced by "true" messages.[12] In other words, the adoption of these signifiers is purely utilitarian, obliterating any truth-value that the code might otherwise carry: "the butter is fresh" conveys no reliable information about the butter but only describes the war. In these instances the coded meaning takes over, replacing the normal meaning of the words by rendering them irrelevant. For the senders of those messages, in other words, there is only one significant level of meaning; the code is purely an instrument, and the coded performance does not signify apart from this instrumentality.[13]

In the instances of coding with which we are concerned in this essay, on the other hand, the performance is already meaningful, whether or not a coded element is understood. Both the ostensible meaning and the "hidden" meaning are true; one does not necessarily replace the other but supplements or enhances it or gives it a new twist. Black slave spirituals, for example, sing of freedom and the Promised Land. Ostensibly, they are about the freedom of Heaven; surreptitiously, they are about the freedom from slavery on earth. Yet the second meaning does not necessarily erase the first; there may still be a longing for the ultimate freedom of a heavenly Promised Land. Butter does not, in other words, relate necessarily to war, but spiritual freedom and material freedom are intertwined. Because cases like the spirituals are entirely plausible performances whether or not they carry coded messages, it is difficult to "prove" that coding is taking place. Consider, for another example, the sexual iconography that has been associated with the flower paintings of Judy Chicago and Georgia O'Keeffe. Chicago has openly proclaimed her flowers to be genital images, while O'Keeffe vehemently denied the presence of sexual imagery in her own paintings. Yet many of Chicago's images are very like O'Keeffe's; the difference of acknowledged intention yields no necessary difference in form. Both remain representations of flowers whether or not either is also a representation of genitalia. In the absence of O'Keeffe's explicit acknowledgment, viewers and critics are left to their own inferences, which they make on the basis of their construction of the context in which the performance has taken place. This indeterminacy of implicit coding is, of course, only an intensification of the larger problem of meaning in language raised by contemporary thought. The intensification occurs because to name something as coded is necessarily to make a statement not only about the text but also about its originating individual or community.

Even when interpreters agree on the fact of coding, there may be no agreement on how to read the coded message—that is, what attitudes and values it conveys. *What* was Minnie Wright encoding into her disarranged kitchen and her missewn squares: mere distractedness and nervousness or angry mockery of her domestic role? A study of women in art contains a turn-of-the-century photo titled "Buy Some Apples," depicting a nearly nude, full-breasted young woman holding a tray of apples well above her waist. A more recent photo on the opposite page, captioned "Buy Some Bananas," shows a nude young man holding a tray of bananas well below his waist. Obviously, the second photo comments on the first, but whether "Buy Some Bananas" is meant to be taken as a friendly joke, a mockery of male anatomy, or an accusation against sexism in advertising is unclear.

We believe it is theoretically feasible to argue that intentionality is built into communicative contexts; with careful and respectful scholarship grounded in the *specific cultural context* of the performance, it seems feasible to posit at least the possibility that an act of coding has occurred. We suggest that a context for implicit coding exists when there is a situation of oppression, dominance, or risk for a particular individual or identifiable group; when there is some kind of opposition to this situation that cannot safely be made explicit; and when there is a community of potential "listeners" from which one would want to protect oneself. Sometimes, some context of danger or taboo is recognized first and coding is inferred on this basis, as when the women's recognition that Minnie probably killed her husband leads them to read Minnie's kitchen as a set of clues. In the absence of explicit evidence of coding, one has to demonstrate that a coded reading is plausible.

At the same time, the suggestion of implicit coding must ultimately remain an act of inference—one that has potential consequences for individuals and communities and therefore should not be undertaken without care. Who is to say whether coding has taken place in a given context? Who is to say what the decoded meaning is? What are the relations of power in which such judgments are made? If coding is a strategy adopted (consciously or not) for concealment, what will be the consequences of uncovering an act of coding? These are not merely academic questions; they involve the safety, reputations, and well-being of individual women and entire communities. We may not do any serious harm to Georgia O'Keeffe if we insist that her flower paintings are genital images, though we may be violating her integrity. If, however, the creator in question is not a famous artist but a dependent housewife in whose performances feminist scholars are publicly reading signs of resistance, our reading of her activities as coded may risk her sense of identity and even her safety. Perhaps this need for safety is what led her to coded actions in the first place, but it may not have led her there consciously. The search for coded feminist messages thus offers especially sharp reminders that interpretation is a powerful and literally consequential activity.

While the status of individual texts and performances must remain ambiguous, there seem to be certain strategic patterns in women's cultural practices that lend themselves to the coding of feminist messages. We offer a provisional typology of these formal strategies for encoding feminist (and other subversive) messages, illustrating them with examples from material life, folklore, literature, and the arts. We acknowledge that the specific acts of coding we identify might not necessarily be considered such by other interpreters. But in giving names to some available forms of resistance and subversion, we hope to make it easier to identify hidden feminist messages and to hear voices that might otherwise have gone unnoticed. We propose these examples of (possible) coding, then, as contestable sites of meaning, recognizing with Chris Weedon that while all meanings may be provisional, even provisional meanings have "real effects."[14]

The typology of coding strategies we offer here is neither complete nor necessarily the best one possible. As far as we know, there is no other existing typology, but others both inside and outside feminism have given name to some practices that we would call coding: Barbara Babcock's "inversion," Maya Angelou's "Principle of Reverse," Luce Irigaray's "mimicry," Sandra Gilbert and Susan Gubar's "palimpsest," Marie Maclean's "oppositional practices," the concept of *signifying* in African-American culture, and so forth.[15] We will mention these where they intersect with specific strategies identified below. Although we necessarily describe each of these strategies separately and sequentially, many instances of coding combine two or more of these formal practices.

Appropriation

By this term we designate coding strategies that involve adapting to feminist purposes forms or materials normally associated with male culture or with androcentric images of the feminine. What we are calling *appropriation* encompasses some aspects of Barbara Babcock's notion of *symbolic inversion*,[16] and Luce Irigaray's concept of ironic *mimicry*, in which a patriarchally designated feminine position is repeated with exaggeration in order to expose it.

Devon Hodges identifies a form of appropriation in literature when she suggests that a major option for the woman writer is "to transgress literary structure from within—demonstrating the inadequacy of the paternal narrative by opening it up to what it excludes."[17] This destabilization of narrative can also be seen to take place in women's oral tales. Peig Sayers, the great storyteller of Ireland's Blasket Islands, owed part of her renown among folklorists to the fact that having learned much of her repertoire from her father, she told many of the long and intricate kinds of tales normally told only by men.[18] Since her father's versions of these stories were never collected, we cannot be absolutely sure that Peig's tellings represent alterations of them; but judging from some versions collected from male neighbors and kin, it seems likely that she made major changes of pace, tone, and emphasis in the stories to focus attention on the hard lot of women, their courage, and their need to stand by one another in a patriarchal world. (In her old age, she commented to a visitor, "Since the time I was married I have never known a day that I was entirely happy.")[19] Her extensive detailing of the patient sufferings of wife and widow in the story of the woman who rescues her husband from Hell (AT 425J),[20] contrasted with the cursory treatment of these same topics in other local versions, seems to reflect her own sensibility.[21]

The process of appropriation, of opening up the paternal narrative to what it excludes, also occurs frequently in literature. Marie-Jeanne Riccoboni's *Letters of Juliette Catesby* (1759)[22] undermines the eighteenth-century heroine's traditional alternatives, marriage or death, by inscribing marriage in the language of death.[23] Not only does the new husband take his wife's pen after the wedding to announce that "there is no more Juliette Catesby," but Juliette herself uses phrases of suffocation and entrapment, seemingly in jest, to report the nuptial event. In Gloria Naylor's *Linden Hills* (1985) Luther Nedeed's abused wife begins to understand the horror of the family tradition into which she has married, and the sufferings of previous Mrs. Nedeeds, when she discovers a trunkful of coded evidence through which she can reconstruct generations of female misery. Luwana Packerville Nedeed has appropriated the 1837 family Bible, for example, and undermined its patriarchial messages in a "fine webbed scrawl that was crammed onto the gold-edged tissue paper that separated one book from another." On those Bible pages normally allocated to family recordkeeping, Luwana has recorded the growth of her despair as wife and mother. Although her "delicate, curled scroll" finally does lead her to write the uncoded assertion that "there can be no God,"[24] her appropriation of a Bible as her own journal—and particularly her choice of the family record pages—already constitutes a coded rejection of patriarchal religion and the patriarchal family.

Strategic appropriations may range from a simple borrowing and refashioning of male forms (Peig Sayers's tactic), to subversions of these forms (*Juliette Catesby*'s "humorous" inscription of marriage as death or Luwana Nedeed's rejection of the very book she is writing in), to outright parody, in which powerful feelings are coded and softened by a humorous tone (see our fifth strategy, trivialization, below). A dramatic case of parody in folk tradition is a surprise fortieth birthday party a woman in Washington, D.C., recently gave for her husband. It was a fairly rowdy and Bacchanalian example of its genre and culminated in the arrival of a huge cake, out of which popped—of course—a stripper. After the initial roars and cheers as she rose up from the icing, there was a startled silence. The stripper was not a luscious young thing; she was a middle-aged woman proudly modeling her lived-in body, sags, stretch marks, and all: a joke to most of the men present, but for the wife and some other women, a pungent commentary on a husband's mid-life fantasies. Here a male form is appropriated through parody, and humor is used to render ambiguous the seriousness of the parodist's intent.

When women are moving into roles that have previously belonged to men, appropriation is often an effective tactic. Cheryl L. Keyes demonstrates that African-American women of the 1980s gained their place in the predominantly male rap music industry by separating themselves from the outmoded "soft" style of rap and imitating—with significant adaptations—the dress, voice timbre, and "hard" performance mode of the male rappers of the time. Their "male" behavior established their competence and gained them commercial recordings and airtime; but they were able, at the same time, to inject into their raps significant rebuttal of the male rappers' attitudes towards women.[25]

Appropriation is a powerful coding strategy in many cultures. Some Native Americans, for example, have recently adapted their traditional beadwork to the ostentatious decoration of such mass-produced popular items as baseball caps, sneakers, Bingo markers, and Bic lighters and ballpoints. As Rayna Green has explained, the makers thereby perform "riffs on the white world," expressing "rebellion, laughter, and resilience" through artifacts that outsiders see as tacky and irrelevant corruptions of "traditional" Indian culture.[26] To the Indians these creations are far from irrelevant; they represent "the recapturing of identity.... They say, 'I am Indian, but on my own terms.'...[They speak loudly] about Survival, about the refusal to accept loss, assimilation, Removal and Relocation by the government, even analysis by scholars who want Indians to stay fixed in time, in place, in the past."[27] Similarly, in Maya Angelou's *I Know Why the*

Caged Bird Sings, a Black man performs a "Sambo masquerade" to con his white audience. The con man's actions would probably be recognized as code by much of the adult Black community but not by those whites unconscious of their own racial stereotyping. Angelou's character describes this turning of a negative stereotype against the stereotypers —another aspect of appropriation—as "the Principle of Reverse."[28]

A feminist parallel would entail appropriating not a masculine practice but an androcentrically feminine one, thereby converting "subordination into an affirmation" to dismantle "the place of [woman's] exploitation by discourse."[29] Linda Pershing's study of a recently created subversive "Sunbonnet Sue" quilt, for example, examines the parodic conversion of a traditional faceless, childlike feminine image into a figure of adult sexual rebelliousness; the patriarchally designated sweet, cooperative female comes into her own as a mature woman.[30] Barbara A. Babcock suggests that in the guise of reviving women's traditional figure pottery, women in the western pueblos have in fact encroached on male territory, creating representations of men's sacred rituals from which women are excluded.[31]

Juxtaposition

Because interpretation is a contextual activity, the ironic arrangement of texts, artifacts, or performances can constitute a powerful strategy for coding. An item that in one environment seems unremarkable or unambiguous may develop quite tendentious levels of meaning in another.

Given the multiple media of folk performances and material traditions, coding by juxtaposition can take a greater variety of forms in folklore and in spatial genres than in temporal genres like literature. A bridal quilt, pieced, patched, and quilted by a group of women and presented to one of its members on the occasion of her marriage, may represent an ironic coded message as it covers her marriage bed; symbolic of the group's intimacy, it becomes a reminder of the bride's removal from that intimacy by her new primary duties to her husband. In Sylvia Plath's *The Bell Jar,* a reminiscence about Buddy Willard's mother yields an even richer ambiguity:

> Once when I visited Buddy I found Mrs. Willard braiding a rug out of strips of wool from Mr. Willard's old suits. She'd spent weeks on that rug, and I had admired the tweedy browns and greens and blues patterning the braid, but after Mrs. Willard was through, instead of hanging the rug on the wall the way I would have done, she put it

down in place of her kitchen mat, and in a few days it was soiled and dull and indistinguishable from any mat you could buy for under a dollar in the five and ten.

And I knew that in spite of all the roses and kisses and restaurant dinners a man showered on a woman before he married her, what he secretly wanted when the wedding service ended was for her to flatten out underneath his feet like Mrs. Willard's kitchen mat.[32]

For the narrator, Esther Greenwood, Mrs. Willard's mat encodes only her oppression as wife, but we read in the mat a coded rebellion against the oppression Mrs. Willard seems to accept. What Mrs. Willard has done might be seen as both appropriation and juxtaposition. She has converted her husband's suits—a male form—to her own cultural purposes. We can imagine her asserting that the sturdiness of the heavy wool material fits it ideally for the hard wear the mat will receive on the kitchen floor. Nonetheless, once she has placed the mat in the kitchen, in her own utterly female space, who is stepping on whom? A woman who has no doubt devoted much time and care to cleaning her husband's clothes is now free to grind them (and, symbolically, him) into the muck under her feet. As the difference between our reading of the mat and Esther's suggests, juxtaposition is a particularly ambiguous coding strategy. It may go unnoticed or be dismissed as an accident; if noticed, it may be read in contradictory ways.

In written literature, juxtaposition may be effected through titles, epigraphs, the placement of stanzas, voices, or paragraphs. Two interrelated examples may be illustrative. In *A Room of One's Own,* Virginia Woolf lambastes Charlotte Brontë for prose that is "deformed and twisted" by angry "sex-consciousness."[33] Her evidence is a famous passage from chapter 12 of *Jane Eyre,* in which the narrator cries out for the physical and spiritual freedom of men. The irony is that although Woolf castigates Brontë for including this complaint, she herself validates it by quoting the passage at length and letting it speak the overt anger that Woolf herself so carefully avoids. Brontë's own placement of this passage in *Jane Eyre* also shows coding through juxtaposition. Immediately after the "digression" about women's need for freedom, in what Woolf criticizes as an "awkward break,"[34] Jane tells us that "when thus alone, I not infrequently heard Grace Poole's laugh. . . ." But "Grace Poole" is actually Bertha Mason, the "mad" wife confined to Rochester's attic, and the juxtaposition suggests that Jane's own confinement at Thornfield may not be as auspicious as it appears.

Distraction

We use the term *distraction* to describe strategies that drown out or draw attention away from the subversive power of a feminist message. Usually distraction involves creating some kind of "noise," interference, or obscurity that will keep the message from being heard except by those who listen very carefully or already suspect it is there. Annis Pratt, who uses the term *drowning* for this phenomenon, gives an example from African-American slave culture: when slaves wished to sing a particularly bold song like "Oh Freedom," instead of a hymn with more indirect lyrics like "Go Down Moses," they would bang on pots to cover up their words.[35] Frances Harper's novel *Iola Leroy* presents just this scenario.[36]

Although distraction is easier to accomplish in a performed genre than in a written one, the avant-garde writing of prewar, expatriate Paris provides two ready examples of distraction in literature. The first is Djuna Barnes's *Ladies Almanack* (1928), a text that celebrates and also parodies the society of lesbians that centered around Natalie Barney in Paris in the 1920s.[37] The language of *Ladies Almanack* is so dense and baroque that only the persistent or the initiated are likely to read it at all. Yet among sentences that seem impenetrable one will find blatant sexual and political comments.[38] Indeed, at one point *Ladies Almanack* actually describes the phenomenon of distraction that it enacts: "It would loom the bigger if stripped of its Jangle, but no, drugged such must go. As foggy as a Mere, as drenched as a Pump; twittering so loud upon the Wire that one cannot hear the Message. And yet!"[39] One might also consider the writing of Gertrude Stein, which often buries "sense" within "nonsense" so that as one is reading pages of cryptic phrases ("patriarchal means suppose patriarchal means and close patriarchal means and chose chose Monday") one suddenly finds a piece of sharply obvious feminist analysis: "Patriarchal poetry is the same as Patriotic poetry is the same as patriarchal poetry is the same as Patriotic poetry is the same as patriarchal poetry is the same."[40]

In literature, the "noise" that drowns out the message is stylistic; in folklore, where the medium need not be verbal, one component of the performance (like the beating on the pot) can work to obliterate another. In lullabies, for example, a distressing text is frequently smothered by soothing melody and rhythms.[41] Bess Lomax Hawes has suggested that the American lullaby, "on one of its deeper levels," represents "a mother's conversation with herself about separation."[42] "Hush, little baby, don't you cry, / You know your mama's bound to die. . . ." Similarly, this example from South Uist in the Hebrides reflects immediate anxieties:

> What, love, will I do for you,
> For I have no breast milk for you?
> I fear that you will get the croup
>   From the softness of the potatoes.[43]

Music, rhythmic accompaniment, and other modes of heightening and marking performance styles may be the most common folkloric means of distraction from subversive messages. Angela Bourke has described how social and sexual complaints occurring in the traditional Scottish waulking songs, performed by groups of women during the laborious fulling of woolen cloth, would be nearly drowned out by the noisy chant and the rhythmic slapping of the cloth,[44] and how Irish women's oblique protests against their husbands' stinginess and violence were submerged in the wild cries of their traditional laments for the dead.[45] But powerful ideas may be as distracting as sounds. Joanne B. Mulcahy reports that because Native midwives on Kodiak Island, Alaska, used their Russian Orthodox ideology to explain and encode their healing knowledge as a gift of God, their potentially threatening claim for the superiority of Native (and female) medical traditions became acceptable.[46]

Indirection

Our fourth kind of coding may be the most common one of all, especially in oral and written texts: strategies of indirection or distancing. Here we include the many ways in which, as Emily Dickinson put it, one can "tell all the Truth but tell it slant."[47] Since indirection is so vast a category, we want to distinguish within it at least three modes: *metaphor, impersonation,* and *hedging*.

Metaphors, from single images to elaborate fantasies, may create both distance and ambiguity. It is not surprising, then, that women often use metaphors for expressing forbidden sexual and political impulses. It has been alleged, for example, that there is "no sex" in the novels of Virginia Woolf. Yet the following passage from *Mrs Dalloway* is surely a description of orgasm:

> She could not resist sometimes yielding to the charms of a woman . . . she did undoubtedly then feel what men felt. Only for a moment; but it was enough. It was a sudden revelation, a tinge like a blush which one tried to check and then, as it spread, one yielded to its expansion, and rushed to the farthest verge and there quivered and felt the world come

closer, swollen with some astonishing significance, some pressure of rapture, which split its thin skin and gushed and poured with an extraordinary alleviation over the cracks and sores! Then, for that moment, she had seen an illumination; a match burning in a crocus; an inner meaning almost expressed. But the close withdrew; the hard softened. It was over—the moment.[48]

An elaborate metaphor structures Charlotte Perkins Gilman's *The Yellow Wallpaper* (1892), whose narrator tries to free a woman she believes is trapped behind the pattern of the wallpaper in the room where she herself is confined. Her "madness," indeed, is the "madness" of mistaking the metaphoric for the literal.[49]

Metaphor abounds in folk legends. Rosan A. Jordan has demonstrated convincingly that legends about vaginal serpents encode Mexican-American women's fears of sexual violation and childbearing.[50] Pointing out similar metaphoric messages in the games played by Mexican girls "as rehearsal for adult life," Inez Cardozo-Freeman indicates that such coding can be subconscious: "None of the women who gave me these games was aware of the symbolic meaning inherent in them until it was pointed out. The women generally stated that they remembered the games because of their pretty melodies and because singing and playing them brought joy to their lives."[51]

In Adrienne Rich's "Aunt Jennifer's Tigers," a woman's art is seen as a metaphor for her anger:

> Aunt Jennifer's Tigers stride across a screen,
> Bright topaz denizens of a world of green.
> They do not fear the men beneath the tree;
> They pace in sleek chivalric certainty.
>
> Aunt Jennifer's fingers fluttering through her wool
> Find even the ivory needle hard to pull.
> The massive weight of Uncle's wedding band
> Sits heavily upon Aunt Jennifer's hand.
>
> When Aunt is dead, her terrified hands will lie
> Still ringed with ordeals she was mastered by.
> The tigers in the panel that she made
> Will go on prancing, proud and unafraid.[52]

Rich's comments about "Aunt Jennifer's Tigers" reveal a second strategy of indirection: *impersonation*, or the substitution of another persona for the "I." In "When We Dead Awaken: Writing as Re-Vision," Rich explains that she invented Aunt Jennifer, a figure from another generation, because she needed "a person as distinct from myself as possible."[53] Rich goes on to identify other female and male personae adopted, she believes with hindsight, to create distance in her poetry.

Clearly, any kind of third-person substitution or any use of another person's discourse provides a form of distancing. The strategy of indirection also includes, then, the use of folk genres that are by definition impersonal, such as the ballads compiled by Francis James Child. A woman singer performing "Our Goodman" (Child ballad 274), for example, may be reflecting her own impatience in her marriage as she sings, in the role of the ballad wife to the ballad husband, "You blind fool, you crazy fool." Polly Stewart has shown that traditional Anglo-American ballads present women with strategies for survival in a brutal, patriarchal world and that women have sung these to each other as deliberate warnings about the consequences of careless behavior and as lessons about how to outsmart men.[54]

Folk narratives may function as impersonal statements about personal beliefs, as do the legends about the deaths of young children that Janet L. Langlois has examined.[55] In the rural Cáceres region of Spain studied by James M. Taggart, villagers of both sexes tell one another folktales about courtship and marriage as "a culturally approved means of reflecting on themselves and their world" that "allows them to express deep feelings through the safety of fantasy." In their telling of "The Innocent Slandered Maiden" (AT 883A), for instance, men tend to blame the female victim for creating temptation. The women's versions of this story, on the other hand, represent their anger at men's suspicions about the conduct of women and at the fact that men—socialized from childhood as sexual predators—nonetheless make the ultimate moral judgments.[56]

The direct "I" can also be evaded sporadically, at particular moments or in particular sentences, as it is in *A Room of One's Own* when the narrator describes her anger at being barred from the Oxbridge library: "That a famous library has been cursed by a woman is a matter of complete indifference to a famous library."[57] On the other hand, some texts struggle visibly to suppress the "I": Harriet Wilson's *Our Nig* (1859), the first novel by an African American to be published in the United States, casts its narrative in the indirect, third-person form, but the titles of the early chapters retain the unmasked "I."[58]

Art historian Mary D. Garrard's studies of the seventeenth-century Italian painter Artemisia Gentileschi provide an example of coding by impersonation in visual art.[59] Garrard traces in Artemisia's early pictures her history as the victim of sexual intimidation, public humiliation, and rape. But Artemisia's paintings are biblical subjects, not self-

representations; through her sympathetic portrayal of Susanna's innocence and terror in *Susanna and the Elders,* she encoded her own
experience of sexual threat, and later, in her violent rendering of
Judith Decapitating Holofernes, she represented her own anger at her
rape.

A third kind of indirection, which we call *hedging,* encompasses a
range of strategies, most common in verbal texts, for equivocating
about or weakening a message: ellipses, litotes, passive constructions,
euphemisms, qualifiers. Such forms have been identified by some
linguists as characteristic of "women's language" or "language of the
powerless."[60] For example, in *A Room of One's Own,* passive constructions allow Woolf to avoid blaming the oppression of women on
men.[61] The first paragraph of Toni Morrison's *Sula* uses passive forms
and the impersonal "they" to avoid accusing the white power structure
for leveling what was "once a neighborhood."[62] The narrator of *The
Yellow Wallpaper* continually qualifies her early assertions with phrases
like "personally" and "perhaps."

Verbal hedging is also common in folklore. In the African-American
lullaby "Hushabye," the slave mother, lulling a white infant to sleep
with dreams of "pretty little horses," disguised the bitterness of her
anger that "Way down yonder, in the meadow, / Poor little baby's
crying 'Mammy'" by leaving out the words that would identify that
abandoned child as her own. In the Irish lament tradition studied by
Angela Bourke, a keening wife might mention that her husband used
to beat her, but she would hedge the accusation with excuses for his
behavior.[63]

Trivialization

Trivialization involves the employment of a form, mode, or genre that
the dominant culture considers unimportant, innocuous, or irrelevant.
When a particular form is conventionally nonthreatening, the message it carries, even if it might be threatening in another context,
is likely to be discounted or overlooked. Consider women's self-
deprecating use of the culture's trivial names for their expressive
genres: "Oh, we're just gossiping"; "That was only 'woman-talk.'"
Such phrases can be strategies to avert attention from topics of conversation that are in fact crucially important to the speakers.[64] Seemingly
trivial activities can also carry important messages. Although their
woodsmen husbands laugh impatiently, a group of middle-aged women
in a Maine logging community continue to knit doll clothes and dress
baby dolls for display and sale. Margaret R. Yocom has shown how

these women enact their longing for the days of childhood and motherhood and express their own aesthetic and cultural values in resisting the pressures of tourism and social change.[65]

Perhaps the most frequent mode of trivialization is humor, and women use it in many contexts to buffer the seriousness of what they are saying. Studies by Carol Mitchell, Nancy Walker, and Regina Barreca have shown that women interpret, select, and tell jokes differently from men and often express hostility toward men through their joke telling.[66] Feminist jokes and comic putdowns—"Adam was a rough draft"; "It's not kosher to be a male chauvinist pig"; "A woman who tries to be a man's equal lacks ambition"—blunt with humor the subversive stab of their messages. Verbal folklore about housework is often rebellious, but its sharpness tends to be softened by humorous parodies: "All work and no pay makes a Housewife"; "Ring around the collar? Wash your neck." Like other strategies of coding, trivialization (particularly through humor) can buffer the acerbity of a message not only for the audience but also for the performer herself. The "Scandalous Sue" quilt, for instance, has been seen as primarily humorous not only by the quilters' husbands but also by the quilters themselves, who prefer not to regard it as a statement of social protest.

Although trivialization has a wider range of possibilities in folklore than in literature, women writers have used this strategy by exploiting or hiding behind the very forms that men already consider nonliterary or inferior—the letter, the diary, children's literature, and the "women's" novel—to express ideas those same women might never express in an essay or a poem. The narrator of *The Yellow Wallpaper* claims that she can criticize her husband only because she is writing privately, for herself: "John is a physician, and *perhaps*—(I would not say it to a living soul, of course, but this is dead paper and a great relief to my mind)—*perhaps* that is one reason I do not get well faster. You see he does not believe I am sick!"[67] That "you" is a giveaway, signaling the purely strategic nature of the diary form. And what is one to make of the scraps of paper on which Emily Dickinson wrote her poetry?

Incompetence

In claiming or demonstrating incompetence at conventionally feminine activities, women may be expressing their resistance to patriarchal expectations. Examples abound of women who, declaring their inability, simply do not cook, sew, or knit. The upshot may be outsiders' pity or scorn, but incompetence is usually not regarded as culpable. In contrast, women who refuse outright to perform "women's" functions often run considerable risks. Brett Williams reports a suit for divorce brought in an Illinois court by the husband of a migrant Mexican-American woman, whose grounds—supported not only by his own kin but also by his wife's—were that his wife refused to cook him tamales. She refused to perform a key female function, which in the migrant culture serves to bind together kin groups and to enlist the support of powerful members of the community. It was her refusal that was the rub; she *could* do it, but she would not.[68] Susan S. Lanser's essay discusses incompetence as a contemporary coding phenomenon and suggests ways of interpreting folktales about "lazy," incompetent, and super-competent wives as coded protest.[69]

Women may either claim incompetence verbally or illustrate it by spoiling their own attempts, as in Marge Piercy's poem, "What's That Smell in the Kitchen?"

> All over America women are burning dinners.
> It's lambchops in Peoria; it's haddock
> in Providence; it's steak in Chicago
> tofu delight in Big Sur; red
> rice and beans in Dallas.
> All over America women are burning
> food they're supposed to bring with calico
> smile on platters glittering like wax.
> Anger sputters in her brainpan, confined
> but spewing out missiles of hot fat.
> Carbonized despair presses like a clinker
> from a barbecue against the back of her eyes.
> If she wants to grill anything, it's
> her husband spitted over a slow fire.
> If she wants to serve him anything
> it's a dead rat with a bomb in its belly
> ticking like the heart of an insomniac.
> Her life is cooked and digested,
> nothing but leftovers in Tupperware.
> Look, she says, once I was roast duck
> on your platter with parsley but now I am Spam.
> Burning dinner is not incompetence but war.[70]

Claims of literary incompetence pervade women's literature; only rarely does one encounter outright war, as in this delightful attack on the male literary establishment by the nineteenth-century "domestic" novelist Fanny Fern: "Should any *dictionary on legs* rap inopportunely at the door for admittance, send him away to the groaning shelves of some musty library, where 'literature' lies embalmed, with its stony eyes, fleshless joints, and ossified heart, in faultless preservation."[71]

Generally, however, claims of incompetence at literature differ sharply from claims of incompetence at cooking or needlework; literature, after all, is male turf. In the eighteenth century, a woman writer's proclamation of literary incompetence in a preface was a conventional strategy by which the woman writer could say on her own behalf what she expected her audience to think: that she had little right to be writing and that her work was bound to be inferior. In this way, she deflected criticism for undertaking the "masculine" act of writing and set the stage for surprised pleasure that she could in fact write well.

There are, however, occasions when women have turned a claim of incompetence at male literary forms into a refusal to perform according to the dictates of men. In Marie-Jeanne Riccoboni's *L'Abeille* (1762), the author constructs a *Spectator*-style offering in which she tells various stories and anecdotes, including stories that criticize the place of woman in European society. Right in the middle of an epistolary narrative—a form commonly used by women novelists and the form in which she herself nearly always wrote—Riccoboni intrudes on her own letter-writing character with the following sentences: "To continue a work of this sort one must never have read the admirable pages of Mr. Addison. I examine myself, I judge myself, and I stop myself."[72] But Addison did not write romantic epistolary tales, and what Riccoboni is in fact stopping is a *feminine* form. In the guise of incompetence at a male form, then, she is actually refusing to do women's work. In a similar double play, Jane Austen used the following claim of incompetence to tell the Prince Regent's clergyman why she could not undertake the clerical novel he proposed: "I think I may boast myself to be, with all possible vanity, the most uninformed and unlearned female who ever dared to be an authoress."[73] Beneath the discourse of incompetence, of course, lies the steely authority—"boast," "vanity," "dared"—of a woman who knows her own gifts. It is no wonder Austen is almost alone among women novelists of her time in not writing any prefaces at all, since to write a preface would have obliged her either to inscribe or to defy the conventional claim of female incompetence.

If we give this strategy of incompetence yet another turn, we are led back, ironically, to the beginning of our typology: the appropriation of male forms. Incompetence at "women's" activities is virtually a signifier of masculinity, something men conventionally brag about, and a woman who claims such incompetence may in fact be appropriating a male stance. (One might recall a popular poster of Golda Meir that was captioned, "But can she type?") From another angle of vision, then, incompetence at the feminine could be described as an appropriative act.

That incompetence may also be appropriation indicates how complex the interpretation of a coded act can be. Strategies overlap, interweave, blend into one another. Elaine J. Lawless's discussion of Pentecostal women in the American South, for instance, illustrates their use of several coding strategies to gain access to the pulpit in a church that insists on the subservience of women.[74] Indirection is essential. Women preachers must be wives and biological mothers first and represent their pastoral identities metaphorically as mothers of their congregations. Impersonation protects them from the censure of the male deacons who govern the church; they must ascribe their vocation to an unbidden call from God. Women preachers routinely trivialize their own abilities ("I kinda hope you all aren't expecting too much. . . . Now, I want you to know that I never thought about these things on my own. I prayed and the Lord revealed these things to me. I have not got that much sense in my own head. . . . I'm not intelligent."). Calling themselves "handmaidens of the Lord," they appropriate the writings of St. Paul, principal authority for the *silencing* of women in churches, when he echoes the prophecy of Joel that in these "last days," God will pour forth His spirit upon all flesh, sons, daughters, servants, and handmaidens, that they may prophesy. All of these tactics distract from the fact that women are serving in powerful public positions normally occupied by men, not only as traveling preachers but also as pastors of congregations.

We have been suggesting throughout this essay that coding may allow women to communicate feminist messages to other women of their community; to refuse, subvert, or transform conventional expectations; and to criticize male dominance in the face of male power. At the same time, because ambiguity is a necessary feature of every coded act, any instance of coding risks reinforcing the very ideology it is designed to critique. A ballad, however extreme its portrayal of the victimization of women, may still be heard as a pleasingly poignant old song; a joke, however pointed, can be laughed off; a woman who burns dinner may be dismissed as a woman who just can't cook. For all the ingenious uses women, or any dominated peoples, may make of coding, then, the need for coding must always signify a freedom that is incomplete. By inscribing into the new context of feminism the evidence of coding by women for whom openly feminist messages would be impossible, taking care to respect the cultural and individual differences and human needs that coding signifies, feminist scholars may help to bring about a social order in which coding will no longer be necessary.

Notes

An earlier version of this essay appeared as "The Feminist Voice: Strategies of Coding in Folklore and Literature," *Journal of American Folklore* 100, no. 398 (1987): 412–25.

1. Susan Glaspell, "A Jury of Her Peers," in *American Voices, American Women,* ed. Lee Edwards and Arlyn Diamond (New York: Avon, 1973), 373. Glaspell first wrote this narrative as a one-act play, *Trifles* (1916).

2. It is important to distinguish between complex symbolic communication and the coded communication of subversive messages. An example of the former is *tifaifai,* the piecework and appliqué textile art through which women in Polynesia represent their identities and their feelings. In designing a single *tifaifai,* a woman may express kinship relationships, regional identity, religious affiliation, and aspects of her roles as artist and woman. The creator of *tifaifai* can thus make a complex series of statements, but this self-expression is not in our sense "coded" because its signs are accessible to all members of the culture and reinforce their shared values. See Joyce D. Hammond, "Polynesian Women and *Tifaifai:* Fabrications of Identity," *Journal of American Folklore* 99, no. 393 (1986): 259–79.

3. See, for example, Barbara Babcock, ed., *The Reversible World: Symbolic Inversion in Art and Society* (Ithaca, N.Y.: Cornell University Press, 1978); Claire R. Farrer, ed., *Women and Folklore* (Austin: University of Texas Press, 1975); Judith Fetterley, *The Resisting Reader: A Feminist Approach to American Fiction* (Bloomington: Indiana University Press, 1978); Sandra M. Gilbert and Susan Gubar, *The Madwoman in the Attic: The Woman Writer and the Nineteenth-Century Literary Imagination* (New Haven, Conn.: Yale University Press, 1979); Rosan A. Jordan, "The Vaginal Serpent and Other Themes from Mexican-American Women's Lore," in *Women's Folklore, Women's Culture,* ed. Rosan A. Jordan and Susan J. Kalčik (Philadelphia: University of Pennsylvania Press, 1985), 26–44; Annette Kolodny, "A Map for Rereading: Gender and the Interpretation of Literary Texts," *New Literary History* 11, no. 3 (1980): 451–67; Tania Modleski, "Feminism and the Power of Interpretation," in *Feminist Studies/Critical Studies,* ed. Teresa de Lauretis (Bloomington: Indiana University Press, 1986), 121–38; Annis Pratt, "The New Feminist Criticisms," in *Beyond Intellectual Sexism,* ed. Joan Roberts (New York: David McKay, 1976), 175–95; Adrienne Rich, "When We Dead Awaken: Writing as Re-vision," in *On Lies, Secrets and Silence: Selected Prose 1966–1978* (New York: Norton, 1978), 33–50; and Dale Spender, *Man Made Language* (London: Routledge, 1980), chapter 3.

4. See, for example, Lawrence W. Levine, *Black Culture and Black Consciousness: Afro-American Folk Thought from Slavery to Freedom* (New York:

Oxford University Press, 1977); and Henry Louis Gates, Jr., *The Signifying Monkey: A Theory of Afro-American Literary Criticism* (New York: Oxford University Press, 1988).

5. Frances E. W. Harper, *Iola Leroy; or Shadows Uplifted* (Boston: Beacon, 1987), 9.

6. *I Know My Own Heart: The Diaries of Anne Lister 1791–1840*, ed. Helena Whitbread (London: Virago, 1988; New York: New York University Press, 1992). Lister devised a set of private symbols that included mathematical signs and Greek letters.

7. For a discussion and the text of this letter, see Susan S. Lanser, "Toward a Feminist Narratology," *Style* 20, no. 3 (1986): 341–63; rpt. in *Feminisms,* ed. Robyn Warhol and Diane Price Herndl (New Brunswick: Rutgers, 1991), 610–29.

8. Although we use here the terms *author* and *text,* we mean any originator/creator and any realized product or performance.

9. Rich, "When We Dead Awaken," 33–49.

10. *The Poetics of Biblical Narrative: Ideological Literature and the Drama of Reading* (Bloomington: Indiana University Press, 1985), 9. As an anonymous reader of this essay has observed, psychoanalytic theory would complicate this discussion of the unconscious, desire, and intentionality. Imagine, for example, a Lacanian reading of "A Jury of Her Peers" *d'après* the "Seminar on 'The Purloined Letter.'"

11. Complicit coding seems to be rare among women, perhaps because, as Simone de Beauvoir has argued, women live "dispersed among the males" and have not historically tended to see themselves as a political community, a "we." See the Introduction to *The Second Sex,* trans. H. M. Parshley (New York: Knopf, 1952), xviii–xix.

12. Actually the bride's surface letter, which proclaims marital happiness, carries very complex messages that a careful reading shows to be more than fictional. See Lanser, "Toward a Feminist Narratology."

13. The medium for coding is not without significance, but it is significant only *as* a medium.

14. Chris Weedon, *Feminist Practice and Poststructuralist Theory* (London: Basil Blackwell, 1989), 86.

15. Babcock, *The Reversible World;* Maya Angelou, *I Know Why the Caged Bird Sings* (New York: Random House, 1969); Luce Irigaray, *This Sex which Is Not One,* trans. Catherine Porter (1977; Ithaca, N.Y.: Cornell University Press, 1985); Gilbert and Gubar, *The Madwoman in the Attic;* Marie Maclean (following Michel de Certeau), "Oppositional Practices in Women's Traditional Narrative," *New Literary History* 19, no. 1 (1987): 37–50; Gates, *The Signifying Monkey.*

16. "'Symbolic inversion' may be broadly defined as any act of expressive behavior which inverts, contradicts, abrogates, or in some fashion presents an alternative to commonly held cultural codes, values, and norms be they linguistic, literary or artistic, religious, or social and political." Babcock, *The Reversible World,* 14.

17. Devon Hodges, "*Frankenstein* and the Feminine Subversion of the Novel," *Tulsa Studies in Women's Literature* 2, no. 2 (1983): 155–64.

18. J[ames] H. Delargy, "The Gaelic Storyteller, with Some Notes on Gaelic Folktales," The Sir John Rhys Memorial Lecture, *Proceedings of the British Academy* 31 (1945): 3–47; reprinted by the University of Chicago for the American Committee for Irish Studies (January 1969), 7, 15.

19. Robin Flower, *The Western Island, or the Great Blasket* (London: Oxford University Press, 1944), 59.

20. Seán O'Sullivan, ed. and trans., *Folktales of Ireland* (Chicago: University of Chicago Press, 1966), 151–64. The AT number refers to numbering in Antti Aarne and Stith Thompson, *The Types of the Folktale: A Classification and Bibliography,* Folklore Fellows Communications No. 184 (Helsinki: Academia Scientiarum Fennica, 1973.)

21. Joan N. Radner, "The Woman Who Went to Hell: Coded Values in Irish Folk Narrative," *Midwestern Folklore* 15, no. 2 (1989): 41–51. See also James M. Taggart's study of "the ways women feminize stories normally told by men and the way men masculinize stories normally told by women" in villages in the Cáceres region of Spain, *Enchanted Maidens: Gender Relations in Spanish Folktales of Courtship and Marriage* (Princeton, N.J.: Princeton University Press, 1990).

22. Marie-Jeanne Riccoboni, *Lettres de Milady Juliette Catesby à Milady Henriette Campley, son amie* (Paris: Desjonquères, 1983).

23. Susan Lanser, "Plot, Voice, and Narrative *Oubli: Juliette Catesby*'s Twice-Told Tale," in *Proceedings of the Hofstra Conference on Eighteenth-Century Women in the Arts,* ed. Frederick M. Keener and Susan E. Lorsch (Westport, Conn.: Greenwood, 1988), 129–40. See also Lanser, *Fictions of Authority: Women Writers and Narrative Voice* (Ithaca, N.Y.: Cornell University Press, 1992), chapter 2.

24. Gloria Naylor, *Linden Hills* (New York: Penguin Books, 1986), 117, 93.

25. "'We're More than a Novelty, Boys': Strategies of Female Rappers in the Rap Music Tradition," herein.

26. Remarks at the American Folklore Society Annual Meeting, October 18, 1989.

27. Rayna Green, "Beaded Adidas," in *Time and Temperature: A Centennial Publication of the American Folklore Society,* ed. Charles Camp (Washington, D.C.: American Folklore Society, 1989), 66.

28. Angelou, *Caged Bird,* 214–15, quoted in Modleski, "Feminism and the Power of Interpretation," 129. For another example of "Sambo masquerade," see Ralph Ellison, *Invisible Man* (New York: Signet, 1952) chapter 20, 373.

29. Irigaray, *This Sex which Is Not One,* 76.

30. "'She Really Wanted to Be Her Own Woman': Scandalous Sunbonnet Sue," herein.

31. "'At Home, No Womens Are Storytellers': Potteries, Stories, and Politics in Cochiti Pueblo," herein. This essay originally appeared in *Journal of the Southwest* 30, no. 3 (1988): 356–89.

32. Sylvia Plath, *The Bell Jar* (New York: Bantam Books, 1972), 69.

33. *A Room of One's Own* (New York: Harcourt Brace, 1929), 72.

34. Ibid.

35. Pratt, "New Feminist Criticisms," 183.

36. Harper, *Iola Leroy,* 13.

37. Djuna Barnes, *Ladies Almanack* (New York: Harper and Row, 1972; New York: New York University Press, 1992).

38. Susan S. Lanser, "Speaking in Tongues: *Ladies Almanack* and the Discourse of Desire," in *Silence and Power: A Reevaluation of Djuna Barnes,* ed. Mary Lynn Broe (Carbondale: Southern Illinois University Press, 1991), 156–68.

39. Barnes, *Ladies Almanack,* 46.

40. Gertrude Stein, "Patriarchal Poetry," in *The Yale Gertrude Stein* (1927; New Haven: Yale University Press, 1980), 110, 116. We are not suggesting that Stein's writings can be read entirely within the framework of distraction, for like other modernists her theories of language are far more complex and her insistence on "nonsense" is a philosophical position. But we do argue that feminist coding is one of the causes or effects of Stein's practices.

41. See Margaret B. McDowell, "Folk Lullabies: Songs of Anger, Love and Fear," *Feminist Studies* 3, no. 1 (1977): 205–18; Shimon L. Khayyat, "Lullabies of Iraqi Jews," *Folklore* 89, no. 1 (1978): 13–22.

42. Bess Lomax Hawes, "Folksongs and Functions: Some Thoughts on the American Lullaby," *Journal of American Folklore* 87, no. 344 (1974): 71.

43. Margaret Fay Shaw, *Folksongs and Folklore of South Uist* (London: Oxford University Press, 1977), 143.

44. *Working and Weeping: Women's Oral Poetry in Irish and Scottish Gaelic,* Women's Studies Working Papers No. 7 (Dublin: University College Dublin Women's Studies Forum, 1988).

45. "More in Anger than in Sorrow: Irish Women's Lament Poetry," herein.

46. " 'How They Knew': Women's Talk about Healing on Kodiak Island, Alaska," herein.

47. Emily Dickinson, Poem 1129, in *The Complete Poems of Emily Dickinson,* ed. Thomas H. Johnson (Boston: Little, Brown, 1960), 506.

48. Virginia Woolf, *Mrs Dalloway* (New York: Harcourt Brace, 1925), 47.

49. Charlotte Perkins Gilman, *The Yellow Wallpaper* (Old Westbury, N.Y.: Feminist Press, 1973).

50. Jordan, "Vaginal Serpent."

51. Inez Cardozo-Freeman, "Games Mexican Girls Play," *Journal of American Folklore* 88, no. 347 (1975): 22.

52. "Aunt Jennifer's Tigers" from *The Fact of a Doorframe, Poems Selected and New, 1950–1984,* by Adrienne Rich, is reprinted with the permission of the publisher, W. W. Norton and Company, Inc., and the author. Copyright © 1984 by Adrienne Rich. Copyright © 1975, 1978 by W. W. Norton and Company, Inc. Copyright © 1981 by Adrienne Rich.

53. In *On Lies, Secrets and Silence,* 40.

54. "Wishful Willful Wily Women: Verbal Strategies for Female Success in the Child Ballads," herein.

55. "Mothers' Double Talk," herein.

56. *Enchanted Maidens*, 9, 41–58.

57. Woolf, *A Room of One's Own*, 8.

58. Harriet E. Wilson, *Our Nig: or, Sketches from the Life of a Free Black* (New York: Random House, 1983).

59. *Artemisia Gentileschi: The Image of the Female Hero in Italian Baroque Art* (Princeton, N.J.: Princeton University Press, 1989); "Artemisia and Susanna," in *Feminism and Art History: Questioning the Litany*, ed. Norma Broude and Mary D. Garrard (New York: Harper and Row, 1982), 147–71.

60. This question is a controversial one among feminists. There are at least three areas of dispute: whether there is in fact a "women's language," whether what has been called "women's language" is more properly a "language of the powerless," and whether this language is a negative phenomenon. On these questions, see especially Robin Lakoff, *Language and Woman's Place* (New York: Harper and Row, 1975); Spender, *Man Made Language;* and William M. O'Barr and Bowman K. Atkins, " 'Women's Language' or 'Powerless Language'?" in *Women and Language in Literature and Society*, ed. Sally McConnell-Ginet et al. (New York: Praeger, 1980), 93–110.

61. J. Christine Salem, "On Naming the Oppressor: What Woolf Avoids Saying in *A Room of One's Own*," *Women's Studies International Quarterly* 3, no. 43 (1980): 209–19.

62. Toni Morrison, *Sula* (New York: Knopf, 1973).

63. "More in Anger than in Sorrow: Irish Women's Lament Poetry," herein.

64. Richard Bauman, *Verbal Art as Performance* (Prospect Heights, Ill.: Waveland, 1984), describes a related concept, "disclaimer of performance"—"a surface denial of any real competence [at narrative performance]"—among the techniques by which a performance may be "keyed" to "include a range of explicit or implicit messages which carry instructions on how to interpret the other message(s) being communicated" (15–22).

65. " 'Awful Real': Dolls and Development in Rangeley, Maine," herein.

66. Carol Mitchell, "The Sexual Perspective in the Appreciation of Jokes," *Western Folklore* 36, no. 4 (1977): 303–29; Mitchell, "Hostility and Aggression toward Males in Female Joke Telling," *Frontiers* 3, no. 3 (1978): 19–23; Mitchell, "Some Differences in Male and Female Joke Telling," in *Women's Folklore, Women's Culture*, ed. Jordan and Kalčik, 163–86; Nancy Walker, *A Very Serious Thing: Women's Humor and American Culture* (Minneapolis: University of Minnesota Press, 1988); Regina Barreca, *They Used to Call Me Snow White... But I Drifted* (New York: Viking, 1991). See also Robbie Davis Johnson's study of the ways the madam of a Texas whorehouse uses jokes to control her male customers: "Folklore and Women: A Social Interactional Analysis of the Folklore of a Texas Madam," *Journal of American Folklore* 86, no. 341 (1973): 211–24.

67. Gilman, *Yellow Wallpaper*, 9–10.

68. Brett Williams, "Why Migrant Women Feed Their Husbands Tamales: Foodways as a Basis for a Revisionist View of Tejano Family Life," in *Ethnic and Regional Foodways in the United States: The Performance of Group Identity*, ed. Linda Keller Brown and Kay Mussell (Knoxville: University of Tennessee Press, 1984), 113–26.

69. "Burning Dinners: Feminist Subversions of Domesticity," herein.

70. "What's That Smell in the Kitchen" from *Circles on the Water*, by Marge Piercy, is reprinted with the permission of the publisher, Alfred A. Knopf (U.S.) and Routledge Kegan Paul (U.K.) and the Wallace Literary Agency, Inc. Copyright © 1982, 1983 by Marge Piercy and Middlemarch, Inc.

71. Nina Baym, *Women's Fiction: A Guide to Novels by and about Women in America 1820–1870* (Ithaca, N.Y.: Cornell University Press, 1978), 33.

72. Marie-Jeanne Riccoboni, *L'Abeille*, in *Oeuvres complètes*, vol. 3 (Paris: Foucault, 1818), 487.

73. Letter to James Stanier Clarke, December 11, 1815, in *Jane Austen: Selected Letters 1796–1817*, ed. R. W. Chapman (Oxford: Oxford University Press, 1985), 185.

74. "Piety and Motherhood: Reproductive Images and Maternal Strategies of the Woman Preacher," *Journal of American Folklore* 100, no. 398 (1987): 469–78.

PART ONE

Women in the Patriarchal Household

Home is often represented as the place where women can be "most themselves," least on guard. As Barbara Holland put it, "The house is my flesh and blood, my second skin." In most cultures, it is the woman's arena, her domestic domain, where she has traditionally maintained the greatest power. Yet when women live in households with men, that power is often hedged and restricted—and Holland, significantly, made her comment in an essay explaining how she hates housework.[1]

This book begins with the patriarchal home, with studies of how women learn, teach, and negotiate their domestic activities in relation to husbands, children, relatives, and in-laws. Intimacy between men and women does not simplify situations of sexual dominance; it may sharpen aggravations and make them frequent and repetitive, and at the same time it may increase the danger of a woman's free expression. One could speculate that the greater the power difference between husband and wife, the greater the need for coding. In many households, a wife's open speech on her own behalf is impossible. Many considerations may silence her. She may, of course, withhold expressions of protest because she fears divorce or abuse, but she may also be muted by her felt obligation to fulfill conventional role expectations. "Moreover," as Sheila Rowbotham has written, "the relationship of man to woman is like no other relationship of oppressor to oppressed. It is far more delicate, far more complex. After all, very often the two love one another. It is a rather gentle tyranny. We are subdued at the very moment of intimacy."[2] Robert Frost's sonnet image of a perfectly balanced woman, "loosely bound / By countless silken ties of love and thought," finally portrays her as "aware" of her "bondage."[3]

A woman's creative skills may offer her an outlet for domestic frustration. When Martha Mitchell of Huntsville, Texas, married in 1920, for instance, she found her life sharply and specifically restricted. Her response was not complaint or direct rebellion; instead, she sought relief in the coded, buffered form of handiwork: "I became Mrs. Mitchell instead of me. You were trained to do that. . . . I didn't like to be told what to do, though I . . . think I made Mr. Mitchell very happy as a dutiful wife, but there were times when I absolutely rebelled. I just rebelled against all of this ownership of women. I could take a lot of that out in my hobbies: in my quilting, and in my art work."[4]

One extreme of the range of women's strategic performance is marked by coding so private that no one but its maker can read it. A nineteenth-century mother speaks of making a particularly significant quilt:

> It took me more than twenty years, nearly twenty-five, I reckon, in the evenings after supper when the children were all put to bed. My whole life is in that quilt. It scares me sometimes when I look at it. All my joys and all my sorrows are stitched into those little pieces. When I was proud of the boys and when I was downright provoked and angry with them. When the girls annoyed me or when they gave me a warm feeling around my heart. And John, too. He was stitched into that quilt and all the thirty years we were married. Sometimes I loved him and some-times I sat there hating him as I pieced the patches together. So they are all in that quilt, my hopes and fears, my joys and sorrows, my loves and hates. I tremble sometimes when I remember what that quilt knows about me.[5]

At the other end of the spectrum from such esoteric coding lie situations in which a potentially antagonistic home audience is able to decode a woman's message but is unwilling to do so. In such a close and enduring group as the family, it can be dangerous not only for a woman to express anger or frustration but also for a man to admit that his partner is frustrated or angry. To pay attention to women's subver-sive feelings is, in a sense, to validate them—and potentially to lose power or self-esteem; acting as if one is not receiving their messages, on the other hand, is a way of silencing women, of screening out their power to disrupt. Men may thus collude with women's coding; they may read some of the messages but may not acknowledge their understanding. Because women's coding mutually protects them from confronting difficult issues, it can on occasion serve the wishes of both sexes.

Martha Mitchell's reminiscences about her marriage again provide a relevant example. Distrusting and denying her love of colorful clothing, her husband, eight years her senior, "wanted me to wear something rather somber, as an old married lady would do, and not attract any attention from anybody else." Occasionally, she found ways to circumvent his restrictions: "One time one of the neighbors gave me a dress that had some green in it. I just loved that dress; it was a kind of a taffeta, a pretty material, and I went ahead and made a dress out of that and wore it. And he couldn't say anything about it because it was given to me by the neighbor."[6] Here Martha Mitchell was protected by indirection; although the green dress allowed her to express her love of color, *she* had not desired the dress but had to wear it to maintain neighborly relations. At the same time, Mr. Mitchell was spared the necessity of a potentially damaging confrontation. Even though his wife was contravening his principles, they remained unchallenged; he lost no face. Coding by indirection, in this instance, may have been just as important for him as it was for her—an ironic reminder of the complex interweavings of resistance and disempowerment.

The studies in this section illustrate a range of coded expression that women have devised in response to the restrictions, the repetitive duties, and the power imbalances of their domestic lives. Susan S. Lanser's "Burning Dinners: Feminist Subversions of Domesticity," which extends and deepens the brief discussion of the tactic of incompetence in "Strategies of Coding," examines women's claims or enactments of incompetence at such domestic activities as sewing, cooking, and cleaning. In many cultures, domesticity is the defining competence of "real" women, and in folktales, even "female intelligence is ultimately harnessed to domestic ends." The strategy (conscious or not) of claiming incompetence permits a woman to avoid unwanted chores and may encode protest against the restrictions of the role to which she is expected to conform. Lanser raises the crucial question of the linkage between coding strategies and class and race status, pointing out that the claim of domestic incompetence is most successful for women in comfortable economic circumstances, which permit them to employ poorer (and often racially different) women to do the tasks they "cannot" perform. Her discussion emphasizes the urgent political challenge "to erase all expectations of competence and incompetence based in class, race, and sex."

Lanser's essay also proposes that the impersonal discourse of folk narratives, in particular, has allowed women to encode tendentious personal and political messages. She suggests that folktales—often told by women—about incompetent, superlatively competent, or "lazy" wives can carry double messages. For those who expect to hear cautionary lessons about domestic diligence, such tales can reinforce traditional assumptions about gender roles. But when the stories portray women who are not punished for avoiding domestic tasks, listeners who choose may hear instead a message that subverts dutiful homemaking.[7]

Coding by indirection through another genre of folk narrative is the focus of Polly Stewart's essay, "Wishful Willful Wily Women: Verbal Strategies for Female Success in the Child Ballads." Stewart combines a structural examination of traditional Anglo-American oral ballads, delineating the cautionary examples they offer women, with a study of accounts of women's singing at home in Appalachia. The ballads teach women that they are vulnerable in many ways to men both inside the family and out and that if they are to survive, they must outsmart the men and the patriarchal system that would victimize them. Learning the ballads within their families as children, these women all their lives "study out" the songs for the wisdom they contain, find in them appropriate warnings about the ways of the world, and sing them to family members to communicate that wisdom. Singing of the tragedies of legendary times in the voices of impersonal narrators, women code with indirection the survival messages they send past listening husbands, brothers, and boyfriends, to the girls and women in their families.

Notes

1. "The Day's Work," in *Pulling Our Own Strings: Feminist Humor and Satire,* ed. Gloria Kaufman and Mary Kay Blakely (Bloomington: Indiana University Press, 1980), 52, 45–52.

2. *Woman's Consciousness, Man's World* (Harmondsworth, England: Penguin Books, 1973), 34.

3. "The Silken Tent," *The Poetry of Robert Frost* (New York: Holt, Rinehart and Winston, 1969), 332.

4. Melvin Rosser Mason, "'Every Stitch Is a Loving Stitch . . .': Martha Mitchell, Quiltmaker," unpublished manuscript, 13–14. I am very grateful to Professor Mason for sharing his research with me.

5. Marguerite Ickis, quoting her great-grandmother, in *Anonymous Was a Woman,* Mirra Bank (New York: St. Martin's Press, 1979), 94. Another example of esoteric personal coding is the diary of Anne Lister, discussed in "Strategies of Coding in Women's Cultures," herein.

6. Mason, " 'Every Stitch,' " 15.

7. Lanser's study complements the observations of Marie Maclean in "Oppositional Practices in Women's Traditional Narrative," *New Literary History* 19, no. 1 (1987): 37–50.

Burning Dinners: Feminist Subversions of Domesticity

SUSAN S. LANSER

One of my favorite childhood rituals was Sabbath dinner at my grandparents' house. Our tribe of close-knit cousins would pass the time before dinner playing in gleeful abandon in the spare room, paying scant attention to the preparation of food for which our services were not required. By the time we were called to the table, my grandfather would be carving the roast chicken or the brisket of beef, and so it is my grandfather's image that sustains my recollection of those meals. Only as an adult did I learn that this image was more apt than I realized, for my grandfather apparently not only carved but also cooked those roasts. My grandmother, my father told me, was not much of a cook.

I do not know by what coded or uncoded actions Sabbath dinners became my grandfather's turf: whether my grandmother made excuses to avoid preparing them, botched meals until my grandfather stepped in, or simply bowed (as one aunt recently suggested) to a husband who loved to cook. I do not know whether my grandfather cooked other, less ceremonial dinners, nor do I know by what process I came to assume that my grandmother had cooked the Sabbath meals. My father insisted that his mother *could not* cook; remembering the woman who so often sat engrossed in her Yiddish books and took avid part in political and cultural organizations, I now imagine a woman who *would not* cook, a woman engaged in the subversive use of incompetence to extricate herself from a traditionally female performance that was not much to her taste.

If my grandmother did in fact avoid cooking dinners, then she was also avoiding an ideal of womanly competence that had changed little in her journey from the outskirts of Warsaw to the Chicago neighborhoods where she and her children raised their families. In the folklore of many cultures at least in Europe, the Middle East, and Euro-America, for several centuries and across situational differences, female competence seems to have been virtually coextensive with competence at domestic tasks.[1] Consider, for example, the tales in which a man is instructed to choose a bride according to how carefully she can cut cheese or scrape the kneading trough, demonstrating at once her frugality and her skill;[2] tales in which a woman gets a husband because she spins so well or makes a soup no one can replicate; ballads celebrating women who can bake cherry pie; and proverbs mapping the way to a man's heart.

Such definitions of women's value can be found in folklore from the ancient and sublime to the modern and obscene. At one extreme, there is the passage in the Hebrew Bible that equates "valiant woman" with capable wife: after thirty chapters on the diverse qualities that make men virtuous, the Book of Proverbs concludes (31:10–31) by detailing the virtues of women who labor skillfully from dawn to dark. At the other extreme, yet born of similar assumptions, are jokes like the one that posits the ideal wife as a lady in the parlor, an economist in the kitchen, and a prostitute in bed—or, in a far more vulgar formulation, the definition reproduced uncritically in a collection of urban folklore, of a wife as "a gadget you screw on the bed to get the housework done."[3] Whether with admiration or contempt, then, the folklore of many cultures equates female value with domestic industry. An Israeli tale concludes with this typology: "And since then, until today, there have been three kinds of women. There are stupid, lazy, and obstinate women. . . . There are bad, bickering, and shouting women. . . . But happy is the man blessed with a clever, quiet, and diligent woman. She is the true daughter of Noah the Righteous One."[4]

It is worth noting that this tale and many others, at least in their extant English translations, call on women to be "clever" as well as industrious. Associated in its early definitions with manual skill, the word *clever* retains its connection with neatness and dexterity rather than with pure intellect. This body of folklore does recognize the value of female intelligence so long as it is bounded by domestic purposes. Daughters and wives (like servants of both sexes) can sometimes even be smarter than the men around them, if they use their wit in the service of their duller relatives. "The Clever Peasant Girl" (AT 875) describes a set of tales from several European cultures in which a clever daughter solves a riddle to win riches for her family and sometimes a rich husband for herself. In one Israeli tale, a husband is so incompetent that he forgets which woman is his wife, but the wife's intelligence protects the husband from harm. Although such a woman may trick her husband to demonstrate his foolishness, there is no question of her turning her superior intelligence to antipatriarchal ends; after all, as a neighbor woman counsels in the Israeli tale, "It is better to have a husband like that than no husband at all."[5] "Clever Else," on the other hand, gets so tangled in abstraction that she cannot do the simplest chore competently. Sent downstairs for beer to serve the man who is courting her, she remains there for hours weeping that if she marries him, and they have a child, and the child comes down to the cellar, the axe sticking from the rafter will fall on him and kill him; later she agonizes over whether to work first or eat first; finally, she is not even certain who she is: " 'Is it me, or isn't it me?' . . . She did not know what to answer."[6] Here, a woman's attempt at abstract thought turns "cleverness" to sad irony.

Indeed, the one exceptional tale I have encountered in which a woman's wisdom seems to be permitted a nondomestic outlet finally ends up proving the old rule. Italo Calvino records the Italian tale of "Catherine the Wise," in which a brilliant and learned young woman, grief-stricken over her mother's death, is allowed by her shopkeeper-father to open her own school. The school is a kind of socialist-feminist democracy: "both boys and girls" are admitted free of charge and sit "side by side, without distinction. . . . 'The coal merchant's son must sit beside the prince's daughter.' " Catherine runs a rigorous classroom, and when "the prince himself decide[s] to attend" and turns out to be a dunce, Catherine "dealt him a back-handed blow."[7] The story takes a swerve when the enraged prince asks Catherine to marry him, she immediately accepts, and he ties her up and locks her in a pit because she refuses to repent the slap. The rest of the tale recounts episode after episode in which Catherine must use her intelligence to outwit her husband, escape from the traps he continues to set, and fool him entirely over a period of years, so that he keeps abandoning her and marrying a "new" princess, who is actually Catherine in disguise. Finally, all identities are revealed and the husband asks forgiveness, but Catherine's school and scholarship are never mentioned again. Even in this anomalous story of a woman scholar, female intelligence is ultimately harnessed to domestic ends.

This rechanneling of a woman's abilities suggests that domestic competence is not simply a part of the definition of female competence but virtually the whole of it. If female competence is domestic competence, the corollary is that in most areas that are *not* associated with domesticity, to be a "woman" is, traditionally speaking, to be (presumed) incompetent or minimally competent. As Joan N. Radner and I note in "Strategies of Coding in Women's Cultures," male and female incompetence are often inversely defined, so that men may demonstrate their manhood when they boast of incompetence at precisely those behaviors that signal female capability—hence the proverbial husband who can't sew on a button or boil an egg. Both women and men, of course, may reinforce this system; Patricia Andrews, for example, quoted in Ann Oakley's *Woman's Work,* says of men's participation in housework, "I'd rather do it myself, because they don't do it properly anyway."[8] An entire tale-type (AT 1408) is devoted to stories about "The Husband Who Would Mind the House," in which men and women reverse roles and the men turn out to be incompetent at domestic chores that they had refused even to define as work.

In cultures with oppositional definitions of masculine and feminine, it is not surprising that these domestic attributes that get defined as "+ female" also get defined as "– male," just as the competencies designated "+ male" are understood as "– female." But the structure of value associated with these oppositions is not wholly parallel because, as Simone de Beauvoir observes, men are not only the positive term in the sex-gender system but the neutral term as well. Thus, what is male is male, but what is human is also male, "as is indicated by the common use of *man* to designate human beings in general."[9] As a result, women's success *or* failure at traditionally male tasks bears a negative charge: the stereotypes of the superfeminine woman who cannot change a tire and the unfeminine woman who can have both been more equivocal than the image of the domestically incompetent or supercompetent man. A "real" woman does women's work and not men's work, just as a "real" man does men's and not women's work. So far, the parallels to men obtain. But a woman who cannot do men's work is "only" a woman, while a man who cannot do women's work is not "only" a man because in such a system there is nothing better than being a man. A man can, of course, do certain kinds of "domestic" work, like cooking or weaving, if he does it outside the home. Such professionalized activities are often distinguished linguistically: the "cook" and the "seamstress" are women, the "chef" and "tailor" men. Competence and incompetence thus participate as cultural values in a nexus of gender arrangements that delineate confining expectations for both sexes but leave women diminished in status and opportunity when they take the "appropriate" avenue.

Precisely because it is safe, indeed immensely serviceable as competencies go, domestic performance so validates a woman that it can mask or justify her appropriation of male turf. In Mary Wilkins

Freeman's story "The Revolt of 'Mother'" (1891), a New England housewife takes over her husband's new barn after he reneges on his promise to build her a new house. In language that gives masculine status to her domestic accomplishments, Freeman makes Sarah a "masterly keeper of her box of a house," an "artist so perfect that he [*sic*] has apparently no art."[10] In her moments of hottest resentment, Sarah still bakes her husband's favorite pies and painstakingly irons his shirts. What appears at first to be yet another enactment of a woman's silent, literally inconsequential resentment becomes instead the ground that justifies the takeover of Adoniram's barn. Sarah is presented as so skillful and industrious, so concerned for her home, that her daring appropriation of male space can be read as the perfection of her domesticity. Sarah's "mastery" is not only justification, then, but also coded distraction: surely a woman who keeps cooking and cleaning so dutifully cannot really be a threat. Both justification and distraction may also be operating in the behaviors of contemporary "superwomen" who succeed in traditionally male work spheres but are determined not to sacrifice a strand of the domestic enterprise. I thought of Freeman's story recently when I read a blurb in my physician's office listing her credentials in medicine and concluding with her marital status and the number and sex of her children. I recalled my inordinate pride at having sewn, during my first semester in graduate school, an extremely elaborate three-piece Halloween costume for the oldest of my three small sons.

While domestic ability is expected of all but the most privileged women, domestic competence is also, of course, constructed in terms of social class. In folktales, domestic competence may be so powerful that it allows women to cross class barriers. It is not only a servant girl's beauty but also her housewifery that can earn her marriage to a prince. Cinderella herself was as industrious as her stepsisters were lazy, and in another Grimms' tale, a man marries the servant of his bride-to-be because she is a more industrious spinner than the bride.[11] Such narratives stand, however, in cruel tension with social experience, for it is not the marriage of women servants but their seduction that pervades history. After all, a rich man does not have to marry competence to reap its benefits, and if the servant girl does get the prince, she will surely be freed from the domestic service for which the man allegedly married her.

Indeed, the ideal of domestic competence is exposed and complicated by class, for not all women have been expected to demonstrate the same degree of competence either in folktales or in life. In many cultures, domestic incompetence seems to be a sign of class status;

certain women get to be as incompetent as men, but their domestic ineptness only makes them more feminine. This is especially true in cultures where physical labor structures class (and thus often racial) differences. In the antebellum U.S. South, for example, domestic incompetence distinguished the white "lady" from her black slaves. Marriah Hines, interviewed in the 1930s at the age of 102, recalls that during her slave days on a plantation owned by "good . . . white folks," the master did not allow the slaves to work on Sunday. Yet "lots of times we slaves would take turns on helping 'em serve Sunday meals just 'cause we liked them so much. We hated to see Missie fumbling round in the kitchen all out o' her place."[12] This kind of class and race complexity continues to structure domestic work, so that it remains entirely acceptable and is no sign of failed femininity for an upper-class woman to hire another woman, very likely a woman of color, to clean and maintain her house. Indeed, the status of (under)paid domestic labor in many, if not most, countries gives the lie to the alleged value of domestic competence; if domestic skill is what makes a woman worthy, it does not make her worthy of much.

Because domestic competence is ultimately of limited cultural value even though it is of urgent cultural necessity, and because so many societies still expect most women to share a common set of domestic interests and skills and to spend much of their time performing them, domesticity has surely become, at least for some women some of the time, a source of limitation, constraint, and downright misery. One would expect, therefore, to find in some traditional settings the traces of women's resistance to the tyranny of daily domestic demands. I am interested here especially in those traces that take the (coded) form of proclaimed or enacted incompetence, like the resistance in which I imagine my grandmother engaged—that is, what Radner and I describe in "Strategies of Coding" as claims or demonstrations of incompetence through which women extricate themselves from traditionally female responsibilities without openly refusing them.

Women claim incompetence when they assert that they cannot cook, bake, knit, sew, or keep a clean house (the latter often under the label "disorganized," since sweeping and scrubbing are usually considered unskilled labor within anyone's competence). Women demonstrate incompetence when they do one of these tasks poorly—leave it incomplete, neglect it, or spoil it in some way. Our hypothesis is that such performances may function as coded rejections not only of the task in question but also of a culturally constructed female role. Like all coded phenomena, strategic displays of incompetence are inevitably double-voiced and double-edged, but precisely for this reason they allow a woman to say "I can't" when she means but cannot say "I won't." The claim or enactment of incompetence does require the woman to declare herself a failure in traditional terms (which may be one of several reasons why women usually declare their incompetence only in selective areas), but the declaration also has a certain traditional savor because it plays on notions of female helplessness and delicacy like those associated with the upper-class white "lady" of the antebellum South. Besides, to fail at what is womanly, as Radner and I suggest, is in some cultural sense to be more like a man. In *The Woman Warrior*, Maxine Hong Kingston recalls that as a child she "refused to cook. When I had to wash dishes, I would crack one or two. 'Bad girl,' my mother yelled, and sometimes that made me gloat rather than cry. Isn't a bad girl almost a boy?"[13]

Given the weight of cultural ideology and the social and economic arrangements of traditional marriage, the open refusal of heterosexually married women to perform necessary domestic activities has been and perhaps still remains largely a luxury of class or circumstance. An acquaintance of mine, the widow of a renowned sculptor, recalls that as a new bride she received only one piece of advice from her mother-in-law: choose one domestic skill that you do not know how to do and never learn it, thereby exempting yourself from its performance for life. She chose laundry. There was, however, sufficient money to have the laundry sent out. I also knew a woman who had no stove; she bought her house without one and just never put one in. But she was a professional woman, divorced, and without children, and although her stovelessness may have annoyed the man with whom she was keeping company, she could afford to have a kitchen that screamed rebellion in this way. Where women are able to live in lesbian partnerships or in heterosexual relationships that do not subscribe to traditional domestic ideologies, domestic competence becomes another issue entirely. As humorist Gail Sausser writes of her lesbian household, "If the house gets too dirty, we throw a party. Everyone becomes motivated to vacuum, wash dishes and scrub sinks so others don't think we are slobs."[14]

On the other hand, there are contexts in which even very selective refusals can be dangerous. In "Strategies of Coding," Radner and I note the more circumscribed refusal documented in Brett Williams's report of a divorce suit brought by an Illinois Mexican-American man on the grounds that his wife refused to cook tamales. Although what infuriated the husband was that the woman could make tamales but would not, probably a claim of incompetence would have been of no use at all, for the woman would simply have been told to learn from the other women in the community what any woman in her culture would be considered able to do. Indeed, Williams notes that the husband had "the full support of his wife's kin as well as his own."[15]

The degree of privilege that even coded refusals entail is clearest when women bound to domestic work for a livelihood fail to do at home what they do successfully in the labor force. Juliet Warren, cited in Ann Oakley's study, describes her mother as an incompetent housekeeper—"very muddly, very disorganized . . . erratic and mad in the way she keeps house"—but this mother turns out to have "had a job cleaning" every morning from 5:00 to 7:30 and also to have had the full care of an invalid son.[16] "Incompetence" at home may well have been a way to protest, where protest was possible, the kind of work expected of her for low pay in the workplace and no pay at home. In this case, the daughter's own experience as a wife and mother did lead her to reread her own mother's (lack of) domesticity: "I've changed completely in my reaction to her and the way she keeps house. When I go down there I just accept it and think, 'Well, poor woman she works,' and I realize what it's all about now perhaps—it's an insight into the way she was, having a baby myself. How she coped, I do not know. When I think of the terrible things one felt about one's own mother! I can see how it all makes sense now, because I find I'm slackening *my* standards."[17]

Incompetence practiced at an early age, like Kingston's behavior as a "bad girl," may also be a strategy for avoiding a future of such low-paying and deadening work. Francie Coffin, the narrator of Louise Meriwether's novel *Daddy Was a Number Runner,* is an African-American adolescent growing up in Harlem in the 1930s, whose mother does domestic day-work. Each evening Francie's mother "would come home and try to keep up with our messy house since I wasn't much help. I cooked the dinner every day and washed the dishes, but after I dropped a sheet into the backyard while trying to hang it on the line and burnt up one of Daddy's good shirts with the iron, I didn't have to help with the laundry no more. I wasn't very good at cleaning up the house either. Mother said I daydreamed too much and she could do it faster without my help so just get on out of her way."[18] Francie's "incompetence" is an act of survival, her preservation from a life her mother has not been able to avoid. The danger of domestic achievement is made clear when Francie's high-school sewing teacher tells her that

> "if you would take more time with your backstitch, Francie, you might make a good seamstress one day."

> "I don't think I'd like it, Mrs. Abowitz. I want to be a secretary when I grow up."
>
> "Well, Francie, we have to be practical. There aren't many jobs for Negroes in that field. And while you're going to school you should learn those things which will stand you in good stead when you have to work."
>
> "I like shorthand and typing, Mrs. Abowitz," I said, suddenly stubborn, "and I'm gonna be a secretary."
>
> She sighed. "I don't know why they teach courses like that to frustrate you people."[19]

If Francie is to avoid this kind of "tracking" as her mother could not, it is better to be incompetent. Contemporary American folk wisdom suggests that girls should refuse to learn typing for the same reason that Francie refused to sew: if you can do woman's work, the logic goes, you'll be forced to do it. In fact, when Francie takes on a one-day domestic job in a desperate moment, it becomes clear that she is indeed capable of housework, just as she is eventually able to cook rice for her father (who knows enough about cooking to teach her how but is clearly unwilling to cook it himself: "it was a goddamn shame a man couldn't get a decent pot of rice in his own home").[20] Francie's coded displays also find a certain parallel in folktales like the Grimms' "Clever Gretel" (tale 77, AT 1741), in which a servant uses her wits to appropriate for herself the food she has just cooked for her master.

Francie's domestic failures are excusable because she is still a child. Although most heterosexual adult women probably could not get away with such broad performances of "incompetence," one common strategy is to declare incompetence in certain areas but to offset this by demonstrating special competence in another, perhaps less essential or more creative domestic art. Liz Smith, editor of *The Mother Book,* says that her mother "detested cooking" but made candy perfectly and cooked it as a kind of compensation to her family.[21] Many women declare themselves "disorganized," thereby excusing themselves from the most repetitive domestic chores, while performing other acts of housewifery with pleasure and skill. By designating areas of competence and incompetence, a woman distracts her family from confrontations; pleasing them in one area may "drown out" absences in another. She also gains some control over the shape, if not the fact, of her domestic identity. Since, as I have said, self-proclaimed domestic incompetence is largely a male prerogative, selective in/competence makes a woman a kind of domestic androgyne, "feminine" in certain areas and "masculine" in others.

Somewhere on an undeclared line between refusal and incompetence lies a tradition of folktales in which the key word is laziness. One group of such tales can be found within the category Antti Aarne and Stith Thompson call "The Lazy Woman Is Cured" (AT 902), a variant of "The Shrewish Wife Is Reformed" (AT 900–904). In the prototype, a lazy woman ends up becoming industrious. But there are also tales about lazy women in which this resolution fails to occur. Linda Dégh records a Hungarian tale in which a girl renowned for her laziness is married off to an unsuspecting man from another village. Since her parents have given her an enormous trousseau, it takes an entire year for the husband to find out that his wife has been burning her dirty clothes instead of washing them. He then returns her—and her dowry—to the parental home. This particular telling omits the reform of the lazy wife and even any indication that she is distressed at being sent home. From the beginning, the anxiety is the mother's. It is the mother who nags the girl constantly that she will never get a man, and when the bride returns home, it is the mother's unhappiness, not the bride's, that the story records. Dégh notes the tale is intended "to point a moral concerning the proper conduct of the village girl" in a "peasant community" where "no lazy girl will ever find herself a husband."[22] The tale *as told,* however, proffers no such moral, allowing an interpretation that rejects the necessity to find and keep a man.

Another variant of AT 902, the Grimms' "The Lazy Spinner," suggests that laziness is not precisely what is at stake. In this tale, the wife "never wanted to do any work" and always left her spinning and her household in a mess.. Each time the husband complains, the woman tricks him into believing the failures to be his own, and finally he gives up asking her to spin. But clearly it is not industry but housework she wants to avoid, for she is willing to expend enormous energy avoiding domestic work. Once again, there is no punishment for the wife's waywardness; indeed, she is rewarded with the very freedom from domesticity that she sought: "in the future he no longer mentioned yarn and spinning." As if recognizing its own incompleteness, the Grimms' version ends with this metacomment: "But you yourself must admit that his wife was a nasty woman."[23] Such a conclusion seems to mark the teller's or editor's effort to impose a penalty where the plot itself does not.

An even more overt sanction for female incompetence structures the Grimms' "The Three Spinners," in which three "deformed" old women help a young woman spin an impossible amount of flax. The girl, "a lazy maiden who did not want to spin,"[24] attracts the queen's attention because her mother is beating her for her laziness and the queen hears the cries. The plot is set in motion by a false claim of competence: the mother says she is beating the girl for wanting to spin more yarn than the family can afford. This prompts the queen to challenge the maiden to spin herself into marrying the prince, a challenge she meets only because the three women help her. When these women appear at her wedding and the prince asks them to explain why they are so ugly, each woman attributes her deformity to an excess of spinning, whereupon the prince promptly forbids his beautiful bride to spin for the rest of her life. Since the girl was both poor and lazy in the first place and is rewarded with not only the prince but also lifelong liberation from the work she had once refused to do, the story provides a double reward for incompetence. Such a tale may well be mocking those stories in which the industrious servant girl is the one who gets the prince.

All of these examples suggest that *lazy* may be a coded word, a cover-up, appropriated from the culture's moral discourse and employed for subversive ends. These stories have seemed to support traditional domestic values because they rely on a cultural context in which laziness is negative, obedience virtuous, and marriage both necessary and desirable. Since they do not explicitly verbalize such values, however, the tales are able to function as coded discourse with a double voice. To the extent that the hearer brings traditional cultural assumptions to the listening and hears the stories *as if* they were saying what the dominant culture expects, they can be heard as innocuous tales reinforcing the status quo. But they function as subversive tales to the extent that the hearer is ready to mark the absence of punishments and reprimands. I find it highly suggestive that all these double-voiced versions I have cited have a woman teller as their source. It is certainly possible that the tellers' conscious or unconscious ambivalence about domestic competence has led them to coded performances. This also means that hidden beneath the patriarchal typology of Aarne and Thompson's index, there may lie a countertradition of (coded) tales in which the "lazy wife" is not cured and the "shrew" is a woman who knows her own mind.

All of the examples I have cited thus far focus on the individual woman's efforts to avoid domesticity but do not openly challenge domestic ideology. The set of folktales I referred to earlier as "The Husband Who Would Mind the House" (AT 1408) does challenge a cultural notion that work in the home is unskilled labor accomplished much more easily and quickly than manly work; a man who complains about his own work or his wife's housekeeping is made to exchange roles with her and completely botches the enterprise. These tales not only make domestic work at least equal to work outside the home but also mock the demands of husbands who have no understanding of what women do. The undermining of the demanding husband is bolder still in an Egyptian tale presented by Hasan M. El-Shamy, in which a husband is looking for an excuse to beat his very competent wife so that he can show her (and the community) who's boss. His friends advise him to give her some fish to cook and then to find fault with the way she prepares it. Alerted to the trap, the capable wife cooks the fish in three different ways, so that when he complains about one dish, she is able to produce an alternative. Finally, the man becomes so flustered that he orders her to serve him shit, and it so happens that their infant son has just produced some beneath the dinner table. This woman's "competence"—which, ironically, is finally demonstrated in the "incompetence" of not yet having cleaned up the mess beneath the table—disarms the man and exposes his domestic "need" as a capricious exercise in mastery.

Although most of the folktales I have cited have been published with little information about the contexts in which they are told and passed on, El-Shamy's notes to this tale suggest that the telling itself may be a coded act. The Egyptian woman who told this story had, "after finishing her housework and lacking a place to go," been lingering in the doorway of her home while the men of the village told their tales. When she finally asked if she could tell one too, her husband agreed, if the tale were not recorded: "We are fellahin; this would be too serious [an offense] in our community."[25] Finally allowed to speak, this woman, who lived under patriarchal rule, used an act of indirection—telling a story about someone other than herself—to criticize male dominance. The woman said that she had heard her mother tell this story to a group of women when she was a child; the husband admitted that in fifteen years of marriage he had never heard the tale.[26] Perhaps the tale collector's presence gave the woman a context of safety for telling the aggressive and subversive story she had heretofore considered fit only for women's ears. If subversive tales like these are usually told only among women, we must wonder how many of them no folklorist has yet heard and whether women collectors are more likely to hear them than men are.

This Egyptian tale begins in modest ways to deconstruct the very concept of *domestic competence*. It makes the necessity for perfect performance a patriarchal quirk and an act of incompetence a woman's way out. A further erosion of domestic competence is enacted in folklore that exposes household work as beyond anybody's competence, that echoes Patricia Andrews's remark that "housework is a waste of time, really. . . . You do it, your husband comes home, and it all gets mucked up again."[27] This is the sentiment represented in the traditional North American ballad "Housewife's Lament," in which a woman, having spent her whole life in a war against dirt, is finally defeated when she lies down, dies, and is buried in it.[28] A related phenomenon is the negativity about domestic work that in the 1960s yielded Peg Bracken's *I Hate to Cook Book* and *I Hate to Housekeep Book,* designed to help women "make yourself do things you don't like to do," "go that last long mile and cook dinner," and "keep up a good front."[29] I recently found a turn-of-the-century precursor of these books in an article proposing to help New England women make time for a daily "study hour." The advice: "Do not put off, but take less time for each thing. The secret to be learned about housework, is how to slight it, and yet do it well." There follows a host of tips for speeding up washing, cooking, ironing, dishes, dusting, and "blacking the kitchen range."[30] Such texts do not constitute outright refusals of domesticity and may not free women from much domestic work, but they do undermine the notion of domestic excellence as a measure of woman's worth. It is no accident that these writings appear during periods in which higher education for women is on the rise.

A more radical deconstructive strategy that appears to be fairly recent reverses the equation of women with domestic competence by implying that domestic life actually *makes* women incompetent. This idea was already implicit in turn-of-the-century radical feminism and articulated by writers like Charlotte Perkins Gilman, who contrasted the utopian women of Herland with U.S. women, who, she argued, had become stunted by domesticity.[31] In more recent renditions, there surfaces from beneath the image of the superwife-and-mother a counterfigure of the housewife/mother as nattering wreck. A few years ago, for example, M. Catherine Burns published in an anthology of Maine humor a set of anecdotes in which the narrator is driven crazy by the care and feeding of three sons. After each incident, the narrator presents herself as "a babbling lunatic sitting in the corner" and as having to find a hobby "to divert what's left of my mind."[32] There is an edge of hostility in this humor; for instance, when one of the children gets lost just before a camping trip and the narrator finds him "packed away in the very front of a U-Haul trailer," she considers it a sign of her "insanity" that "I only spent five minutes enjoying all the blissful possibilities before letting him out."[33] I recently came across a commercial mug that bore the slogan "Insanity is inherited; you get it from your kids." If children and housework make the domestically competent woman incompetent, domesticity subverts itself.

Yet as I have suggested, these displays of incompetence risk reinforcing the notion that women really are incompetent. Strategic incompetence can work subversively only to the extent that the performer—or the performer's political community—has interpretive control of the display. The coded performance of a feminist message may, in the eyes of the receiver, simply reinscribe an existing folklore of female ineptitude found, for example, in men's jokes about their mothers' bad cooking—such as the ballad parody that "You can't chop your mama up in Massachusetts, / Not even if you're tired of her cuisine"—and in the cultural stereotype of the inept housewife that gets enacted in advertisements for floor cleaners and fabric softeners. Conversely, the coding may be too obvious, so that what a woman represents as incompetence is recognized and treated as a rebellious act. Since no one can control the interpretive process, even the cleverest act of strategic incompetence walks a fine line. On the one hand, it can be derided as mere female ineptitude; on the other, it can be exposed for the act of refusal on which it is based.

Moreover, especially in industrial societies where heterosexual domestic life isolates women from one another, even the most radical performance of coded incompetence risks remaining an isolated personal act. Such a private action may effect an individual liberation without openly challenging the legitimacy of a female domestic sphere. When Katharine Hepburn says, for example, that "being a housewife and a mother is the biggest job in the world" but that she herself "would have made a terrible parent," she gets herself off the hook but leaves the mystique of domesticity intact.[34] If the performance of incompetence does not embrace a refusal to work—if the woman says she cannot do things but does them anyway or does them badly without any savings of time or energy—then the performance may relieve emotional pressure but may not significantly change the material realities of her life.

Individual acts of coded resistance do, however, become the grounds for feminist revolution when they can be articulated within a theoretical frame. Marge Piercy's poem "What's That Smell in the Kitchen?" (quoted in "Strategies of Coding," p. 21) offers more than a witty catalogue of the different kinds of dinners being burned "all over America"; it creates a model for re-presenting these actions as a collective, coded resistance.[35] In the fashion of a classic feminist analysis, the poem builds an understanding of cause and effect from the observation of multiple individual experiences. Piercy exposes incompetence as a rejection of not only the required daily dinner but also the entire performance that constitutes a traditional woman's daily life, and on the basis of this understanding, she reconceives incompetence as war. This kind of analysis is, of course, also one task of feminist folklore: to gather and analyze individual moments, decoding and renaming them as political acts, Once they are exposed as feminist messages, such performances can no longer function as coded strategies; they become instead the folklore that supports more open resistances.

Even collective resistance to compulsory domesticity carries serious dangers if it does not challenge the larger social system that embeds these notions of competence. Proclamations and displays of domestic incompetence by professional-class women in the United States are as acceptable today as they were once embarrassing, *so long as one can pay someone else to do the work.* Some women have begun to represent domestic competence as a sign of human *in*competence, acceding to the traditionally masculine convention that a competent person can- not or would not want to do "women's work." Since much of this work is physical labor poorly rewarded in both money and status in the United States and most other technological societies, such a devaluation of domestic competence necessarily denigrates other women and, by displacing domestic work onto women of a less privileged social class, ends up reinforcing the same gender/class divisions that structured such reactionary and racist societies as the antebellum South. This kind of middle-class feminism has already caused painful schisms among women, as Audre Lorde suggests in issuing this chal- lenge to feminists in the academy: "If white american feminist theory need not deal with the differences between us, and the resulting differences in our oppressions, then how do you deal with the fact that the women who clean your houses and tend your children while you attend conferences on feminist theory are, for the most part, poor women and women of Color?"[36]

Clearly, the challenge is to erase all expectations of competence and incompetence based in class, race, and sex. Insofar as the necessity of domestic competence has functioned as a leveler, requiring women of different backgrounds, interests, classes, and races to learn and prac- tice similar skills, women's history could be the basis for understand- ing that just as there is no sphere for a sex (as Elizabeth Cady Stanton put it in refusing the belief that woman's place was in the home), so there is no sphere for a race or a class. In this way perhaps domestic work can become neutralized both in folklore and in social practice as sometimes necessary, sometimes pleasurable, and sometimes onerous work worthy of respectable status and, when performed for wages, respectable reward. Only those practices that do not transfer domestic competence to an underclass of women—or men—will offer genuinely feminist messages, messages that might yield in turn a new folklore in which "valiant women" can make policy and "real men" can make rice, tamales, and quiche.

Notes

1. I have not found this focus on domestic competence in American Indian, African, or African-American folklore, but my research is not sufficient to draw any conclusions from this absence. As will become clear, these equations of femininity with domestic competence also do not apply to leisure-class women (a term defined variously in different cultures and different bodies of folklore).

2. This is the "Bride Test," AT 1452, exemplified in the Grimms' tale 155, "Choosing a Bride," and in North Carolina and Missouri versions reported by Richard Dorson, *Buying the Wind: Regional Folklore in the United States* (Chicago: University of Chicago Press, 1964), 146–48. For citations from the Grimms' tales, I am using *The Complete Fairy Tales of the Brothers Grimm*, trans. Jack Zipes (New York: Bantam Books, 1987). AT numbering refers to the index of Indo-European tale plots catalogued in Antti Aarne and Stith Thompson, *The Types of the Folktale: A Classification and Bibliography*, Folklore Fellows Communications No. 184 (Helsinki: Academia Scientiarum Fennica, 1973).

3. Alan Dundes and Carl L. Pagter, *Work Hard and You Shall Be Rewarded: Urban Folklore from the Paperwork Empire* (Bloomington: Indiana University Press, 1975), 50. While I find it disturbing that this definition is passed along without any critical context, I am equally disturbed by the equivocal commentary Dundes and Pagter do attach, for example, to a piece of racist folklore in the same book (127).

4. "The Only Daughter of Noah the Righteous," no. 52, in *Folktales of Israel*, ed. Dov Noy (Chicago: University of Chicago Press, 1963), 135.

5. "The Two Husbands," no. 69, in *Folktales of Israel*, ed. Noy, 188. The tale type is AT 1406, "The Merry Wives' Wager."

6. "Clever Else," no. 34, in *The Complete Fairy Tales of the Brothers Grimm*, trans. Zipes, 132.

7. "Catherine the Wise," no. 151, in *Italian Folktales, Selected and Retold by Italo Calvino*, trans. George Martin (New York: Pantheon, 1980), 541.

8. Ann Oakley, *Woman's Work: The Housewife, Past and Present* (New York: Random House, 1974), 111.

9. Simone de Beauvoir, *The Second Sex*, trans. H. M. Parshley (New York: Bantam, 1961), xv.

10. Mary Wilkins Freeman, "The Revolt of 'Mother'" (1891), in *The Revolt of Mother and Other Stories* (Old Westbury, N.Y.: Feminist Press, 1974), 121. The story is widely anthologized.

11. "The Leftovers," no. 156, in *The Complete Fairy Tales of the Brothers Grimm*, trans. Zipes, 511–12.

12. *Voices from Slavery,* ed. Norman R. Yetman (New York: Holt, Rinehart and Winston, 1970), 167. Hines adds, "We didn't have to [help in the kitchen]; we just did it on our own free will." The notion of *free will*—which I have no doubt was experienced in this way by these slaves—is a perfect example of the workings of ideology to make what is culturally demanded seem desirable and freely chosen.

13. Maxine Hong Kingston, *The Woman Warrior: Memoirs of a Girlhood among Ghosts* (New York: Random House, 1976), 56.

14. Gail Sausser, *Lesbian Etiquette: Humorous Essays* (Trumansburg, N.Y.: Crossing Press, 1986), 31.

15. Brett Williams, "Why Migrant Women Feed Their Husbands Tamales: Foodways as a Basis for a Revisionist View of Tejano Family Life," in *Ethnic and Regional Foodways in the United States: The Performance of Group Identity,* ed. Linda Keller Brown and Kay Mussell (Knoxville: University of Tennessee Press, 1984), 114.

16. Oakley, *Woman's Work,* 123.

17. Ibid., 123–24.

18. Louise Meriwether, *Daddy Was a Number Runner* (Englewood Cliffs, N.J.: Prentice-Hall, 1970), 162–63. This unjustly neglected novel, long out of print or classified as a "juvenile" book, was reissued by the Feminist Press in 1988.

19. Ibid., 144.

20. Ibid., 108.

21. Liz Smith, *The Mother Book* (New York: Doubleday, 1978), 269.

22. Linda Dégh, ed., *Folktales of Hungary* (Chicago: University of Chicago Press, 1965), 319. The tale is "Lazybones," no. 12, 142–47.

23. "The Lazy Spinner," no. 28, in *The Complete Fairy Tales of the Brothers Grimm,* trans. Zipes, 455–57.

24. "The Three Spinners," no. 14, in *The Complete Fairy Tales of the Brothers Grimm,* trans. Zipes, 55.

25. "Reason to Beat Your Wife," no. 56, in *Folktales of Egypt,* ed. Hasan M. El-Shamy (Chicago: University of Chicago Press, 1980), 216.

26. El-Shamy notes that "two additional variants of this anecdote are available in Egyptian archives; both were told by females from rural areas" (299).

27. Oakley, *Woman's Work,* 113.

28. "The Housewife's Lament," no. 67, in *Folksongs of North America,* ed. Alan Lomax (New York: Doubleday, 1975), 133.

29. Peg Bracken, *The I Hate to Housekeep Book* (New York: Fawcett, 1962), ix.

30. Adelaide F. Chase, "A Study Hour for the Housewife," *American Kitchen Magazine* 9, no. 7 (1898): 211.

31. Charlotte Perkins Gilman, *Herland* (1915; New York: Pantheon, 1979).

32. M. Catherine Burns, "Dr. Sock," in *Ladies' Choice: A Collection of*

Humor by Maine Women, ed. Mavis Patterson (Thorndike, Maine: Thorndike Press, 1982), 18; "On Surviving Three Sons," ibid., 19.

33. Burns, "On Surviving Three Sons," 19.

34. Quoted in *The Mother Book,* ed. Liz Smith (New York: Doubleday, 1978), 58.

35. Marge Piercy, "What's That Smell in the Kitchen?" in *Circles on the Water* (New York: Knopf, 1983), 288.

36. Audre Lorde, "The Master's Tools Will Never Dismantle the Master's House," in *Sister Outsider* (Trumansburg, N.Y.: Crossing Press, 1984), 112.

Wishful Willful Wily Women: Lessons for Female Success in the Child Ballads

POLLY STEWART

Among poetry scholars, a remark attributed to Robert Frost floats in the oral tradition. "All art is synecdoche," he is supposed to have said. "All an artist needs is samples." It is not difficult for folklorists to apply this fetching observation to their own field. However sliced, folklore, like other art, can teach as well as delight. Folklore informally teaches by supporting and reifying belief systems—as well as by controlling people, since males and females learn from their culture's folklore what is proper and possible for them—yet any genre or traditional performance could in itself impart the learning. As with Frost's samples, an individual item, process, or body of folklore has analytic potential as a window to the whole tradition.

One such body of folklore is the Child ballads, so named because of their compiler, the Harvard scholar Francis James Child (1825–96). These ballads are sung poetic narratives that originated and developed in the British Isles between the Elizabethan period and the early nineteenth century. They share a number of prosodic features and address common familial, social, historical, and other concerns. In the course of Child's decades-long ballad research, he amassed several thousand texts, from which he extrapolated, numbered, organized, titled, and annotated 305 separate ballads. His findings were published over a period of sixteen years in a five-volume compendium known as *The English and Scottish Popular Ballads* (1882–98).[1]

The present study has two purposes. The first is to examine the treatment of women characters in certain of the Child ballads (the rationale for selection will be given below), pointing out cultural lessons that these texts may be imparting to and about women. Not the least of these lessons should be noted at the outset: while a large number of ballads have no women at all in them, the ballads that do depict women also depict men. More bluntly, women are absent from Child ballads unless in some kind of social or filial relationship with men. If this observation about Child ballads is startling for being heretofore unstated, it is so only until we recall that women have always been relegated to an ancillary position in Western culture. Moreover, it will be shown again and again that the women characters in Child ballads are caught in the bind that has been made evident through the feminist critique of the patriarchy: females in a male-dominated world are subject to oppression whether they act or do not act. Engrained in the very fabric of our cultural experience, this lesson too is expressed synecdochically in the Child ballads. In rare cases, a ballad woman escapes that bind through verbal quickness, as will be shown.

While the first purpose of the study will be realized in an examination of Child ballad texts, the second will be met in speculating on possible rhetorical uses to which such ballads may be put by female tradition-bearers who perform them in modern settings. Just as women in ballads might on occasion circumvent oppressive situations by means of verbal or other mental agility, so might women ballad singers use these songs to send coded messages to women audiences—an agile use of traditional material, message within message.

Lessons in Ballad Texts

The ballads that Child collected came from two distinct origins, oral and non-oral, but only oral ballads will be included in the present study. The oral ballads were created and communally re-created without reference to literacy and were passed orally from one performer to another. Persuasive criteria for differentiating the oral from the non-oral ballads have already been established.[2] Under the terms of these criteria, only 135 of the 305 Child ballads are oral. Of these, about a hundred depict women—again, always in a male-female relationship of some kind. (The sole exception to this convention is found in "Bessy Bell and Mary Gray" [201],[3] in which two women, who have shared a home, have died of the plague and are to be buried together.) As the plots of these ballads unfold, we discover that the women in them are in agonistic situations—they have something to protect or something to gain.

While the three dozen or so ballads examined here are representative of this group, it must be acknowledged that a very small number of oral ballads depicting women present the women not in agonistic situations but in what we might call situations after the fact. For

example, in "Lord Randal" (12) and "Edward" (13), a mother questions her son only after a murderous act has been committed; when
"The Cherry-Tree Carol" (54) opens, the Virgin Mary is already with
child; women are not mentioned in "Sir Patrick Spens" (58) until after
the death of the hero and his men; in "The Death of Queen Jane"
(170), the queen is well on her way toward death when the story
opens; and in "Queen Eleanor's Confession" (156), the queen thinks
she is dying and is unaware of any conflict her confession might
engender. These after-the-fact plot situations are not addressed here,
nor are plots driven entirely by supernatural elements, as in "Thomas
Rhymer" (37), stolen from this earth by a fairy woman; "The Wee,
Wee Man" (38), who takes the narrator on a tour of Faerie without ill
effect; "The Queen of Elfan's Nourice" (40), a mortal woman enjoined
to nurse a fairy child; "Clerk Colvill" (42), whose headaches, caused by
his jilted otherworldly lover, result in his death; and "The Great Silkie
of Sule Skerry" (113), a seal who has fathered a son upon a mortal
woman and who predicts both his and his son's death at the hands of a
mortal hunter.

This study is thus limited to those oral Child ballads in which a
woman is depicted agonistically with a man or with a male-headed
authority structure. (Occasionally the antagonist is the woman's whole
family.) So far as I am aware, the present study is the first to examine
these ballads to find out what the women in them do, and to what
ends, and how successfully.

It is important to understand the narrow and ironic sense in which
I am using the word *success*. In the tightly bounded world of the
ballads, a woman's range of options is much more restricted than we
have become accustomed to thinking of in connection with the term
success, and a woman's achievement of something approximating success for herself is often accompanied by its opposite, failure, in the
expectations of the larger society. This is so because in the society
depicted in the ballads, male prerogatives, including all those commonly found within the patriarchy—decision making, sexual control,
ownership of family, and the assumption that the best place for a
woman is in the nuclear family, propagating the race—are primary.
Men are not punished for assaults on women; the family is initiated by
the man, often without the woman's consent. An unmarried woman
is fair game. A married woman, as chattel, takes any initiative at her
peril. (Not surprisingly, the heterosexual bias is pervasive; the one
ballad in the Child collection that tells of two women who have made
a home together, "Bessy Bell and Mary Gray" [201], shows also that
they have succumbed to the plague.) The irony is that within such a

restricted framework, a woman who seeks goals of her own, if these goals run counter to the social and cultural expectations established for her, will thus be achieving personal success only by effecting cultural failure in denying or escaping her designated role.

Success and failure understood in this way can be analyzed in the ballads on two levels, the cultural and the personal, yielding a four-part paradigm. Inasmuch as the prime cultural goal expressed in the ballads is that the expectations of men will be met first, irrespective of the cost that might be incurred in meeting them, ballads that end in the achievement of this goal may be said to evince *cultural success,* and ballads whose events interfere with it, *cultural failure.* For a female ballad character, *personal success* consists in averting harm—death, rape, abandonment—or in reaching a goal; personal success is achieved by means of internally controlled stratagems and may involve deviant behavior that is in some instances outrageous. A woman's *personal failure* consists in being subjected to harm, as above, or in failing to reach a goal. Personal failure can occur if she is unavoidably in a passive role or is somehow unable to control external conditions; it can also occur if her behavior is unacceptably deviant. (The narrator rarely moralizes about the characters in a ballad, however unsettling their actions may be, tacitly inviting the audience to draw its own conclusions.)

Again without addressing any question of audience approval or disapproval, we can observe that in some ballads a woman experiences personal failure in a situation that ends in cultural success, while in others a woman triumphs but her personal success results in cultural failure. In a sizable number of ballads women fail both personally and culturally, and in a very few they succeed both personally and culturally.[4] From the vantage point of women's efforts to control situations, the present survey yields a kind of spectrum. On the one end are a number of personally unsuccessful women whose circumstances are beyond their control. On the other are personally successful women whose control over situations is invariably due to their mental quickness, verbal or otherwise. In the middle are women actively trying to exercise control but with mixed success. The analysis suggests a broad inverse pattern: the better a woman is at marshaling internal resources to confront external threats or obstacles, the less likely she is to be harmed or thwarted.

Personal and Cultural Failure

In this first category is an array of lachrymose ballads about doomed women who end up dead or damned, whether through someone else's actions or through their own. When people cluck their tongues and wonder aloud why the old ballads have to be so sad, they are thinking of these. A classic illustration is the story of Bonny Baby Livingston (222), who is abducted and raped. Though able to send a message to her lover at home, she dies before he can come to her aid. As another example, Fair Janet (64) has borne Willie's child, but he chooses another woman to be his wife; at the wedding, Fair Janet dances with him, then dies at his feet. In a third example, a ship's captain gets Bonnie Annie (24) with child, then manipulates her into committing a crime (stealing money from her parents) and running away with him. When a violent storm comes up at sea, Bonnie Annie accepts the blame for it and is thrown overboard in expiation.

In "The Cruel Brother" (11), a would-be bride is punished by death despite her effort to observe social rules. She tells her suitor that before they can marry he must gain permission from her entire family. She names each member and specifies, "dinna forget my brither John" (B, I:146).[5] Yet, as the narrator tells us,

> He has asked her father, the king:
> And sae did he her mither, the queen.
> And he has asked her sister Anne:
> But he has forgot her brother John. (B, I:146)

The suitor's failure to carry out a simple instruction, more pointedly in light of its place following a series of properly observed instructions, may seem an appalling display of ineptitude but is not at all untypical of events in folk narrative and is, moreover, needed to further the plot. What is important to note is that the victim of the slighted brother's wrath is not the suitor but the bride. As the wedding comes to a close, John sets his sister on a horse; "It's then he drew a little penknife, / And he reft the fair maid o her life" (B, I:146). In "Lizie Wan" (51), too, a brother murders a sister. Here the point of conflict is incest. While she cannot be morally defended for her complicity in this matter, she pays more dearly for it than the brother. Upon her disclosure of pregnancy to him, "he pulled out his wee penknife, / And he cut her fair bodie in three" (B, I:449). The brother's punishment, self-elected, is mere exile.

Families engage in collective violence against daughters whose loves they disapprove of. "Andrew Lammie" (233) tells of a young woman who has fallen hopelessly in love with a man beneath her social station. Once her family members learn she will not give him up, they punish her so harshly that she dies:

> Her father beat her cruellie,
> Sae also did her mother;
> Her sisters sair did scoff at her;
> But wae betide her brother!
> Her brother beat her cruellie,
> Till his straiks [strokes] they werena canny [gentle];
> He brak her back, and he beat her sides,
> For the sake o Andrew Lammie. (A, IV:303)

In "Lady Maisry" (65), a Scottish heroine's family plays a similar role in punishing her for refusing to renounce her love for an English lord, though here the method is burning at the stake.

The number of oral Child ballads in which a hapless female is thus treated is five times greater than those featuring a clearly victimized male—"Lord Randal" (12), in which a man is fatally poisoned by his sweetheart; "Sir Hugh, or, The Jew's Daughter" (155), in which a young boy is lured into a garden and murdered; and "The Sweet Trinity (The Golden Vanity)" (286), in which a cabin boy is betrayed by his ship's captain and left in the sea to drown.

Personal and cultural failure occur in some ballads because of a woman's use of violence or unsanctioned sex, or both. In "Young Hunting" (68), a woman stabs her lover to death upon learning he is interested in someone else, though he cannot be credited for diplomacy in his manner of telling her: "The very sols of my love's feet / Is whiter then thy face" (A, II:144). The woman hides the body in a river and, when the body is discovered, tries to blame her lady-in-waiting for the crime. She is burned at the stake. In another ballad, "The Cruel Mother" (20), a woman stabs to death and buries the twin boys she has borne out of wedlock, apparently in an effort to deny her sexual activity: "She's put them aneath a marble stane, / Thinking a maiden to gae hame" (I, I:224). Later the twins appear as revenants, naming her as their murderer and predicting she will be punished in Hell. A third ballad, "Mary Hamilton" (173), is so variously attested that, as Child notes, "It is impossible to weave all the versions into an intelligible and harmonious story" (III:380). Common to all versions, however, is that Mary, a member of the royal court, has had a child by a man of the highest nobility, has murdered the infant—in some versions she has previously tried to abort the child, and in others she denies having had a baby at all—and is now to be executed.

"Bonny Barbara Allan" (84) tells of no overt act of violence, though it implies that Barbara has caused Sweet William to sicken to the point of death because she thinks he has slighted her. No guesswork about whether she has purposely sickened him is really necessary, however, for it is made clear that she is responsible for his death simply by her rejection of him:

> "If on your death-bed you be lying,
> What is that to Barbara Allen?
> I cannot keep you from [your] death;
> So farewell," said Barbara Allen. (B, II:277)

Only after Sweet William's death does Barbara experience remorse; then she too dies.

Ballad women are rarely seen taking the initiative in matters of sex, but a disastrous exception is the adulterous woman in "Little Musgrave and Lady Barnard" (81), who aggressively invites a man to her bed:

> I have a hall in Mulberry,
> It stands baith strong and tight;
> If you will go to there with me,
> I'll lye with you all night. (E, II:249)

He agrees to the assignation after she assures him that her husband is away. But a footpage who has witnessed these negotiations rushes off and reveals to the absent husband the pair's adultery. The husband returns and confronts them at the foot of the bed in which they are lying. In the duel that ensues, Little Musgrave is killed. The wife, too, will be killed, but only after guaranteeing her death by responding defiantly to her husband's question, doubtless asked in an attempt to find some reason to forgive her, about which of the two men she prefers:

> Full well I love your cherry cheeks,
> Full well I love your chin,
> But better I love Little Sir Grove, where he lies,
> Than you and all your kin. (I, II:254)

In a final example, Proud Lady Margaret (47) refuses to marry at all—evidence of cultural failure—unless her suitor can answer riddles she poses. Several men have tried, failed, and been killed for their pains. Margaret is guilty of two mortal sins, pride and greed, and the ballad's narrator predicts that she will suffer in Hell.

Personal Failure and Cultural Success

The women in the first category fail personally—all die or are to be punished after death—and they are in situations which, for any number of reasons, thwart the cultural prescription for propagation of the species. By contrast, women in the second category, though they experience personal failure (often by being raped or by having to be rescued), end up in culturally successful situations.

In "The Broom of Cowdenknows" (217), a passing gentleman accosts a milkmaid. After failing to lure her by pretext away from the safety of her ewe pen, he uses force:

> He took her by the milk-white hand,
> And by the green gown-sleive,
> And thare he took his will o her,
> Bot o her he askit nae leive. (D, IV:196)

(The verse is found, in variation, in most of the rape ballads in the Child collection. Sometimes it is not the victim of whom "he askit nae leive" but her family.) Several months later the rapist returns unrecognized and taunts his victim about her pregnancy before disclosing that he is a nobleman who intends to marry her. Another ballad, "Fair Annie" (62), tells of a woman, kidnapped as a child, who has borne her abductor seven children out of wedlock, but now he announces that he intends to marry someone else. The wedding does not take place, but only because the prospective bride turns out to be Fair Annie's sister.

The heroine in "Gil Brenton" (5) is sent to be Gil Brenton's bride. Upon arriving, she learns that he has already had seven brides, all of whom he has mutilated (by cutting off their breasts) and sent away because they were found not to be virgins. Knowing that she is not a virgin, she substitutes her bower-woman, who is intact, in the bridal bed. Gil Brenton asks the sheets, blankets, and pillows on the bed if the woman with him is "a maid." They reply, "It's nae a maid that you ha wedded, / But it's a maid that you ha bedded" (A, I:68). Upon hearing of this, Gil Brenton's mother angrily confronts the bride, who explains that in her own country she had been deflowered against her will. She shows the mother the tokens the rapist had given her, which are the same tokens the mother had earlier given her son. The child that the bride is carrying is thus Gil Brenton's child, and the situation is saved.

In "The Knight and Shepherd's Daughter" (110), a knight accosts a shepherdess and has his will of her. She goes to the king and accuses the knight of robbing her of her maidenhead. The king decrees that the knight must marry her. Not wishing to marry so far beneath him, the knight tries to bribe his way out of the sentence, but she will have none of his gold. Seeing no recourse, he grudgingly accepts his fate. It turns out that this "shepherd's daughter" is really a noblewoman, so her persistence and pluck have paid off not only for herself but for her bridegroom as well.

Other women in the second category require rescue. After the rescue a marriage can take place. The best-known ballad of this type is "The Maid Freed From the Gallows" (95), though Child may have been incorrect in assigning that name to it, for in the minds of many traditional singers the main character is male, not female.[6] In other ballads, however, the issue is unambiguous. Brown Adam (98), returning secretly from banishment, discovers his lady being threatened by a false knight. He rescues her by disarming and wounding the knight. In "Johnie Scot" (99) a woman, pregnant by Johnie, is imprisoned by her family as punishment. Johnie rescues her after fighting a duel. In "Glenlogie, or, Jean o Bethelnie" (238), Jean falls in love at first sight with Glenlogie, though he is already promised to another. Jean is dying of grief, but a sympathetic chaplain sends Glenlogie a letter explaining the situation; Glenlogie agrees to save Jean from death by marrying her:

> Her spirit revived to hear him say sae,
> And thus ended luckily all her great wae;
> Then streight were they married, with joy most profound,
> And Jean of Bethelnie was sav'd from the ground. (F, IV:343)

Personal Success and Cultural Failure

In "Willie's Lady" (6), a mother—whom the narrator, in an unusual bit of editorializing, calls "that vile rank witch of vilest kind" (A, I:86)—has worked a spell that is preventing Willie's young wife, who is in labor, from giving birth. The spell is broken upon the advice of the Belly Blind, a beneficent household familiar. Because the mother's efforts are unsuccessful, "Willie's Lady" actually belongs in the second category. But its plot situation—a mother's efforts to destroy the love affair or marriage of her son—is identical to that of three ballads in the third category. In these three the mother succeeds.

In the first, "The Mother's Malison, or, Clyde's Water" (216), Willie rejects his mother's blandishments to stay at home with her, as he intends to cross the Clyde and spend the night with Margaret. The mother cries, "Clyde's water's wide and deep enough; / My malison drown thee!" (B, IV:188). Mindful of his mother's curse, Willie makes a difficult passage across the Clyde, but when he reaches Margaret's door he is unaccountably refused entry, presumably because of the curse. In his attempt to recross the Clyde he drowns, as does, in some versions, Margaret in a belated effort to follow him. In the second, "The Lass of Roch Royal" (76), a mother mendaciously impersonates her son to thwart the son's reunion with his sweetheart and their baby. The mother succeeds in this effort but at great cost, as son and sweetheart and baby all die as a result.[7] Finally, in "Prince Robert" (87), a son begs for his mother's blessing of the marriage he has made, but she replies, "Instead of a blessing ye sall have my curse, / And you'll get nae blessing frae me" (A, II:284). She kills him with poisoned wine; later, when the widowed bride asks only for Prince Robert's ring, the mother refuses her even that, "Tho your heart suld burst in three" (A, II:285). (It does.)

These plot summaries help remind us that in the third category a woman may achieve personal success by getting what she goes after, but in the process she violates the marriage-and-propagation mandate for cultural success. Perhaps the best-known example of this type of ballad is "The Gypsy Laddie" (200), in which a nobleman's wife is so taken by the sweet singing of a gypsy, or company of gypsies, that she decides to renounce her baby and all the perquisites of marriage in favor of the uncertainties and vicissitudes of the wandering life:

> Yestreen I lay in a weel-made bed,
> And my gude lord beside me;
> This night I'll lie in a tenant's barn,
> Whatever shall betide me. (F, IV:70)

In some ballads a woman preserves her virginity (that is, achieves personal success), but in so doing she violates the norm for cultural success, since no pregnancy or marriage will occur. In "The Baffled Knight" (112), for example, a maiden is seen bathing in a forest pool; the passing knight desires her sexual favors on the spot. She convinces him that her father's hall will be more commodious, but when they get there she locks him out. This ballad has two of the best lines in all ballad literature, both of them plays on words: "She says, I am a maid within, / You're but a knave without, sir" (E, II:488), and "If you will not when you may / You shall not when you will, sir" (B, II:484). In another example, "The Gardener" (219), a man proposes marriage by offering, poetically, to clothe the woman in the flowers of summer; she rejoins with a cold counteroffer to clothe him in the snow and wind of winter.

In a third example, "The Elfin Knight" (2), a knight catches the attention of a young girl by blowing his horn at the top of a hill. She speaks aloud her desire to have both horn and knight, and he appears immediately at her bedside. Having placed herself in sexual danger because of words, she now extricates herself in the same way, establishing at once that she is capable of verbally topping her visitor. He begins by remarking that she seems rather young to be wanting to marry, to which she replies, "I have a sister younger than I, / And she was married yesterday" (A, I:15). The knight then says that if she wishes to marry him, she must first perform an impossible task—make a shirt for him that has no seams or needlework out of cloth that has not been cut with scissors. She responds, "If that piece of courtesie I do to thee, / Another thou must do to me" (B, I:16), and she sets him a whole series of equally impossible tasks—variously plowing with his horn an acre of land "Atween the saut sea and the sand" (C, I:16), sowing it with a peppercorn, reaping the crop with a knife, stacking it in a mousehole, and so on. "And when that ye have done your wark, / Come back to me, and ye'll get your sark" (B, I:16). The knight, verbally bested, quits the field with a lame utterance about his wife and seven children. The young woman has the last word: "My maidenhead I'll then keep still, / Let the elphin knight do what he will" (B, I:16). In some versions of this ballad, the knight is the devil in disguise; in others, the devil is absent and the colloquy is between mortals. In either case the woman gets the upper hand, and in so doing she goes against cultural expectations.

It could be argued that in ballads like this one the heroine does not cause cultural failure, because she may be preserving her virginity against a possible future marriage with an appropriate partner. There is, after all, no textual indication that she intends never to propagate the race. In the absence of evidence one way or the other, this question is impossible to address. It does, however, force us to recognize that the structural categories outlined here are subject to blurring. In "Lady Isabel and the Elf-Knight" (4), for example, Lady Isabel, to keep from being murdered by a man who has already killed her sisters, claims modesty when he orders her to remove her costly gown before he pushes her into the water to drown. He averts his eyes, and she seizes the moment to push him in instead. While the personal-success component is obvious here (a quick-thinking woman saves her own life), the ballad contains no hint of the cultural-success component. A related ambiguity is found in the different versions of "Riddles Wisely Expounded" (1), in which a young woman answers a series of riddles to gain something she wants (a husband), to fend off something she does not want (a demon), or, in one version, to no stated end. Whatever the narrative situation may be, she succeeds in naming what is whiter than milk (snow), louder than a horn (thunder), higher than a tree (heaven), more innocent than a lamb (a babe), and so forth. Here the focus is purely on the heroine's verbal cleverness.

Personal and Cultural Success

This final category comprises women who gain what they want and who also meet cultural expectations for success. In "Child Waters" (63), a young woman goes to extraordinary lengths to keep her lover. She is pregnant by him, but he will travel nonetheless and does not care to have her as his equal. She accompanies him dressed as a footpage, walks barefoot alongside his horse, swims across a river, takes care of his horses, bears his child in the stable. Such devotion is finally so impressive to Child Waters that he renounces all other loves and says he will marry her. In "The Famous Flower of Serving-Men" (106), a woman also dresses as a man, though for different reasons. The young heroine, of noble birth but widowed early and impoverished, disguises herself as a serving-man and is taken into the royal court, where she performs so ably that the king makes her his chamberlain. One day, when the king is away hunting, she confides to an old man her true circumstances. When this information is conveyed to the king, he marries her at once: "The like before was never seen, / A serving-man to be a queen" (II:431).

Finally, in "Captain Wedderburn's Courtship" (46), a marriageable woman keeps her suitor at bay by requiring him to answer six riddles before she will be his. He answers all six, but then she exacts three more answers before giving her consent at last.[8] That Child recognized the similarity of this ballad to "Proud Lady Margaret" (47), presented above as an example of the first category, is apparent in his having numbered the two ballads consecutively.

Setting aside the monstrous mothers in the third category, whose success is destructive, the ballad women who achieve personal success—irrespective of whether they achieve cultural success—can do so by appropriating the masculine decision-making prerogative, as in "The Gypsy Laddie" (Category 3), or by appropriating masculine dress, as in "Child Waters" and "The Famous Flower of Serving-Men" (Category 4). Most, however, achieve personal success by their clever use of words. (Even the adulterous and doomed Lady Barnard of Category 1 gets quick results from her verbal performance, a twisted sort of success.) Ballad men, too, can use language cleverly to serve their own ends, as in "Trooper and Maid" (299), in which a soldier gives his one-night sweetheart the brush-off. She asks him when they will see each other again, and he replies, "When cockle shells turn siller bells" (C, V:174). Overall, however, the women outwit the men by a rather large margin.

The reason for this lopsided distribution is surely attributable to the fact, noted at the outset, that when women do appear in ballads they are almost invariably depicted in some kind of male-female relationship. I have been discussing these women politically, in that the term as used here denotes the manipulation of power in the battle of the sexes. The battle lines are drawn on a field of cultural expectations, the most prominent of which is that the species must survive. However—as the ballad texts tell us repeatedly—this worthy goal, when it is met at all, is likely to be met at the price of extreme sexual and social oppression of women. A further irony is that a woman who takes control of the reproductive treasury by avoiding marriage or rape is acting against the cultural norm. The deck is stacked. In the world of the Child ballads, in which men have main strength, the double standard, and the force of authority on their side, the women who take advantage of verbal quickness to outmaneuver the men are the only ones likely to succeed personally, for, as demonstrated in the texts, women's wit is their only sure resource.

Here we may remind ourselves of the powerful teaching function of folklore. What are the lessons women might learn from these ballads? That a man will take from a woman what he can and will punish her for being his victim; that a woman's needs are not a primary consideration either for her family or for men outside her family; that, for a woman, stepping outside the house is a dangerous act; that a woman's resources for protecting her interests are slim indeed. By horrible example, a woman learns how not to get killed.

Not surprisingly, other genres of folklore besides ballads can carry the same cultural lesson. In the folktale known as "The Robber Bridegroom" (AT 955),[9] a woman marked for death not only saves her own life but also exposes the murderous intentions of her husband-to-be through the clever marshaling of her slim resources, through the use of words. Feminist critic Marie Maclean, in her commentary on this and similar folk narratives, takes note of the contribution Michel de Certeau has made to contemporary criticism in providing new life to the military concepts of *strategy* and *tactics*. Strategy is the resource of the strong and dominant, tactics the leftovers, available to the Other—precisely as we see gender roles played out in the ballad texts. Tactics, according to de Certeau, "is wile. In sum it is an art of the weak."[10] This very useful concept may also be seen to operate in the performance of old ballads by modern-day singers, as will be suggested below.

Tactical Performance of Ballads

When people from the British Isles settled in America during and after the colonial period, they brought their cultural freight with them. For many, this freight included a stock of ballads, which the settlers sang and passed along to their descendants. (Two things should be pointed out at this juncture: first, not all of the oral Child ballads discussed in the present study have survived in the New World; second, settlers in the New World created new ballad texts along the existing Child–ballad pattern.)[11] In regions of the country that experienced little interference from the outside, ballads flourished within the families that had brought them and played an integral part in their daily lives—and continued to do so until very recently, as attested in the autobiographical narratives of traditional singers Jean Ritchie, Almeda Riddle, and others.[12]

These autobiographical narratives provide valuable information about the learning and transmission of song materials and about the contexts in which they were performed—in the household and in the bosom of the family. The Ritchie family, for instance, sang while churning butter and performing other kitchen tasks, sang while cultivating corn, sang to soothe an injured child, sang at corn shuckings and other social events, sang in the evening at home. Jean Ritchie re-creates the atmosphere of such evenings as one of her earliest memories: "I have never been able to decide which times I liked better, those winter evenings around the fireplace, or the summertime twilights when the song and tale-telling moved out onto the front porch. Even before I was old enough to take much part in anything else the grownups did, I was doing my share in singing the moon up on those soft summer nights."[13] Almeda Riddle recalls learning songs by overhearing others singing, by having her parents, relatives, friends, and husband teach her songs directly, and by studying songbooks and clippings. The learning was most intensive in her earliest years ("I learned 90 percent of my songs by the time I was eighteen"), and it often occurred in work situations, as in this reminiscence about a widowed neighbor with whom she often stayed as a child: "Aunt Fanny, she used to pick cotton. They had a small patch of cotton and we used to go out in the cotton patch and I picked cotton with them and she'd sing me songs while we were picking cotton. I can just see her out there singing 'Barbara Allen.'... She taught me the song—I first heard it from Aunt Fanny Barber."[14]

A reading of these singers' autobiographical narratives imparts a strong sense that as very young girls they were hearing, in the songs of their childhood, complicated social messages and were imaginatively using the information in the songs to prepare themselves for adulthood. Riddle recalls a sad song that her mother used to sing, "Ten Thousand Miles Away": "I can remember yet what I'd think when she'd sing this. I'd think maybe this was a girl that had married and gone away from her mother and she was a-crying to go back. I always had a fierce imagination—'fraid I still do have—and she was trying to go back to see her mother and probably it wasn't pleasing her husband."[15] Similarly, Ritchie provides an early recollection of her deep emotional involvement with the story of "Lord Thomas and Fair Annet" (73), a ballad about love, betrayal, and death: "And so I died, as Fair Ellender, but even death seemed lovely and romantic in that song; I could imagine how the wedding guests gathered around as I lay with my pale hair spread about me on the floor, everybody weeping and saying how beautiful I was, even in death. I gave myself up completely to wonderful dreams, forgetting until tomorrow that life was not really like that. For even though I was only six, I had begun to have my troubles. . . . "[16]

The emotive and teaching power of the ballads is well illustrated in Riddle's memory of the sad songs in her own childhood: "I don't want to think that I was a morbid-minded child, but still I loved these sad songs. . . . I think maybe that our best songs are our ballads. You know, happy things that tell us good news don't make the papers as often as sad news. And most of the ballads, didn't you ever notice that, are written about sad occurrences."[17] Whether sad or happy, however, songs that teach are the ones that Riddle values most: "I don't care a thing in this world . . . for a song that doesn't tell a story or teach a lesson."[18]

To return to the lessons of the Child ballads in the present study. Though none of the autobiographical narratives refers to particular ballads examined here, we get a sense of the general admonitory properties of ballads in the words of Buna Hicks, a traditional singer from Tennessee: "I guess sometimes it might help a body to watch out. Some [ballads] that's sung might be a good warning to people sometimes, the lovesongs would. They really, I think, might be to warn somebody if they just take heed and study these songs out."[19]

Just as a singer can learn from "studying out" a ballad, so also can she use a ballad to teach someone else, by performing it in an appropriate context. Here Michel de Certeau's concept of *tactics* as "an art of the weak" must come into play. Because ballads when sung before others are public expressions, they are potentially accessible to all, and men are just as likely to be in the audience as women. But sometimes a singer might want to convey a lesson to only part of that audience. To do so she will have to encode the message by her selection of the song—a tactic to hide the lesson from all but the one for whom it is intended. Traditional singer Hattie Presnell tells a story from her youth that illustrates this principle. Her sister was "a-talkin'" to a young man whom the family did not trust; they asked young Hattie if she would sing, in company, a particular song ("Pretty Polly," an American ballad not included in the present study) describing the murder of a too-trusting young woman by the man who was supposed to marry her. In Hattie's account, the family wanted Hattie to notify her sister about their uneasiness regarding the man she was seeing—without letting the man himself in on the message. Hattie declined the request, in retrospect tersely acknowledging the song's power to influence an attuned listener: "It wasn't none of my business." A song performance of this type, she allows, "might cause a lot of [people] to be careful about goin' off with people."[20]

The sending of messages by means of coded ballad performance provides a way for women to teach other women not only about the values of the culture, which are, as the texts of the present study repeatedly demonstrate, largely negative where women are concerned, but also about how to survive in the environment that prevails as a result of those values. The coding is useful because of the men in the audience. It would not necessarily be wise to say overtly that the only safe way to deal with a man is to outsmart him, but singing a ballad in which a female character does outsmart a man could get the message across in a socially acceptable way.

Appendix

Below, arranged into the four categories created for purposes of discussion in the present study, are the 96 oral ballads in the Child collection that depict women characters in agonistic situations involving men. Category assignments have been made on the basis of plot analyses of texts in Child.

Category 1: Personal and Cultural Failure (41 titles)

- 7 Earl Brand
- 9 The Fair Flower of Northumberland
- 10 The Twa Sisters
- 11 The Cruel Brother
- 20 The Cruel Mother
- 24 Bonnie Annie
- 47 Proud Lady Margaret
- 51 Lizie Wan
- 52 The King's Dochter Lady Jean

64 Fair Janet
65 Lady Maisry
67 Glasgerion
68 Young Hunting
69 Clerk Saunders
73 Lord Thomas and Fair Annet
74 Fair Margaret and Sweet William
75 Lord Lovel
77 Sweet William's Ghost
78 The Unquiet Grave
79 The Wife of Usher's Well
81 Little Musgrave and Lady Barnard
83 Child Maurice
84 Bonny Barbara Allan
85 Lady Alice
88 Young Johnstone
89 Fause Foodrage
90 Jellon Grame
93 Lamkin
173 Mary Hamilton
178 Captain Car, or, Edom o Gordon
199 The Bonnie House o Airlie
212 The Duke of Athole's Nurse
213 Sir James the Rose
214 The Braes o Yarrow
221 Katharine Jaffray
222 Bonny Baby Livingston
231 The Earl of Errol
233 Andrew Lammie
235 The Earl of Aboyne
243 James Harris (The Daemon Lover)
272 The Suffolk Miracle

Category 2: Personal Failure and Cultural Success (24 titles)

5 Gil Brenton
6 Willie's Lady
15 Leesome Brand
25 Willie's Lyke-Wake
41 Hind Etin
44 The Twa Magicians
62 Fair Annie
95 The Maid Freed From the Gallows
98 Brown Adam
99 Johnie Scot
100 Willie o Winsbury

110 The Knight and Shepherd's Daughter
217 The Broom of Cowdenknows
226 Lizie Lindsay
228 Glasgow Peggie
238 Glenlogie, or, Jean o Bethelnie
251 Lang Johnny More
264 The White Fisher
277 The Wife Wrapt in Wether's Skin
279 The Jolly Beggar
280 The Beggar-Laddie
281 The Keach i the Creel
293 John of Hazelgreen
299 Trooper and Maid

Category 3: Personal Success and Cultural Failure (16 titles)

1 Riddles Wisely Expounded
2 The Elfin Knight
4 Lady Isabel and the Elf-Knight
14 Babylon; or, The Bonnie Banks o Fordie
43 The Broomfield Hill
76 The Lass of Roch Royal
87 Prince Robert
112 The Baffled Knight
155 Sir Hugh, or, The Jew's Daughter
200 The Gypsy Laddie
216 The Mother's Malison, or, Clyde's Water
219 The Gardener
248 The Grey Cock, or, Saw You My Father?
274 Our Goodman
275 Get Up and Bar the Door
278 The Farmer's Curst Wife

Category 4: Personal and Cultural Success (15 titles)

17 Hind Horn
39 Tam Lin
46 Captain Wedderburn's Courtship
53 Young Beichan
63 Child Waters
96 The Gay Goshawk
97 Brown Robin
105 The Bailiff's Daughter of Islington
106 The Famous Flower of Serving-Men
182 The Laird o Logie
209 Geordie
218 The False Lover Won Back

232 Richie Story
236 The Laird o Drum
240 The Rantin Laddie

Notes

1. Ballads and ballad history are well known to folklorists. For the uninitiated, two accessible and evenhanded introductions to the subject are David C. Fowler's *A Literary History of the Popular Ballad* (Durham, N.C.: Duke University Press, 1968) and M. J. C. Hodgart's *The Ballads,* rev. ed. (London: Hutchinson's, 1962), from which this brief overview has been derived. Child's five-volume opus, *The English and Scottish Popular Ballads,* is readily available in reprint paperback (New York: Dover, 1965) and reprint hardback (New York: Cooper Square, 1965).

2. J. Barre Toelken, "An Oral Canon for the Child Ballads: Construction and Application," *Journal of the Folklore Institute* 4 (June 1967): 75–101.

3. In the present study, parenthetical numerals in connection with a ballad title refer to the number Child assigned to the ballad.

4. See appendix.

5. Parenthetical material following a quoted passage locates the passage in Child. (B, I:146) refers to version B of the ballad found on page 146 of the first volume of the five-volume *English and Scottish Popular Ballads.* Because the ballads exist in variation, the textual examples are illustrative, not definitive. Child avoided emending texts that came his way, retaining their idiosyncratic spellings.

6. Eleanor Long, *"The Maid" and "The Hangman": Myth and Tradition in a Popular Ballad,* University of California Folklore Studies, 21 (Berkeley: University of California Press, 1971).

7. In the United States, a fragment of "The Lass of Roch Royal" survives under the title "Who's Gonna Shoe Your Pretty Little Foot?" Barre Toelken, *The Dynamics of Folklore* (New York: Houghton Mifflin, 1979), 173–76, presents an informative contextual discussion of both the ballad and the fragment.

8. Some of the riddles in "Captain Wedderburn's Courtship" have been retained in the widely known American folksong "I Gave My Love a Cherry." Toelken discusses the song's sexual connotations in *Dynamics,* 209–11.

9. The parenthetical notation refers to the number assigned to this folktale in Antti Aarne and Stith Thompson, *The Types of the Folktale: A Classification and Bibliography,* Folklore Fellows Communications No. 184 (Helsinki: Academia Scientiarum Fennica, 1973).

10. Michel de Certeau, "On the Oppositional Practices of Everyday Life," trans. Fredric Jameson and Carol Lovitt, *Social Text* 3 (1980): 6; cited in Marie Maclean, "Oppositional Practices in Women's Traditional Narrative," *New Literary History* 19, no. 1 (1987): 40.

11. Tristram P. Coffin's study, *The British Traditional Ballad in North*

America, rev. ed. (Philadelphia: American Folklore Society, 1963), shows which of the Child ballads have been transplanted to the New World. Traditional New World ballad creations based on the old pattern are presented in G. Malcolm Laws's *Native American Balladry,* rev. ed. (Philadelphia: American Folklore Society, 1964).

12. Jean Ritchie, *Singing Family of the Cumberlands* (1955; Lexington: University Press of Kentucky, 1988); Roger D. Abrahams, ed., *A Singer and Her Songs: Almeda Riddle's Book of Ballads* (Baton Rouge: Louisiana State University Press, 1970); Thomas G. Burton, *Some Ballad Folks* (Johnson City: East Tennessee State University Press, 1978).

13. Ritchie, *Singing Family,* 15.

14. Abrahams, *A Singer,* 87.

15. Ibid., 40.

16. Ritchie, *Singing Family,* 20.

17. Abrahams, *A Singer,* 33.

18. Ibid., 112.

19. Burton, *Some Ballad Folks,* 24.

20. Ibid., 30.

PART TWO

Women Together

Building on her analysis of "the dailiness of women's lives," Bettina Aptheker has called for a "re-visioning of ourselves as women" through a philosophical standpoint she calls "the lesbian connection": "an invitation into a female-centered world, a standpoint from which to take up women's experience and with it weave a different cloth. That is, rather than always seeing women in relationship to men, as adjuncts to the political, cultural, and social movements organized and led by men, it is possible to treat women as independent human beings who have formed, and in turn, been informed by all social relations." Aptheker believes that this "re-visioning" is underway, that "women have begun, cautiously, tentatively, and with many contradictions, to change the balance of power relative to men in each other's everyday lives: employing, evaluating, provisioning, nurturing, supporting, networking, reconnoitering, protecting each other." Although the need for this philosophical struggle extends to all women regardless of sexual orientation, at present it may be in lesbian communities and households that the vision of "ourselves as women divested of our colonized and servile status" can be most nearly realized in free and open communication.[1] Women who live with awareness of their dependence on men, on the other hand, often censor themselves and rely on coding even when no men are present.

The essays in this section represent some common situations in which those women who live "dispersed among the males" (as Simone de Beauvoir put it) gather together: as mothers of young children, exchanging information and watching play groups; as friends sharing a hobby; as collaborators in the production of community events—church bazaars, parades, rummage sales. In such gatherings, one might expect to find the steam valve for the frequent muting of women in their own homes; for this reason, Dale Spender argues, "one of the most salient features of our social organization has been the *isolation* of women."[2] Chilean *arpilleristas* recount that when, driven by the necessity of their poverty, they began to attend the meetings of their needlework movement, "the men wouldn't let us go out," and there were bruises and black eyes. But at the meetings, one woman recalled, "it was such a great joy to see and talk with all those people, and to look at the themes of the pictures and analyse them. . . . With this work I learned to grow as a person, to have an opinion, to criticize, to understand. Women are at home, just keeping everything going. They don't know how to do anything else, people who are just physical, and in the head, nothing."[3]

Among themselves women often tell different stories, voice different ideas, adopt different attitudes from those they may display in mixed company.[4] They can share their dislike of housework and of the endless demands of husbands and children, their irritation at male domination, their frustration on the job. Together they can create art—narratives, handiwork, songs—that encodes messages they cannot speak elsewhere. In "Mothers' Double Talk," Janet L. Langlois explores a set of legends about inept mothers who cause the deaths of their children. These tales seem cautionary, warning women about proper mothering strategies (control your temper with a child; don't leave babies unattended on changing tables or in bathtubs; and so forth). But the young mothers who tell the stories to each other are also aware of an encoded subtext: a criticism of U.S. culture's patriarchally defined institution of motherhood, which unreasonably demands that a woman care, alone, for several children.

The "Bee There" quilters of Austin, Texas, began their Scandalous Sue project as a joke, to tease one of their members whose fondness for the "sweet" Sunbonnet Sue pattern they found excessive. In "'She Really Wanted to Be Her Own Woman': Scandalous Sunbonnet Sue," Linda Pershing shows that the project became a means of self-expression for the quilters, as each of them created a square depicting Sue doing something "naughty." In rejecting the uniformity of the traditional faceless appliqué pattern, they consciously rejected the bland, child-like stereotype of women (and especially of quilters) that the pattern represents; *their* Sue would be "a modern woman," "an independent person," doing "all the bad things a woman isn't supposed to do."

The Maine women about whom Margaret R. Yocom writes in "'Awful Real': Dolls and Development in Rangeley, Maine" first played with dolls and knit doll clothes as children at home, learning from their mothers. Now, with their own children grown, they turn to one another for affirmation as they knit and sew for gift shops, church sales, raffles, and the annual summer doll parade. Although their crafts seem rather childlike and trivial to their logger sons and husbands, and "cute" and "pretty" to the summer tourists, for the knitters the doll clothes encode important personal history and the values of the local women's community. They express female identity and self-worth in a culture where men's more visible lives are associated with danger and occasional family violence; soft, fragile creations unlike the hard, wooden crafts and chain-saw carvings of the men, they bespeak the needs of children for protection and care. Their homemade individuality speaks against the commercialism that has come to Rangeley with recent economic development.

Most of the women discussed in these essays would not call themselves feminists, and their meetings are not the consciousness-raising groups of the 1970s. They do not intend to decode all the potentially disturbing meanings in their own words and actions or to tease out and highlight the strands of oppression in their lives. On the contrary, although they may speak more freely among themselves than any would in the family or in the community, their friendships are for comfort, not revolution, for cooperation in an established pattern of life, not its deconstruction. So there may be necessary silences in such groups—silences that come not only from the members' choices not to speak (out of feelings of privacy, propriety, shame) but also from their subconscious and necessary choices not to *know*. Since open acknowledgment of inequity and domination can be disturbing and painful, this awareness may not be welcome. In "A Jury of Her Peers," the new (and unsought) understanding to which Mrs. Peters and Mrs. Hale come causes them not peace of mind but distress, as they realize the extent to which they, as well as Minnie Wright, have been willing accomplices in their own muting and oppression in the service of menfolk. Their first action as a result of this understanding—the deception that protects Minnie—brings them not relief but anxiety. Their decoding of Minnie Wright's kitchen has brought them (particularly Mrs. Peters, the sheriff's wife) a conflict of loyalties they might never have chosen and an awareness of how dangerous the consequences of their new knowledge can be; after all, they have just tacitly condoned the murder of a husband by his wife (their "peer").

Although the young mothers who exchange versions of the legend studied by Janet L. Langlois may well recognize its subversive nature at some levels, they may not wish to plumb all its possibilities with equal openness. The legend highlights the isolation of a woman with small children and overtly cautions women to be more careful mothers;

its speakable subtext blames the system that isolates mothers, not the mothers themselves. But finally, Langlois suggests, the tale also encodes the unthinkable: it can express women's hostility to motherhood and even to their own children.

The Bee There quilters insisted that they "weren't making a statement" but were "just making a gift for a friend and being creative." Indeed, as they recognize, their "Scandalous Sue" quilt is minimally scandalous, telling the story of a girl who committed the teenage indiscretions of the quilters' own generation and finally married and bore children, as they have done. The Austin quilters deliberately chose not to create squares that showed Sue "going too far"—but their revisions of the traditional pattern imply the possibility of further revision, more serious disruption (as has been depicted in "alternative Sue" quilts by other groups), and more fundamental questioning of their lives.

The knitting women of Rangeley also maintain boundaries and do not read their coding as extensively as a folklorist might. Yocom suggests, for instance, that a woman who places in her gift shop a teddy bear dressed in a pastel knit outfit next to a logger's black bear hewn by chain saw from a pine tree can by this juxtaposition "soften" the carved bear and render it toylike, thus making the implicit claim that men's skills and women's are equal in quality and worth. This claim is not overt, though. In a culture where, according to a staff member at the Portland Family Crisis Shelter, "men believe they have a right to have power and control over their partners,"[5] women gloss over their troubles with phrases like "when things get complicated," and they do not read some of the latent self-assertion in their own art. In these essays, Langlois, Pershing, and Yocom, analyzing artistic creations and contexts from an explicitly feminist consciousness that their women informants often do not share, are careful to delineate and occasionally to restrict their own scholarly interpretations and not to infer tendentious coded messages, whose publication might cause difficulties for those who have trusted them as friends and fieldworkers.

Notes

1. *Tapestries of Life: Women's Work, Women's Consciousness, and the Meaning of Daily Experience* (Amherst: University of Massachusetts Press, 1989), 119–20.

2. "Woman Talk: The Legitimate Fear," in *Man Made Language* (London: Routledge and Kegan Paul, 1980), 106–37.

3. Guy Brett, *Through Our Own Eyes: Popular Art and Modern History* (Philadelphia: New Society Publishers, 1987), 32–34.

4. One area that has been of some interest to folklorists is joke telling in women's groups. See, for instance, Rayna Green, "Magnolias Grow in Dirt: The Bawdy Lore of Southern Women," *Southern Exposure* 4, no. 4 (1977): 29–33; Carol Mitchell, "Some Differences in Male and Female Joke-Telling," in *Women's Folklore, Women's Culture,* ed. Rosan A. Jordan and Susan J. Kalčik (Philadelphia: University of Pennsylvania Press, 1985), 163–86; and Regina Barreca, "The Laughter in the Kitchen: Growing Up Female and Funny," in *They Used to Call Me Snow White... But I Drifted* (New York: Viking, 1991), 101–22.

5. "Domestic Violence Up," *Maine Times,* July 27, 1990, 2.

Mothers' Double Talk

JANET L. LANGLOIS

For scholars and activists interested in feminist theory and its implications and for women in their daily lives, mothering is at the center of
debate on gender politics. On the dark side, a line stretches from
Simone de Beauvoir's *Second Sex* through Adrienne Rich's *Of Woman
Born* to Nancy Chodorow's statement in *Women, Culture and Society*
that "women's motherhood and mothering role seem to be the most
important features in accounting for the universal secondary status of
women."[1] On the brighter side, perhaps, French feminists, such as
Hélène Cixous, Luce Irigaray, and Julia Kristeva, have invested the
maternal with a powerful presence radiating through layers of personality development, literary criticism, and culture.[2]

Within this chiaroscuro of debate, I would like to set discussion of
a horror story that has been told by mothers about a mother who
inadvertently causes the death of her child or children. The story that
I have labeled "The Inept Mother" has oral and written versions that
form the data base for the discussion.[3] I think the story, disturbing on
many levels, addresses the issue of ambiguity that Joan N. Radner and
Susan S. Lanser find to be the central problem in decoding domestic
incompetence as a strategy women use to resist patriarchal institutions,
the Law of the Father.[4] Although all the readings that follow are
cultural ones, I call those in section 1 primarily sociopolitical, those in
section 2 psychoanalytical, and those in section 3 metaphysical.

1

I first heard "The Inept Mother" in 1978 from Alice Marie Thomas, a
friend since we went to Colorado State University together as under-
graduates in the mid-1960s. Always interested in my folklore studies,
she contacted me after she had heard *two* versions of the same anxiety-
producing story. She set the context for the first narrative perform-

ance in Colorado Springs, Colorado, in 1968. At that time, she was twenty-two and worked in the proofing department of the First National Bank downtown. Older women in the department had taken her under their wing, and they often had lunch and coffee breaks together. One day, Alice walked with Carol and Linda to the Walgreen's drugstore next to the bank for a coffee break. While there, Linda, who was from Oregon, told the other two women the story, which Alice recounted in a later interview:

> [Linda] told the story about some family in her hometown, supposedly; they didn't know the family—it was like a friend of a friend—and the mother had brought home the baby boy. . . . and they had a three-year-old daughter who was very curious about the new baby and, when the little girl was watching her mother change his diaper, she asked the mother, she said, "What is that?" [pointing to the baby's penis]. And Mom said, "Oh, that's just something the doctor forgot to cut off." And, then Mother had forgotten the powder or something needed, left the little girl watching the baby on the changing table, went to get it. When she came back, the little girl had gone to the kitchen, gotten a butcher knife and cut off his penis. And the Mom was trying to, had to take the child to the Emergency Room, but, of course, the baby bled to death.[5]

Alice recalled her response the first time: "I remember feeling shock and horror and thinking how terrible that must have been and what a tragedy it was. And just thinking how awful that mother must have felt . . . and I believed this story absolutely."[6]

The second time Alice heard the story was in 1978, shortly before she first told me. By then, she was married, was teaching in a school system in Albuquerque, New Mexico, and had a new baby boy herself. Friends who also had a new baby invited Alice and her husband over for dinner. While they were sitting around the table talking about the concerns of new parents, the hostess, Theresa, told a version of the story Alice had heard ten years earlier in Colorado Springs. This time, since Theresa was from Boston, the mother and children were known to Theresa's family there, and the story had the additional tragic ending that the mother, in her haste to get the bleeding baby to the hospital, backed the car out of the garage and ran over her daughter in the driveway so that *both* children died.

Although Alice might have been doubly affected by the double tragedy, she was now aware of the story as a narrated event: "as soon as Theresa started telling the story—the bells went off—and I thought, 'I HEARD this story before. I KNOW what's coming. I KNOW HOW THIS STORY IS GOING TO END.' And so I was not horrified. I was not shocked. . . . But the other people around the table, especially the fathers, . . . were very uncomfortable."[7] Hearing the story a second time made Alice aware of what folk narrative specialists would recognize—that she was a participant in two legend-telling sessions.[8] The twice-told tale cued her to its narrative possibilities. She no longer believed the story to be literally true as she once had, but she wondered about its effects and meanings. *Why* were women telling and listening to it?

Because Alice had changed from a participant in a legend event to an analyst of the folk process by the time I formally interviewed her in 1988, her stretched-out responses reveal some of the meanings listeners and tellers might construct around and through these narrative performances. When Alice first heard the story in 1968, her sympathy lay with the mother's tragedy. By 1988, however, her sympathy had shifted away from the mother and toward the children. Now a child development specialist and kindergarten teacher in the Woodland Park, Colorado, school district, she has come to the conclusion that the mother's incompetence was inexcusable.

In the 1988 interview session, we explored those incompetencies. I focused on the mother's linguistic mistake—most hearers of the story know that a tragedy is imminent the minute the mother says, "Oh, that's something the doctor forgot to cut off." Alice focused on the mother's caretaking mistake—no competent mother would leave a newborn baby on the changing table with only a small child in attendance. Subsequent ineptness includes the mother's failure to administer immediate first aid for severe bleeding, and, in the case of the second version, her failure to check her rearview mirror before backing out of the garage.

Like all legends, this legend issues a warning; in this case, it is a "don't" list for the competent mother in our culture. In fact, the nameless mother, whose inept responses to her children serve as negative exempla, is very much aligned (and maligned) with an American suburban housewife, Joanne Michulski, who killed the youngest two of her eight children in 1974 and whose story Adrienne Rich portrays so powerfully in the last chapter of *Of Women Born*, "Violence: The Heart of Maternal Darkness." Rich says that Michulski, as she was portrayed in the media, "became a scapegoat, the one around whom the darkness of maternity is allowed to swirl—the invisible violence of the institution of motherhood, the guilt, the powerless responsibility for human lives, the judgments and condemnations. . . ."[9] The same reading can be applied to the inept mother of the legend, even though she did not actually murder her children.

Rich writes further about the Michulski case that "reading of the 'bad' mother's response to an invisible assault on her being, 'good' mothers resolve to become better, more patient and long-suffering, to cling more tightly to what passes for sanity. The scapegoat is different from the martyr; she cannot teach resistance or revolt."[10] Rich thus reads this mother-as-scapegoat image in classic functionalist terms: as the steam valve diffusing what she calls women's need for "lucid rebellion" against the cultural structures/strictures of motherhood as an *institution*.

Hearing the "bad" mother's "wrong" response to a domestic crisis in the legend, mothers may resolve to be "good" mothers, to be more competent, more vigilant, and more careful in their "powerless responsibility for human lives," instead of reorganizing childcare responsibilities, for example. Rich's interpretation of the Michulski story and, by extension, "The Inept Mother" story, then, reaffirms patriarchal space for readers and listeners. This interpretation may be valid. Witness Alice's move from sympathy to censure, for example. Barbara Babcock, a discussant on the conference panel where I first presented a version of the present essay, even questioned if these legend versions might not have been deliberately planted by antifeminist groups to offset the rising women's movements in the United States in the 1960s and 1970s.[11]

Yet Rich's analysis itself suggests alternative readings. She presents Joanne Michulski's story sympathetically and is implicitly asking Alice, all of us, to return to sympathy. She asks us not to condone children's deaths but to see these unfortunate mothers in the full context of their lives. She sees Joanne Michulski as one example of the mother-as-martyr, who desperately tried to *speak* through the sacrifice of her children about "the invisible violence of the institution of motherhood." Taking Rich's lead, let us look again at Alice's responses to "The Inept Mother" and see if they can possibly bring us to reading "lucid rebellion" encoded in tragedy.

First, let us explore the issue of linguistic incompetency. Here, the mother fails because she speaks figuratively when she says the baby's penis is something the doctor forgot to cut off and her three-year-old daughter understands her literally. The mother, in wanting to avoid a discussion of sex, does not recognize that the child is too young to understand the social use of metaphor and wordplay. A circumlocution becomes a castration.[12] Alice said to me, "And this is all tied up with sexuality and sex education. And how we deal with our children's sexuality—which this mother clearly doesn't want to [do]. But, I guess, perhaps, because I'm not as comfortable with that either [laughing]... I can forgive her for saying something that DUMB to her child [more] than I can forgive her for leaving the baby unattended."[13]

Alice shows how typical is this mother's evasive response to her child's typical question by telling a humorous story of her own. When her son was about the same age as the daughter in the legend, he asked her, "Why is my penis so hard?" when he had an erection. Alice, who had taken a course on sexuality for parents, was not as prepared to answer as she thought: "and he wanted to know, right now, you know. And, like this rather dumb mother's response, I said to him, 'I DON'T KNOW!' [laughing] and did not answer the question because I was embarrassed."[14]

Informal samplings of mothers' talk about their children embarrassing them at home or in public often show children disregarding the conventions of silence concerning sexuality and sexual difference.[15] Alice's coda to the above account—"*I hope I would have said something else* but, obviously, there are times when I don't say, especially when it concerns sexuality"—signals a complex response to "The Inept Mother" that challenges Rich's conception of the "good" mothers' resolve to submerge themselves in the system. Alice recognized, as we all might, the deeply internal Victorian cultural codes still operating for her, but she hoped she would not "suffer and be still" but speak openly, yet responsibly, about sexual difference to a curious child. The implication is that in speaking out, mothers demystify the unspoken assumptions that allow a patriarchal system, with its concomitant gender codes, to be maintained. The message is that the child, or children, would have been protected, less vulnerable, and allowed to grow to adulthood if the mother had spoken of difference and so broken an authoritarian discourse.[16]

Second, let us explore the issue of the chain of caretaking incompetencies following from the mother's linguistic blunder. A third version of the legend will help bring an alternative reading to light. In the spring of 1982, Sarah Chandler, my graduate assistant in Wayne State University's Folklore Archive, recorded an exchange she shared with Janny, a neighbor in Royal Oak, Michigan. At the time, both women had a daughter and a son the same age as the children in the legend. One day when the two mothers were talking as they watched their children playing, Sarah brought up the legend she had learned through my research: "There are such awful stories about older sisters castrating their baby brothers. Did you hear the one about the mother who was changing her baby boy's diaper, and had to leave the room to answer the phone or something and when she came back her little girl had castrated the baby with a pair of scissors?" Janny's response surprised her:

> Yes, I did. Only that's not the way I heard it. I heard that the mother had *three* children, and that she was giving the newborn baby a bath in the tub when she heard the little boy screaming in the next room. She dropped the baby and ran into see what the trouble was and found her little girl had cut off the little boy's penis. She was so upset that when she tried to grab the scissors away from the girl, that the girl fell on them and got stabbed. So all three of her children were killed. . . . The baby drowned. The little boy bled to death, and I think the little girl died from the scissors. Can you believe that?[17]

Believable or not, the baby's drowning in Janny's story adds one more link in the chain of incompetencies to mark a triple tragedy. (Note that the mother's linguistic blunder is missing from both these versions.) Yet, at the same time, it highlights, through sheer repetition, the mother's terrible isolation and resultant panic. Alice made this observation, once she had heard this version in our interview session: "and the other element of all this—the baby left in the bathtub. It does point out that *mothers are all by themselves—alone with children*—and there's no other grownup upon which they can call and say, 'I need to run do this, the baby's in the bathtub'—something. . . . "

Rich's reading of Joanne Michulski's story corresponds to Alice's recognition of the institutional pressures exemplified in "The Inept Mother."[18] Rich noted that Joanne Michulski's bouts of mental illness "took place when she was left alone with the children. Aware that the situation was deteriorating, Michulski stuck to his decision to 'keep the family together'—that is, *to leave his wife all day long responsible for eight children.*"[19] The mothers who heard this story in my sample resolved not to be alone all day with small children. That resolve, in itself, is a revolutionary act, more open, it is true, to white, college-educated, professional women than to others and involving much more than the availability of babysitters or day care centers. That resolve demands a shift in mindset that both recognizes and accepts other options. It demands altering family and cultural dynamics and restructuring basic social relationships, so that caretakers are within an extended network of support and without patriarchal dichotomies. The revolution in childcare will continue to be one of the major issues of the 1990s.

The ambiguity lies, of course, in which reading is read by whom and when. If the legend text is a warning to conform within the system, then its subtext is a warning to subvert that system. Alice has heard both. So have I. The paradox of legend makes the failed mother a "disorderly woman," one who can outline the conventional through her failures or one who can open up the deeply radical through others' recognition of her untenable position in the system that entraps her.[20] These alternative readings constitute the first layer of mothers' double talk.

2

The second layer of mothers' double talk lies on the border of the sociopolitical and the psychological. Normally seen as two distinct arenas for thought and action, the two collide in recent discussions of psychoanalysis and women's development. Before turning to further analysis of the story at hand, let us first take a look at a decidedly nonfeminist, but thought-provoking, reading of the "The Castrated Boy" legend by Michael P. Carroll in a recent issue of *Folklore*.[21] Since *women* usually tell and listen to the urban legend of the boy castrated in a public men's restroom while his mother waits outside, Carroll builds a case for seeing this urban legend as an expression of women's fantasies of male castration tied to the women's movements of the 1960s and 1970s rather than as an expression of ethnic tension and fear of crime:

> In summary, then, I am arguing that the dramatic increase in public discussions concerning the need to eliminate the glaring social inequalities between the sexes reactivated in the minds of many females the infantile memory of their *first* experience of sexual inequality, which involved their perception that they lacked a penis. In the unconscious of some women, however, this memory was associated with a resentment against the father, and a consequent desire to castrate the father. These infantile memories would therefore also be reactivated by this increased emphasis upon the social inequalities between the sexes. A reactivated desire to "castrate the father" would express itself in the form of a general desire to castrate a male, and—at one level at least—it is this desire to castrate a male that is being gratified in the ["Castrated Boy"] story and that therefore accounts for its popularity.[22]

Carroll's reading depends on a Freudian model of children's psychosexual development, a model that has increasingly come under attack by feminist scholars for not considering sexual difference and one that Carroll has had to modify himself to include discussion of *women's* castration symbolism.[23] It also depends on subordinating the importance of sociopolitical movements by positing them as mere catalysts for psychological states. Yet his chilling conclusion that the legend text expressing "the parents' natural concern over the safety of their children" masks a subtext of its exact opposite—women's unconscious desire to castrate—is at the heart of the ambiguity issue being developed here.[24]

Carroll's interpretation might be applied to versions of "The Inept Mother." I particularly have in mind the texts Jan Harold Brunvand includes in his 1986 collection of modern urban legends, which are clearly related to those discussed in section 1 but which express quite a different family dynamic.[25] Edward Eulenberg, a retired Chicago newspaper reporter, sent Brunvand the first text, remarking that the most horrible tale he remembered was about "the little boy who wet": "Depending on the version, he was two or three years old. Despite scoldings, he resisted toilet training until his exasperated mother warned: 'If you don't learn, I'm going to cut it off.' Unfortunately, she was overheard by the boy's older sister. So one day, when the children's mother was away, the boy wet again, and the girl took up a pair of shears and cut it off. He almost bled to death."[26] Eulenberg recalled a double context for the telling of this story. Middle-aged "ladies" of his mother's generation talked over coffee and cake when they visited each other's homes and when they met each other shopping in neighborhood stores in 1930s Chicago, and his mother told him the story she had heard from them.[27]

Brunvand includes a second text from Rodney Dale's recent collections of British urban legends. No specific social contexts for performances are given. Here, the British mum can't get her unruly boy to sleep. She finally shouts, "If you don't go to sleep I'll . . . I'll . . . cut off your willie." Needless to say, "her angelic daughter" does the job for her with a dressmaking shears, and the mum runs over her as she is going to the hospital, to mark the familiar double tragedy.[28]

Don Holt, from Mobile, Alabama, recently sent Brunvand a third text of the story, which he had heard many years ago but for which he gives no other particulars. Here, the mother catches two-year-old Reggie masturbating and says, "If you don't stop that I'm going to cut it off with a knife." While she is bathing six-month-old Clarice in the tub, four-year-old Hattie cuts off Reggie's penis and announces the fact to her mother. The mother rushes Reggie to the doctor's office too late, runs over Hattie in the driveway, and forgets Clarice, who drowns in the bathtub, to mark the triple tragedy we have come to expect.[29]

In these versions, all reported by men (which would support a Freudian reading of castration anxiety certainly), the mother is inept, not because she gives an inappropriate response to her daughter as she did in section 1 but because she gives an inappropriate threat to her son and her daughter enacts it. The mother's hyperbolic statement is taken literally, innocently or not, by the older sibling. In fact, Brunvand appropriately labels this section of his book "The Mother's Threat Carried Out." Holt's comment that "I don't believe anyone ever said it was true or not, but it certainly says that *one should never say bad things to one's children*" marks the legend text, what Carroll would call its manifest content, as a warning, here to use other ways of disciplining children if one is to be a good mother. There is even a hint that this message is a middle-class comment on perceptions of working-class approaches to child rearing; a middle-class parent's goal would be to further reason with the child, not to threaten violence, for example.[30]

The legend's subtext, however, seems even more apparent here than it does in "The Castrated Boy." Women's latent fantasies of castration seem much more obviously gratified; the mother actually threatens castration instead of just inadvertently causing it; the daughter does it, at just the age Freud suggested girls first see they lack a penis and when they are old enough to verbalize their actions and therefore presumably old enough to understand their mothers' meaning. Here, the mother and daughter, caught in what Freud would call a preoedipal situation, carry penis envy to its extreme. They make concrete Carroll's assertion that adult women regress to the unconscious desires of their childhood through external stimuli. No wonder the young fathers who heard the story recounted in section 1 were so uncomfortable.

Yet these versions put Carroll's reading to a number of tests. First, the women's liberation movement in the United States in the 1960s and 1970s does not account for the Eulenberg and Holt versions predating that decade or the Dale versions, which are British. Women have been telling this story longer and in more places than either Carroll or I first recognized. Second, and perhaps more important, it is possible to flip Carroll's analysis upside down by showing a somewhat different configuration of sociopolitical or cultural and psychological components underlying these narratives. I arrived at the following feminist readings independently of Carroll's study, but I find them interesting counterpoints to his analysis.

Nancy Chodorow rereads Freud's model of child development as a *cultural* sequence rather than a biological one. It depends on early mother-child relationships instead of the Oedipus complex to create gender identities forged by the time the child is three. (Note that this is the age of the daughter in the stories in section 1.) For Chodorow, mothers see their daughters as extensions of themselves and so identify with them in a deeper way and for a longer time than they do with their sons, who must separate from them to gain a male identity. For psychoanalytic theory and for the culture at large, Chodorow recognizes that the autonomous self, the self that can differentiate from others, the male self, is privileged. The relational self, the self that defines itself in connection to others, the female self, is not privileged yet is essential in the cultural process of nurturing daughters, who will become mothers, and sons, who will separate from them.

For Chodorow, then, this lack of boundary maintenance between mother and daughter perpetuates sexual stratification, the earmark of a patriarchal system. Because the daughter never completely differentiates from her mother, she is filled with ambivalence, both toward her mother and toward others. She experiences penis envy, then, not because she feels herself a castrated son, as Freud maintained, but because the penis is both a sign of differentiation from her mother and a desire for the status and power being male entails.[31] (Note that the daughter is older in the stories in section 2; her age, approximately four or five, corresponds to the onset of penis envy.)

With this revised model in mind, it is possible to read the subtext of "The Mother's Threat Carried Out" in a different way. We see the mother and daughter deeply identified at the very moment their joint act of castrating the son/brother reveals their frustration with their subordination. They are literally and metaphorically "getting even" and so, presumably, gratifying symbolically those mothers and daughters listening to the story who are also caught within the system they subvert.

Another related reading grows out of feminists' positive evaluation of this mother-daughter bond. Chodorow herself has surveyed anthropological studies of past and present cultures where feminine bonding of this type is a valued one; Carol Gilligan makes a case for seeing the empathy developed in this type of bonding as important for our culture now; Cixous, Irigaray, and Kristeva see "la différence féminine" as a way to transcend patriarchal dichotomies in the future. They positively value the preoedipal stage and the bonding posited there between mother and child and so deny the value of the oedipal crisis, especially for the daughter.[32]

If we look through the horror and accept a desire or wish for maternal, if not matriarchal, bonding at the base of "The Mother's Threat," then the mother's and daughter's actions make symbolic sense. Both mother and daughter desire a more feminine world. The mother threatens castration, and the daughter does it in three areas where the son transgresses that world. He refuses to be toilet trained, a child's developmental task and a parent's child-rearing one that most people in our culture see is sooner done by girls than by boys. He is rowdy at bedtime and refuses to settle down, again marking our cultural assumptions about boys' activities. And he masturbates, the erect penis symbolizing masculinity. The boy is castrated not because of penis envy but because his mother and sister want him to be more like them; a castrated boy does become a girl in an ironic reversal of Freud's position.

The feminist readings, taken together, are themselves ambiguous and feed into a debate alluded to in the opening paragraph of this essay. Are women's conditions now the powerless "imperfect present," as the first reading suggests, or have they the powerful potential of the "future perfect," as the second reading suggests? A case can be made for seeing "The Mother's Threat" as one of "those complex stories of the interweavings of women's power" that Diane Christian asks us to examine and interrogate. Here, at least, women do not harbor secret desires to unsex males because of public discussions about sexual inequality, as Carroll theorizes, but they do want that sexual inequality to be eradicated. That eradication is *symbolized* by castration of the phallus, the system that disregards difference. The incompetent mother, then, becomes strangely competent through the paradox of metaphor.[33]

3

The concluding set of readings I find the most painful for it deals specifically with the metaphysical dilemma of motherhood, only hinted at in the preceding sections. Let us look briefly at two more versions of the all-too-familiar story, this time separated by thousands of miles and at least four centuries, to see that parenting has a built-in double bind and a corresponding double vision that may well span Western culture. This sweeping statement and the underlying methodology of historic-geographic tracings of parallels are justified here, I think, as explorations rather than conclusions.

Maria Tatar writes that one tale appearing in the Grimms' 1812 *Kinder und Hausmärchen* was mercifully left out in subsequent editions:

"How Children Played Butcher with Each Other," the most ghastly tale in the Grimms' collection, happily never entered the pages of the second edition of the *Nursery and Household Tales.* In the first edition the Grimms went so far as to offer two different versions of it. The first describes the fatal consequences of a children's game, which takes a tragic turn when one boy "playing" butcher slaughters another "playing" swine. The second version offers a chain of events even more lurid. A boy who takes the butcher's role murders his brother; his mother, witnessing the event from a window, is so enraged and distraught that she plunges a knife into the heart of her son; she returns to the house to find that the child she had been bathing has drowned in her absence; in the end, she hangs herself, and her grief-stricken husband dies shortly thereafter.[34]

Jack Zipes, who reprints both versions in his recent edition of the Grimms' fairy tales (but leaves the sex of the children open), confirms that the versions were deleted from the 1819 edition because "the tales were too gruesome."[35]

Yet Dieter Richter writes something that we know: this tale has not been so easily deleted from oral tradition. He shows that the Grimms' source for the second version of special interest here is Martin Zeiller's *Miscellen,* published in Nuremberg in 1661, but that the story can be traced to late antiquity and to Protestant sermon exempla in the sixteenth century in one direction and to nineteenth- and twentieth-century contemporary narratives in the other.[36] I can only guess at the shifting contexts and shifting meanings the story has held for its tellers and listeners over the centuries. There is some indication that the sermon exempla connection may be the one that fascinated Wilhelm Grimm, who is said to have remembered hearing this tale as a child, most probably as a cautionary tale and so fitting within the patriarchal sphere. That nineteenth-century German bourgeois parents, the major audience for *Kinder und Hausmärchen* originally, objected to this tale suggests the reading public found its framework either too archaic or too subversive for its taste.

Yet the tale persists in oral tradition, usually told by mothers in the legend contexts we have explored. This twentieth-century version comes from the Folklore Archives at the University of Utah in Salt Lake City. Its immediate context, like those of other versions, mirrors the tale's content—mothers with babies are talking about mothers with babies. Susan S. Wolf, a student in an introductory course in folklore, summarized the story performance she heard on March 26, 1986, when she and two friends with newborns were talking about "bad things that can happen." Both mothers Susan recorded believed the story and had heard it had happened "back East":

A mother with three small children was giving her six-month-old baby a bath in the tub when her two-year-old cut himself very badly. She couldn't leave her baby in the water, so she told her six-year-old to run across the street to the neighbors and get help. It took so long that she left the baby to help the two-year-old who was unconscious by now. She hears sirens, thinking help was there, but they were there because her six-year-old had been hit by a car. In the meantime, the baby in the tub drowned and the two-year-old bled to death. So she lost all three of her children in 20 minutes, *through no fault of her own.* [37]

These texts are different from those discussed in previous sections. First, the element of castration, raising issues of the mother's culpability and sexuality, is absent. Second, gender differences of the children are absent also, most clearly in the recent version and in some translations of the Grimms' tale, so that possible sibling rivalry and developmental differences do not seem to be the issue. Third, the versions present the extreme form of the tragedy—all three children are killed in a chain of inexorable causality. These versions highlight the fact that the mother loses all of her children *due to circumstances beyond her control.* In the Grimms' version, the mother loses control through her anger at the child, who turned a common rural game—playing at pig slaughtering—into the real thing. In the Utah version, the mother loses control simply through accident. Rich's statement already quoted—the mother's recognition of her "powerless responsibility for human lives"—is literally dramatized here, in a most elemental and abstract way.

These mothers, whether the seventeenth-century German farmwife or the contemporary American suburban housewife, experience what every mother fears; these stories encapsulate the dreadful anxiety for the lives of their children that is one of the most difficult aspects of parenting. As Alice Thomas remarked, "It seems to me that children have been at risk always; there've always been things that hurt children, take children away, no matter how good a mother you are. That is one of the big dangers of being a mother and it's one of the greatest fears. All mothers fear that."[38]

Another reading, related to the subtextual readings already discussed, demands that we look through the horror at the change in the woman's condition in the texts. She is an overburdened mother at the beginning of the tale and a childless woman at its end. Domna Stanton opens her article in the 1986 *Poetics of Gender* with a quote from Rimbaud: "When the infinite bondage of woman will be broken, when she will live *for herself and by herself . . . ,* she too will be a poet." In criticizing French feminists' use of maternal metaphors, Stanton suggests a metonymical approach to women, one in which their differences are played out in many connections. The woman is an "I" with many relations, the mother-child relation just one of a number of options. Stanton admits, however, that this approach is hypothetical because of the nature of Western metaphysics.[39]

This metaphysical dilemma, this existential crisis of being a woman, is at the heart of "The Inept Mother" legend complex. The narrative in all its versions is a sign or symbolic (re)presentation of the "double vision" of parenting, which Bess Lomax Hawes and Barre Toelken discuss so well in their analyses of the paradox of lullabies in Western cultures. Mothers sing words, such as "When the bough breaks, the cradle will fall, and down will come baby, cradle and all," possibly expressing their wish to be free from parental responsibilities. That desire, embedded in the lyrics, corresponds to mothers' desire for freedom *as women* I read in the legend process above. At the same time, mothers sing these words to soothing melodies designed to help loved children sleep safely through the night. The melodies are musical antidotes to the maternal anxiety about protecting children and warding off danger I also read in this legend process.[40]

Bess Lomax Hawes offers another reading when she asks, "Must we then conclude that American mothers are really expressing hostility toward their infants when they . . . put them to bed to . . . a lulling refrain that actually suggests that the babies should go off somewhere else?" Hawes responds to her own rhetorical question with a "Maybe, but that's only one of the possibilities." She concludes that the mother sings about the double bind in which she finds herself:

On the one hand, she must train her baby to be the active, exploratory, happily vocalizing—in sum, independent—little character that our culture prefers. On the other hand, she must do this without assistance from anybody else because our society is most unique in its insistence that mothers —and mothers alone—take care of babies. Thus, she must simultaneously try to separate her baby from herself . . . while at the same time she remains in maximum physical proximity to him. No wonder American mothers sing to their babies—and more especially, probably, to themselves—about separation and space and going very far away.[41]

If we refer back to Chodorow's distinctions in child development patterns, Hawes's comments are more applicable to a mother's separation from her son than from her daughter. Yet, for Hawes, the mother in this scenario is culturally forced to think of separation from her child, whatever her own wishes.

I read the legend as complex thinking about the thinkable— protecting the child who must leave you—and about the unthinkable —being a woman not defined in relation to motherhood. Barre Toelken writes that "The Inept Mother" does not mean "that mothers have a streak of secret aggression against their kids, but that we often can use a metaphor, or joke, or, in this case a legend, to experience vicariously the unthinkable."[42]

Hawes's reading of lullabies as "a mother's conversation with herself about separation" pulls together all the ambiguities of the legend discussed in the preceding sections. I hear the same echoes of mothers' isolation, separations, and double desires encoded in song and narrative. I do not hear a resolution, however. Mothering is one domestic task in which both competence and incompetence are double-edged swords.

Notes

1. Simone de Beauvoir, *The Second Sex*, trans. and ed. H. M. Parshley (1952; New York: Vintage Books, 1974); Adrienne Rich, *Of Woman Born: Motherhood as Experience and Institution* (1976; New York: Norton, 1986); Nancy Chodorow, "Family Structure and Feminine Personality," in *Women, Culture and Society*, ed. Michelle Zimbalist Rosaldo and Louise Lamphere (Stanford: Stanford University Press, 1974), 45.

2. See Elaine Marks and Isabelle de Courtivron, eds., *New French Feminisms* (New York: Schocken Books, 1980), and Joanne Trebilcot, *Mothering: Essays in Feminist Theory* (Totowa, N.J.: Rowman and Allanheld, 1984), for a general overview; Domna C. Stanton reviews French feminists' positions on the value of the mother in her "Difference on Trial: A Critique of the Maternal Metaphor in Cixous, Irigaray, and Kristeva," in *The Poetics of Gender*, ed. Nancy K. Miller (New York: Columbia University Press, 1986), 157–82. My own interest in this issue is not purely academic; my child, now seven years old, was not quite three when I gave the first version of this paper in the panel "Women and Folklore: Empowering Marginality" at the 1987 American Folklore Society Meeting in Albuquerque, New Mexico.

3. At this point, I do not know how widespread this legend complex is, but I have considered all the versions that have come to my attention. Whether all the texts I discuss are, in fact, the same story or related stories can be the focus of further discussion. I thank Jan Harold Brunvand, Donald Haase, and Janet Bennett for their contributions.

4. Joan N. Radner and Susan S. Lanser, "Strategies of Coding in Women's Cultures," herein; Susan S. Lanser, "Burning Dinners: Feminist Subversions of Domesticity," herein.

5. Interview with Alice Marie Thomas, Detroit, Michigan, on June 10, 1988. See also personal communication in 1978, 1982, and 1987; and Janet L. Langlois, "Mothers' Double Talk," *Folklore Women's Communication* 29 (Spring 1983): 7–8.

6. Interview.

7. Ibid.

8. See Linda Dégh, "The 'Belief Legend' in Modern Society: Form, Function and Relationship to Other Genres," in *American Folk Legend: A Symposium*, ed. Wayland D. Hand (Los Angeles: University of California Press, 1971),

55–68; Dégh, "Folk Narrative," in *Folklore and Folklife: An Introduction,* ed. Richard M. Dorson (Chicago: University of Chicago Press, 1971), especially 72–80; and Dégh and Andrew Vázsonyi, "Legend and Belief," in *Folklore Genres,* ed. Dan Ben-Amos (Austin: University of Texas Press, 1976), 93–124.

9. Rich, *Of Woman Born,* 277.

10. Ibid., 278.

11. American Folklore Society Annual Meeting, October 1987. Further research is needed on these important points of transmission. At this point, response to the Michulski case and to the legend event generally is hypothetical, as is the possible origin of the legend.

12. Barre Toelken gives this reading: "The sister is not old enough to have had her sibling rivalry socialized through association, observation and inference; she *is* old enough to understand language, but not socialized enough to understand wordplay, thus she understands only the manifest content of the mother's . . . remark and does not catch that it's hyperbole" (personal communication, March 13, 1988). The issue of sibling rivalry is one that I considered earlier but did not focus on in this essay. A recent letter to the editor of the *Detroit Free Press* urged parents to consider the effect of metaphor on children, who take such expressions as "I could have died laughing" literally.

13. Interview.

14. Ibid.

15. See, for example, Danielle Roemer, "Children's Indiscretions and Women's Narratives," *Folklore Women's Communication* 27–28 (Fall–Winter 1982): 3–5.

16. See Luce Irigaray, "The Blind Spot of an Old Dream of Symmetry," in her *Speculum of the Other Woman,* trans. Gillian C. Gill (Ithaca, N.Y.: Cornell University Press, 1985), 13–129.

17. Langlois, "Mothers' Double Talk," 8.

18. It is fair to question whether I brought Alice to this recognition and so skewed her response toward this reading; at this point, I don't believe so.

19. Rich, *Of Woman Born,* 258 (emphasis added).

20. See Natalie Zemon Davis, "Women on Top: Symbolic Sexual Inversion in Early Modern France," in *The Reversible World: Symbolic Inversion in Art and Society,* ed. Barbara Babcock (Ithaca, N.Y.: Cornell University Press, 1977), 147–90, for the model of the disorderly woman who both confirmed and subverted cultural expectations.

21. Michael P. Carroll, " 'The Castrated Boy': Another Contribution to the Psychoanalytic Study of Urban Legends," *Folklore* 98, no. 2 (1987): 216–25.

22. Ibid., 222.

23. See, especially, Chodorow, "Family Structure and Feminine Personality," and Irigaray, "The Blind Spot in an Old Dream of Symmetry."

24. Carroll, " 'The Castrated Boy,' " 219.

25. Jan Harold Brunvand, *The Mexican Pet: More "New" Urban Legends and Some Old Favorites* (New York: Norton, 1986), 72–73.

26. Ibid., 72.

27. Ibid.; personal communication with Edward Eulenberg, 1987.

28. Rodney Dale, *The Tumour in the Whale* (London: Duckworth, 1978), 151–52, and *It's True, It Happened to a Friend* (London: Duckworth, 1984), 90–91, as cited in Brunvand, *The Mexican Pet*, 72–73.

29. Personal communication from Don E. Holt to Jan Harold Brunvand, 1988.

30. Ibid. For a literary reworking of the legend, see Morton Thompson's 1954 novel, *Not as a Stranger* (New York: Scribner), 278–80. In this account, the mother, "dressed in a cheap housedress," tells the doctor in the ambulance that her four-year-old son castrated himself after she told him she'd get his father's razor and cut it off if he didn't stop masturbating. She recalls that she left her year-old daughter in the tub and the ambulance crew found the child drowned. A doctor muses, "Just in a twinkling—the home empties—both kids gone—for nothing! For nothing! Just like that!" French novelist Michel Tournier also has a short story, "Prikli," in his *The Fetishist* (New York: Doubleday, 1973), in which a little boy castrates himself.

31. Chodorow, "Family Structure and Feminine Personality," and *The Reproduction of Mothering: Psychoanalysis and the Sociology of Gender* (Berkeley: University of California Press, 1979); Coppelia Kahn, "The Hand that Rocks the Cradle: Recent Gender Theories and Their Implications," in *The (M)other Tongue: Essays in Feminist Psychoanalytic Interpretation,* ed. Shirley Nelson Garner, Claire Kahane, and Madelon Sprengnether (Ithaca, N.Y.: Cornell University Press, 1985), 72–77; Carol Gilligan, *In a Different Voice: Psychological Theory and Women's Development* (Cambridge, Mass.: Harvard University Press, 1982), 7–9.

32. Chodorow, "Family Structure and Feminine Personality," 60–64; Gilligan, *In a Different Voice,* 24–63; Hélène Cixous, "The Laugh of the Medusa," Luce Irigaray, "This Sex which Is Not One," and Julia Kristeva, "Oscillation between Power and Denial," in *New French Feminisms,* ed. Marks and de Courtivron, 245–64, 99–106, 165–67.

33. Diane Christian, "Commentary," *Journal of American Folklore* 101, no. 399 (1988): 54. See also Jane Gallop, *The Daughter's Seduction: Feminism and Psychoanalysis* (Ithaca, N.Y.: Cornell University Press, 1982), especially 113–31; and Julia Kristeva, "Women's Time," reprinted in *Critical Theory Since 1965,* ed. Hazard Adams and Leroy Searle (Tallahassee: University Presses of Florida, Florida State University Press, 1986), 471–85.

34. Maria Tatar, *The Hard Facts of the Grimms' Fairy Tales* (Princeton, N.J.: Princeton University Press, 1987), 180.

35. Jack Zipes, trans., *The Complete Fairy Tales of the Brothers Grimm* (New York: Bantam Books, 1987), 650–51, 725.

36. Dieter Richter, "Wie Kinder Schlachtens mit einander gespielt haben (AaTh 2401)," *Fabula* 27, no. 1–2 (1986): 1–11. I thank Don Haase for the reference and Ute Klotzek for the translation.

37. Susan S. Wolf, student paper recorded April 8, 1986, Folklore Archives, University of Utah, courtesy of Jan Harold Brunvand.

38. Interview. The *Detroit Free Press* carried this story on July 20, 1988: "2 Ann Arbor children die inside freezer." Part of the copy reads: "An Ann Arbor girl and boy, out of their mother's sight for less than 30 minutes as she cared for their crying infant sister, suffocated Tuesday morning after climbing into an old-style freezer that trapped them inside, police said. . . . Neighbor Ron Odom, 27, said: 'This is a shame. The kids were real friendly. . . . They seemed like well-taken-care-of kids.' "

39. Stanton, "Difference on Trial," 157 (emphasis added), 157–82.

40. Bess Lomax Hawes, "Folksongs and Functions: Some Thoughts on the American Lullaby," reprinted in *Readings in American Folklore,* ed. Jan Harold Brunvand (New York: Norton, 1979), 202–14, especially 212–13, from *Journal of American Folklore* 87, no. 344 (1974): 140–48; Barre Toelken, "Ballads and Folksongs," in *Folk Groups and Folklore Genres: An Introduction,* ed. Elliott Oring (Logan: Utah State University Press, 1986), 147–74, especially 162–65.

41. Hawes, "Folksongs and Function," 212–14.

42. Toelken, personal communication, March 13, 1988.

"She Really Wanted to Be Her Own Woman": Scandalous Sunbonnet Sue

LINDA PERSHING

Idealized images of children in large bonnets and hats have been popular among American quilters since the early 1900s. Often depicted either playing children's games or standing with their arms demurely at their sides, these images have appeared on quilts in a variety of shapes and patterns. Among many contemporary quilters, Sunbonnet Sue—the name commonly given to the stylized figure of a little girl who wears an oversized bonnet—has become a particular favorite. Characteristically, Sunbonnet Sue represents an endearing and senti- mentalized portrait of childhood. Frequently Sunbonnet Sue quilts are made for children or as gifts to celebrate the arrival of a new baby. Given the conventional associations of Sunbonnet Sue with inno- cence and youth, it would be surprising to encounter a Sunbonnet quilt that showed young Sue engaging in a series of controversial activities, such as burning a bra, skinny-dipping, or showering with a male. But this was precisely what I discovered when I attended the October 1986 quilt show of the Austin Area Quilt Guild, where I first saw a quilt entitled "Scandalous Sue." This essay is an analysis of the complex messages conveyed by the creation and presentation of the Scandalous Sue quilt. I suggest that by appropriating and inverting a symbol of feminine domesticity and propriety, the quiltmakers expressed resistance to dominant cultural norms in a way that was both acces- sible and safe for them.

The Development of Sunbonnet Sue

American women have been making Sunbonnet Sue quilts for at least a century. Researchers have suggested that from the end of the 1800s through the 1930s, the proliferation of quilts depicting children in large hats and bonnets seems to have been spurred by commercial advertisements and illustrations.[1] The work of the British artist Kate Greenaway, whose illustrations in children's books were extremely popular from 1885 into the early 1900s, may have created the impetus for the development of similar quilting patterns.[2] Commercial artist and illustrator Bertha Corbett, well known for her drawings of busy children whose faces were hidden by large hats, produced so many figures of this kind that she became known as "the mother of the Sunbonnet babies." *The Sunbonnet Babies Primer,* illustrated by Corbett in the early 1900s, sold over a million copies. Corbett's work also appeared in several other prominent children's readers and in countless magazines and postcard series (see Figure 1). A third commercial artist, Bernhardt Wall, was also recognized for his illustrations of bonneted children much like Corbett's, including a variety of little boys in wide-brimmed hats, who later became the male counterparts to Sunbonnet Sue in popular illustrations and subsequently in quilts.

The evolution of Sunbonnet Sue quilts exemplifies the complex interweavings of popular or mass culture and folk culture and suggests

Figure 1: Postcard designed by Bertha Corbett, a well-known illustrator who became known as "the mother of the Sunbonnet babies." The postcard is undated, but it was postmarked 1907. (Courtesy of Dolores Hinson; photo by Linda Pershing)

the necessity for scholars to study them as interrelated processes. Whether the fascination with children in oversized bonnets had its origins in folk tradition or a trend in commercial art (and the latter appears to be more likely), each perpetually influenced the other.[3] The signed and anonymous work of dozens of commercial artists at the turn of the century reflected the sunbonnet craze and was used to sell a variety of products. For example, the illustrations of Jessie Wilcox Smith (born in 1879) appeared on the cover of *Good Housekeeping* magazine for fifteen consecutive years, certainly enough time for many quilters to recognize and integrate her images of childhood into their own quilting patterns.[4] Quilt researcher Dolores Hinson observes that "it was anonymous work, however, that was copied most often by quilters, who saw in the fill-in illustration, the small picture ads, and the needlework or women's interest column illustrations the basis for many needlework ideas."[5]

This became a reflexive process as magazine and commercial patterns were used and adapted by women, who altered them to meet their needs and, in turn, passed them on to other quilters. Other individuals who liked the general Sunbonnet genre of quilting no doubt designed their own distinctive patterns, which were also circulated. In turn, as patterns became popular, they were published in magazines in the 1920s and 1930s as an incentive to subscribe.[6] With the passing of time, Sunbonnet patterns became adaptations of adaptations of adaptations, influenced by a combination of commercial art, folk distribution, and personal preferences.

In the 1920s and 1930s, Sunbonnet Sue images became so popular in the United States that they appeared not only in book illustrations, magazine advertisements, and embroidery and appliqué quilting kits but also on pillowcases, dishtowels, potholders, curtains, greeting cards, chinaware, and pottery and as trademarks and paper dolls. The Morton Salt Girl holding the big umbrella and the Dutch Cleanser Girl, the latter designed by Corbett, likely had their roots in the Sunbonnet Sue patterns of their day.[7] Although there were far fewer Sunbonnet quilts by the end of the 1930s and 1940s, when quilting in general fell out of favor, there was a later resurgence of interest in Sunbonnet imagery. Modernized versions of Sunbonnet Sue reappeared in the 1970s in the form of "Hobbie Holly" and again in the "Strawberry Shortcake" of the present.

Conventionally, Sunbonnet Sue patterns are an abstraction of a clothed, female form, usually that of a young child.[8] Sue wears an oversized bonnet or hat, which completely covers her face and hair.[9] Although she has also been called the Dutch Girl or Dutch Doll,

Figure 2: "Saying Grace," a 1905 postcard drawn by Dorothy Dixon in the sunbonnet style that was popular in her time. (Courtesy of Dolores Hinson; photo by Linda Pershing)

when given a first name, she is almost always called "Sue."[10] The patterns of little boys have more widely varying names, including Overall Bill, Farmer Boy, Sombrero Boy, Overall Andy, Sunny Jim, Fishin' Freddie, Cowboy, Peter Prim, and Li'l Jake.[11] Sunbonnet children may be stationary, often depicted from a side view with a single arm and foot shown, or they may be busily engaged in a variety of childhood play activities. Both Sunbonnet Sue and Overall Bill commonly are shown working in the garden, fishing, swinging, or playing with a toy. A popular series of poses from the early 1900s, however, depicted Sue engaged in domestic tasks, including washing windows, sweeping, washing and hanging laundry, baking, ironing, and mending. Sunbonnet Sue quilts with similar designs were made for young girls, apparently to inculcate in them the value of these domestic activities.[12] Passed down and adapted through generations of women to reflect the gender norms of the day, Sunbonnet Sue became a generic representation of feminine ideals and behavior.

Above all, the Sunbonnet Sue image is "cute" and sentimentally sweet, conjuring up all that is adorable and innocent about children.

She may be curious, but never dirty, aggressive, or disagreeable—a perfect display of stereotypical feminine attributes at an early age (see Figure 2). Indeed, it was the contravention of this norm that made the Sunbonnet Sue quilt designed by a group of Austin women all the more remarkable.

The Making of "Scandalous Sue"

The Bee There quilting bee of Austin, Texas, originated in 1984, when one member of the Austin Area Quilt Guild identified and organized other quilters in her neighborhood who were interested in meeting regularly. During the first year of the bee's existence, nine of the members lovingly conspired to make a "scandalous" quilt for Karen Horvath, the newest addition to the group. In 1984, when the quilt blocks were made, all of the bee members except Karen were fulltime homemakers, ranging in age from thirty to their sixties. Most of their children were teenagers or already grown. Until 1988, these women, all of whom are white and middle or upper-middle class, met in one of their homes every Tuesday afternoon, sharing quilting, conversation, and companionship, although by 1987, the year of my research, the group had disintegrated somewhat.[13] The six quilters I interviewed, however, repeatedly described the bee as a "support group," a gathering of friends whose love and humor encourages their development of self-confidence as they stitch and talk together about their quilting and their lives. Bee member Judy Woolley described the group by commenting, "The quilt was done with love and a sense of humor, and that's how we operate all the time."

The making of the Scandalous Sue quilt illustrates the interrelationship of tradition and innovation in form and process. As is common practice in quilting bees, each month the women wrote their names on a slip of paper and placed them in a hat. One name was drawn, and each of the other bee members made the winner a quilt block using her choice of color and pattern. Karen desperately longed for a Sunbonnet Sue quilt, thinking the pattern "cute" and appropriate for herself, as the mother of three daughters. Month after month, she hoped her name would be drawn. As time went by and her name was not selected, Karen became increasingly demonstrative about her disappointment, talking incessantly about Sunbonnet Sue and bringing Sunbonnet Sue patterns to the meetings. The other bee members pretended not to notice. What she did not know was that behind her back they had secretly slipped her name out of the hat so it could not be chosen.[14] Weary of her pestering, they were making her a Sunbonnet Sue quilt that would finally silence her requests.

To celebrate Karen's fortieth birthday, they surprised her during their regular get-together with a party, complete with Sunbonnet shaped cookies and decorations; each bee member covered her head with a sunbonnet or scarf. The completed quilt blocks were individually wrapped as birthday presents, and as Karen opened them one by one, the others laughed uproariously. Sweet Sue had turned scandalous (see Figure 3). "Scandalous Sue," as the group named the quilt, retains certain traditional elements of Sunbonnet Sue patterns. In each square Sue's face is hidden and a bonnet is shown. Some of the figures are squat and relatively shapeless, and most show her from a side view, as do many traditional Sue patterns. Here the similarities end, though. Instead of the traditional saccharine images, often depicting Sue watering flowers or playing with a dolly, Scandalous Sue is burning her bra, dancing a can-can, reading "dirty" books, drinking a martini, skinny-dipping, smoking, necking in the back seat of a convertible, taking a shower with Overall Bill, and, finally, taking her wedding vows as a pregnant bride.

Each quilter designed and stitched one block, using fabrics to blend with the blue trim. The group spent months on their clandestine project, and the time and attention they devoted to the quilt are a tribute to their affection for Karen (see Figure 4). As Susan Karnes, the youngest member of the bee and the originator of the idea for the quilt design, remarked, "Well, when you think about it, it [the quilt] is just the ultimate gesture on our part because it's one-of-a-kind, and it's going to receive a lot of recognition, and we haven't gone to that much trouble for anybody else, for anybody else's birthday. So, really, it's a really big compliment to Karen and, you know, how we feel about her that we went to all the trouble that we did."

After the party, Karen decided the placement of the squares in the quilt and was encouraged to make up a story to explain Sue's behavior. The following—which seems to meet with the approval of the other mischievous bee members—is the narrative that she now tells about Scandalous Sue:

> I truly believe it all started with the Women's Liberation Movement—that is when she got into burning her bras. From Women's Lib she did an about face and became a Las Vegas show girl. After feeling very guilty for exploiting her body, she then became a librarian. However, her true nature kept popping out and she would sneak behind the bookshelves and read her trashy novels.[15] Then one thing led to another, first she took up drinking martinis, she then joined a nudist camp and really enjoyed swimming in the buff, and next she took up smoking, (cigarettes

Figure 3: "Scandalous Sue," the quilt made by the Bee There quilters of Austin, Texas, 1984–86. Bee members presented the quilt to Karen Horvath for her fortieth birthday. The blocks are (*top row, left to right*) Sue Burning Her Bra, by Diane Lott; Sue Dancing the Can-Can, by Kathy Anderson; Sue Reading "Dirty" Books, by Cathryn Phillips; (*middle row*) Sue Drinking Champagne, by Paul Hazel Larson; Sue Skinny-Dipping, by Susan Karnes; Sue Smoking, by Judy Woolley; (*bottom row*) Sue Necking with Overall Bill, by May Ross; Sue Showering with Overall Bill, by Mary Ellen Barrett; and Sue Taking Her Vows as a Pregnant Bride, by Elinor Owensby. (Photo by Linda Pershing)

Figure 4: Karen Horvath, recipient and owner of the Scandalous Sue quilt. (Photo by Linda Pershing)

I think). And then came Bill! From parking in Lovers' Lane in the back seat of a red convertible to using the excuse of saving water by taking showers together. And last, but not least, the ultimate scandal of becoming a pregnant bride.[16]

Interpreting "Scandalous Sue"

The analysis that follows is not necessarily the view of any of the Austin quilters but rather is my own exploratory interpretation of the Scandalous Sue quilt based on contemporary feminist theory. The women who created the quilt see it as innocent fun and an amusing sign of genuine affection for a bee member. Karen Horvath, especially, stresses the gifting and supportive aspects of the project, noting that "we really weren't making a statement. They [the Bee There quilters] were just making a gift for a friend and being creative." In response to my analysis of the quilt, she has made it clear that she does not regard the making of "Scandalous Sue" as an expression of protest or social commentary. It was, Karen explained, "innocent fun poked at a fictional character and at myself for wanting a simple gift. These . . . are bright, intelligent, and creative women who happen to be very happy with their individual lives—they don't speak for anyone else through my quilt."[17] In the process of learning about the Scandalous Sue quilt and interviewing these women, I came to admire the love they have for one another and the fun they have had while quilting together. My analysis—which is strictly my own and not one that was offered or is shared by the quilters themselves—began with this appreciation. My thinking about "Scandalous Sue" developed further, however. It seemed from my angle of vision that the quilters' ingenuity extended not only to their ability to make an unusual and humorous quilt but also to their skillful response to the complexity of their experiences as contemporary American women. Appreciation for their work led me to the following analysis, which suggests a wider range of communicative possibilities than just a surface reading of "Scandalous Sue."

In contrast to the saccharine notoriety of the traditional Sue, Scandalous Sunbonnet Sue is about violating rules, social norms, and taboos. When I came through the front door of Karen Horvath's home to interview her about the quilt, the first thing she said to me was, "I have to keep her hidden away upstairs, she's so bad." During the interviews with Bee There quilters, Scandalous Sue was also called "naughty," "wrong," and "sinful." "Scandalous Sue" catches our attention because encoded in this negotiation of tradition is a complex set of cultural messages. Given that in American culture quilting in particular—and needlework more generally—is considered women's work, these messages are gender-specifically esoteric; their humor and commentary rely on a knowledge of a medium developed and transmitted by women.[18] Frequently perceived as a harmless, if not trivial, way for women to pass the time, decorate their homes, and care for their families, quilting provides a nonthreatening medium for women's social commentary.

In searching for a theory that accounts for women's culture beyond the boundaries of genre and medium, Joan N. Radner and Susan S. Lanser have proposed a typology of coding strategies used by women to covertly express ideas and experiences that the dominant culture (at times including women themselves) would find disturbing or threatening if expressed more overtly.[19] They suggest that processes of coding often found in women's folklore and literature are the result of enormous social pressures on women to conform to particular roles and ways of being, speaking, and behaving and that strategies enabling women to transform, subvert, or refuse conventional expectations have arisen with the devaluation and disauthorization of women's expressive forms.

Their discussion of coding as the adoption of a system of complex signals that protects the creator from the dangerous consequences of directly stating a particular message can help shed light on the significance of "Scandalous Sue." Several of the coding categories defined by Radner and Lanser are simultaneously in evidence, including juxtaposition (for example, ironically using a traditionally saccharine image in the role of transgressor), indirection (for example, utilizing Sunbonnet Sue as a metaphor for "everyquilter" or "everywoman"), and trivialization (for example, cloaking the makers' commentary about the changing roles of women in the supposedly innocuous form of a humorous quilt).[20]

The primary coding strategy at work in "Scandalous Sue," however, is what Radner and Lanser call "appropriation," that is, expressive processes "that involve adapting to feminist purposes forms or materials normally associated with male culture or with androcentric images of the feminine." In "Scandalous Sue," it is a woman's form that is appropriated by women to comment on not only the strictures imposed on them by men but also the ways in which women as quilters have incorporated compromising images of women into their own artistic expression. For the Bee There quilters, appropriation involves anthropomorphizing and personalizing Sunbonnet imagery; the makers call both the character Sue and the quilt itself "she," as though these have taken on lives and personalities of their own. Karen refers to herself as "Sue's Mother" and has expressed her concern over "Sue's [the quilt's] first trip away from home."[21]

The appropriation and consequent transformation of Sunbonnet imagery was also personalized in each quilter's choice of design and stylistic features. Some (but not all) bee members depicted scenes directly related to their own personal experiences. For example, Judy Woolley, the only smoker in the bee, made the block depicting Sue smoking (see Figure 5). This tendency toward personalization is characteristic of many types of needlework, in which women choose particular fabrics and patterns to remind them of people, places, and events in their lives. Quilting mothers frequently make Sunbonnet Sue's dresses and bonnets out of swatches of fabrics from their daughters' clothing.[22] Jean Ray Laury, author of three cartoon-style books about Sue as a compulsive quilter,[23] suggests that Sunbonnet Sue has become a symbol of the self for contemporary quilters, providing a vehicle for self-revelation that can "lead quiltmakers all over the world to their own discoveries—as self-revealing to them as mine were to me."[24]

Figure 5: Detail of Sue Smoking, one of the blocks in the Scandalous Sue quilt. Made by Judy Woolley, the only smoker in the Bee There quilting bee of Austin, Texas. (Photo by Linda Pershing)

Contemporary quilters like Laury have adopted Sue as a form of self-representation, often tailoring Sue's dress, features, or activities in their quilts to suit their own personal agendas.

Appropriation, as outlined by Radner and Lanser, sometimes takes the form of symbolic inversion: expressive behavior in which cultural categories are simultaneously adopted and reversed or negated. In her important work on the subject, Barbara Babcock defines symbolic inversion as "any act of expressive behavior which inverts, contradicts, abrogates, or in some fashion presents an alternative to commonly held cultural codes, values, and norms be they linguistic, literary or artistic, religious, or social and political."[25] All within the context of a block quilt, a brazen woman (Scandalous Sue) has paradigmatically replaced her childlike counterpart (traditional Sunbonnet Sue). Two simultaneous and competing sets of metacode signals are thereby communicated: on the one hand, through elements of traditional form, we are told this is a Sunbonnet Sue quilt; on the other, by virtue of the ways in which innovation overshadows tradition, we are told this is *not* a Sunbonnet Sue quilt as conventionally conceived.[26] Symbolic inversion implicitly involves negation, demonstrating through the inversion that the taboo can be discussed. By humorously altering traditional Sunbonnet imagery in such a way as to make it self-contradictory—"sweet" Sue becomes a "loose" woman—the Bee There quilters offered a palatable way to express dangerous messages, one of them being that women are intentionally breaking the rules.

Babcock notes that one type of symbolic inversion is parody, in which satirizing society is implicitly done by lampooning its most popular, banal, or repetitive forms of expression.[27] In parody, a conscious discrepancy is set up, often to comment on the original or to suggest some contrast between the new and the original form. The parody, however, must resemble a well-known original closely enough that no doubt exists concerning the referent.[28] The Bee There quilters wanted, first and foremost, to make a humorous quilt to surprise Karen on her birthday. As Judy noted, "How can you abuse a basket quilt pattern and make it funny?" Because Sunbonnet Sue is the image of a human form rather than, for example, an inanimate object, she is easily manipulated for humorous treatment; because she is a female figure, quilters can readily identify with her. Moreover, in parody, symbolic inversion may operate as a form of criticism or self-criticism, allowing quilters, in the case of "Scandalous Sue," to comment to themselves about themselves using traditional quilting imagery.[29] When I asked whether the quilt was created in response to the overly sweet connotations of traditional Sue, bee member Peggy Meathenia responded that Scandalous Sue is "a modern woman, she's not putting up with all this stuff anymore," reflecting her own predilections about the changing roles of women. She also was commenting on social conformity and the sexual revolution. In parodic form, Scandalous Sue is happily indulging in the freedom to exercise her own sexuality. In contrast to her traditional counterpart, this unruly woman is funny, amoral, and full of life and energy, and because she does not conform to gender-specific cultural norms, she automatically becomes a social critic and commentator.[30]

The characteristics of the inversion are carefully selected. Scandalous Sue has grown up. No longer a little girl, she is depicted as an adolescent or older, possibly reflecting the fact that most of the quilters were raising teenagers at the time the quilt was made.[31] Although she retains her sunbonnet, it is clear from her activities that Scandalous Sue has been modernized.[32] Elinor Owensby described Scandalous Sue's transformation by noting, "She's becoming an independent person, doing her own thing." Contrasting Sue's traditional "sweetness" with the realities of modernity, Karen added, "She was supposed to be sweet. And she's not really. That's probably the other side of her. She really wanted to be unconventional, be her own woman. This is probably the way she would look. This is Sue of the '80s."

But most of all, Scandalous Sue is unapologetically mischievous, a transformation largely accomplished by stripping the image of undue sentimentality. Susan explained, "We just tried to think of things that would go against social mores." Symbolizing the contravention of popular moral authority, Scandalous Sue dabbles in activities unbecoming to "a lady." She is no longer passive, involved in the supposedly innocent pastimes of childhood, or practicing the virtues of inculcated domesticity dictated by tradition.[33]

Several aspects of gender role inversion that could have been shown are conspicuously absent, however, indicating that the inversion process is neither random nor accidental. There is no evidence, for example, of the type of hierarchical inversion depicting women-on-top or husband-dominator imagery cited by Natalie Zemon Davis in her well-known study of symbolic sexual inversion.[34] In the Scandalous Sue quilt, women are not portrayed aspiring to occupations traditionally ascribed to men, nor are they mocking men, except perhaps indirectly by mocking the moral strictures men impose on women.

In fact, one of the most striking features of the quilt is the *conservative* nature of Sue's scandals. Bee member Susan Karnes noted that there was a conscious effort on the part of the makers to stay within the boundaries of "good taste" and that some designs discussed in the earliest stages of the project (for example, Sue smoking marijuana instead of a cigarette[35]) were ruled out by individuals in the group who thought this would be "going too far." Given the consensual nature of the designing process—the motif for each block was discussed and approved by the entire group—and the fact that each block was signed by its maker, some of the more controversial images were abandoned for the sake of propriety. Smoking, skinny-dipping, necking fully clad in the back seat of a convertible, and reading D. H. Lawrence are the "scandals" of an earlier era, not the 1980s. Instead, they chose to make Sunbonnet Sue scandalous by modernizing her, depicting Sue doing the same sorts of things that the Bee There quilters themselves might do. Reflecting on Sue's behavior, Karen remarked, "I don't find her radical at all. I just find her just a normal, everyday woman growing up in today's society. And maybe it's not today's society. It could be ten or twenty years back before you could call it scandalous," to which Susan retorted, "After all, even [the television evangelist] Pat Robertson's bride was pregnant!" Scandalous Sue may be sexually active, but her behavior falls within the boundaries of the quilters' own experiences and sense of moral equilibrium. Accordingly, Sue is not shown, for example, as a drug addict, child-abuser, or violent criminal. Even the story Karen created to explain Scandalous Sue could have been saucier; as Peggy remarked, "It was plain vanilla compared to what it could have been."

All but two of the squares deal with sexual behavior, implicitly conveying the message that what is really scandalous about Sue is the violation of sexual taboos. Even the two blocks not explicitly so—drinking Sue and smoking Sue—have sexual overtones. Women who drink alcohol in excess are conventionally portrayed as "loose women," and the figure of smoking Sue is the most voluptuous of the lot, with padded buttocks hanging out of her hotpants and shapely legs accented with high heels (see Figure 5). The bee members I interviewed agreed that smoking Sue, made by Judy Woolley, was the most creative and original block in the quilt. Although they denied that there were any deeper messages intended by the prevalence of sexual themes (Peggy remarked, "No, it was just for pure fun," and Judy added, "We were just being ourselves and not trying to please anybody else"), Peggy also acknowledged that violation of sexual norms occurred because "that's the last thing left, you know, to expose." Because Sunbonnet Sue has often been used by quilters as a symbol of self-identification (Karen calls Sunbonnet Sue her "trademark"), the Bee There quilters may have used sexual subject matter to encode messages about their own desire to be identified as sexual beings rather than stereotypical "little old ladies who sit in rockers." Some of the bee members commented that when their husbands—who are usually bored by their quilting—saw what they were making, they became enthusiastic about the project because of its "racy" subject matter.[36] Through processes of appropriation and inversion, "Scandalous Sue" refutes the asexuality of quilters for an outside audience in much the same way that the "dirty" jokes frequently told by bee members refute this dehumanizing notion for the quilters themselves.[37]

It is important to keep in mind that "Scandalous Sue" is parodic in form, for it is only in the context of traditional quilting patterns, which are appropriated and inverted, that Scandalous Sue lives up to her name. Babcock cogently argues that symbolic inversion, by virtue of its propensity to violate the "don'ts" in culture, can be seen as an attack on control, on closed systems, and on the arbitrary nature of what is conventionally taken as a given.[38] While relying on enough similarity with traditional form and process to accomplish its parody, the Scandalous Sue quilt is mildly iconoclastic, taking an irreverent poke at tradition. Like all symbolic systems, it is multi- and polyvalent, addressing a set of ideal norms that seem to operate in the society at large. These "ideal norms," however, include a double standard by which the behavior of women and men is differentially judged, and the absence of a single unitary moral system in American life results in ambiguity and mixed messages capable of portraying differentiation and continuity at the same time.[39]

The mixed messages encoded in the making of the quilt also reflect the quilters' own ambivalence. After reading my interpretation of the quilt, Karen remarked, "I don't believe any of these squares isn't something that we all haven't done in our growing up years. 'Scandalous' is only in someone else's eyes, really. You wouldn't necessarily call yourself scandalous, you would just be participating in life doing all those things. I don't think she was set out to—I don't know if we were making a statement, saying that these things were supposedly so scandalous, that they were unacceptable." Bee members chose the term *scandalous* for the title of the quilt, although in my most recent conversation with them they explained that they selected this primarily because of its alliterative qualities (they wanted a word that started with *s*). When questioned about her views on the changing roles of women in American society, Karen affirmed her belief in equality for women by talking about freedom of choice: "I think it's fine for the individual. I think everybody can pretty much do what they want as long as they don't hurt anybody else or cause anybody harm. My philosophy is: I don't want any man telling me I can't do something." At the same time, for Karen, the quilt represents a moral reminder of "all the bad things a woman isn't supposed to do." Discontinuity between philosophy and practice is evident in Karen's claim that Scandalous Sue should have the right to do any of the things depicted in the quilt and in her contradictory relief that none of her three daughters has followed Sue's example: "So far, none of them have, not that I know, even hit one square yet. Maybe they're drinking martinis, I'm not so sure about that. They may have read a few books also." Karen told me she offered to let her sixteen year old daughter keep the quilt on her bed "to remind her of all the things she shouldn't do. It's kind of a subtle way of saying, 'Mother's watching you. Just be careful.'" Similarly, Elinor, who made the pregnant-bride block, told the group how much fun she and her husband had laughing about her square while she was working on it, but later she added in all seriousness, "More than anything, mine was just a moral: this is what's going to happen if this sorta thing, if this goes on, this is going to happen."

Alternative Sunbonnet Sue Quilts

While "Scandalous Sue" obviously violates certain aspects of traditional Sunbonnet imagery, this is not simply an idiosyncratic piece. There are other quilts across the country in which the conventional image of Sunbonnet Sue has been altered and manipulated to express women's contemporary concerns. The makers of these "alternative Sue" quilts express three typical complaints about Sunbonnet patterns. First, they contend that traditional Sunbonnet Sues are too simple, boring, and repetitive. Bee There member Diane Lott commented, "That's the most elementary pattern anybody learns to quilt, that's the first image they learn, and also an Overall Bill. None of the clubbers like them because they are just used over and over and over again."[40] Dolores Hinson, who appreciates and defends the pattern, acknowledged, "Now I'm tired of it because I have lectured and gone all over the country teaching them, so I always get a certain percentage of Sunbonnet Sues. I get a certain percentage of Double Wedding Rings. I get a certain percentage of Crazy Quilts. And after you've said how fine the work is, there's nothing much to say after the five-hundredth one. You know, the quilts themselves are wonderful, it's just that I'm tired of them."[41]

Second, other quilters are uncomfortable with the exaggerated sentimentality that Sunbonnet Sue represents, feeling that she is *too* cute, corny, trite, and syrupy for their tastes. This was largely the motivation behind the making of the Scandalous Sue quilt, as Judy noted: "We were, like, if we hear Karen say [mimics a shrill voice], 'those cute Sunbonnet babies!' one more time, we were just going to gag!" As one quilter pointed out, transforming the Sunbonnet image gave "alternative Sue" makers an outlet for "their suppressed desires to eliminate the 'Goody Two-Shoes' in their pasts."[42]

Third, other contemporary quilters are offended by the old-fashioned aura of Sunbonnet Sue's image. In her prairie bonnet, shapeless skirts, and aprons, she seems out of date, absorbed in domesticity in a way worrisome to many modern American women.[43]

Sharing these criticisms, a few contemporary quilters scattered across the country have launched an impromptu, multifaceted attack on traditional Sunbonnet Sue imagery. This trend was started in 1979[44] when nationally known quilter and researcher Barbara Brackman and her friend Laurie Metzinger were finally nauseated past endurance by the Sunbonnet Sues that perpetually appeared at the "show and tell" sessions of the Eastern Kansas Quilt Guild meetings "doing sappy things like feeding kittens and watering little flowers."[45] During one of these meetings, shortly after the Jonestown, Guyana, mass suicide, Metzinger muttered, "I'd like to see Sue get some of that purple Kool-Aid."[46] Deciding to strike "a blow against the cute," Brackman explained, "We drew a sketch of Sunbonnet Sue in her stereotypical pose, hands rigidly at her side, face demurely hidden. We drew an arrow in her back and laughed. We showed it to our quilting friends; they said it gave them ideas. We showed it to our nonquilting friends; they said they'd learn to quilt."[47] What resulted was a twenty-block quilt (appropriately, set together using black and blue fabrics), depicting the demise of Sunbonnet Sue. In each block Sue is killed off in a different and hideous way, as a means of contesting female images of passivity, conformity, and propriety. They called it "The Sun Sets on Sunbonnet Sue" (see Figure 6).

"The Sun Sets on Sunbonnet Sue" evoked varied reactions from other quilters. While some found the quilt hilariously funny, others were shocked and outraged. There was a report of a woman whose friends, "knowing she was a fan of Sue and offended by this quilt, made her a block of Sunbonnet Sue praying the rosary for the souls of all the poor dead Sues" depicted in "The Sun Sets on Sunbonnet

---

Figure 6: "The Sun Sets on Sunbonnet Sue," the quilt made by a quilting group called the Seamsters Union Local 500, in Lawrence, Kansas. The blocks are (*top row, left to right*) Self-immolation, by Cathy Dwigans; Dr. LaFong's Cure for Cuteness, by Bryan Anderson; O.D., by Nadra Dangerfield; SkyLab Accident, by Carol Gilham; (*second row*) Sunbonnet Soup, by Bette Kelley; Strangled by a Sunflower, by Patty Boyer; Food for Worms, by Nadra Dangerfield; Sunbonnet Sioux, by Bonnie Dill; (*third row*) Three Mile Island, by Georgann Eglinski; Eaten by a Snake, by Nadra Dangerfield; Mummified, by Chickie Hood; Struck by Lightning, by Carol Gilham; (*fourth row*) Tied to the Tracks, by Georgann Eglinski; Lost in Space, by Bette Kelley; Sunbonnet Sue-icide, by Barbara Brackman; Squashed by a Rock, by Barbara Brackman; (*bottom row*) Suestown, Guyana, by Laurie Schwarm; Jaws III, by Nancy Metzinger; Died for Love, by Nadra Dangerfield; and Run in with the Mob, by Georgann Eglinski. (Photo by Linda Pershing)

Sue."[48] Brackman describes the heavy opposition to the quilt that was expressed at a quilt show in the Sunflower State Expo in Topeka: "although the judges awarded the quilt second prize in its class (there were two entries), the head of the textile exhibits confiscated our ribbon and refused to display 'The Sun Sets on Sunbonnet Sue.' She told 'The Topeka Daily Capital,' which gave front-page space to the story on the slap in Sue's face, that she found nothing humorous in a quilt she characterized as sick."[49] Expressing a similar reaction, Dolores Hinson said, "I thought that the idea of it and the doing of it was in extremely poor taste. The doing of it was in much worse taste than the ladies that had gone on doing the same pattern for years and years. That [traditional pattern] merely showed lack of imagination. This showed lack of good will, and I don't like that."[50]

Interpreting "The Sun Sets on Sunbonnet Sue" as an inappropriate poke at tradition and as ridicule of other quilters, Hinson responded by writing a book that offers a wide variety of Sunbonnet patterns. She explained, "Well, they said right out that they were trying to kill her off because they were tired of her. They were just tired of that pattern. And so they felt that if they made fun of it, people wouldn't make it anymore.... The one thing you do not do—any pattern that hundreds and hundreds of people do is—you don't make fun or sneer about their taste. That is, not if you want them to change—you give them constructive criticism. And that's what my book is, is constructive criticism. Don't go on making the simple ones; here's all these beautiful ones!"[51]

Other quilters responded to "The Sun Sets on Sunbonnet Sue" with sympathetic, yet revisionist concerns. Natalie Edwards, who commented that she "did not mind how she [Sue] was presented in that quilt, except for the Jonestown Square, which I found gross and in poor taste," designed "Alive and Free in '83." She invited friends to make blocks of contemporary Sue, stipulating only that the designs "pertain to today's world."[52] Her friends responded by making quilt blocks that depict Sunbonnet Sue engaged in a variety of activities, from driving a car to hot-air ballooning; in many blocks Sunbonnet Sue is explicitly portrayed as an adventurer.

Odette Goodman Teel of Long Beach, California, thought that "The Sun Sets on Sunbonnet Sue" was "very funny; however several friends thought it was dreadful."[53] She designed an alternative, "Ms. Sue: Alive and Liberated,"[54] as a humorous answer that would also give her friends "equal time" to bring Sue back to life (the invitation to participate accordingly requested that green fabric or embroidery be included somewhere in each block to symbolize "life and growth").[55]

She wrote to quilters she knew from across the country, and forty-two of them made blocks depicting·Sue as a "liberated woman." Participants were allowed to show Sue's face and could replace her outdated bonnet with something more appropriate, but her old sunbonnet had to appear somewhere in the block.

Teel responded to my question of whether there was conscious feminist intent in making the Ms. Sue quilt with an unqualified yes. It was her feeling that even the more conservative participants were making a statement about equal rights for women and that quilting provided the participants a medium for expressing views in a way that was comfortable and familiar to them. Mindful of the quilt's performative aspects, she wrote, "After I began the quilt, I found myself much more interested in the feminist movement and in statements by feminists. I am not the type to march in a parade or to be dragged off by police as a protestor, but I did enjoy making this quilt to be in a show and to be seen by as many people as possible." Amused by the humorous potential of Sunbonnet Sue "because she [Sue] is so old fashioned," Teel worked in 1989 in collaboration with other quilters on "Sunbonnet Sue by Great Artists," in which Sue was being substituted as the subject of famous paintings. Some of the blocks include *Nude Descending a Staircase* by Marcel Duchamp, *Madame X,* and *American Gothic.* [56]

Other alternative Sue quilts may exist, and given the networking that occurs among quilters, it is likely that additional quilts will emerge in response to those already mentioned. This is not to suggest, however, that this sort of deviation is the norm with Sunbonnet quilts; those who have stepped beyond the bounds of convention are a small group constituting only a limited segment of the quilting community. [57]

Conclusion

"Scandalous Sue" is more than just an amusing quilt, although the makers are reluctant to discuss the possibility of encoded meanings. They were more comfortable talking about the technical aspects of making the quilt than about the reasons for making it or what it means to them. In some cases they markedly disagreed with my interpretations. [58] I feel that this affectionate joke played by a group of quilters on one of their bee members had wider cultural significance, however. Encoded in the Scandalous Sue quilt are women's attempts to speak their truths about society. The Bee There quilters are middle-class, suburban women who do not use the word *feminist* to describe themselves and are not actively involved in the women's movement.

Precisely because these women have filled traditional roles, the quilt is all the more significant for them; their feminist messages are not expressed overtly but through a coding process of appropriation and inversion, providing both a "safe" and critical commentary on social and gender-specific norms. Babcock and the authors of *The Reversible World* have convincingly demonstrated how inversion may operate as a means of social control, social protest, social change, and social deviance.[59] By synthesizing needlework and parodic process in the making of "Scandalous Sue," the quilters found a way to comment on conventional expectations and to express their own sense of ambivalence about prevalent images of women.

The creation of this quilt attests to women's willingness to manipulate convention to negotiate their own expressive needs and to the emergent and reflexive nature of contemporary folklore as it sometimes arises in American life. In the recent revival of scholarly interest in quilting, much has been written about the ways in which quilting serves as a metaphor for women's creativity and maintenance of community.[60] This is essential to understanding the social nature of women's needlework, and it deserves further attention. But there has been little investigation of the ways in which quilting allows women to contest social roles or comment on cultural norms. The parodic elements of "Scandalous Sue" are gender-differentially encoded. Only those with "competence" in the vocabulary of quilting, those who can identify the symbolic association of Sunbonnet Sue with female innocence and docility—and hence perceive the drastic nature of the manipulation of her conventional appearance—can fully appreciate the messages of the quilt.

In her study of symbolic sexual inversion, Natalie Zemon Davis notes that sexual or gender inversions are most likely to appear in hierarchical and conflictive societies, reminding us of the necessity of grounding studies of symbolic inversion in historical context.[61] Alternative Sue quilts, not surprisingly, appeared across the country during the Reagan era, a time when there were repeated attempts to turn back the clock on equal rights, affirmative action programs, and pro-choice legislation—all while increasing numbers of women were working outside the home and family life was changing dramatically. Davis maintains that when gender roles are being challenged and reassessed, symbolic inversions have the potential to go beyond simply commenting on social mores, offering a glimpse of new possibilities.[62] The creation of Scandalous Sue, the unruly woman in traditional guise, suggests there are alternative ways of conceiving social structure by both confirming the double standard that subjugates women and

Figure 7: Detail of Sue taking her vows as a pregnant bride, a block from the Scandalous Sue quilt. Made by Elinor Owensby, a member of the Bee There quilting bee of Austin, Texas. (Photo by Linda Pershing)

depicting resistance to it. Bee There quilter Susan Karnes commented that feminist ideals were not the motivating factor in making the quilt but that their pervasive cultural influence permitted bee members to move beyond the imagery of traditional Sue. In addition, the evolution of alternative Sue quilts—in reflecting the changing roles of women and contributing to a developing tradition of resistance and critique—made the Bee There quilters' option to be "scandalous" more conceivable.

In appropriating and critiquing Sunbonnet imagery, alternative Sue quilters have chosen varying strategies. Some have attempted to eradicate images of an oppressive past by literally killing Sue over and over again in their quilt blocks. These women have rejected the notion that their traditional arts may be used only to support and sustain conventional notions of female identity. In particular, Sunbonnet Sue's passivity and inability to move beyond the strictures of gender roles have become the targets of feminist critique. Taking a more moderate stance, other quilters have tried to claim Sue as a part of their own conflictive history and revise her to meet present needs. On a symbolic level, the Scandalous Sue quilt is a product of the latter approach, for here women have chosen not to eliminate "sweet Sue" but to reclaim her as their own and then transform her into a joker figure who, though recognizable, is also raucous and incorrigible. The last quilt block depicts Sue as a pregnant bride, "carrying on another generation" (see Figure 7).[63] Significantly, here Sue's potential for change is symbolized in her intention to reproduce, fulfilling a maternal role, but outside the customary boundaries of propriety. More reformist than the victimized images of "The Sun Sets on Sunbonnet Sue," Scandalous Sue is very much alive and well, perpetuating life as an agent of mischief and transgression.

Notes

After seeing "Scandalous Sue" at the 1986 Austin Area Quilt Guild exhibit, I arranged to interview the quilt's owner, Karen Horvath, the following April at her home in Westlake Hills (Austin, Texas). In September 1987, I met at bee member Judy Woolley's home with Karen, Judy, Susan Karnes, Diane Lott, Peggy Meathenia (who joined the bee after the blocks for the Scandalous Sue quilt were made), and Elinor Owensby to conduct a group interview that lasted approximately two hours. My tape-recorded interviews with these women provided much of the data for my analysis. In February 1988, after I had written an initial draft of this essay, I again met collectively with Karen and the bee members mentioned above to get their comments and suggestions on my work, which I have attempted to incorporate in my revisions. Throughout this process, the warmth and humor of the "Bee There" quilters made researching this topic a delight, and I sincerely thank them for sharing with me their stories and insights about Scandalous Sue. Although women's needlework and textile arts are a primary interest of mine, I am not a quilter, and I thank Austin quilters and researchers Kathleen McCrady and Dolores Hinson, who gave me a broader understanding of the Sunbonnet Sue tradition. I am also grateful to Joan Radner and Suzanne Seriff for their most helpful comments and suggestions on earlier versions of this essay.

1. For a more complete description of the historical development of Sunbonnet Sue, see Betty J. Hagerman, *A Meeting of the Sunbonnet Children*

(Baldwin City, Kans.: Betty J. Hagerman, 1979); and Dolores Hinson, *The Sunbonnet Family of Quilt Patterns* (New York: Arco Publishing, 1983). Hinson notes that there are late Victorian-style crazy quilts with either appliquéd or embroidered Sunbonnet Sues dating around 1900 (7).

2. The work of commercial artists predating Greenaway suggests the general popularity of the genre. Bertha E. Blodgett (1866–1941), for example, drew similar images, sometimes depicting two children, one whose face was hidden, one whose face was exposed. Hinson, *The Sunbonnet Family,* 9.

3. One of the clearest examples of a Sunbonnet Sue pattern copied directly from commercial art can be found in a pattern Dolores Hinson recently adapted from a 1911 postcard, with a notation citing its source. Hinson, *The Sunbonnet Family,* 236.

4. Ibid., 9.

5. Ibid., 13.

6. Hagerman, *A Meeting of the Sunbonnet Children,* 47.

7. Ibid., 38, 46.

8. There are also Colonial Ladies, Balloon and Pantalette Girls, and Umbrella or Parasol Ladies, closely related to Sunbonnet Sues, which are frequently older in appearance. See Hagerman, *A Meeting of the Sunbonnet Children,* for a typology of these patterns.

9. Hagerman includes a few rare exceptions to this rule. See pp. 7, 39, for a general discussion of Sue's covered face; p. 37, for a pattern of Sue with her full face showing; and pp. 44, 45, for partial faces on both boys and girls. Researcher Dolores Hinson showed me a quilt she made in 1977 that depicts Sunbonnet Sue with her face showing. She explained, "When I was little, it bothered me that you couldn't see their faces. It just bothered me so. So, for my own pleasure I made 'Peeking Sue' " (cf. Hinson, *The Sunbonnet Family,* 7, 89). The facelessness and anonymity of the female child raises semiotic questions beyond the scope of this essay; however, it is interesting to consider Hagerman's observation that Corbett, "the mother of the Sunbonnet babies," was not so preoccupied with hiding the faces of the boys as she was the girls' (*A Meeting of the Sunbonnet Children,* 16, 31). Showing Sue's face was one of the taboos broken by some of the other "alternative Sue" quilters, although not by the makers of the Scandalous Sue quilt.

10. The Dutch Doll has become another generic name for Sunbonnet Sue, perhaps originally associated with the 1920s and 1930s fad for collecting patterns and objects inspired by the Netherlands. This name is widely used in the South (Hinson, *The Sunbonnet Family,* vii, 13). I have also seen patterns for a cowgirl, Pantalette Prudence; Li'l Jenny, a "squaw"; and Aunt Jemima that are obviously derivations of Sunbonnet Sue.

11. Hagerman, *A Meeting of the Sunbonnet Children,* 16, contends that, in general, the boys have not been as widely adapted as the girls have and are not found in as many varieties of seasonal clothing as their female counterparts are.

12. One popular trend in dishtowels and postcards shows Sue doing a

different job each day of the week. See ibid., 12; and Hinson, *The Sunbonnet Family*, 2, 7 (see Figure 1).

13. The passage of time has dramatically changed the composition of the bee. Karen Horvath was the only bee member employed outside the home when I first interviewed her in April 1987. By September of the same year, three bee members were working outside jobs, making it difficult for the group to find a mutually convenient time to meet on a regular basis. Since 1984, three members have moved out of Austin, one died, and others no longer participate.

14. Diane Lott, one of the bee members, suggested that making the scandalous quilt "was just something to do for Karen, to put her in her place," to which another member added, "to get her off our backs."

15. The titles embroidered on the books are *Lady Chatterley's Lover* (which Sue is reading), *The Happy Hooker, The Joy of Sex, Marquis de Sade,* and *Madame Bovary.*

16. From Karen's correspondence with nationally known quilter Jean Ray Laury, March 31, 1987. Karen recounted a very similar oral rendition to me in an interview on April 15, 1987.

17. Karen Horvath, personal correspondence, February 13, 1992.

18. See Patricia Mainardi, "Quilts: The Great American Art," *Feminist Art Journal* 2 (1973): 1, 18–23.

19. Joan N. Radner and Susan S. Lanser, "Strategies of Coding in Women's Cultures," herein.

20. Radner and Lanser note the simultaneous multifunctionality of the categories they propose: "Although we necessarily describe these strategies separately and sequentially, many instances of coding combine two or more of [them]."

21. In 1986, Karen decided not to send the quilt to a national show in Houston since she could not attend. She told me, "I really wasn't ready to send her down there. I didn't want her left there. I didn't want to be without her, or trust it being there. . . . She hasn't been in a plane by herself."

22. Barbara Brackman observed that this practice may be one of the reasons some quilters reacted so negatively to "The Sun Sets on Sunbonnet Sue," a quilt depicting the death of Sunbonnet Sue. Perhaps for them this quilt symbolically suggests an untimely death for their own children—all too personal an assault. Brackman, telephone conversation, September 13, 1987.

23. Jean Ray Laury, *Sunbonnet Sue Goes to the Quilt Show* (San Francisco: Quilt Digest Press, 1985); *Sunbonnet Sue Gets It All Together at Home* (San Francisco: Quilt Digest Press, 1987); *Sunbonnet Sue Makes Her First Quilt* (San Francisco: Quilt Digest Press, 1987).

24. Jean Ray Laury, "Sue Makes a Comeback," *Quilter's Newsletter Magazine* 193 (June 1987): 20. Interesting in this regard is Karen's suggestion that it is only fitting Sue's face not be shown on Sunbonnet quilts, "so she could be yourself, or anyone you want."

25. Barbara Babcock, "Introduction," in *The Reversible World: Symbolic*

Inversion in Art and Society, ed. Barbara Babcock (Ithaca, N.Y.: Cornell University Press, 1978), 14.

26. Barbara Babcock, " 'Liberty's a Whore': Inversions, Marginalia, and Picaresque Narrative," in *The Reversible World,* ed. Babcock, 99.

27. Ibid., 100. Radner and Lanser also briefly mention parody in their discussion of appropriation ("Strategies of Coding," herein).

28. Barre Toelken, "Ballads and Folksongs," in *Folk Groups and Folklore Genres: An Introduction,* ed. Elliott Oring (Logan: Utah State University Press, 1986), 165.

29. Clifford Geertz discusses the dynamics of this type of metacommentary by a group in "Deep Play: Notes on a Balinese Cockfight," in *The Interpretation of Cultures: Selected Essays* (New York: Basic Books, 1973), 412–53. See also Babcock, "Introduction," 21, for her discussion of this phenomenon and its relationship to symbolic inversion.

30. See Natalie Zemon Davis, "Women on Top: Symbolic Sexual Inversion and Political Disorder in Early Modern Europe," in *The Reversible World,* ed. Babcock, 147–90. Davis's discussion of "the unruly woman" is relevant to Scandalous Sue, who, anthropomorphized by her makers, demonstrates many of the characteristics of the unruly woman, including the reflexive capabilities of the social critic.

31. In my interviews with Karen and the larger group, their teenage children were mentioned each time I inquired about how Scandalous Sue and her activities differed from traditional patterns. While describing their depiction of Sunbonnet Sue, one bee member told me, "Ours was older, more teenage. I think most of us had teenagers at the time."

32. For examples of ways in which Sunbonnet Sue's clothing was updated by quilters of the past to look contemporary with their own times, see Hagerman, *A Meeting of the Sunbonnet Children,* 33, 36, 38.

33. Although Dolores Hinson could recall no example in the past of Sunbonnet patterns depicting Sue doing naughty or mischievous things, I did find precedent for this notion in several patterns, including a pattern for "Mischievous Kids" (Hinson, *The Sunbonnet Family,* 13); kissing Sunbonnet children and Dutch dolls (ibid., 31, 54d, 155); and two nude sunbonnet children of an early date (Hagerman, *A Meeting of the Sunbonnet Children,* 17).

34. Davis, "Women on Top."

35. Despite this decision, the suggestion that Sue is smoking marijuana crept back into Karen's narrative about the quilt, as reported above.

36. Diane Lott commented, "Well, most of our husbands, those of us who have husbands, think that quilting is just the biggest drag in the world. It's really pretty boring, except for Elinor's [husband], so when we came forth with this, they kinda thought it had a little bit of spark to it—we weren't totally boring."

37. One of the bee members had a reputation for her outrageous jokes. Diane explained, "Our friend was one of our older members, and just a dear, dear person. And she was the sweetest looking, and the sweetest person. And

when she walked in the room, she could tell the best jokes in the world, off-color. . . . " When discussing joke-telling among bee members, I asked, "How many of them were off-color?" and was told, "Oh, about ninety-nine per cent. You think we're all sweet little old ladies . . . !" Diane then told a story about a prominent quilter in the guild whose jokes "are just about filthy," to which Peggy retorted, "And they are *funny.* " For a discussion of the links between quilting, joking, and sexuality, see Lorre Marie Weidlich, "Quilting Transformed: An Anthropological Approach to the Quilt Revival" (Ph.D. dissertation, University of Texas at Austin, 1986), 87ff, 159ff.

38. Babcock, "Introduction," 17.

39. Roger D. Abrahams and Richard Bauman, "Ranges of Festival Behavior," in *The Reversible World,* ed. Babcock, 193–208.

40. *Clubbers* refers to quilters who are active bee or guild members. Diane's comment provoked some discussion among other bee members during my interview. While most agreed they were tired of Sunbonnet Sue, they also acknowledged that each of them has made a Sunbonnet quilt for one of her own children or one has been given to them by a female relative and that some of the bee members no longer meeting with the group still like to make Sunbonnet quilts.

41. Interview, September 16, 1987.

42. Barbara Brackman, "Quilts with a Sense of Humor," *Quilter's Newsletter Magazine* 148 (January 1983): 41.

43. Laury, "Sue Makes a Comeback," 18.

44. Barbara Brackman heard years ago there was an alternative Sue quilt that predated her "The Sun Sets on Sunbonnet Sue," but she was unable to verify this. Rumor had it that it was a "Nazi Sue, in which all the Sues had swastikas on their helmet/hats and were goosestepping." Barbara Brackman, personal correspondence, September 9, 1987.

45. Barbara Brackman, telephone conversation, September 13, 1987.

46. Barbara Brackman, "The (Un)Making of Sunbonnet Sue," *Open Chain: The Magazine for Threadbenders* (October 1983): 24.

47. Ibid., 2.

48. Barbara Brackman, personal correspondence, September 9, 1987.

49. Brackman, "The (Un)Making of Sunbonnet Sue," 24. During a quilt show in Colombia, Missouri, another woman approached Brackman and drew a crowd of people around her while explaining with great emotion why the demise quilt upset her so. Because of the quilt, Brackman has also been accused of supporting child abuse, told that Sue is like a "real person," and informed that "The Sun Sets on Sunbonnet Sue" would be funny if the events it depicts never happened to real people, but they do. Brackman, telephone conversation, September 13, 1987.

50. Interview, September 16, 1987.

51. Ibid.

52. Natalie Edwards, personal correspondence, September 26, 1987.

53. All quotes from Odette Goodman Teel are taken from personal correspondence, September 23, 1987.

54. Teel mused that by using the word *liberated* in the title of her quilt, those friends she had sought to include were too intimidated to participate ("Not one had time to make a block!"). Eventually she contacted other quilters from around the country, who were amused by her idea and eager to make a block for the quilt.

55. Teel observed that "some of these friends dearly love the old fashioned Sue: Betty Hagerman wrote a book about her; Jeanie Cuddy used to give a Sunbonnet Sue quilt show every year in Minnesota; Norma Locke makes miniature Sue quilts to sell and give as gifts. Some of my friends enjoyed the satire: Nancy Halpern's Sue is sawing up those dumb bonnets (Nancy learned to use a chain saw at Haystack, Maine, that year!); Barbara Brackman's block which proves that a liberated woman will wear a bikini if she wishes, no matter what her figure type; Judy Robbins' nude on the beach. That last one really bothered a little old lady at one of my lectures."

56. Brackman, personal correspondence, September 9, 1987.

57. For a useful discussion of the boundaries of disruption and the contravention of ideal norms in a community, see Abrahams and Bauman, "Ranges of Festival Behavior."

58. Karen Horvath emphasizes that "this quilt was designed and created ... by a group of fun-loving, multi-talented women all of whom I consider dear friends" and feels very strongly that what I am "trying to implicate in their hidden meaning does not exist" (personal correspondence, February 13, 1992).

59. Babcock, "Introduction," 30–31.

60. See, for example, Joyce Ice, "Quilting and the Pattern of Relationships in Community Life" (Ph.D. dissertation, University of Texas at Austin, 1984); Susan Roach, "The Kinship Quilt: An Ethnographic Semiotic Analysis of a Quilting Bee," in *Women's Folklore, Women's Culture*, ed. Rosan A. Jordan and Susan J. Kalčik (Philadelphia: University of Pennsylvania Press, 1986), 54–65; and Elaine Showalter, "Piecing and Writing," in *The Poetics of Gender*, ed. Nancy K. Miller (New York: Columbia University Press, 1986), 222–47.

61. Davis, "Women on Top."

62. Ibid.

63. In comparing "Scandalous Sue" with "The Sun Sets on Sunbonnet Sue," Karen remarked, "This one ['The Sun Sets on Sunbonnet Sue'] is really bad." When I asked further, "Do you think this is worse than yours?" Karen replied, "Yes, I mean, they kill the poor thing several times. At least mine's still living and giving birth—she's reproductive. I mean, she's carrying on another generation."

"Awful Real": Dolls and Development in Rangeley, Maine

MARGARET R. YOCOM

In the logging country of northwestern Maine that I have been visiting for fifteen years now, two things stand out for me: the chain-saw carved wooden bears and the baby dolls with their hand-knit dresses. The bears conjure up the white pines that the loggers drag out of the forest and then haul through towns on thirty-five-ton rigs that rattle and roar. When I think of the baby dolls, I remember church basements or quiet living rooms and women telling tales of their children to the rhythmic click of knitting needles.

I am studying a three-generation family of loggers and homemakers, woodcarvers and knitters from Rangeley. When I began, it was the logging and the chain-saw wood carving that caught my eye. My fieldnotes spill over with stories about work in the woods, details about how to drag logs out of the forest with a skidder and the proper use of a birch hook, and reasons why a carver turns from a life-size chain-saw figure to carve a half-inch bunny out of a chip of basswood. I had always been aware of the baby sweaters in yellow or green or aqua lying half-finished in a yarn bag alongside a living room easy chair, but it took me several months in Rangeley to begin to see that the dolls had a vital story of their own.

During my fieldwork in the winter of 1985, I worked in the woods with the men. I learned how to operate the skidder. I bounced around in the truck delivering pulp to the mill—sometimes two loads a day. And I would come home with pitch and sweat all over, covered with a weariness that often responded only to beers and jokes at the Wagon Wheel Restaurant or dancing at the Rangeley Inn. Then I would return to the world of women, with their clean clothing in their warm homes, knitting soft pastel yarns into doll dresses. I felt as if I were crossing over into the Twilight Zone. I did not feel comfortable with

Lucille Richard with two of her baby dolls.

Rodney Richard with two of his chain-saw carved wooden bears.

my reactions to the world of the women in those early months: their work seemed so easy compared with the work I had just done. The male world of the loggers was exotic and seductive. And there were other reasons, more personal ones, that colored my early view of Rangeley.

Being a woman fieldworker and studying dolls is both a blessing and a curse. It is a blessing because my own childhood experiences with dolls undoubtedly helped me pay attention to the dolls and their clothing. The curse comes with the complicated associations that dolls call up. Dolls revive childhood memories. They stir up feelings about our mothers and our relationships with them. Ultimately, they urge us to question who we are as women. In a doll's face, we see ourselves as children, as teenagers leaving dolls behind, as women having or not having children, and as women. They are mirrors of our souls. They invite us to turn inward. Studying dolls, like studying housework, involves women fieldworkers in a long, sometimes joyous, sometimes painful journey home to visit and, perhaps, embrace another part of our selves.

As my days in Rangeley went by, I began to see the many ways that dolls—and always baby dolls—entered into the life of the community. The windows of Mo's Variety Store and Jannace's Clothing, for example, almost always feature dolls and stuffed animals as people celebrate holidays and such community events as Girl Scout Week and the Blueberry Festival. When the Logging Festival Field Days Committee offers awards to young girls at the Little Miss Woodchip contest, it gives baby dolls. One of the first summer festivals, the Fourth of July, is celebrated in Rangeley not with a parade of local bands and fire engines but with a parade of dolls. In nearby Dummer, New Hampshire, Mildred Smith decorates her yard with dolls, 125 of them.

So, in the summer of 1987, I turned to the dolls and decided to learn what I could from them. For me, they have become multivocal objects encoding women's values and their protests against changes that they perceive they can neither accept nor stop. As the women face economic changes brought on in part by a tourist-driven economy, they inscribe their protests in the baby doll by choosing her over the more expensive dolls brought in by "people from away." The knitters turn from the model-thin Barbie and the Cabbage Patch doll with its flattened face because the former calls forth to them a self-absorbed woman devoid of nurturance and the latter reminds them of children who have been abused. The women's continued use of dolls signals a statement of their values and their belief in maternal power in the face of a patriarchal world that so often trivializes them and their creations.

If we look at the knitters of the generation born in the late 1920s and early 1930s first as girls, then as women with husbands and young children, and finally as older women living in a tourist town filled with strangers, we can read in their stories and their stitches how knitting has taken on layer upon layer of meaning.

Girlhood

When Lucille Haley Richard, Bertha Lamb Haines, and other knitters were growing up in the Rangeley area in the 1930s, most people lived on farms. Franklin County was rich farmland, with 220,777 acres being tilled for crops. Of the 9,670 adults working in the county, 1,785 worked the land.[1]

Lucille Richard, born in 1927, tells of working her father's pea and potato fields, weeding rows that stretched longer than she could see. She preferred indoor work, though, and learned to sew and knit from her mother. Her story about learning from her mother shows how women learned from working closely with one another and how they, as girls, began to develop a doll craft aesthetic. As Lucille considers why knitting doll clothes is important to her today, she discusses the role of dolls in her life as a young girl on a Maine farm:

> I like knitting dolls' things and small children's, really, better than I do adult items, although I've done quite a few adult sweaters.
>
> And I particularly like little girls' things, even though I never had any little girls. The three were all boys.
>
> I think that maybe some of it stems back from the fact that I always loved dolls growing up and I had dolls till I was . . . probably older than most kids today. I was probably eleven or twelve and still getting dolls at Christmas. And perhaps living on a farm, where you weren't close to the town and didn't have a lot of activities and getting together with a lot of other kids.
>
> Because I remember sitting with my mother. She often did make cloth dolls and dolls' clothes *for me* because most of my sisters . . . liked the outdoor work and they really could care less about dolls. I guess I was probably the only one that really, really enjoyed dolls. So she used to sit with me and make the dolls, make the dolls' things.
>
> I probably started knitting when I was twelve or fourteen. Probably started just some simple knitting because my mother used to knit a little. She used to knit our mittens and she used to knit sweaters without patterns. They were just plain cardigans, is what she'd make. Probably I started from watching her and then I progressed buying books.[2]

Traditional learning among women in rural Maine thus consisted of learning by sitting close to another woman, watching her, and receiving instructions as the process went on. As women like Lucille learned to make dolls and their clothing, they also learned and internalized a set of values that prized careful handwork, baby dolls that a girl could nurture, the tutelage of another woman, and careful work:

> I think kids really had more of the baby doll types. And we didn't have the—like Barbies—the stylish dolls like they have now. We had more that looked like babies. They were bigger sized. Or, occasionally you had a cloth-bodied one or the cloth ones that were *made* at home. Not like Kens and the Barbies and a lot of the model dolls, I'm trying to say thin dolls, small dolls that they have now.
>
> [My mother] always made the dolls and made the dolls' hair out of yarn. And she had no patterns or anything. She did everything by newspapers. She would just take newspapers and shape out the doll's head, the arms, legs. I think she made them all separate and then sewed the legs on and the arms on and the head on. But she would use, like, an old sheet, that's what she would use for the doll.
>
> And I really don't remember what we would use for the stuffing. It was probably some old cotton, like, maybe some old pillowcases and sheets.
>
> She would embroidery the face and then she would take yarn for the hair and she would either make the curls or the pigtails.

Lucille's story about the time her family's house burned down and she saved her one big doll emphasizes the importance of dolls in her life and illustrates one of the first challenges to her values:

> They were quite big. We might have used some small baby clothes because I remember one in particular. It was a pretty big one, so it might have taken six-months-sized clothes. Cause I remember we had a fire at our house and my mother never got over it: that was the first thing I grabbed of all the things to grab to save. The big doll was the thing that I picked up first. [laughs]
>
> And my father either: "Of all the things to save, you saved that first!"
>
> But I suppose I hadn't had it that long. She hadn't made it that long ago.

Lucille's story is echoed in those of other women, such as Bertha Haines, who learned from her mother-in-law, Blanche, when both families lived together on the Haines farm: "We'd sit by the old kitchen stove and sometimes in the living room, like sometimes half the afternoon. We had no radio or anything. And she'd say, 'Well I guess it's time we have a little knitting bee.' And knitting! She wouldn't think anything of knitting for two, three hours at a time. And I got so

I could knit pretty fast." As girls, then, the Rangeley knitters began work in the women's sphere with its relational, affiliative values and developed a liking for baby dolls that would deepen with the years.[3]

Young Wives and Mothers

In the late 1940s, the 1950s, and the early 1960s, the Rangeley region underwent rapid change. For ninety-one years, the town had been governed by a board of selectmen, but in 1946, a town manager form of government began to handle the increasingly complicated affairs of the town. Motels and small, private summer cabins multiplied. With the opening of Bald Mountain Ski Area in 1959 and Saddleback Ski Area in 1960, Rangeley became a major four-season resort.[4] The number of farms dropped rapidly. In 1945, Franklin County had 1,351 farms and 180,405 acres in farmland; in 1964, 451 farms remained, with 121,705 acres of land.[5]

During this period, many of the women of Lucille Haley Richard's generation worked in the drug stores, restaurants, and motels of Rangeley that served both local people and the ever-growing tourist and summer resident trade. Lucille worked at the soda fountain of Riddle's Rexall in 1946 and then waited on tables at Doc Grant's Restaurant from 1947 until 1953. When her youngest son started college in 1977, she returned to waitress work.

In 1951, Lucille Haley married Rodney Richard of Phillips, a town just forty-five minutes down the mountain from Rangeley. They settled in Rangeley and raised their sons there: Rodney, Jr., was born in 1955, John in 1956, and Stephen in 1959.

During the 1950s, Lucille began to knit more. "I didn't do a lot of knitting," she says, "until my kids were small." She made some sweaters for the boys, but mostly she knitted children's clothes for the church fairs.

By knitting children's clothing and thus clothing that could fit on baby dolls, the women were able to give such dolls to their children, a purposeful choice in their minds:

BERTHA: I just like the baby dolls that they could play with ———
LUCILLE: Yes! I did too.
BERTHA: ——— and put into a doll's crib. I mean Sheila would play for—Lucille knew it—wash those doll clothes till they were about worn out.
LUCILLE: And she'd put them on a bed ———
BERTHA AND LUCILLE: ——— cover them up ———
BERTHA: ——— and kiss them ———

Lucille Haley Richard, on the right, at her first waitress job, Riddle's Rexall, 1946. (Courtesy of Lucille Richard)

LUCILLE: —— and she'd lie down with them.

BERTHA: I said I think nowadays that if some parents, some mothers felt like she did, as much love for children as she did for a doll that there'd be ——

LUCILLE: —— less child abuse.

BERTHA: I guess not!

LUCILLE: And then when Butch was little, I can remember, I had a little basket on wheels and Bertha would come over and visit and help a little. And Sheila, she'd get there. And oh, if the little stocking wasn't up just right or wasn't even, she'd pull on them.

BERTHA: Yeah, straighten them ——

LUCILLE: —— pull his shirt down ——

BERTHA: —— tuck his shirt in ——

LUCILLE: —— and touch his hair. Oh! You'd think it was a living doll. Had to have everything just so ——

BERTHA: —— just so ——

LUCILLE: —— on it. He'd kick a bootie off, she'd have that bootie on.

Doc Grant's Doll Carriage Parade, begun by "Doc" and Lelia Grant in 1946, underscored the importance of dolls and homemade doll clothing. The Grants invited little girls from all over the region to put on a special dress, decorate a doll carriage, and push their dolls down Rangeley's Main Street. One year Doc had 103 little girls and their carriages in his parade. "Many parents would start a month or two before," Lucille explains. "Some of the carriages would be really elaborate. Most of them were handmade with many, many hours of handwork."

A few years later, the Grants added a children's parade so boys and girls could participate by riding their tricycles and bicycles. Doc gave prizes and gifts to all the children; he also fed them ice cream from a big barrel. "And he talked to every one of those kids himself," Norma Keep adds. Doc hung poster-size pictures of the award-winning children all over the walls of his restaurant. "Oh, that was quite a parade, the biggest event Rangeley ever had," Norma recalls.

Doc Grant ran the parade every year until his death in 1964. "He had a little son whom he lost at about two years old," Lucille Richard explains, "and they never had any more children. So he thought this was one way he could start something for children. They never adopted a child because they said they were very bitter over the loss of their child and I'm sure it took a while to accept it and get back on with their lives. So doing this seemed to be honoring him."

In the late 1950s, while the doll carriage parade was still going

DOC GRANT'S 1952 CHILDREN'S DAY & DOLL CARRIAGE PARADE
RANGELEY LAKES, MAINE

Program book cover from the Doc Grant's Children's Day and Doll Carriage Parade, 1952. (Courtesy of the Rangeley Lakes Region Historical Society)

strong, the Barbie doll appeared in Rangeley. The knitters greeted her with disgust. "I have made Barbie Doll clothes," Lucille admits, "but they're not easy. They're so tiny, so few stitches on them. And you usually have to use the very fine yarn. And then to sew them together and turn them right side out ———. Uh! I don't enjoy doing them. I've done it, but I don't enjoy them. I'd rather knit the baby doll clothes."

This opinion of Barbie and her clothes is shared by several knitters in Rangeley, among them Kay Morgan:

> KAY: My granddaughter's into Barbie things right now. She's *into* Barbies. She would like this baby doll and she would lay it on her bed and go play with Barbies.
> LUCILLE: You like knitting for Barbie? I hate doing it ———.
> KAY: Oh! I *hate* doing it.

To the knitters, then, the Barbie clothes are painstakingly troublesome to make and the Barbie doll itself represents a strong shift away from the values of the baby doll. Barbie, with her sexual if not anorexic figure, her expensive cars and houses, and her career and evening clothes, models a type of woman that a girl can fantasize becoming, not a baby that a girl can nurture.

Talk about Barbie also encodes messages about child abuse, messages so strongly felt that sometimes they erupt into explicit speech, as they did with Bertha and Lucille. The women are aware of the increasing child abuse statistics in Franklin County; Child Protective Services of the Maine State Department of Human Services reports that in 1986, the Lewiston office, which includes Franklin County, received 3,120 referrals of sexual, physical, and emotional abuse of children and accepted 842 cases.[6] Barbie, a doll more likely to be held up to a mirror than to be cuddled, is just the kind of woman, in my interpretation of the knitters' visions, to be more likely to abuse her children. Through their knitting, their participation in the doll parade, and their consistent use of the baby doll, the knitters speak for the kind of love and attention they believe children deserve.

Older Women with Grown Children

From the 1970s, the Rangeley Lakes region has continued to grow as a commercial and resort area, leaving its agricultural heritage behind. By 1982, the number of acres in farmland had fallen to 51,046,[7] and only 424 farm laborers remained in 1986. The 812 seasonal homes located in Franklin County in 1940 mushroomed to 3,334 in 1980, an increase of 310.6 percent.[8] As of 1985, Rangeley's year-round population stood at 1,150 and, during the peak tourist season, the total population of residents and visitors reached 6,700.[9] From 1984 to 1988, real estate sales tripled to three hundred annually, and six new condominium projects were proposed.[10] In 1988, Saddleback Ski Area began plans for a major expansion, many rental cottages were sold as condominiums, and there was talk of a convention center. In 1986, real estate in Rangeley was valued at $58,116,475, almost double the figure for 1983, when a revaluation of property was done.[11] Despite all this growth, the 1979 median family income of Rangeley stood at $14,904, 12 percent lower than state average.[12] Many local people saw the late 1980s as the time to sell. Along a mile-long stretch of town, five year-round residents had For Sale signs on their lawns.

For the Richard family, tourism brings mixed blessings. In 1984, they opened a little shop on the edge of their property to sell their carvings, knit goods, and the handmade work of other friends in the region. Now, as they look out their front window toward Rangeley Lake, they see not an open field but condominium units going up and the specter of a two-hundred-unit motel that a developer is planning.

In these times, the women of Rangeley knit even more. Lucille continues to work at the Good Shepherd Episcopal Church Fair with her neighbor Bertha Haines, as she has done every year for twenty-eight years. The fairs, though, have changed. Local people used to form the greater part of the audience. "Now," Lucille explains, "a big percentage of people who come to the fairs and different events to buy the stuff are strangers or some tourists." As the women look around them at the newcomers to Rangeley, they often speak of knowing no one. They are becoming strangers in their own hometown.

As her sons matured and tourism increased, Lucille Richard's knitting changed. "Once in a while when the boys were young," she remembers, "people would see something I had done for the church fair and I would occasionally take an order." Now, though, she takes many more orders and sells some of her creations in the family's craft shop.

Orders are not her favorites. She does not like the pressure involved in getting things just right for people and getting them done at a particular time. She is also quite aware of the low price—fifteen to twenty dollars—she gets, considering the time she spends. Raffles, however, are something else. "I like to knit things on raffles," Lucille explains. Since she believes that helping others through charities is how people should live, she has knitted many a bunny and teddy bear

Lucille Richard's and Bertha Haines's knit goods table at the Good Shepherd Episcopal Church Fair. (Mrs. Richard is at the far right.)

outfit and is now planning doll outfits for both the Farmington Hospital Auxiliary and for the Logging Museum.

Raffles also satisfy a good knitter because they show how her accomplishments are recognized throughout the community. Often people scoop up raffle tickets without even seeing the knitted prize. Just knowing that it is the work of Lucille or another fine knitter is enough. Lucille's outfits often bring about seventy-five dollars at a raffle. Even though she earns no money, Lucille enjoys raffles because through them she can see her work go for the monetary value she believes it deserves. Like other women knitters, however, Lucille faces a dilemma: for her work to realize its greatest economic power, she herself must earn nothing.

As Lucille increases her orders and her benefit work, she and the other knitters continue to strengthen their ties within the women's sphere. As adults with grown children, they teach others to knit. Lucille remembers when her niece Julie was ten: "Some evenings Julie and I would just sit here and she'd go get my needles and say, 'Would you help me?' What I tried to start her on was dolls' things because they would be small and she wouldn't get too discouraged. We would do a doll's scarf or something real plain, in the beginning. And then we'd go to a little doll's sweater and from there on to bigger things. I'd be knitting at the same time. And I think that's why she'd want me to show her: sometimes, I was probably knitting and she wanted to do the same thing."

The women's sphere also encompasses women knitters' visits with one another. When Lucille visits her neighbor Bertha Haines or sees Kay Morgan, who fashions the buttonholes on Lucille's sweaters, talk focuses on knitting as they praise each other's work, discuss the challenging details on a sweater or a doll dress, trade information about where to get materials, consider how to get the best price for the time spent, and take a few swipes at the dolls and doll clothing they all dislike.

At the church fair, a major part of the women's sphere in Rangeley, women compliment each other's work as they pick up the sweaters, clothes, potholders, afghans, clothes hanger covers, toilet roll covers, and pin cushions on the knit goods table—"My, what a lot of beautiful things you've got here." "Look at these! Are these yours?" "A lot of work in these!" The knitters' expertise is clear, especially in their talk about sizing mittens for children. With ease, they recommend one size for one child, one size for another.

In the aisles between the tables, women hug and kiss. Summer residents greet local people and each other after long absences. Others throw kisses and wave to the many babies and children in the room. A local woman who owns some cottages greets Lucille, and, amidst the praise for her work, they comment on the summer people they both depend on and disparage:

> WOMAN: Hi, Lucille. Thanks so much for making those sweaters for my friend. They were beautiful! She was so pleased!
> LUCILLE: How are the camps this year?
> WOMAN: Well, good. Some people are saying the motels aren't full, but our people have to book ahead, so they come rain or whatever. "Is it always like this?" they ask. "So rainy?"
>   What do they expect? Doesn't it rain where they come from? [laughs] I want to say, "No, it just rains over you; there's a grey cloud that follows you around. Just you."
>   Honestly, you think they could take what they get like we do.

From the ranks of the older women in town came a few who, disturbed by the end of the Doc Grant's Doll Carriage Parade in 1964, lobbied to have it begin again. "We older ones," Rose Quimby explained, "thought it was something they shouldn't drop. I talked to them [the women at the Chamber of Commerce] several times. It was nice, something for the kids in Rangeley to participate in. You know, there's not too much for the Rangeley kids to do."

Jane Linnell, then at the Chamber of Commerce, had been talking about the parade with her friend Joan Blythe. "I was interested in new things to attract people to town," she explained, "things to do. And when you could bring people from Connecticut—that was something." Jane, Joan, and Rose began the parade again around 1974. "This time, though," Rose added, "we called it the 'Children's Day Parade' [from the start] so boys and girls could enter it. This way everybody could participate."

Enthusiastically, Lucille and her friends entered grandchildren and the children of friends. Though the parade certainly gave the children something to participate in, it also provided the Rangeley knitters with a major public space to exhibit their creations and declare the values inherent in baby dolls, hard work, and handmade goods. This time, however, Lucille and like-minded others encountered competition from mass-market doll products. The parade became a visual dialectic between contesting sets of values. "I entered Meredith [Larry and Eileen's girl] for three years, 1980, '81, '82," Lucille pointed out:

> The first year she was only six months old, so we decorated a big baby carriage and sat her in it but we made it all white. Rodney hand carved a husky dog and a friend of mine made a sled the exact replica to go along with the size of the dog carving. We put her in sponsored by the Saddleback Motor Inn and we put a little crown on her head. It was cute.
>
> And then the second year, she was a year and a half and her mother dressed her all in a little pink smock dress and I made the doll carriage all in pink. I used a little stroller and put a big doll in it and then the bottom part of the stroller formed her gown. And that was really pretty. I decorated the carriage with crepe paper. I made a frame and put sheeting around it. Then you sew your crepe paper to the sheet— you'd have to hand sew it on. And when you finally got it fit around the frame, you'd sew one seam to keep it on. I waited until I got it onto the carriage and then I embroideried little rose buds with yarn all the way around it. It was a lot of work. But it was cute.
>
> And then the third year, the final year, I dressed her as a bunny and made her carriage an Easter basket and filled it full of toys and Easter eggs.
>
> One year when we put Meredith in, another little girl got first prize and her carriage was just a tin carriage from Sears and Roebuck that was a Strawberry Shortcake and her dress was a Strawberry Shortcake, also from Sears and Roebuck so there was no work involved. I don't know

how they judged it first except that they thought it was cute. It was the first year Strawberry Shortcake had come out, but there was no work in it. And Meredith's, I'd spent days on her carriage. To me, there's not an equality in judging when they do it that way. And when you're judging, you really ought to consider the amount of hours that somebody put in, even if it's not quite as cute or pretty as another that was put together in a short length of time.

Not everyone greeted the new parade with enthusiasm. As Rose Quimby, who organized the parade for several years, comments, "The parents now don't take the time, don't have the imagination. They say they don't *have* time. I called a lady in Oquossoc: 'Why don't you put your three in the parade?' 'Well, what could I do?' she said. 'Dress them up like Indians. The two boys and a princess. Call them O-squaw-sic.' Get it? Oquossoc. They won a prize. But I had to give her the idea."

Though the Chamber of Commerce continues to support the parade, the 1989 head of the chamber reminded me that the parade was "always really more of a local parade than anything for the visitors. More for the people who live here year round."

This much smaller doll parade thus faced challenges from the different priorities of young parents, from increased emphasis on the differences between locals and "people from away," and from a greater use of mass-produced rather than handmade costumes. A greater challenge to the values of the Rangeley knitters, however, was on its way: the late 1970s witnessed the whirlwind arrival of the Cabbage Patch dolls.

"I don't see how kids could love them," exclaims Lucille to her neighbor, Bertha, who agrees with her:

BERTHA: They're homely things. Yes, they look like something stepped on their face, almost like an animal or horse or foot had stepped on their face and flattened the face right back.
LUCILLE: I like the baby dolls, the fat little baby dolls.
BERTHA: Oh, I know it.
LUCILLE: I still got the one that you people bought Steve for his second birthday. That's the big one, the big baby doll that I usually put doll sweaters on down to the shop.
    I had a lot of uneasy pros and cons on the Cabbage Patch doll, that people were making too much of the adoption part. And that if kids broke them or set them aside or neglected them, it would be like a real kid they were doing it to. Or if they got dirty. I don't think the whole thing was good for kids psychologically.
BERTHA: I just like the baby dolls that they could play with.

Rose Quimby echoes Lucille's and Bertha's position as she, too, speaks for baby dolls and against the injustices brought about by popular, widely advertised, expensive dolls: "I like the baby dolls: they're so soft. And cute. Not at all like those Cabbage Patch. What a farce! Cloth dolls, too, but forty dollars! And not good-looking either, their faces. Did you hear about the birthday party? One woman had a birthday party for her daughter and invited only those who had Cabbage Patch dolls. Imagine. Forty dollars! Well, not everybody can *afford* that. There were a lot of little girls crying because they couldn't go to the party."

As they had done with the Barbies earlier, the knitters made Cabbage Patch clothes, but they displayed the clothes on baby dolls or teddy bears—never on a Cabbage Patch Doll itself. Neither did they put up any signs to mark the clothes as Cabbage Patch clothes; buyers either recognized the sizes as appropriate or they asked a knitter, who would usually reply, "Yes, and they also fit teddy bears and baby dolls." The knitters continued to praise the doll they cared for most: the baby doll. As Lucille discusses her preference, she also outlines her belief in the value of dolls for young girls:

> [Baby dolls] are more appealing to me. They're cuter and *more appealing.* Their little faces, the expressions on them. And sometimes their little hands and feet are so real looking.
>
> I think [children] did more then [with dolls], had dolls for a longer age. But now the kids after they're seven, eight years old feel like they're being sissies—or a lot of kids tell them they are—if they get dolls. They are too mature at such a young age.
>
> I hate to see them get too mature too early because I think they lose—Rodney and I both say—a lot of their youth too quickly and they think they're older and they want to work and do things. Then sometimes these kids later in life want to revert back to a childhood they've missed.
>
> And some parents will encourage their kids to be grownups ahead of their time. They'll either dress them older or encourage them to go to dances at a young age and rush them into being teens when they're just kids. I don't mean that they should try to keep them as a baby or an immature child, but I think there's no harm in a little girl having dolls say at eight or nine or ten years old.
>
> I think sometimes if they really liked dolls, they would make a good mother.
>
> So I try to encourage Eileen or any of our friends. I say, "Look, if your little girl really wants a doll for Christmas, go buy it for her. She'll have years enough that she doesn't want them and wants to feel mature." That's my feeling.

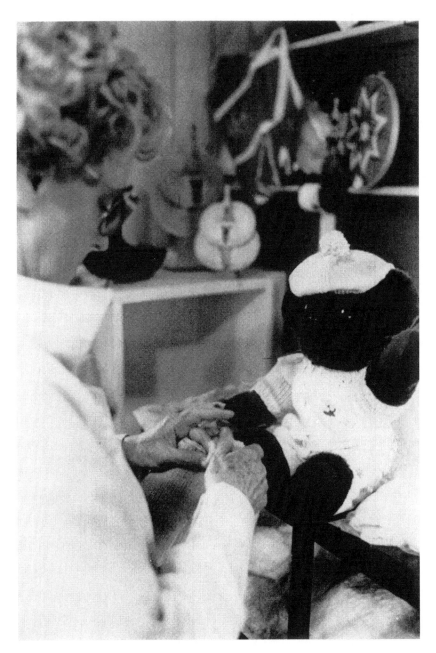

Lucille Richard dresses a teddy bear.

There is much support for Lucille's opinion in and beyond Rangeley. Merchants often decorate their windows with baby dolls. Parents support the Logging Museum talent show for girls between six and eight years of age—the Little Miss Woodchip Contest—where every contestant receives a baby doll and, often, a doll dress knitted by Lucille. Southwest of Rangeley, down the Androscoggin River through the logging country of New Hampshire, lies the tiny town of Dummer, where Mildred Smith decorates her front yard with 125 dolls.[13] Mildred's use of dolls cues us to strategies that, in my opinion, enable her and the Rangeley knitters to grow older, creatively, in a society that undervalues all women but especially older women.

Some of Mildred Smith's dolls are dressed as riders atop motorcycles, some are arranged like vignettes from such childhood stories as "Goldilocks and the Three Bears" and "Jack and Jill," some stand with masks in place of lost heads or with stuffed stockings for a lost arm, and some just stand. Mildred's dolls grab the attention of all who drive past.

"Four times a year," Mildred explains, "I change [their clothes] for summer, fall, winter, and then spring":

> I change them for the whole four seasons. Now school will be starting up in another month or so, September, so by next month, August, I'll be changing their outfits to their fall clothes. I change their pants, their shirts, and if I have the light jackets, I'll put light jackets on them—until winter.
>
> Then I'll start changing them to their heavy jackets and ski pants and skidoo suits that I got. I take all the toys in. Then I start putting sleds and stuff out with them. They'll all be changed.
>
> I'll take their clothes off out on the porch there and I'll take them in and I'll have the hot water right there at the sink. I'll start cleaning them right up and brushing their hair . . . I got to wash their wigs.

When I comment about the time Mildred devotes to her dolls, she laughs and says, "I *love* the dolls anyways. The faces look *so real,* they look awful *real.* Oh, when I see a doll I fall in love with it right away [quietly]. I can't go out to the stores; I'd buy it. [laughs] If I don't have no money I can't buy it, so I don't go in the store. I stay out of the stores."

Mildred was born in 1924. "We were so poor when we were small," she remembers, "all we could have was one doll and that was it. And I still ain't got that doll that I had." Now, Mildred has a thousand more dolls inside. She gets many from family and friends. Some are given to her by strangers. "This doll with the note attached was left on my

Andrea Brackett, Little Miss Woodchip, 1988.

Mildred Smith of Dummer, New Hampshire, and some of her dolls.

doorstep," she explains. " 'Please take care of me. I need a home. Suzi.' " Some dolls she picks up at tag sales or at the dump. She tells everyone she meets, "The more the merrier. Don't throw them away, throw them my way."

If we saw just Mildred's dolls, or just the Rangeley Children's Day Parade, or just the Little Miss Woodchip talent show, or just a knitted doll's outfit in a craft shop filled with chain-saw animals, we would probably not ask ourselves much about dolls in this region of loggers. Taken altogether, however, the dolls with their open, though silent, mouths speak many cultural truths.

These baby dolls, produced and discussed within the women's sphere, give the older knitters—usually bound to silence by politeness and humility—the opportunity to pronounce their own ideals, to say what they want to in their own voice. The dolls speak for the value women place on the period of childhood, before the tumult of adolescence and sexual maturity, and on the importance of play that teaches children to nurture others and to be good parents. The women's belief in careful handwork also shines through the stitches of the doll clothes. In these real-life dolls, mothers set before their daughters their aesthetic that is based on realism. By raising them in the knitting world, then, the mothers of Rangeley teach their daughters to be women.

The baby dolls also speak for the value the women place on their spheres of influence in the community. The women defend their choice of dolls and stress how others enjoy viewing their work. "At first my sons, they thought it was weird of me doing the dolls," Mildred Smith explains:

> I said, *"Weird? What?"* I says, *"Everybody's* got a *hobby,"* I says. There's *guys* that *play* with *trains;* they pick trains up. My youngest daughter's husband, he collects model airplanes. He goes to these model airplane shows. He pays two, three hundred dollars for his projects. I says, *"Well,* I collect *dolls."*
>
> In Milton Mills where I lived before I came here, people from California and all over came down to see them. Even by the *bus loads,* the *van loads* and everything to see the dolls. And I was on the main highway where the school bus goes by, so the kids used to look forward to seeing the *dolls* and the changing of their clothing. Then a nursing home, Edgeworth Manor from Portsmouth, they come up by the busloads to see the dolls.

Talking pointedly against mass-produced dolls enables the knitters to state their positions more forcefully.[14] The knitters scorn Barbie. Her clothes, a drudgery to knit, do not provide the relaxing, shared experience the women want for themselves and their daughters. With Barbie, girls do not learn to nurture babies; they learn to want to become Barbie. Strawberry Shortcake fares no better with the knitters because this self-contained doll who needs no dresses cannot show young girls the importance of careful handwork.

For the Rangeley women, however, the Cabbage Patch doll is the most pernicious, for it is ultimately a perversion of baby doll ideals. Soft and cuddly, able to be dressed in real baby-sized clothing, this doll represents some of the women's values. But its price tag makes the reality of class differences, already uncomfortable in a small town, even more uncomfortable, and its face reminds the women of ugly, pushed-in, flattened faces and elicits comments on child abuse.

For me, the women's emotion-filled comments on the flattened faces of Cabbage Patch dolls encode messages of protest about spouse abuse, too. Though the knitters themselves have marriages free from physical abuse, they read of the new women's shelters in the larger towns of Franklin County, and they have seen the results of spouse abuse when they visit the service organizations in Farmington and Rumford to give them donations from knitting sales, raffles, and rummage sales. Encouraging girls to play happily with smiling, bright-faced baby dolls is their way of creating a vision of the kind of relationships they would like to see throughout the world.

The use of baby dolls also shows the strategies these women use as they face growing older in a society that undervalues older women. Through baby dolls, the women encode that time when, as young women and new mothers, they received more attention and favor. Such messages foreground maternal power and serve not only to console but also to empower women as they present images, in code, of their continuing strength and creative abilities.

Conclusion

"One of the major challenges for Rangeley," 1988 town manager Bill MacDonald said, "is adjusting to the fact that the town is changing rapidly and . . . thinking how they're going to face the changes." The knitters of Lucille's and Bertha's generation indeed see that change is upon them. Condominiums, timberland sales, second-home buyers from Boston are now common in Rangeley; Barbies and Strawberry Shortcakes and Cabbage Patch dolls grow in popularity; independent loggers struggle to earn a living wage; and more and more women and children suffer physical and emotional abuse. Since most of these are not changes the knitters feel they can "adjust" to—and they also do not see how they can stop the changes—they meet change through the dolls. They clothe the dolls in their own values and give them knitted, handmade exteriors. They also keep urging the baby doll upon as many children as they can.

The worlds that immediately surround the knitters—the male world of logging and construction as well as the world of tourists and land development—do not hear the voices of the women as they speak through the dolls. But it may be exactly this choice of the dolls—a seemingly trivial but safe form—that allows the women to be so expressive and creative in their own world. In the dolls, they have selected texts that are fully available only to those who share their ideals or are sympathetic to them as women. Their selection of a "trivial" form may be, as Joan N. Radner and Susan S. Lanser suggest, a coded message, a message that minority groups—such as local women in a male- and tourist-oriented community—often adopt, a "set of signals—words, forms, behaviors, signifiers of some kind—that protect the creator from the consequences of openly expressing particular messages."[15]

Many of the women's actions do confront, albeit through coding, the other worlds of Rangeley and their conflicting values. Each time the women put Cabbage Patch doll clothing on a baby doll or a teddy bear, each time they enter a meticulously prepared doll carriage in a parade or give a baby doll for an award, they speak out for their own positive valuation of women's role in their world as they know it.

Their actions stand up in the face of the sons who think their mothers "weird" for collecting dolls, the fathers who think it incredible to save a doll from a fire, and the husbands who comment, "What do you think of a wife who still plays with dolls?" Their actions also stand up against the mass-produced dolls that, like the tourists and summer residents and real estate developers, bring a host of alien assumptions to town.

And for me, when Lucille takes a teddy bear dressed in a little knit outfit of aqua or lavender or pink with teddy bear buttons and sets it in the shop next to one of her husband Rodney's carved wooden bears, a shift in perspective occurs. Rodney's bears soften. His bears, carved in pine with a chain saw to look like the powerful, agile, wide-ranging Maine black bear, look more like toys. Through this juxtaposition, Lucille calls attention to her own work and points out the similarity between her knitting and her husband's carving, both in subject matter and in quality. She transforms part of the male world into the female world.

Through the dolls, the knitters create a world of their own, a model world. "The miniature," as Gaston Bachelard writes, "deploys to the dimensions of a universe. Once more, large is contained in small."[16] Dressing the baby doll and thinking of her even as Cabbage Patch doll clothes spill from their needles, the women of Rangeley reenact a time of pleasure, the moments when they enjoyed their nicely dressed babies, cared for them, and showed them to their friends. A time when others smiled on them as new mothers. A time when their power as women who carried on their husbands' lineage in a male-oriented community was strongest. A time when they were not strangers in their own hometown.

The baby dolls re-create the happiness and power of motherhood. "A miniature," Susan Stewart proposes, "is a material allusion to a text which is no longer available to us, or which, because of its fictiveness, never was available to us except through a second-order fictive world. Its locus is nostalgic."[17] Baby dolls are texts that select and celebrate one part of the experience of being a mother.

The use of the miniature helps people order, understand, and control their world, especially a world that may seem to be changing rapidly beyond their control. "The cleverer I am at miniaturizing the world," Bachelard notes, "the better I possess it."[18] Similarly, Stewart reminds us that the miniature presents a "diminutive and thereby manipulatable version of experience."[19]

The world of the dolls in Rangeley also represents a reaction to change. Within this world of the baby dolls, adults always love children, and children look adorable, cute, happy, and well cared for. They do not die of crib death; they do not get shot while hunting. They are ever alive, ever young. Their faces do not bear signs of the anger of adolescence. They do not grow up to choose lives different from their parents' or careers that lead them away from parenting. Spouses and children are never abused. Mothers always want to be mothers, and fathers always want to be fathers.

Yet, for me, the world of the dolls has another side, hinted at by the knitters' comments on abuse and the eerie stillness of Mildred Smith's dolls. Her lawn full of dolls makes chillingly manifest the dialectic on life and death that dolls embody. Even as the dolls look so alive with their wide-open eyes and their outstretched arms, their silence reminds us of death. The eternal happiness of their faces calls to mind the opposite, the faces of children when they fight, cry, get abused, and die.

The continued use of the baby doll may also be understood in terms of Annette Weiner's discussion of reproduction and regeneration. For her, *reproduction* refers to the "cultural attention and meaning given to acts of forming, producing, or creating something new," such as children, and *regeneration* refers to the "cultural attention and meaning given to the renewal, revival, rebirth, or re-creation of entities previously reproduced," such as dolls. For Weiner, the regeneration of reproductive forms constitutes "an unrelenting attempt to counteract the constant threat of deterioration, degeneration, infertility, and eventual or immediate loss."[20]

When I asked Mildred why she displays and tends the dolls, she paused and then said forcefully:

> Well, after raising a big family and then you got nothing else to do and they're all gone and there's no others around, only your grandchildren to come visit. The dolls keeps *my mind* occupied 'cause we're so used to having kids around, you know? It's hard, but I make use of it. Hard, when you're by yourself, you're all alone. Your kids ain't here to come in and say, "Ma give me this, Ma give me that," you know? That's *hard*.
>
> I have fifteen, eleven boys and four girls. Plus, there's two boys and a girl gone. One died at the age of four months. The other one was pretty near a year old. The other one was nineteen; he was shot outside the woods and they call it an accident. It was no *accident* because the kid was standing right beside him and blew his stomach out. A *moose* is more important than a human being's life. You got to pay a stiff fine for a moose, but when you kill a human being's life. . . .
>
> And he's my Labor Day baby, born the first of September.

I see the dolls on the lawn standing as if desperately trying to stay alive and cheerful while their rubbery flesh bleaches, hardens, and decays with the season. "They are real," Mildred Smith comments, "awful real." Popular tales, such as "Pygmalion" and "Pinocchio," show just how much we want dolls to be alive. Perhaps the life and death we see in them is also our own. For me, the dolls signify women's lives creatively contending with forces—economic and patriarchal—that would drag them down to a life not worth living. And, on Mildred Smith's lawn, the battle scars show.

Perhaps because change, danger, financial hardship, and death swirl around the women so often, perhaps because they push so hard to be creative and alive in a world that does not fully welcome them, it is life that Mildred Smith and the knitters of Rangeley focus on when they speak of the dolls.

When Lucille's nephew, Randy Brackett, was almost killed two years ago in a logging accident, she donated a teddy bear with a knit outfit to a raffle to raise extra funds for him. "I had the little teddy bear and I dressed it," Lucille says. She goes on to explain:

> A little knitted suit. It seems like it was in the fall, near a holiday season and I made his outfit out of red or green.
>
> [My nephew] drove a big truck. He had parked his truck and it was on a little bit of ice and when the sun came out in early afternoon, it [melted and] moved the truck. It was his big logging truck. And he went to jump down offen it to keep it from rolling and when he did, this big piece of wood from the guy loading [a man on the bucket loader was loading wood into the bed of the logging truck] struck the back of his head and knocked him down.
>
> It was about an hour and a half before the ambulance could get there, then another two hours to drive him down [to the hospital].
>
> He was really quite critical. They didn't expect him to live at first. And he still has a hearing problem to this day. Very bad. He hears very little. He mostly reads lips. But he's lucky to be alive because it cracked his skull in two places.
>
> Must have been two years ago, at least two years ago. It was real serious. It was in Bemis, way in the back shore of Bemis and it would have been harder except that they have radio towers and so there was somebody right there at the garage that they called right into to get the ambulance started down, otherwise you'd have to wait until somebody could get to a phone or get somewhere to get help and it would have been many hours later.
>
> It was a serious accident.

Lucille's teddy bear puts life and death before us. This toy bear, surrounded by silky, warm yarn, calls forth the world of living children tucked safely in bed and also quietly acknowledges and protests the dangerous work that takes the limbs and lives of many Rangeley men and brings hardship to their families.

It also signifies the life that creative women fashion for themselves in the midst of forces that could bring about a death of the spirit. "Lots of times I like to pick up my knitting before I do the day's work," Lucille explains. "After I have breakfast, I feel a little bit lazy and rather than get out the dishpan, I go down and put the laundry in real quick and I just pick up my knitting, knit a few rows, set it down, then go work on something. And lots of times I pick it up after lunch. Quite often, later in the evening. Because if I get keyed up or need to sit down for a few minutes to relax, I go get my knitting. It gets my mind off other things. [laughs] When things get complicated, I grab my knitting and my needles and just sit."

The knitters of Rangeley speak to us through the dolls they love and the dolls they hate. Their baby dolls are cultural texts that present us with multilayered stories of personal change and responses to the economic development of the region. Through their dolls, the women act against and react to the worlds that seek to circumscribe them. "The need for such coding," Radner and Lanser remind us, "must always signify a freedom that is incomplete."[21] The messages, however, are there in the stitches for careful readers to receive, and they show us the survival strategies of women who, faced with the strictures of their community, find in creativity a measure of freedom, self-expression, and strength.

Notes

My thanks to Rodney and Lucille Richard and their family and friends in Rangeley, Maine, for sharing their time, lives, and insights with me. Thanks, also, to Joan Radner for her careful editing and her continuous encouragement.

1. Richard Barringer, Charles Colgan, Lloyd Irland, John Joseph, Frank O'Hara, and Kenneth Stratton, *The Western Mountains of Maine: Toward Balanced Growth* (Augusta, Maine: MaineWatch Institute, 1987), 20, appendix 2.

2. All interview material in this essay comes from tape recordings and journal notes from the summers of 1987 and 1988.

3. In speaking about the women's sphere, I am drawing from such literature as Carroll Smith-Rosenberg, "The Female World of Love and Ritual," in *Disorderly Conduct: Visions of Gender in Victorian America* (New York: Oxford University Press, 1985), 53–76, and Elaine Showalter, "Feminist Criticism in the Wilderness," in *The New Feminist Criticism,* ed. Elaine Showalter (New York: Pantheon, 1985), 243–70. Smith-Rosenberg uses the term *female sphere;* Showalter uses *woman's sphere.* I am using the *women's sphere* to better designate the culturally specific group of women in this essay—the twentieth-century Rangeley knitters.

4. Edward Ellis, *A Chronological History of the Rangeley Lakes Region* (Farmington, Maine: Rangeley Lakes Region Historical Society, 1983), 75–87.

5. Telephone conversation, U.S. Bureau of the Census, Washington, D.C., August 1988. I thank Thomas Vesey of the New England Agricultural Statistics Service for his help.

6. Correspondence, Child Protective Services of the Maine State Department of Human Services, August 1988.

7. Telephone conversation, U.S. Department of Commerce, Office of Regional Economic Statistics, Washington, D.C., August 1988.

8. Barringer et al., *Western Mountains of Maine,* 21.

9. Androscoggin Valley Council of Governments, *Comprehensive Plan: Town of Rangeley, Maine* (Auburn, Maine: AVCOG, 1987), 8.

10. Scott Allen. "Uproar in Rangeley," *Maine Times,* July 8, 1988, 18–20.

11. Annual Town Report of Rangeley, Maine, 1970–1987.

12. Androscoggin Valley Council of Governments, *Comprehensive Plan*, 23.

13. For other folk environments that older women have created using dolls, see Seymour Rosen, *In Celebration of Ourselves* (San Francisco: California Living Books, 1979), 82–87, 156–58, and Verni Greenfield, "Silk Purses from Sow's Ears: An Aesthetic Approach to Recycling," in *Personal Places: Perspectives on Informal Art Environments,* ed. Daniel Franklin Ward (Bowling Green, Ohio: Bowling Green State University Press, 1984), 133–47.

14. Woman's protest against mass-produced dolls has a history in the United States. See Miriam Formanek-Brunell, "With Pins and Patents: Mothers' Resistance to the Toy Store, 1870–1900," a paper presented at the Second Annual Feminist Roundtable, George Mason University, April 9, 1988.

15. Joan N. Radner and Susan S. Lanser, "Strategies of Coding in Women's Cultures," herein.

16. Gaston Bachelard, *The Poetics of Space* (Boston: Beacon, 1958), 157. I thank Leslie Prosterman, who brought this quotation to my attention.

17. Susan Stewart, *On Longing: Narratives of the Miniature, the Gigantic, the Souvenir, the Collection* (Baltimore: Johns Hopkins University Press, 1984), 69.

18. Bachelard, *The Poetics of Space,* 150.

19. Stewart, *On Longing,* 69.

20. "Reproduction: A Replacement for Reciprocity," *American Ethnologist* 7, no. 1 (1980): 71–72.

21. Radner and Lanser, "Strategies of Coding," herein.

PART THREE

Women in the Larger Community

It is a commonplace that women tend to be confined to the home and the domestic sphere, while men occupy public, visible community roles. In every community, however, men and women share public space and responsibilities differently; the essays in this section illustrate some of the range of difference. Sometimes women's voices are audible in the community, chiefly in formal and circumscribed roles, as was the case with the rural Irish women discussed by Angela Bourke. But when, in times of economic or political change, women have entered realms previously dominated by men, they have often eased their entrance and communicated their own points of view in the buffered form of coded creative expression.

No matter how muted women are in extreme patriarchal societies, they may be able to express even subversive ideas through their formalized, stable public roles—singing, delivering ritual greetings, lamenting the dead, supervising children—which protect them from debate or censure. The situation reported of Araucanian women in Chile is a dramatic example:

> The ideal Araucanian man is a good orator.... Men are encouraged to talk on all occasions, speaking being a sign of masculine intelligence and leadership. The ideal woman is submissive and quiet, silent in her husband's presence. At gatherings where men do much talking, women sit together listlessly, communicating only in whispers or not at all. On first arriving in her husband's home, a wife is expected to sit silently facing the wall, not looking anyone directly in the face. Only after several months is she permitted to speak, and then, only a little.... The

one means by which women can express their situation is a form of social singing (*ulkantun*) in which mistreatment, disregard, and distress can be expressed.[1]

Although their subservience to men was less extreme than among the Araucanians, women in rural eighteenth- and nineteenth-century Ireland spent most of their lives in domestic activities, and their voices were muted outside the home. They performed certain public functions, however, prominent among which was assuming responsibility for the dead. Their traditional ritual laments (*caoineadh,* or keen), discussed by Angela Bourke in "More in Anger than in Sorrow: Irish Women's Lament Poetry," enacted and stimulated community expression of grief. The passionate outcry of the keen carried a sophisticated, spontaneously composed poetic address to the dead man, praising him and describing and commenting on the details of his life. At such times of societal inversion, noisy and highly charged with emotion, women in public could blame as well as praise. They could criticize others and even protest the dominance, stinginess, and abusiveness of men. Bourke's examination of the surviving *caoineadh* texts uncovers evidence for a hidden, double-voiced tradition of rural Irish women's protest against the conditions of their lives.

In periods of marked political change, gender roles also tend to shift, and male and female spheres of influence are renegotiated. Joanne B. Mulcahy's research, presented in "'How They Knew': Women's Talk about Healing on Kodiak Island, Alaska," documents the power of Native women to sustain traditional culture and covertly express its value while adapting to extreme social and political change. Healing and midwifery, traditionally important public functions of Kodiak women, have been progressively displaced by Western, male-dominated medical practice since European contact in the mid-eighteenth century. Unobtrusively, however, and supported by the preferences of Native women, village midwives have kept alive the traditional female institution—and, symbolically, Native identity itself. Until very recently, they needed to use coding to continue their practice. Like the Pentecostal women preachers studied by Elaine Lawless,[2] the Kodiak healers ascribed their powers and their vocation to God; thus they brought their practice under the protective patriarchal screen of Russian Orthodoxy, central to community life on Kodiak. However, the current generation of midwives, working in an era of open Native political and cultural assertion, freely states a preference for Native, female ways. For this generation, coding is unnecessary. Although religious observance is still prominent in Kodiak culture, these midwives explain their medical powers in terms of aptitude and secular apprenticeship.

When women choose to enter public realms that have been exclusively or predominantly male, they often seek "authenticity" that will gain them credibility and acceptance. Appropriation of male forms and styles is a common strategy. Cheryl L. Keyes discusses a complex pattern of appropriation in " 'We're More than a Novelty, Boys': Strategies of Female Rappers in the Rap Music Tradition." To get their music recorded and on the air, the women rappers of the 1980s found they had to imitate the "hard" style—dress, behavior, and vocal timbre—of the established male rap musicians; claiming their art was identical to that of their male contemporaries, some female rappers denied that such a thing as "women's rap" existed. Yet while they were masquerading in the male aesthetic, they were converting it to female form. Black leather was tailored into skirts, heavy gold necklaces gave pride of place to heavy gold earrings, and behind the tough-guy voices of the women were variations on a decidedly feminist message: men insult and undervalue women and will take advantage of them whenever they can. Avoiding the more direct male styles of insult, the women rappers have retaliated against male "sounding" by "signifying," a tactic of verbal dueling character-ized by indirection. Such strategies have established the commercial viability of female rap musicians and won them a respected place in the tradition.

For Helen Cordero and other potters making *Storyteller* figures in the New Mexico pueblos, culture change seems to have brought an opportunity for the assertion of female power. Cordero and the women potters who have followed her example seem to be reviving a female tradition of making and selling figure potteries to Anglo tourists as souvenirs. The traditional figurines were female, however, whereas Helen Cordero's innovative *Storytellers* are male, representing her grandfather and, symbolically, the tradition of sacred discourse controlled by and reserved for men. In " 'At Home, No Womens Are Storytellers': Potteries, Stories, and Politics in Cochiti Pueblo," Barbara A. Babcock traces a complicated history of appropriation and reappro-priation of the powers of fertility and reproduction, showing that in representing men's storytelling in pottery, the women "have contrived to tell stories about storytelling, to subvert masculine discursive control, and to disturb the distribution of power profoundly." Cloaked in ambiguous coding as a revival of women's commercial figure pottery making and as a necessary boost to the Pueblo economy, the *Storyteller* image is in fact so "dangerously liminal," such a potent trespass on male authority, that the Cochiti tribal council in 1982 considered banning the women potters from exhibiting and demonstrating their work. Helen Cordero's assertion of her own creative and economic power depends on the multivalence of the *Storyteller* symbol, but there is no ambiguity in her attitude toward her innovation: "I'm getting me what I always wanted," she told Babcock.

Various communities, past and present, are represented in this section, their diversity pointing to the need for sensitivity to cultural difference when we interpret women's folklore. Women's issues intersect their communities in different ways. In rural Ireland, the lamenting women—simultaneously sustaining their community in times of crisis and criticizing some of its patriarchal norms—ran into opposition from the church, whereas religious beliefs served as protection for the customs of earlier Kodiak Island midwives. On Kodiak, where the practices of the women healers represent the worldview of the Native peoples, preference for women's ways is intertwined with assertion of Native culture. In Cochiti Pueblo, on the other hand, Helen Cordero's work has in some ways challenged traditional gender roles. For African-American women, entering the commercial rap scene has demanded aggressive resistance to male rappers' strident disparagement of women.

Feminism and its messages are thus not uniform and certainly do not take everywhere the configurations they have among contemporary Western women of the academy. As feminist researchers respectful of a spectrum of life experience, we may emulate the scholarly model offered by Bettina Aptheker in *Tapestries of Life:* "to pivot the centering, to let each woman's story or poem or experience or idea stand on its own merit," and in this "juxtaposition of stories" to understand the complex constructions and achievements of women's lives in their communities.[3]

Notes

1. Dell Hymes, "Models of the Interaction of Language and Social Life," in *Directions in Sociolinguistics: The Ethnography of Communication,* ed. John J. Gumperz and Dell Hymes (New York: Holt, Rinehart and Winston, 1972), 42, drawing on Sister Inez Hilger, "Araucanian Child Life and Its Cultural Background," Smithsonian Miscellaneous Collections, 135, Publication 4297 (Washington, D.C.: Government Printing Office, 1957).

2. "Piety and Motherhood: Reproductive Images and Maternal Strategies of the Women Preacher," *Journal of American Folklore* 100, no. 398 (1987):

469–78; see also the discussion in Radner and Lanser, "Strategies of Coding in Women's Cultures," herein.

3. *Tapestries of Life: Women's Work, Women's Consciousness, and the Meaning of Daily Experience* (Amherst: University of Massachusetts Press, 1989), 20.

More in Anger than in Sorrow: Irish Women's Lament Poetry

ANGELA BOURKE

In many parts of the world, death is as much women's responsibility as birth is. Women take care of the practical business of preparing a body for burial or cremation and also orchestrate and perform the funeral ritual. A funeral is not just a farewell to the dead; it is also a highly marked interaction among the living, a ceremony of transition. Funerals are characterized by marginality and can accommodate behavior not normally tolerated, but what goes on at them is always highly structured and vividly remembered.[1]

In societies as far apart as Greece, New Guinea, and India, women are the composers and singers of powerful and sophisticated oral lament poetry.[2] Women poets formally and publicly express their own and the community's reaction to death, piecing traditional motifs together to provide a musical and verbal accompaniment to grief and to the dislocation that follows any death.

The Irish lament is called *caoineadh,* the origin of the English word *keening.* [3] It was performed loudly and publicly and was regarded as essential to the honor of the dead person. Using a traditional meter and verbal formulas, the lament poet—always a woman—lavishly praised the dead person's character, family, and home in a poem that could be remembered and quoted for generations.

Not all the sentiments she expressed were positive. Some women poets gave vent to anger at powerful people, publicly criticized their own relatives and in-laws, and gave graphic accounts of personal violence and miserliness, all in the course of lamenting. They did so with relative impunity and in ways that have largely been ignored by scholars—but until very recently no scholar has taken a feminist approach to this material.[4]

Feminist analysis of lament traditions in other cultures shows that laments are often a part of the marriage ceremony as well as of funerals and that the feelings they express are frequently ambivalent.[5] Both Anna Caraveli Chaves and Constantina-Nadia Seremetakis have shown in their analysis of funeral ritual that Greek women use the lament to articulate their own view of the world in opposition to men's. According to Chaves, lament poets in Crete use their poetry as "a means of airing their grievances against their relatives or society," and she writes, "A common category of grievances to be aired is that of afflictions which are peculiar to women in a male-dominated society."[6] In Inner Mani, according to Seremetakis, women lamenting at funerals create "a domain of cultural power from which men . . . must necessarily keep their social and physical distance."[7]

In Ireland, women's traditional responsibility for funeral ritual brought them into conflict with the (male) Catholic clergy. In 1670, a synod of archbishops and bishops ordered that each priest in the country should do all in his power to end the wailings and screams of female keeners who accompanied the dead to the graveyard. Other such pronouncements, issued between 1631 and 1800, threatened keeners with excommunication and forbade priests to take part in funerals where the "heathenish" and "savage" custom was practiced. In spite of this, several accounts tell of sharp verbal exchanges between lament poets and priests in which the women came out best.[8] This is an obvious example of the lament poets' ability to challenge authority, but a more thorough examination of the *caoineadh* tradition will show the various ways Irish women poets could manipulate the themes and verbal formulas of the lament to construct and transmit a rhetoric of resistance to male domination in general.

The vast majority of known laments in Irish were composed about men, by women, so the opposition of women's experience to men's, expressed in female discourse about male activity, is a central theme of the tradition. The lament poetry considered in this essay contains messages that would have been intelligible to an inner circle of women but not necessarily to the rest of their audience. These messages—particularly the ones protesting men's violence and stinginess—were variously disguised. The most devastating criticism could be made to seem quite innocuous by clever turns of the traditional formulas. Like the piecing of a quilt, verbal art always involves the skillful placing and combining of ready-made motifs, and a talented artist could use the formulas and conventions of a common tradition in a variety of ways and with a variety of meanings.

The practice of *caoineadh* resisted church opposition for centuries, but it was gradually displaced by increasing modernization. It survived as formal ritual in remote areas until early in this century but has now died out. Field recordings of lament poetry are therefore not available, and any study of its content and context must depend on the record found in historical, literary, and folklore sources. Some accounts of Irish funerals and wakes were written by travelers who were ignorant of the Irish language and therefore paid no attention to the poetic content of the lament.[9] On the other hand, scholars of Irish studying lament poetry have focused on the available texts, often to the neglect of their contexts.[10] Between these two extremes lies a large body of other evidence. I shall draw on songs and narratives about death from the oral tradition of Ireland and Scotland, descriptions of death in medieval saga literature, and accounts of traditional Irish society by its own members and by folklorists, anthropologists, and other writers.

Keening Performances at Funerals

The communities where *caoineadh* was practiced have been greatly changed by increased industrialization and the spread of the English language and urban values. Even in the late twentieth century in the west of Ireland, however, there have been funerals where older women, skilled in verbal art and anxious to do full honor to the dead, have wept longer, louder, and with more rhythm and conscious artistry than some observers have thought seemly.[11] *Caoineadh* is still one of the normal terms used in Irish for weeping of any kind, but most members of Irish-speaking communities readily recognize this kind of outburst as belonging to the ritual lament, and many remember hearing it as children.

Women and men still living are familiar with the conventions of the *caoineadh* tradition, and some can recite passages of rhymed, rhythmic lament poetry, celebrated and remembered over generations as the work of particularly skilled keeners. From them, and from literary sources, we learn that the lament was performed by groups of women: a soloist who established the rhythm and sang or chanted alone, and two, four, or more other women who listened carefully and answered her in chorus.[12]

The chief mourner was usually a close woman relative of the dead person, but if no woman of the family could undertake the task, a semiprofessional lamenter, who might also be a midwife, was called in and paid for her services in salt, tobacco, or whiskey, or occasionally in cash. So strong was the belief that lamenting was a necessary part of the funeral ritual that even an itinerant vendor, a stranger to the community, was mourned with praise poetry where he happened to die, for to do otherwise would be to dispose of him "like a cow or a horse."[13]

One of the funerals described by J. M. Synge, writing in 1911 about the Aran Islands off the coast of Galway, was that of an old woman: "While the grave was being opened the women sat down among the flat tombstones, bordered with a pale fringe of early bracken, and began the wild keen or crying for the dead. Each old woman, as she took her turn in the leading recitative, seemed possessed for the moment with a profound ecstasy of grief, swaying to and fro, and bending her forehead to the stone before her, while she called out to the dead with a perpetually recurring chant of sobs."[14] Synge's play *Riders to the Sea* later introduced the image of the keening woman to generations of theatergoers.

Writers from Giraldus Cambrensis in the twelfth century to Edmund Spenser in the sixteenth and William Carleton in the nineteenth described and commented on Irish wakes and funerals.[15] Visitors to Ireland recorded their horror at the "abuses" they witnessed during funeral "orgies," whereas native commentators more often described the merry wake with nostalgia.

James Joyce's punning on *funeral* as *funferall* in *Finnegans Wake* reflects the fact that wakes were times of licence and hilarity. Tobacco and whiskey were freely provided, there was a great deal of noise and sexual pairings, and various games were played. Many of the games were judged obscene by observers, and some were so elaborate that they resembled small plays, often parodies of solemn ceremonials. As one observer remarked, "The whole trick was to make everything and everyone as ridiculous as possible."[16]

During this sort of wake, the world was turned upside down, recalling the carnivalesque of medieval and renaissance Europe. The marginal time of the funeral and wake represents what Mikhail Bakhtin calls "the people's laughter" of universal upheaval and renewal.[17] As in carnival, images of fertility and new life were found at wakes, along with images of death and decay, and both were treated ambiguously and ambivalently.[18] Like carnival, the funeral contained elements that were neutral or ambiguous in themselves but could be polarized and made to carry specific meaning. Lament poets were adept at switching the charge of an utterance from positive to negative and back again. *Caoineadh* may be seen as the verbal and musical aspect of a traditional "theater of death," the ritual of the wake and funeral, over which certain skilled women presided and through which the entire community adjusted to death and loss.[19]

The lament poem was only one part of a total performance, and the audience witnessing it was complex and variable. The whole community was expected to be present, but the center of activity shifted as the body was brought from the place of death to its "laying out" for the wake in a house or barn and from there to the church and the graveyard. A wake lasted up to three days, during which people came and went. Besides the clamor of lamenting immediately around the body, there were the competing attractions of games and other activities. It was a major social event, particularly for women. Rosemary Harris quotes a saying from rural Northern Ireland in the early 1950s that "women love a wake just because it gives them the chance to visit neighbours' homes."[20]

Paintings and engravings of Irish wakes, as well as written descriptions, depict crowded scenes in small rooms, as the mourners cluster around the corpse.[21] Joan N. Radner and Susan S. Lanser remark in their essay in this collection that "coding occurs in the context of complex audiences." In the case of the Irish lament, pictorial, literary, and oral sources agree that the jostling audience had at least two parts: an inner circle of active lamenting women gathered around the body, and an outer, less involved group of men, women, and sometimes children.

The women of the inner audience, whom I call "active" for the purpose of this study, would be the relatives of the dead person and other women, paid or not, who had attended many funerals and mourned their own dead. They would join in the chorus of sobs and rhythmic wailing, and each might take a turn at leading the lament by contributing lines, or whole series of lines, of formulaic verse. In this way they would gradually build the *caoineadh*.

While this was going on, the younger women, conscious of a separate, women's tradition of responsibility in the community, would see themselves as apprentices, rather like the young "singers of tales" in Albert B. Lord's Yugoslavian model.[22] These two groups of older and younger women would make up the inner circle, among whom coded messages could be passed under cover of an event in which the whole community participated. The apprentices would therefore be initiated not only into the social ritual of lamenting the dead but also into a private discourse of women's concerns and experience. This situation is paralleled by the waulking song tradition of Scotland, in which younger and older women sang as they worked together in processing woven cloth. The songs accompanying their work combined energetic, rousing melodies with lyrics about every aspect of women's sexual and social life. Like wakes, waulkings were prized social occasions in women's lives.[23]

It is important to remember that rural Irish society in the preindustrial period was not as homogeneous as some commentators, influenced by the romantic nationalism of Johann Gottfried Von Herder and others, would have us believe.[24] Potential members of the audience for the lament belonged to different socioeconomic groups, from the landlord and his guests to the priest, the bereaved family, neighbors, and whatever destitute lamenters or beggars might turn up. Conflicting interests and conflicting interpretations of signs could be expressed in various ways. We find them most notably in the verbal art of the lament poet.

The Lament Poet

According to the stylized accounts given in lament texts, songs, and prose narrative, the woman who composed and performed the *caoineadh* functioned as a tragic actor. Her willingness to experience disturbing emotions to the full provided a catharsis for everyone who witnessed her performance. She used her appearance, her voice, and her poetry to work on the emotions of her audience. The cry of the keener has been described as "blood-curdling," "horrible," and "hideous," yet young girls used to practice to get the right effect.[25] By skillfully articulating anger and the power to shock—the same elements that make this poetry so striking on the printed page and in translation—the lament poet in her oral performance led others through the emotional experience of loss. In the process, she contrived to make memorable public statements about her own and other women's lives.

When the lamenter heard news of her son's or husband's death, she immediately dropped what she was doing and set off. The mother of Dermot McCarthy, whose lament I quote at length later, is said to have walked some twenty miles over rough mountainside to Cork, still carrying the rope she had used to tie her cow. Similar stories are told of other women, including the Virgin Mary.[26] The lamenter does not stop to comb her hair, put on shoes, or change her clothes— sometimes she loosens her hair or tears her clothing, baring her breasts. In her self-presentation she acts out the disorder brought about by death, and her journey takes her not along roads but across country, through wild nature. She does not notice the stones and briars that cut her feet.

Arriving at the scene of death, she takes charge, starting immediately on her poem and loudly berating anyone who laughs at her appearance, attempts to move away, or fails to join in the chorus that punctuates her chanting. If the body is bleeding, she may even drink the blood. This practice is mentioned in texts of *caoineadh* and in several Irish prose texts from the medieval period. Edmund Spenser also describes an incident after an execution in Limerick when an old woman, the foster-mother of the dead man "tooke vpp his heade whilst he was quartered and sucked vpp all the blood running there out."[27]

Everything about the lamenter's behavior marks her as marginal: she embodies the state of transition in which the bereaved community finds itself, and by drinking the blood of the dead man, she allies herself with him against the continuing stability of the living community. In one prose text, "The Romance of Mis and Dubh Ruis," drinking blood is specifically identified as leading to insanity and separation from the community.[28] Yet she speaks to the dead person *on behalf* of that living community. Traditional formulas in her repertoire address the corpse reproachfully, asking why he died and demanding that he get up and come home.

The lamenter's liminal position is expressed as a kind of madness. Irish narratives from medieval to modern times describe madmen (and a few madwomen) as figures who dwell in the wilderness, barefoot, often naked, and unkempt, leaping wildly from place to place and occasionally composing poetry.[29] Lamenting women are also described as leaping, and traditional religious poems recount that even the Virgin Mary "rose, without shame or sense, and leapt over the heads of the guards" or "landed like an idiot without sense or shame."[30]

The "madness" of the lament poet at a wake or funeral would clearly have the effect of protecting her from the consequences of her outspoken behavior. The inner circle of mourners—women who had lamented their own dead and the younger women who listened to learn—must have recognized that there was method in that madness, however. Far from being socially isolated, the lament poet throwing herself into her expression of grief was performing an essential social service—recognized as such by the whole community and not just by women—as the payment of professional lamenters and the continuing currency of their poetry make clear.

The assumed madness of mourning could be used to cloak statements about sexual and personal identity. By baring their breasts and loosening their hair, by referring to sexual pleasure, or the absence of it, in their relations with their husbands, and by frequently referring to pregnancy and childbirth, lament poets asserted their identity as women in a way that contrasts sharply with the accepted norms of modesty and reticence in Irish society. A woman advised by the priest officiating at her son's funeral to accept the will of God and cease lamenting is said to have answered:

> Éist, a Shagairt agus seasuigh díreach,
> Léigh an tAifreann is gheobhaidh tú díol as.
> Níor thug sé trí ráithe in imeall do chroí agat,
> Ná naoi mbliana déag ar fuaid an tí agat.

> [Shut up, Priest, and stand up straight!
> Read the Mass and you'll get paid.
> He didn't spend nine months next to your heart,
> Or nineteen years around your house.][31]

For those who preferred not to hear what the lamenter said, this sort of defiance would provide further evidence of her madness.

Hearing is selective. Given several sounds together, we hear the one we listen for, and one way of disguising subversive messages is by burying them under other sounds.[32] In descriptions of Irish funeral laments written by travelers, the overwhelming impression is of noise. People clapped hands, beat their fists on the wood of the coffin, and wailed. Edmund Spenser wrote of "theire Lamentacions at theire burialls, with disparefull outcryes, and ymoderate waylinges," and other writers referred to "barbarous outcries" and "Irish-like howlings."[33] In oral tradition, too, there is much emphasis on the noise of lament as a horrible and unnerving sound. Peig Sayers, the story-teller from County Kerry who was famous for her mastery of "masculine" genres of folklore, once described a scream of mourning that went "back and forth through my heart as though a knitting-needle had been stuck into my ear."[34] The noise generated and the fact that so few commentators who heard keening at funerals recorded its content make it clear that for all except those listening intently, the words spoken were less audible than the loud wailing and clapping that accompanied them.

The young women of the inner circle—apprentices in the art of lamenting—must surely have listened more carefully. They would need to familiarize themselves with the meter, the verbal formulas, and what in the case of ballad-performance has been called the "architectonics" of the poem.[35] All the women immediately involved needed to pay close attention to the lamenter, because it was their function to help her and because she might well turn her invective on them if they did not. In surviving lament texts and in songs about death from Ireland and Scotland, formulaic curses begin "Woman over there who laughed!" and proceed to wish misfortune on the inattentive.[36]

Mourners who listened carefully would hear in the words of the keener not only praise and grief but also clear statements of identity and protest and a catalogue of women's wrongs. Others listening less carefully or less sympathetically—or the uninitiated, unnerved by the experience—would hear mostly noise or would miss the small verbal clues that gave point to the familiar formulas.

Lament Poetry

Caoineadh was oral formulaic poetry, composed in performance, but the same themes and diction were used from one lament to another.[37] A *caoineadh* for a particular individual, incorporating his name, genealogy, and other personal details, would be sung and sometimes reworked by its composer at funeral after funeral. It would also be recited by others as a fine example of its genre. It is through performances of *remembered* laments, and chiefly through transcriptions of them made over the last hundred years, that we learn most about the poetry of the lament tradition. Some of these transcriptions, like *Caoineadh Airt Uí Laoghaire—The Lament for Art O'Leary*, composed by his wife Eileen O'Connell when Art was shot dead in 1773—are several hundred lines long. It seems likely that they represent collections of orally composed poetry, gathered over time around the core of a single memorable performance.[38]

The lament poem consisted of groups of short, rhymed lines, usually of two or three stresses, each group beginning with a formulaic opening line. This opening might be a call to others present, such as *"Druidigí thart, a mhná"* ("Gather round me, women"), or, more commonly, an exclamation of affection for the dead person, such as *"Mo ghrá go daingean tú!"* ("My constant love!") and *"Mo chara's mo rún tú!"* ("My friend and darling!"). It might be an exclamation of grief or a curse, usually on the dead man's enemies or the people or things held responsible for his death. With the first line of each group, the poet established both the metrical shape of the following lines—the number of stresses, the rhyming end vowel—and the person being addressed. Some accounts say she repeated the first line several times, rocking back and forth as she did so.[39]

The lamenter detailed the dead man's beauty, generosity, bravery, noble ancestry, and skill as a hunter and lover, and she praised his home place in traditional formulas describing its natural beauty and fertility. She exhorted him to get up and come home, as Eileen O'Connell did in *Caoineadh Airt Uí Laoghaire*:

Mo ghrá thú go daingean!
Is éirigh suas id sheasamh
Is tar liom féin abhaile.
Go gcuirfeam mairt á leagadh,
Go nglaofam ar chóisir fhairsing,
Go mbeidh againn ceol á spreagadh,
Go gcóireod duitse leaba
Faoi bhairlíní geala,
Faoi chuilteanna breátha breaca,
A bhainfidh asat allas
In ionad an fhuachta a ghlacais.

[My own beloved dear!
Now get up on your feet
And come on home with me.
It's time to slaughter beef—
We'll organize a feast—
We'll have musicians play,
And I'll make you a bed,
With clean white sheets
And colored patchwork quilts,
To make you sweat with heat
Instead of this awful cold.][40]

The wealth and ease referred to here were perhaps a reality for Eileen and Art, who belonged to a Catholic gentry class, but formulas like these are typical of the *caoineadh* tradition.

When Dermot McCarthy was killed in a fall from his horse in Cork around 1860, his mother was at home, twenty miles away, preparing to milk her cows. According to a man and a woman who grew up in the same area and could recite her *caoineadh* eighty years later, she walked across the mountains to reach him, still carrying the spancel. In her lament she offered to take him home:

Mo chara is mo rún thú!
Bhéarfad liom thú
Go Driseáin chumhra . . .
Meas go glúine,
Ba boga 'búirthigh
Maidin bhog dhrúchta
Ad iarraidh a gcrúdhta!

[My friend and my darling!
I'll take you home
To sweet Drishane . . .
Knee-deep in beech nuts

> Where gentle cows low
> In the morning dew,
> Asking to be milked!]

McCarthy's home, "sweet Drishane," has become a sort of Promised Land; elsewhere in the same text she described it as a land rich in honey and wheat.[41]

The lamenter typically bewailed the fact that she was not nearby when her darling was killed, so that she might have saved him, and referred to a premonitory dream or signs in nature that foretold his death. Commentators on this poetry have emphasized her love and anguish and her celebration of nobility and masculine virtues. Her poetic techniques, however, included curses, invective, and stark and shocking images and contrasts, such as the image of the lover's soft skin and the same skin being eaten by fish after he drowned.[42] She often cursed the dead man's enemies and engaged in verbal contests with other lamenters or with priests.[43] Sometimes, she launched scathing attacks on people who were present, as when Sir James Cotter was hanged in Cork in May 1720, and his old nurse demanded that people stand back and make way for his body:

> *Greadadh oraibh is brón,*
> *A lucht na mbolg mór,*
> *Fanaidh siar go fóill*
> *Is leogaidh Séamus romhaibh*
> *Mar is dó ba chuibhe is ba chóir.*

> [Bad cess to you, and sorrow,
> You big-bellied lot!
> Stand out of the way,
> Let James go before you
> As is his right and due.][44]

Blame is the obverse of praise, and the traditional poetry of keening could be turned to either purpose. There were even cases where the dead man himself was the one criticized.[45]

The Woman Lamenter as Protester

Throughout the *caoineadh* tradition, women protest men's violence and miserliness. Some of this is explicitly stated, but most is expressed in "safe" ways, so the victim is protected from further attack. In the lament for Dermot McCarthy, the poet uses her son's death as an opportunity to complain about her son-in-law's treatment of her daughter. First she talks about his stinginess. He forces his wife to work hard but lets her eat only her child's leftovers, while he collects the butter and eggs that should have been a source of independent income for a farm woman.[46] Then the lamenter addresses her daughter:

> *Mo chara is mo chiall thú,*
> *A's do ghabhadh sé den tsrian ort,*
> *A's d'fhuip naoi n-iall ort,*
> *A's den mhaide i ndiaidh sin;*
> *Níor innsis-se riamh é*
> *Go bhfuaras-sa a rian ort*
> *Ar an leabaidh tar éis bliadhn' ort.*

> [My friend and my dear one,
> He beat you with the bridle,
> With the nine-thonged whip,
> And then with a stick;
> You never told me,
> Till I found the marks on you
> In bed a year later.]

She goes on to address the offending husband, opening with the traditional term of affection but moving immediately to an elaborate curse:

> *Mo ghrádh is mo thaisce thú!*
> *Thugas fiche bó bhainne dhuit,*
> *Lasaid chun fuinte dhuit—*
> *Mo mhallacht in' ionad duit,*
> *Ní id stoc ná it iothalainn,*
> *Ná i dteinteán na teine istig,*
> *Acht id chroidhe agus id chuisleanna*
> *Ad iarraidh do chiorruighthe,*
> *A bhodaigh an domblais!*

> [My love and my treasure!
> I gave you presents—
> Twenty dairy cows,
> A trough to knead bread—
> My curse on you instead,
> Not on livestock or harvest,
> On hearth or on home,
> But in your heart and veins,
> To leave you maimed,
> You sour-tempered lout!][47]

In this case the injured woman is not the one who protests, and her mother insists she learned of her plight only by accident. To state publicly that her daughter had complained of abuse in marriage would be to lay her open to further attack and public disgrace. In other examples, the subversive messages of women's protest are disguised so that the protesting victims are protected.

Sometimes anger is directed at a safe target. A well-known feature of lament poetry is the eloquent cursing of enemies or people defined for the time being as enemies. Eileen O'Connell, in her lament for her husband Art O'Leary, is thus free to express uninhibited anger at the spy who betrayed him. The vocabulary of blame reverses that of praise, and she enumerates the gifts he would have had for his loyalty, as she names Art's gifts to her—but this time with a sneer to show her contempt. She describes Art's physical beauty, but refers to her disloyal brother-in-law as *"An spreallairín gránna, / An fear caol-spágach"* ("The ugly little wretch, / The skinny-legged man").[48] Behind every word of praise lies the threat of its opposite.

Related to this technique are the various types of "hedging" used by lamenters, where a statement is made such that some of its force is blunted. *Caoineadh Airt Uí Laoghaire* is known as a passionate poem of praise and heartbroken love. In three versions its editor gives in an appendix, however, Art's wife Eileen says that he used to beat her with a stick. In one, she says he used a silver-handled whip.[49] She is obviously drawing on the same tradition that the mother of Dermot McCarthy, who denounced her son-in-law in verse, did. In every case, however, she withdraws the accusation as soon as it is made by excusing him: it was her own fault, for she was too extravagant, or it was for her own good, because she nagged too much at his extravagance. But when these lines are read in the context of feminist protest, and presumably when they were heard by women familiar with such references, they say clearly, "He beat me, and I didn't like it."

Lament poets hedged their accusations of niggardliness in similar ways. Lines about plenty and want are very common in this poetry and, according to orthodox interpretations, belong to praise of the dead and blame of the guilty, respectively. Only a syllable of negation or a closing couplet of bitter irony—a small verbal clue—needs to be added to the rhythmic verse to turn praise into blame, or back again.

In yet another version of *Caoineadh Airt Uí Laoghaire*, Eileen says, *"Níor thug tú béal ná bata dhom"* ("You gave me neither mouth nor stick")—that is, "You didn't shout at me or beat me." The negative is there, but so is the vivid image.[50]

Lament poets sometimes express protest using a communal rather than a personal voice, drawing attention to the treatment of all or any women by all or any men. Using traditional formulas about stingy husbands, niggardly in-laws, and domestic violence, lament poets passed a rhetoric of resistance along in the tradition, even if in their own productions they discreetly hedged those formulas with negatives and excuses, saying effectively, "My husband has stopped beating me." It matters little whether the lines about sticks and whips were actually spoken by Eileen O'Connell or only later attributed to her; clearly they were part of the currency of lament poetry.

One of the safest ways of expressing anger is to make a joke of it, and the most uncompromising statements of women's protest are found in humorous laments. These, including the following from a satiric lament in which a wife rejoices at the death of her stingy, violent husband, are parodies of the tradition:

> *Mo chiach agus mo thuirse!*
> *Ar a shon gur mise bhí baineann,*
> *Ní mé a bhí amhlaidh ach tusa.*
> *Is tú a chuireadh na cearca chun socairt*
> *Nuair a thógthá an t-im den chuiginn,*
> *Agus mise ag luascadh do linbh*
> *I gcúil i bhfad ón dtine,*
> *Is ná fuighinn féin teacht 'na ngoire.*

> *. . . Do thugthá domhsa*
> *An ceann ba raimhre den mhaide,*
> *An ceann ba chrua den leaba,*
> *An ceann ba chaoile den bheatha,*
> *Agus é sin 'fháil an fhaid a mhairfinn.*

> *A mhic bhodaigh an domblais!*
> *Do shílinn nár mhiste dom,*
> *Dá dtugainn a thuilleadh duit:*
> *Thugas fiche bó baineann duit,*
> *Tarbh chun a dartha duit—*
> *Chuirtheá an fheoil ar salainn*
> *Go málaibh lín is leathair,*
> *Gheobhadh an[?] a mbolaithe*
> *Is ní bhfuighinn féin a mblaise uait.*

> [My sorrow and grief!
> Though I was the female
> You took women's work.
> You were the one
> Who shut in the hens
> And took butter from the churn.
> I sat in the corner

Away from the fire,
Rocking your child,
Not allowed near them!

. . . You used to give me
The thick end of the stick,
The hard side of the bed,
The small bit of food,
—That was all I expected.

You sour-tempered son of a lout!
I wouldn't have grudged you
More than I gave you:
Twenty dairy cows,
With a bull to serve them;
You used to salt the meat
In linen bags and leather bags
You let me smell it,
But never once taste it.]51

Like the son-in-law denounced by Dermot McCarthy's mother, the husband satirized here had violated convention and contract by denying his wife what was legitimately hers.52

These lines are quoted from a mocking lament—sung with a light-hearted, drinking-song type chorus instead of the usual sobs. Their bitterness is "harmless," because it is all just a joke, but jokes mark points of tension, and as the texts already quoted show, the formulas used can all be found in serious laments. "Light-hearted" poems like these, unlike the *caoineadh* proper, were sung as entertainment, but even this function may have originated within the funeral ritual. The merry wake expressed ambivalent attitudes toward death and, like the carnival, mocked social institutions with abusive language and grotesque realism.53 Mock funerals, including keening by hooded women, were among the games played at wakes, and various parodies of the lament tradition exist.54

Two versions of the "humorous" lament for the stingy husband have been published, both collected from men, though both are said to have been composed by women.55 In the case of the one not quoted here, it was performed as part of a *chantefable*, coupled with a story about a husband who pretended to be dead so as to hear what his wife would say about him. This story, the basis of Synge's play *The Shadow of the Glen,* is told in several versions, one more misogynistic than the next, in the southwestern region from which the lament comes.56 Ironically in this case, the tables have been turned again, and women's protest has been appropriated—and defused—by male tradition.

Conclusion

The Irish lament poet, as the various available sources describe her, occupied a marginal position in society while she mourned. At the time of death, however, margins become central as attention is focused on the limits of human life and culture. Clearly, the lament poet was involved in a very precise contract with the living members of her community. It was necessary and right that the dead should be lamented, so the lamenter was able to demand payment as well as attention for herself and for the dead.

She took charge of the formalities of mourning, and by example, exhortation, and criticism, she let other members of the community know what was expected of them. She controlled a large repertoire of poetic diction and imagery, out of which she constructed memorable and influential texts. She passed the skills of mourning and composing lament poetry on to younger women through active performance, recitation, and discussion. In the process, she also transmitted a rhetoric of resistance to abuse and violence and an assertion of the validity of women's experience.

As Radner and Lanser remark at the conclusion of their essay, "ambiguity is a necessary feature of every coded act."[57] All funeral ritual belongs to liminal time—a time of social upheaval, ambivalence, and ambiguity. Lament poetry is composed and performed in a "world upside down," but its images and diction penetrate the everyday, normally structured world. The women who lament also live in society, and laments are remembered and quoted even when the world is right side up. By her expertise in keening, a bereaved woman could demand attention and support at a time of difficult transition in her own life, and ideally this would facilitate her return to normal living.

The Irish lamenter had license to behave and speak disruptively, but her craziness was not the isolating kind that makes people unable to communicate. If lament poets were crazy, it was surely only in the way a quilt may be crazy—in an articulate and structured way and as a creative response to containment.

Notes

Versions of this essay were read at the Annual Meeting of the American Folklore Society in Albuquerque, New Mexico, in October 1987 and at the

Center for Folklore and Ethnomusicology, the University of Texas at Austin, in February 1988. I am grateful to those who attended for their questions and comments and to Phyllis Gorfain, Siobhán Ní Laoire, and Ken Bourke, who read earlier drafts and made helpful comments and suggestions. I also thank my colleagues at University College Dublin for facilitating research leave and Oberlin College for its generous hospitality.

1. For discussion of transition in human culture, see Arnold Van Gennep, *The Rites of Passage* (*Les Rites de passage,* 1909; London: Routledge, 1960); and Victor Turner, *The Ritual Process* (1969; Harmondsworth, England: Penguin Books, 1974).

2. There are occasional examples of men's participation, but this seems always to have been an exception to the rule. For a short account of lament traditions in different parts of the world, see Maria Leach, ed., *Standard Dictionary of Folklore, Mythology, and Legend,* vol. 2 (New York: Funk and Wagnalls, 1949), 754–57. For studies of lament poetry in Greece, see Margaret Alexiou, *The Ritual Lament in Greek Tradition* (Cambridge: Cambridge University Press, 1974), especially 36–51; Anna Caraveli Chaves, "Bridge between Worlds: The Greek Women's Lament as Communicative Event," *Journal of American Folklore* 93, no. 368 (1980): 129–57; and Constantina-Nadia Seremetakis, "Women and Death: Cultural Power and Ritual Process in Inner Mani," *Canadian Woman Studies/Les Cahiers de la Femme* 8, no. 2 (1987): 108–10. For New Guinea, see Steven Feld, *Sound and Sentiment: Birds, Weeping, Poetics and Song in Kaluli Expression* (Philadelphia: University of Pennsylvania Press, 1982). For northern India, see K. M. Tiwary, "Tuneful Weeping: A Mode of Communication," *Frontiers* 3, no. 3 (1978): 24–27. For Finland, see Lauri Honko, "Balto-Finnic Lament Poetry," *Studia Fennica* 17 (1974): 9–61. For African countries, see Ruth Finnegan, *Oral Literature in Africa* (Oxford: Oxford University Press, 1970).

3. Published texts of *caoineadh* include Seán Ó Tuama, ed., *Caoineadh Airt Uí Laoghaire* [The Lament for Art O'Leary] (Dublin: An Clóchomhar, 1961); Risteárd Ó Foghludha's edition of *Caoineadh Shéamuis Mhic Choitir* [The Lament for Sir James Cotter], "Cé Cheap an Caoine," *Irish Press,* April 27, 1936, 4; and editions of *Caoineadh Dhiarmada mhic Eoghain Mhic Chárthaigh* [The Lament for Dermot McCarthy], ed. Gearóid Ó Murchadha and Caitlín Ní Bhuachalla, *Éigse* 1, no. 1 (1939): 22–28, and *Éigse* 1, no. 3 (1939): 185–90. See also Tomás Ó Concheanainn, *Nua-dhuanaire,* vol. 3 (Dublin: Dublin Institute for Advanced Studies, 1978), 9–13. Translations of *Caoineadh Airt Uí Laoghaire* include Eilís Dillon, "The Lament for Arthur O'Leary," *Irish University Review* 1, no. 2 (1971): 198–210; Brendan Kennelly, *The Penguin Book of Irish Verse* (Harmondsworth, England: Penguin Books, 1970), 78–86; and Kenneth Jackson, *A Celtic Miscellany,* rev. ed. (Harmondsworth, England: Penguin Books, 1971), 268–74.

4. Angela Bourke, "The Irish Traditional Lament and the Grieving Process," *Women's Studies International Forum* 11, no. 4 (1988): 287–91; Bourke, *Working and Weeping: Women's Oral Poetry in Irish and Scottish Gaelic,* Women's

Studies Working Papers No. 7 (Dublin: University College Dublin Women's Studies Forum, 1988).

For general literary studies of lament poetry, see two papers by Rachel Bromwich: "The Keen for Art O'Leary, Its Background and Its Place in the Tradition of Gaelic Keening," *Éigse* 5, no. 4 (1948): 236–52; and "The Continuity of the Gaelic Tradition in Eighteenth-Century Ireland," *Yorkshire Celtic Studies* 4 (1947–48): 2–28 (includes translation). For more recent work, see Breandán Ó Madagáin, "Irish Vocal Music of Lament and Syllabic Poetry," in *The Celtic Consciousness*, ed. Robert O'Driscoll (New York: George Braziller, 1982), 311–31; and Seán Ó Coileáin, "The Irish Lament: An Oral Genre," *Studia Hibernica* 24 (1988): 97–117.

Studies published in Irish include a comprehensive introductory essay by Seán Ó Tuama, in his edition of *Caoineadh Airt Uí Laoghaire*, cited above; a two-part article by Tomás Ó hAilín, "Caointe agus Caointeoirí" [Laments and Lamenters] *Feasta* (January 1971): 7–11; (February 1971): 5–9; and a collection of essays, *Gnéithe den Chaointeoireacht* [Aspects of the Lament], ed. Breandán Ó Madagáin (Dublin: An Clóchomhar, 1978).

5. Rosan A. Jordan and F. A. de Caro, "Women and the Study of Folklore," *Signs* 11, no. 3 (1986): 500–518, give several references on p. 511. The "tuneful weeping" discussed by Tiwary is more strongly associated with marriage than with death, and Honko's "Balto-Finnic Lament Poetry" discusses wedding laments at some length.

6. "Bridge between Worlds," 138. See also Anna Caraveli, "The Bitter Wounding: The Lament as Social Protest in Rural Greece," in *Gender and Power in Rural Greece*, ed. Jill Dubisch (Princeton, N.J.: Princeton University Press, 1986), 169–94. Unfortunately, I did not have access to this essay in time to consider it for the present work.

7. Seremetakis, "Women and Death," 108.

8. Seán Ó Súilleabháin, *Irish Wake Amusements* (Cork: Mercier, 1967), 138–43; Pádraig Ferritéar, "Bean Chaointe á Cosaint Féin" [A Lamenter Defends Herself], *Éigse* 1, no. 3 (1939): 222; Ó hAilín, "Caointe agus Caointeoirí," part 1, 10; Ó Madagáin, "Irish Vocal Music," 315.

9. See descriptions of wakes and funerals by Giraldus Cambrensis, *Topographia Hibernica* (1187), quoted by Diarmuid Ó Muirithe, "Tuairiscí na dTaistealaithe," in *Gnéithe den Chaointeoireacht*, ed. Ó Madagáin, 28; Edmund Spenser, *A View of the Present State of Ireland (A Vewe of the Present State of Ireland Discoursed by Way of a Dialogue betwene Eudoxus and Irenius, 1596, by Ed: Spenser Gent.)*, ed. W. L. Renwick (London: Eric Partridge Ltd., at the Scholartis Press, 1934), 72, 81; and William Carleton, *Traits and Stories of the Irish Peasantry* (Dublin: William Curry, Jr., 1843), 104–14.

10. Lament texts were studied "as poetry," with little reference to their oral origin. In any case the only lament texts available for transcription or recording were performed *outside* funeral ritual. See the references cited in note 3.

11. Ó Madagáin, "Irish Vocal Music," 311.

12. It was stipulated that no woman should be left alone to lament and that the number of lamenters should always be uneven. According to convention expressed in religious songs and in verbal accounts of funeral practice, the ideal number of lamenters was three. See Angela Partridge, *Caoineadh na dTrí Muire: Téama na Páise i bhFilíocht Bhéil na Gaeilge* [The Lament of the Three Maries: The Crucifixion in Irish Oral Poetry] (Dublin: An Clóchomhar, 1983), 127–28; and compare Ó Madagáin "Irish Vocal Music," 313. All works cited by Angela Partridge are by the present author.

13. Ó Súilleabháin, *Irish Wake Amusements*, 134–38; Mr. and Mrs. S. C. Hall, *Ireland, Its Scenery, Character, etc.,* vol. 1 (London: Hall, Virtue, 1841), 229 (quotation). For references to paid mourners and many other points of correspondence between the Greek and Irish traditions, see Alexiou, *The Ritual Lament.*

14. John Millington Synge, *The Aran Islands* (Boston: John W. Luce, 1911), 64.

15. See the references in note 9. Modern studies of wake custom include Henry Morris, "Irish Wake Games," *Béaloideas* 8 (1938): 123–41; E. Estyn Evans, *Irish Folk Ways* (London: Routledge and Kegan Paul, 1957), 289–94; Vivian Mercier, *The Irish Comic Tradition* (Oxford: Oxford University Press, 1962), 49–53; Ó Súilleabháin, *Irish Wake Amusements;* and Nina Witoszek, "Ireland: A Funerary Culture?" *Studies* 76, no. 302 (1987): 206–15.

16. Morris, "Irish Wake Games," 132.

17. Mikhail Bakhtin, *Rabelais and His World,* trans. Hélène Iswolsky (Cambridge, Mass.: Harvard University Press, 1940).

18. See Vivian Mercier's discussion of phallic play and mock marriages during wakes, *The Irish Comic Tradition,* 50–53.

19. Nina Witoszek, in "Ireland," uses the term *theatrum mortis* in referring to Irish funeral and mock-funeral ritual. For a discussion of the therapeutic value of *caoineadh,* see Bourke, "The Irish Traditional Lament and the Grieving Process."

20. Rosemary Harris, *Prejudice and Tolerance in Ulster: A Study of Neighbours and Strangers in a Border Community* (1972; Manchester: Manchester University Press, 1986), 114. Women were otherwise very isolated in this community, as "unrelated women did not visit" (84). Harris gives several accounts of the importance of wakes and funerals in Irish social life and the obligation felt by all neighbors to attend.

21. See, for instance, *The Aran Fisherman's Drowned Child* by Frederick William Burton (1816–1900), at the National Gallery of Ireland, Dublin, and the engravings in Hall's *Ireland.*

22. Albert B. Lord, *The Singer of Tales* (Cambridge, Mass.: Harvard University Press, 1960).

23. Bourke, *Working and Weeping.* For information on the waulking tradition and texts of songs, see John Lorne Campbell and Francis Collinson, *Hebridean Folksongs,* 3 vols. (Oxford: Oxford University Press, 1969, 1977, 1981); Margaret Fay Shaw, *Folksongs and Folklore of South Uist* (1955; Oxford:

Oxford University Press, 1977); and Alexander Fenton, "Waulking the Cloth," in *Gold under the Furze: Studies in Folk Tradition presented to Caoimhín Ó Danachair,* ed. Alan Gailey and Daithí Ó hÓgáin (Dublin: Glendale, 1983), 129–37.

24. See Jennifer Fox, "The Creator Gods: Romantic Nationalism and the Engenderment of Women in Folklore," *Journal of American Folklore* 100, no. 398 (1987): 563–72; and compare Gearóid Ó Crualaoich, "The Primacy of Form: A Folk Ideology in de Valera's Politics," in *De Valera and His Times,* ed. John Caroll and John A. Murphy (Cork: Cork University Press, 1983), 47–61.

25. See Diarmuid Ó Muirithe, "Tuairiscí na dTaistealaithe" [Accounts by Travelers], in *Gnéithe den Chaointeoireacht,* ed. Ó Madagáin, 20–29. For the aesthetics of keening, "good criers and bad criers," see Irish Folklore Collection (University College, Dublin), ms. vol. 815: 183.

26. Partridge, *Caoineadh na dTrí Muire,* 94–95.

27. *A View of the Present State of Ireland,* 81.

28. Brian Ó Cuív, "The Romance of Mis and Dubh Ruis," *Celtica* 2 (1954): 327. Drinking the blood of the dead is also mentioned in Ó Tuama, *Caoineadh Airt Uí Laoghaire,* 35, and in several Scottish Gaelic folksongs. See Campbell and Collinson, *Hebridean Folksongs,* vol. 1, 14.

29. James G. O'Keeffe, *Buile Suibhne (The Frenzy of Suibhne), Being the Adventures of Suibhne Geilt, a Middle Irish Romance* (London: Irish Texts Society, 1913). For a modern rendering of this text, see Seamus Heaney, *Sweeney Astray: A Version from the Irish* (New York: Farrar Straus Giroux, 1983). In an earlier essay, I compared the two categories and pointed out that laments employ motifs normally associated with the literature of insanity and often speak explicitly of the lament poet as mad, crazy, or out of her mind. See Angela Partridge, "Wild Men and Wailing Women," *Éigse* 18, no. 1 (1980): 25–37.

30. Partridge, *Caoineadh na dTrí Muire,* 98–99 (translated).

31. Quoted in Ó hAilín, "Caointe agus Caointeoirí," part 1, 10.

32. See the discussion of the strategy of distraction in Joan N. Radner and Susan S. Lanser, "Strategies of Coding in Women's Cultures," herein.

33. *A View of the Present State of Ireland,* 72; see also Ó Muirithe, "Tuairiscí na dTaistealaithe," 20–21.

34. Mícheál Ó Gaoithín, *Beatha Pheig Sayers* [The Life of Peig Sayers] (Dublin: Foilseacháin Náisiúnta, 110 (translated).

35. David Buchan, *The Ballad and the Folk* (London: Routledge and Kegan Paul, 1972). An analysis of lament texts shows that most follow the traditional paradigm of customary themes as described by Bromwich, "The Keen for Art O'Leary," 242–43. Examination in the light of modern theories of grief shows that many include several changes of mood, incorporating expression of all the "stages" of the grieving process. See Bourke, "The Traditional Lament and the Grieving Process."

36. "A bhean úd thall a rinne an gáire!" is a common opening line in

Scottish Gaelic waulking songs (see Campbell and Collinson, *Hebridean Folksongs*). It is also found in laments and songs in Irish.

37. Ó Coileáin, "The Irish Lament."

38. Ó Tuama's 1961 edition of *Caoineadh Airt Uí Laoghaire* used several sources, chief of which was a transcription made around 1800 from the oral recital of Norrie Singleton, a young woman who lived twelve miles from where Art was shot dead in 1773. Ó Tuama constructed his 390-line text from this text, another collected much later from the same informant, and several shorter texts from oral tradition, some of which were attributed to other lament poets. Whole passages of this poem are almost identical to parts of the lament for Sir James Cotter, hanged in 1720 (see Ó Foghludha, "Cé Cheap an Caoine?").

39. Bromwich, "The Keen for Art O'Leary," 243. Rocking back and forth while repeating a poetic formula may have assisted the lamenter in altering her state of consciousness, like a *mantra* used in meditation. Compare the description by J. M. Synge, quoted earlier.

40. Ó Tuama, *Caoineadh Airt Uí Laoghaire*, 36. The translation and all those that follow are by the author.

41. Ní Bhuachalla, "Caoine ar Dhiarmuid Mac Cárthaigh," 185–90. For the accounts of Dermot's mother's walk across the mountains, see Ó Concheanainn, *Nua-Dhuanaire*, 9, 75, 76.

42. Bourke, *Working and Weeping;* Partridge, *Caoineadh na dTrí Muire,* 90–91.

43. Verbal disputes between lamenters usually involved in-laws. Each woman defended the honor of her own family of origin or asserted the primacy of her own relationship with the deceased.

44. Ó Foghludha, "Cé Cheap an Caoine?"

45. For a similar convention in Greek tradition, see Alexiou, *The Ritual Lament,* 182.

46. For gender-role division in rural Ireland and an account of the economic basis of small-farm life, see Conrad Arensberg and Solon T. Kimball, *Family and Community in Ireland* (Cambridge, Mass.: Harvard University Press, 1940), 202–3 and passim. Land and cattle—the main forms of wealth—were seen as belonging to the male line of the family, to be passed on to male heirs (80). When a daughter married, cattle were given to the new husband as dowry, or "fortune," but these were never the woman's own property; they passed from her father or brother to her husband (107–22, 140–41). A woman who did not marry could look forward to a life without adult status; at fifty she would still be a "girl," while her brother's twenty-five-year-old wife would be a "woman" (66, 216). The wife in a farm family not only had adult status but also earned an independent income of sorts: making butter and feeding hens were her responsibility, and the profit from them belonged to her (48).

For discussions of gender roles in rural Ireland in the 1950s and 1970s, see Harris, *Prejudice and Tolerance;* Nancy Scheper-Hughes, *Saints, Scholars, and*

Schizophrenics (Berkeley: University of California Press, 1979); and Scheper-Hughes, "From Anxiety to Analysis: Rethinking Irish Sexuality and Sex Roles," *Women's Studies* 10 (1983): 147–60.

47. Ní Bhuachalla, "Caoine ar Dhiarmuid Mac Cárthaigh," 188–89. The gifts mentioned would have been the daughter's dowry, a capital contribution made to the marriage on her behalf that was expected to guarantee her a decent livelihood. See the preceding note. The poet quoted here is defending the economic honor of her own family while attacking that of her son-in-law.

48. Ó Tuama, *Caoineadh Airt Uí Laoghaire*, 45.

49. Ibid., 78, 82, 85. Text written down in 1933 from a Mrs. O'Connor, aged sixty-eight, who had learned it from her mother (who died in 1925 at the age of eighty-seven), includes the following lines (ibid., 82):

> *Thugathá ceannas dom,*
> *Rince ar halla dhom,*
> *Párlús á ghlanadh dhom*
> *Is bácús á dheargadh—*
> *'Dtaobh gur leathadh ort*
> *Go dtugathá an maide dhom*
> *Is fuip cinn airgid.*
> *Anois ós marbh duit,*
> *Bainimse barra astu*
> *Ná bítheá in earraid liom,*
> *Mura n'éireodh sparainn duit*
> *Agus bheith ar mhaithe liom*
> *De bharr a laghad a scaipinn ort,*
> *Mar do bhís rabairneach*
> *Agus croí chun caite agat*
> *Agus bhínn á chasadh leat.*

> [You put me in charge,
> You took me dancing,
> Had the parlour cleaned for me
> And the oven heated—
> Because it was said
> That you often took a stick to me
> And a silver-handled whip.
> Now that you're dead
> I can assert
> That you never scolded
> Unless you were angry
> And that was for my own good,
> For I spent so little on you.
> You were extravagant
> With a taste for spending
> And I nagged you because of it.]

50. Alf Mac Lochlainn, "Caoineadh Airt Uí Laoghaire, Leagan as Lámhscríbhinn," *Studia Hibernica* 12 (1972): 116.

51. Angela Partridge, " 'Is Beo Duine tar éis a Bhuailte': Caoineadh Magaidh as Béara" ["A Person Can Survive a Beating": A Mock Lament from Beare Island], *Sinsear* 3 (1981): 70–76.

52. See notes 46 and 47.

53. The lines that follow those quoted above are *"Mo chiach agus mo chreach! / Is tusa féin a íosfadh an cnap / Is ná déanfadh de dhá leath, / Is é a shlogadh siar id' chliabh / Is arís id' thaobh eile amach!* [My sorrow and destruction! / You used to eat the lot / —You never would divide it— / And swallow it down inside / And out the other end!]." For carnivalesque uses of grotesque realism and abusive language, see Bakhtin, *Rabelais and His World.*

54. The following text, from the Irish Folklore Collection (University College, Dublin), ms. vol. 259: 497 (Ring, County Waterford), was apparently composed in English: "If I had you at Christmas / I had you at Easter / And now your old breeches / Lies under the table, / *Ochón ó!*" For mock funerals at wakes, see Morris, "Irish Wake Games," 125.

55. In addition to the text quoted, see Pádraig Ó Siocfhradha, "Caoine Magaidh (A Mock Lament)," *Journal of the Irish Folk Song Society* 19 (1922): 21–23.

56. See Éilís Ní Dhuibhne-Almquist, "Synge's Use of Popular Material in *The Shadow of the Glen*," *Béaloideas* 58 (1990): 141–80.

57. "Strategies of Coding," herein.

"How They Knew": Women's Talk about Healing on Kodiak Island, Alaska

JOANNE B. MULCAHY

When Julia Wolkoff describes her days as a traditional midwife on Kodiak Island, her face grows animated with memory: "You have to have a HEART to do that! Not to be scared . . . you have to be strong." Katherine Chichenoff, one of Kodiak's Native elders, echoes a refrain heard from women throughout Kodiak Island when she recalls the midwife's care during the births of her ten children: "You know Julia Wolkoff? She KNOWS how to do it. I don't know how she learned. Thank God she did. All my babies were born by midwife. They were just clean. . . . Really good! I would never go to a doctor."[1]

Kodiak Native American women's stories about childbirth and midwifery are peppered with phrases about "helping," "knowing," and "having a heart." Through their talk and the central metaphor of "knowing," women re-create and affirm a way of life and a time when Native women held important roles as healers.[2] Since European contact in the mid-eighteenth century, their position and authority have been gradually usurped by Western health care practitioners as part of a broader transformation of Native life. Women, particularly the elders, however, continue to tell stories about the importance of the village midwife, the power of a tribal doctor named Oleanna Ashouwak, and traditional healing based on intuitive "knowing." Further, according to oral testimony and in contrast to the written record, Western and traditional healing systems coexisted into the mid-twentieth century. These stories stress the importance of traditional healing as a metaphor for the Native worldview and identity that women have sustained through periods of rapid culture change.

This essay explores the ways in which Kodiak women's stories communicate the continued importance of this worldview through talk about women's roles as healers. It is based on oral history interviews conducted with women on Kodiak Island between 1979 and 1988. Comparisons are made between the beliefs embodied in the elders' narratives and the emerging stories of a younger generation. Examining women's stories about healing offers insights into aspects of Kodiak's history and culture as well as women's communicative strategies. These narratives provide an opportunity to "read" women's stories critically as expressions of a historically situated set of beliefs. Although women's status cross-culturally has received greater scrutiny from social scientists in the past few decades, analysis has often supported essentialist arguments built on Western cultural categories. Universal explanations of sexual asymmetry or gender equality often ignore actual political, economic, and cultural circumstances and the creative ways in which women deal with them. Many feminist scholars are now looking instead at more culturally specific models and historically based analysis for understanding women's lives. Following this focus, this essay illuminates how Native women have communicated aspects of cultural identity in one particular setting, allowing us to hear the "different voices in which [women] fashion and refashion themselves."[3] Changes in women's self-perception and social roles emerge through generational differences in women's stories about healing. A complete history of gender relations or changes in health care systems on Kodiak is beyond the scope of this essay. Attention here focuses on those aspects of women's narratives that have encoded and maintained Native identity and self-esteem in the face of cultural suppression.

Kodiak women's narratives creatively reproduce and affirm the values of Native culture through talk about women's powers as healers. Midwives held the central position as healers on Kodiak until well into the twentieth century. Among the older generation, whose worldview is dominated by Russian Orthodoxy, women's narratives assert a continued belief in women's power and the superiority of traditional life, including Native healing. This story of traditional midwifery in women's oral narratives is not, however, well represented in the written cultural histories. Since women's experiences have been viewed as supplements to or deviations from the norm, their lives are often absent from recorded oral narratives of Kodiak Natives as well.[4] While Native views of history have been generally neglected, women have been doubly silenced by inattention to those aspects of culture deemed worthy to record in oral histories.

In addition, the Native celebration of a traditional way of life that women's stories express was not an acceptable cultural message until recently. The history of European and then U.S. colonization of

Alaska has followed the all too familiar scenario of alternating exploitation, neglect, and attempted assimilation of Native people. If professions of Native pride have been unacceptable, the assertion that a Native women's healing tradition is superior to Western medicine would have been perceived as doubly threatening. To avoid stigma, older Native women communicate their beliefs through narratives about "knowing" and the power of religious belief. *Knowing* describes an intuitive, religious understanding not easily reducible to Western notions of medical efficacy. Learning to interpret women's stories, one can read their statements as indirect commentary on the hierarchical, tightly structured, and male-controlled Western medical system to which their healing practices and Native way of life stand diametrically opposed.[5]

In contrast, younger women openly assert their desire to maintain and in some cases to re-create Native ways of life, including health care. They also express a preference for women as health providers, despite the continued dominance in Kodiak of a Western male-controlled medical system. They describe practices that combine medical knowledge and Native spirituality, but without the dominant dimension of Russian Orthodoxy so striking in older women's narratives.

Stories of both generations can be read as celebrations of a predominantly female realm. While women on Kodiak would not likely characterize themselves as feminists, their statements clearly establish women's historical power as healers and can be read as intended messages about that power.[6] Through distinct and creative communicative modes, an older generation of women has kept alive important aspects of traditional Native values and identity. To understand the narratives and worldview of Kodiak's elders, it is essential to look among their granddaughters, who are not afraid to straightforwardly assert the superiority of Native ways and are in some cases actually returning to midwifery as part of a general revitalization of Native culture.

The Historical Setting of Kodiak Island

Women's stories about healing are best heard in the context of other versions of history. Kodiak, which lies 250 miles southwest of Anchorage in the Gulf of Alaska, has been a meeting ground of different cultures for centuries. The island's Native people have adapted to turbulent change since the time of Russian contact in the mid-eighteenth century. Written histories of Kodiak reflect a predominantly male perspective built on early ethnographies and ethnohistories, the records of Russian missionaries and early explorers, and the narratives of U.S. military personnel, teachers, and travelers. These accounts chronicle the steady march of "progress" toward modernization and an increased dependence on Western technology. This occurred in tandem with a gradual loss of Native language, culture, and political autonomy.

In this framework, a history of health care traces the early healing roles of the shaman and midwife/herbalist to the present dominance of a Western medical system. In precontact times, shamans, usually male, were called on to cure extreme cases, control weather conditions, foresee the future, and heal in cases that required a manipulation of the spirit forces underlying illness. Everyday healing of both men and women was attended to by the midwife/herbalist. She had an extensive knowledge of plants, midwifery, lancing, and other surgical techniques. Although Kodiak's healers were skilled practitioners, they proved unable to handle the onslaught of such epidemics as smallpox, brought by the Russians colonizing Alaska in the eighteenth and nineteenth centuries.[7] Letters from teachers and other personnel based on Kodiak after the U.S. purchase document the government's attempts to discourage any continued practice by Native healers, often regarded as "witch doctors." Given these attitudes, one could easily conclude that Native healers eventually died out on Kodiak, completely disappearing by the early part of this century. Official history stresses the role of the U.S. government in saving the Native population from the ravages of subsequent infectious diseases, particularly the tuberculosis epidemic of the 1940s and 1950s. The remainder of the century is regarded as a steady and unquestionably progressive movement toward the present health care model.[8] By mandate from the U.S. Indian Health Service operating within a Western medical context, women now deliver their children in the hospital in Anchorage or Kodiak.

Women's stories, in contrast, stress not change but continuity in both Native values and practice. According to oral testimony, there were long periods in which the two medical systems coexisted, particularly in the villages. What is often obscured in historical accounts is that following the U.S. purchase of Alaska in 1867, the government all but ignored the health needs of the territory, and indigenous healers continued to provide primary health care. Infectious diseases continued to decimate the Native population until a centrally administered Western health care system was established in the 1950s. Even after Western physicians became available in the town of Kodiak, many women who either could not afford the doctor's fees or preferred the midwife continued to seek her care. In the villages, some of the midwives and a tribal doctor named Oleanna Ashouwak were practicing until well into the 1960s. Further, in contrast to what one would expect given the written sources, women's stories stress how much healthier people were in the past and how superior their childbirth experiences with the village midwives were.

The Village Midwives

The role of the Kodiak midwife historically and symbolically reflects the importance of childbirth as a biosocial construct with universal, physiological dimensions and cultural richness and specificity. Cross-cultural studies emphasize birth as a process whose form and function vary widely in different societies. It is, as one researcher described, "at once a biological process and a cultural event shaped and defined by attitudes toward women, toward medical knowledge and authority, and toward nature itself."[9] Women's narratives about giving birth place the event in the rich texture of their lives and culture and in relation to other folk medical practices.[10] On Kodiak, women's recollections carry the threads of historical memory back to the earliest women healers. These midwife/herbalists provided a general knowledge of herbs and plants as well as care for more specific ailments. Women best remember the preparation and process of childbirth, however. In a literal sense of healing, to make whole, the midwives eased women through a time of social transition and provided a strong base of support for the process of birth. They brought women to the *banyas* (steambaths, from the Russian for *bath,* or in Alutiiq, *maqiwik*) for prenatal care from as early as three months gestation. These served to foster relaxation and to "fix" the baby's position. The midwives used massage, heat, and steamed alder branches called *wainiiks* to reposition the fetus and ensure an easy delivery. This repositioning of the fetus through massage compares with practices in other areas of Alaska as well as other cultures.[11] Women insist they had short labors and few complications in the days of midwifery. Clyda Christensen of the village of Larsen Bay speaks for many Kodiak women when she insists, "Our babies were just small before. We didn't have problems!"

"People were healthier then" is a repeated phrase, one that links birth as a symbol to women's belief in the superiority of Native ways of life. The midwives helped throughout the delivery and offered several weeks of postpartum care. They often stayed in a woman's home, cooking, cleaning, and helping care for the infant. The sense of being cared for and supported, and of establishing a sense of community through "helping," is an ongoing refrain in women's accounts.

To be a midwife required emotional strength. It was a calling and a respected position in the community. Some midwives were appointed by village elders, but in Kodiak's larger villages, a meeting was called to decide on the apprenticeship of younger women. Nida Chya of Old Harbor recalls, "Before they used to hold a meeting, you know . . . to see if we like this lady to be a midwife. They never used to take just ANYBODY. They have to let the ladies know first, if it's o.k. with them, you know. . . . " There was usually more than one midwife to aid and give support through the birth process.

To be a midwife also required expertise. Women learned midwifery in a variety of ways, ranging from informal observation to formal apprenticeship. Many learned from a mother, grandmother, or another community midwife, although some were self-taught, relying on observation and the experience of bearing their own children. Women learned massage, the use of *wainiiks* in the *banya,* knowledge of plants and medicinal herbs, and a range of other diagnostic and treatment skills. They used herbal teas from local plants and sometimes a drink made of charcoal to ensure the discharge of the afterbirth. Other folk remedies displayed women's ingenuity, a fact they proudly relate in their narratives. Nida Chya tells of rubbing the belly button with oil where the umbilical cord was cut and then placing a raisin over it to induce healing. One midwife from Karluk recalled devising small boxes for placing premature twins in a slightly warmed oven as a makeshift incubator. Women still talk of the older midwives' using a small knife to "lance" above a woman's wrist and then drawing out the "bad blood" with a small horn after childbirth. All of these stories stress women's creative response to their local environment in learning the skills essential to establish both biological and cultural continuity, forging generational ties.

In women's descriptions of learning and practicing midwifery, there is a level of understanding beyond the learning of skills. Knowledge of healing encompasses diagnosis and treatment and is attributed not to worldly instruction but to a spiritual understanding described simply as "knowing." These descriptions of birth as a well-defined ritual that lends order to a process beyond human control are similar to folk practices in many other cultures; they differ substantially from the modern medical model. Oleanna Ashouwak and the village midwives just "knew" how to turn a baby, feel a pulse, and predict a delivery date or a child's sex. Julia Pestrikoff of the village of Port Lions recalls that "in those days, they just feel around and some of them know, too, if it's going to be a boy or a girl, just by feeling. I don't know how they KNEW. . . . " The midwives are also often described as devout Russian Orthodox women whose power came from God.

Ninety-year-old Katherine Chichenoff articulates the importance of the midwife's knowledge: "The midwives before, they were so good! They wouldn't let us up. Eight days we had to stay in bed. They took such good care of you. They were so good. They took care of the babies, wash your clothes, and take care of you. We were really spoiled! . . . The midwife, she KNOWS how to do it. Do you know Julia Wolkoff? She knows how to do it. I don't know how she learned it. Thank God for that. . . . " Mary Peterson of Akhiok offers a more straightforward explanation of how she "knew": "First time by myself, I happened to be home alone when one of the girls was ready to have her baby. I guess it was one of my sisters. So, I delivered her baby and it was like I had been doing it for a long time. I just KNEW, you know, knew what to do, like there was somebody with me, but using my hands and my mind. No fear, no worry, or excitement. Only after the baby was born, when I got everything done, got the mother settled and drinking tea, then I started shaking and sweating all over! When I think about it, it was like coming out of a trance, like it wasn't me. I always think that God was using my hands to help this lady."

Another motif in women's stories that reinforces the sense of knowing as some kind of second sight is that of the blind midwife. Accounts can be heard in every village of the old blind woman who, through an acute sensitivity and knowledge, could simply feel, deliver children, and diagnose a person's condition. Nida Chya of Old Harbor recalls her grandmother's legendary status: "My mother's mother, she used to deliver the babies all by herself. She was blind! She was a blind lady. My cousin remembers her. She got nineteen kids, over seventy grandchildren. . . . Irene used to tell me, 'Your grandmother used to be a great, great midwife!' She delivered babies blind." Clyda Christensen of Larsen Bay relates a similar account, which has counterparts all over the island: "There was my mother-in-law from my first husband, Katherine Melcoulie. She was the midwife for thirty-five years after she got blind! And before that, too, she was the midwife. But she was blind for thirty-five years and was still the midwife. She always used to know someone is sick, just by feeling them. By FEEL, she knew what was wrong, by feeling their pulse, up here, and then here, just feeling and feeling."

Mary Peterson's stories about Oleanna Ashouwak, a woman who was central to the village communities on the southern end of Kodiak, affirm both the historical importance and the religious nature of women's healing power. Oleanna, who lived from 1909 until 1965 and practiced a wide variety of healing techniques, was widely respected by people on Kodiak, though little known beyond the island.[12] Mary

Peterson recalls, "She was really something. She just KNEW! She helped the midwives, too. I guess she just liked taking care of people. She felt that it was her job to do." Rena Peterson of Akhiok, who was raised and subsequently trained by Oleanna, echoes Mary's memories: "She KNEW how to help people. She used a little knife when you have bad headaches, from behind your head, and then they use that cow's horn and suck the blood out." Nina Zeedar, an elder from Old Harbor, recalls that Oleanna learned from her mother, a blind healer in Kaguyak: "Her mother was blind, but she knew what roots to use for medicine. Even though she's blind, she just knew."

Other stories about Oleanna more openly critique Western medicine by pitting traditional against modern ways. Mary Peterson remembers, "Oh, she fixed me once! I had kidney problems so bad that I was like an old person. She checked and took both of my pulses, and she KNOWS! She could tell what's wrong. I didn't tell her, but she knows. She gave me hot packs for three days. After she hot packed me, she sat on top of a pillow, and I'd sit in front of her, and she'd hold my head, feel for the pulse. On the third day after this, I felt like I wanted to run around. I never had any problems since. When I came back up to Anchorage for a check-up, they could never figure out what happened."

In measuring Western against traditional medicine, women also provide covert criticism through selective memory. Children who died in birth are often lost to the distant past, but recollections of the midwives' successes remain as strong as those of the physician's failures. Julia Pestrikoff recounted the births of her four children, only to be reminded by her sister Alice that she had forgotten the one who died in childbirth. "Oh, I always forget," she exclaimed. In contrast, she recalled years later a delivery by a doctor in town that left her with "trouble in my womb." She used a local plant and advice from the midwife to cure herself: "I used to put those over hot water, and just, you know, sit and steam. Other than that, I probably would have had a cancer because my womb was torn in a knot for seven and a half years. When I asked the doctor later why he had sewed it back together, he said, 'How come you decided to ask me after all these years?' I said, 'Well, I just wanted to know if there was an infection.' He said, 'There was but I scraped it and I must have not done a good job.'"

These critiques of Western medicine are based on its alignment with features of life and healing strictly opposed to Native ways: the separation of healer from patient, the cash exchanged for the "service" of childbirth, and the segregation of the birth process from the flow of everyday life. These are in turn part of a broader juxtaposition of two essentially opposing worldviews, one exemplified by Native women's roles as "helpers" in village life, the other by the medical system's "delivery" of the baby in a hospital.[13]

Native Worldview, Russian Orthodoxy, and Western Medicine

Women's descriptions of the midwives' work and of Oleanna's power are part of an overarching Native cultural world in which healing had a central place. Although the importance and skill of Kodiak's indigenous healers has been highlighted in historical documentation, their status as women and the meaning of their roles to the community have never been explored. When women talk about the midwife's work, they treat it as a symbol of traditional life, which they contrast with life today. The past was a time of lush gardens, subsistence living, helpfulness to one's neighbors, shared resources, and uniformly better health. The midwives' knowledge was part of that specifically Native way of understanding the world. In this context, childbirth was a part of community life, not a segregated medical event. The midwives' work was essential to social cooperation, not unlike baking bread for a neighbor, helping bring in a full fishnet, or performing other acts that reflected community spirit. Traditional life is juxtaposed against the "now" of a cash economy, competition for resources, individual struggles for attainment, and such health problems as alcoholism and violence. Elders recount their preference for the old days, when times were better and the world was infused with the elders' knowledge. They use the past, particularly the strong traditions and religious significance of Russian Orthodoxy, to comment on the present. Marina Waselie remembers, "My mother-in-law used to say before, 'These days, these coming years, you hear somebody walking, maybe real good, maybe two, three, four days, and then dead!' She used to say, 'People will die without sickness.' She used to say it. Nowadays, people you see walking, in a week or maybe six days, they're dead. Sure enough. I don't know how they KNEW. They didn't have no school. I don't know how they learned those words. She used to say, 'You believe in God, God and his mother, and they'll help you. If you forget to guard God's words and pray to God, then he won't help you. That's true.'"

The "knowing" of Mary Peterson and the other midwives and of Oleanna Ashouwak is linked to a particular set of cultural and religious beliefs. These mirror practices and beliefs documented in other areas of Alaska. Oleanna's understanding compares with the "second sight" of healers from northwestern Alaska, who apprenticed with tribal doctor Della Keats. Anthropologist Edith Turner, in documenting healing practices at Point Hope, reports that this "direct kind of knowledge" involves a "multitude of senses" and a deep religious faith. At Point Hope, the spiritual dimension is a blend of Native and Protestant beliefs (versus Russian Orthodox beliefs on Kodiak), but the descriptions are otherwise quite similar. Della Keats's second sight allowed her to know a person's illness before seeing him or her. She is quoted as saying, "I just pray to my Good Lord. I pray all night, and before I arrive in sick person's village, my Good Lord tells me what's wrong." Similarly, Della's apprentice, Rose Ella Stone, responded to Turner's question about how she learned healing with "I taught myself. I knew."[14]

These stories reveal the importance of the Russian Orthodox church in Native life on Kodiak and establish a link between women's healing power, the knowledge of the elders, and Native spirituality. In Kodiak's Native identity, it is impossible to segregate strictly Native from Russian beliefs and practices. Although the Russian fur traders who began the colonization of Alaska exploited the Native people, the monks who closely followed tried to mitigate the damage through the creation of schools, an orthography for the Alutiiq language, and a literate creole population.[15] In a turn from cultural domination to synthesis, Russian culture, particularly the spiritual dimension, became part of, not a substitution for, Native identity. Although the place of the Russian experience in Alaskan Native life is not uniformly agreed upon by historians, many have argued that the history of Russian America followed a different pattern than colonization elsewhere in North America. In contrast to the U.S. policies that suppressed most aspects of Native culture and nearly destroyed many Native languages, the Russians encouraged bilingual, bicultural education and literacy. Further, even those historians who argue against the importance of this bicultural identity acknowledge that the legacy of Russian life in Alaska remains most marked today in Orthodox traditions.[16]

"Knowing" to Native women on Kodiak symbolizes a series of complex and often overlapping spheres. It is a distinctly Native understanding, one realized in the elders' worldview. In the realm of health care, it is a specifically female understanding, a powerful symbol of what is most valued by Native women. It embodies community spirit, helping as the heart of healing, and the subsistence lifestyle of precontact village life. In all cases, knowing is infused with the spiritual dimension of Russian Orthodoxy. Traditional healing stands counterpoised to the complex economic system and separate health institutions of the now dominant non-Native culture.

The linkage of the religious symbolism of Russian Orthodoxy to the midwives' knowledge has another layer of significance. Russian Orthodoxy is an inherently ambiguous symbol. It is both an integral part of Native identity and, as an institutional structure, part of the Western, male-dominated cultural system. Coding women's power and "knowing" as religious protects women from attacks on "primitive" Native practices, such as lancing. Since the church is part of the established structure, spiritual "knowledge" becomes legitimate in a way it could not be as a pre-Christian Native power. Further, women's power seems more contained when expressed in the context of a male-dominated institution. It is, however, also an aspect of Kodiak life now well integrated into Native identity. As such, the power of women's knowledge is clearly a specifically Native understanding, one regarded as superior to Western thought. The use of spiritual symbolism allows women to offer an oblique criticism of modernization, including Western health care. Given the history of Russian and U.S. domination of Alaska Natives, the implicit criticism of westernization contained in women's stories likely could not find direct voice. Couched in the language of religion, however, the midwives' power is less threatening to the established order of Western medicine. Using this coding device, Kodiak women protect themselves from possible reprisals while maintaining the integrity of their message about the superiority of Native life for those empowered to hear it.[17]

Changes Today: The 1988 Midwifery Workshop

The ambiguity of Russian Orthodoxy as a symbol allows it to serve as a vehicle for the complexity of women's messages. It is open to the interpretation of the listener to decide how to decode women's messages about "knowing." Further, these are messages that are changing on Kodiak today. Important shifts in the past few decades have altered the nature of women's stories. The current movement to reclaim Native land is paralleled in the cultural sphere. In the wake of the 1971 Alaska Native Claims Settlement Act (ANCSA) and other political developments in Alaska, Native people all over the state are projecting renewed cultural identities.[18] Native groups are revitalizing those aspects of indigenous culture threatened by the Western influences that have permeated life in this century, often with destructive results. Although the written history of Alaskan life records a linear movement toward Western progress, there have been ironic twists in the story. Westernization and increased technology have occurred in tandem with a rise in alcohol abuse and the attendant ills of suicide, violence, and other behavioral illness.[19] Previous assumptions about the benefits of progress are now being questioned as Native people move toward greater autonomy and away from dependence on Western culture. Elders' conferences, often organized through Native non-profit groups, have been held for the past decade by Native groups throughout the state. They serve as important arenas for reassessing the values of traditional culture in new contexts. Given the need to combat alcoholism and violence, one area of particular significance is health care. Traditional healing has emerged as a symbol for community life and Native values and as a metaphor for a more inclusive cultural healing. Indigenous healers, such as Della Keats, are now recognized as significant contributors to the community in unique ways not measurable by Western standards.

On Kodiak, this movement has taken hold more slowly than in other areas of Alaska.[20] Changes in Native self-perception and public expression have been gaining momentum since the early 1970s. These shifts have been reflected in new language and cultural programs, in the increased importance of the Kodiak Area Native Association as a community institution, and in Native participation in political life. Two events in 1988 brought the importance of these changes to greater public awareness. The first Kodiak Cultural Heritage Conference was held in the spring of 1988, bringing together scholars from Europe and the lower forty-eight states to address the importance of Kodiak's cultural legacy. A women's conference, also sponsored by the Kodiak Area Native Association, was held at the same time, and within that context, several of the Native midwives came together to discuss the meaning and significance of their work. Although Native midwifery has not risen as a rival to the now entrenched Western health care system, it is symbolically important that the midwives chose to gather publicly. The differences between these younger women's narratives about Native healing and those of the elders' generation were striking. Strategies for talking about healing and Native culture and the changes in self-perception that younger women's stories reflect had gradually shifted over a period of time. The conference was a public arena in which those changes could be communicated to a larger audience.

One attendant at the session was Rena Petersen of Akhiok, who had been raised and trained by Oleanna Ashouwak. In the past there has been a general air of secrecy surrounding discussions of Oleanna with outsiders and even with Kodiak Natives. Fear of condemnation as "primitive" by medical practitioners, teachers, and other representatives of Western culture kept knowledge of Oleanna's lancing, holding, and other techniques underground for years.[21] Here, however, Rena talked openly about learning how to "hold" a person and feel his or her pulse until a state of health is restored. She was accompanied by Annie Petersen, whom Rena is training to take over the practices that she learned from Oleanna. Both spoke about the importance of carrying on the traditions of Native health care.

In addition to the public nature of the discussion, it was striking how little religion was linked to the explanation of a healer's power. This is particularly noteworthy because religious belief continues to play a powerful part in Native life, especially in the realm of healing. The majority of Native people on Kodiak are Russian Orthodox, although various other Christian groups are gaining converts. Most of the community health aides who now serve the villages in concert with itinerant teams of doctors are religious Native women.[22] While the health care system has changed significantly, these women maintain a position similar in many ways to that of the traditional midwife. A recent issue of the Kodiak Area Native Association newsletter described the health aide's role as that of "doctor, care giver, mother and priest."[23] One community health aide, Betty Nelson of Port Lions, related her own position to that of her mother-in-law, a traditional midwife from the village of Afognak: "I know now just how she felt, having to take care of every little thing!" Further, Old Harbor's health aide Stella Stanley, in describing the stresses of the job, stated, "When I get burnt out, it's going to church that really helps." Given the continued connections between religion and healing, it was surprising that the cloak of religious symbolism for "knowing" was no longer deemed necessary. Women's power is now being asserted as secular Native medical practice without fear of condemnation.

This was evident throughout Rena Petersen's discussion of Oleanna's practice, particularly her diagnostic techniques. Oleanna knew what was wrong with someone, Rena surmised, by the "pounding of the pulse" and through other skills she had learned from her mother. Also noteworthy were the contributions of Barbara Boskofsky of Old Harbor, a woman who learned midwifery from her grandmother and has now begun to practice again. Barbara has delivered the children of her daughter, Juanita, to whom she is passing on her knowledge. Barbara is deeply religious, but she also expressed her belief in Native healing practices quite apart from religion. After she explained that her grandmother had correctly predicted her delivery date, I asked if that was an intuitive kind of "second sight." Barbara responded, "My grandmother, I asked her, you know, how can you tell, how did you KNOW that I was ready to deliver, and she said, 'It depends upon how far my fingers can go into your pelvic bone. When the tips of my fingers can't reach in there to a certain part, then you're ready.'"

In contrast to the knowing described by the older midwives, Barbara and the generation now revitalizing Native practices describe healing knowledge as learned behavior. Women had fewer problems in the past, she pointed out, because they ate Native foods, "especially seal meat because of the iron," and because of the excellent care provided by the midwife, particularly in the steambaths. The women at the Kodiak Women's Conference also seemed comfortable with stating a preference for a woman as well as a Native healer. Kathy Short, a non-Native lay midwife from Kodiak who was present, mentioned that in her work with Mexican women in Texas, she found that they were used to having midwives and opposed to seeing male doctors. She asked, "Is that something that village women have feelings about?" to which Barbara Boskofsky replied, "Right. Right. VERY much!"

Both the Native and non-Native participants were at ease openly comparing Western and indigenous healing and stating a distinct preference for Native practice. These comparisons revealed a new strategy for women's statements and beliefs about their own health care practices: humor. Barbara's daughter, Juanita, told a story about being trained as a community health aide in Old Harbor while receiving prenatal *banyas* from her mother. When she described the warning in medical training manuals about the dangers of steambaths for pregnant women, there was a riotous response. Laughter punctuated the session, particularly following Barbara Boskofsky's account of witnessing her first delivery:

I remember the very first baby that I experienced with my grandmother delivering. It just so happened that a cousin of mine went into labour that night and there was a dentist there from ANS [Alaska Native Services]. Of course, the former health aide that we had in Old Harbor at that time, she stayed completely away from deliveries, so she panicked and she went and got the dentist. [laughter] She insisted, you know, "Well, he's in dentistry and he's got to know something!" [laughter] Well, we let her do what she wanted, she's the health aide, you know.... My cousin that was in labour wanted me there with her so that she would feel better and she wanted my grandmother there, she didn't want the DENTIST there! But this lady kept saying, "Well, he's from ANS!" So he did come to the delivery and he was with the lady, but my grandmother and I did the whole delivery and he just kind of held her knees, kind of supported her. Afterwards he said, "I was so GLAD that you guys were here!" [laughter]

Conclusion

The story of the Kodiak midwives is an unwritten chapter in the documentation of Alaskan history. Beyond enriching our understanding of women's roles as healers, women's stories allow us to see how women have perceived those roles through periods of radical social change. Comparing Barbara Boskofsky's story of her first delivery with Mary Peterson's belief that God guided her hands reveals some important shifts in women's ways of communicating a sense of their own power as healers. The symbolism of Russian Orthodoxy allows Mary and other Kodiak elders to express pride in their cultural heritage and to create a particularly Native understanding of history and women's roles. Suggesting that religion is a type of code does not negate or trivialize the strength of women's faith in Russian Orthodoxy; rather, it explains its cultural tenacity. The interpretation of women's stories as "coded" offers a means of understanding the recurrent but never explicitly defined "knowing" of Native women as a symbol of women's power and Native identity. Religion serves as a vehicle for expressing belief in a powerful, intuitive knowledge closely related to a Native worldview and firmly rooted in "medicine from the land" and traditional practices.

In contrast, younger women, despite continued religious practice, are moving away from the cloak of religious ambiguity as a code for their messages about Native or female power. Though only a generation younger than Mary, Barbara is working in a politically charged era of Native autonomy and cultural pride. She and the other participants at the Kodiak Women's Conference openly pronounced a preference for Native women as healers and compared medical systems without fear of condemnation. They sometimes couch their explanations in Western terms, such as when Barbara describes the elders' understanding of nutritional requirements for pregnant woman. Yet she also asserts the superiority of Native practices quite distinct from Western medicine, as in the case of the *banyas*. Healing remains, as it was for the elders, a symbol of Native life and of women's feelings about their culture. The recent resurgence of interest in traditional healing is reflected in a three-year project (1989–91) conducted by the Kodiak Area Native Association to record and preserve health care knowledge. While not a threat to the dominance of the Western health care model and the continued practice of hospital deliveries, the practices of women like Barbara Boskofsky and Rena Peterson are practically and symbolically central. Reclaiming the right to talk about midwifery and to serve as a midwife openly asserts pride in Kodiak Native women's distinct heritage. Finally, women are finding the strength in traditional life to face such current social problems as alcoholism and suicide. In the aftermath of these kinds of tragedies, what women "knew" and continue to "know" serves as a cornerstone for rebuilding essential aspects of the heritage of all of Kodiak's Native people.

Notes

1. Kodiak Natives employ *Aleut, Koniag,* and, increasingly, *Alutiiq* as terms of self-reference for a unique cultural identity born of contact and intermarriage with Russian fur traders, American frontiersmen, and Scandinavian fishermen. There are differing explanations as to why *Aleut* was adopted in the eighteenth century for the language and culture of Kodiak's people. One version is that the word was mistakenly applied by the colonizing Russians to several groups of Native people they encountered in the early days of exploration. It was adapted from the Russian term for a Siberian coast people, the *Aliutor.* This has been a source of confusion since people on Kodiak differentiate themselves from the Aleuts of the Aleutian Chain, with whom they share some linguistic and cultural traits. There is longstanding conflict between indigenous terms of self-reference and the scholarly classification of "Koniag" as one group among a larger population of Pacific or Southern Eskimos, who along with the Chugaches of Prince William Sound, speak the Alutiiq language. For an overview of the Pacific Eskimo, see Nancy Yaw Davis, "Contemporary Pacific Eskimo," in *Handbook of North American Indians,* vol. 5, ed. D. Dumas (Washington, D.C.: Smithsonian Institution Press, 1984), 185–197. For a more personal view of the changing Alutiiq identity, see Gordon Pullar, "Ethnic Identity, Cultural Pride, and Generations of Baggage: A Personal Experience," *Arctic Anthropology* (forthcoming).

2. Women were the primary traditional healers on Kodiak as midwife/herbalists; men held ceremonial positions as shamans. This was part of a general role division according to gender. Men were maritime hunters, while women gathered and prepared food, made and repaired clothing, and performed other domestic tasks. After two centuries of contact with Western culture, traditional social organization has been significantly altered. Women now participate in the wage economy and in a wider variety of roles. Some traditional patterns continue, however, including the importance of women healers on Kodiak and in many rural Alaskan villages. Even under a Western health care system, where men hold most institutional positions of authority, primary health care today is provided by community health aides, who are predominantly women (see note 22).

3. Barbara Babcock, "Taking Liberties, Writing from the Margins, and Doing It with a Difference," *Journal of American Folklore* 100, no. 398 (1987): 394. See this entire issue for a review of feminist folklore scholarship. For an

overview of feminism and post-structuralist theory, see Joan W. Scott, "Deconstructing Equality-Versus-Difference: Or, the Uses of Post-Structuralist Theory for Feminism," *Feminist Studies* 14, no. 1 (1988): 33–50. See also Jane Flax, *Thinking Fragments: Psychoanalysis, Feminism, and Postmodernism in the Contemporary West* (Berkeley: University of California Press, 1990); Christie Farnham, ed., *The Impact of Feminist Research in the Academy* (Bloomington: Indiana University Press, 1987); and Michaela di Leonardo, ed. *Gender at the Crossroads of Knowledge* (Berkeley: University of California Press, 1991).

4. This lack of attention to women's voices in both written history and the documentation of Native American life histories has been noted in a number of studies. For an overview of life history methods in relationship to the lives of Native American women, see Margaret Blackman, *During My Time: Florence Edenshaw Davidson, a Haida Woman* (Seattle: University of Washington Press, 1982); and Julie Cruikshank, *Life Lived Like a Story* (Lincoln: University of Nebraska Press, 1990).

5. This interpretation of cultural stories is influenced by the intersection of literary theory and developments in anthropology in which both linguistic and cultural constructs are viewed as texts to be interpreted. See Stuart Plattner, ed., *Text, Play, and Story* (Washington, D.C.: American Ethnological Society, 1984); Michael M. J. Fischer and George E. Marcus, eds., *Anthropology as Cultural Critique* (Chicago: University of Chicago Press, 1986); J. W. Clifford and George E. Marcus, eds., *Writing Culture: The Poetics and Politics of Ethnography* (Berkeley: University of California Press, 1986).

6. Rayna Green has explored the issue of Native women and feminism in her introduction to *Native American Women: A Contextual Bibliography* (Bloomington: Indiana University Press, 1983). She cites the activism and recent scholarly activity of many Native women, but she warns that feminist questions are necessarily considered in the broader context of Native issues and that social action takes precedence over theory. For a discussion of intention in women's communication, see Joan N. Radner and Susan S. Lanser, "Strategies of Coding in Women's Cultures," herein.

7. See Robert Fortuine, *Chills and Fever: Health and Disease in the Early History of Alaska* (Anchorage: University of Alaska Press, 1989), for an excellent and balanced overview and history of health care in Alaska.

8. Medical care for Alaska Natives today is provided through a variety of state (Alaska Department of Health and Social Services) and federal (Indian Health Service) agencies. Tribal governing bodies in the villages contract federal services through the regional Native associations.

9. See Nancy S. Dye, "The Medicalization of Birth," in *The American Way of Birth,* ed. Pamela S. Eakins (Philadelphia: Temple University Press, 1986), 21–46.

10. For cross-cultural comparisons of birthing systems, see Margarita Kay, ed., *The Anthropology of Human Birth* (Philadelphia: F. A. Davis, 1982); and Brigette Jordan, *Birth in Four Cultures* (Montreal: Eden Press Women's Publications, 1980).

11. See Jordan, *Birth in Four Cultures;* and Sheila Kitzinger, *Women as Mothers* (New York: Vintage Books, 1980).

12. Oleanna Ashouwak's work is very similar to that of the better-known Della Keats. Keats, an Inupiat healer celebrated throughout Alaska before her death in 1986, successfully integrated traditional and modern medicine. Her use of massage, "poking" to let blood, steambaths, hot springs, and spirituality is remarkably like Oleanna's. As one woman from Kodiak commented, "They both used their hearts and their hands."

13. Events on Kodiak in the early part of this century followed a general pattern of "medicalization" of birth that occurred in much of the United States in the context of nineteenth-century industrialization. *Medicalization* has been described as the process by which a social event comes under the jurisdiction of medical professionals who define disease, prescribe roles, and control the methods, tools, diagnosis, and treatment of some aspect of life. For a historical view of how patterns of childbirth changed in the United States, see Pamela S. Eakins, ed., *The American Way of Birth* (Philadelphia: Temple University Press, 1986). For an exploration of how these changes have been transformed into part of the dominant ideology regarding childbirth and women's reproductive systems, see Emily Martin, *The Women in the Body: A Cultural Analysis of Reproduction* (Boston: Beacon, 1987). Martin analyzes the cultural metaphors of machinery and labor that we have internalized for understanding menstruation, the birth process, and menopause. See also Robbie E. Davis Floyd, "The Technological Model of Birth," *Journal of American Folklore* 100, no. 398 (1987): 479–95.

14. Edith Turner, "Traditional Healing at Point Hope, Alaska," paper presented at the Alaska Anthropological Association meetings, Fairbanks, Alaska, March 1988.

15. *Creole* was a social class that emerged during the period of Russian occupation. It initially included Natives who could trace Russian ancestry on the male side. After 1821, Native Alaskans who became "naturalized citizens" through pledged alligiance to the tsar were considered Creoles. See Archpriest Michael J. Oleksa, "The Creoles and Their Contributions to the Development of Alaska," in *Russian America: The Forgotten Frontier,* ed. Barbara Sweetland Smith and Redmond J. Barnett (Tacoma: Washington State Historical Society, 1990), 185–95. See also Lydia Black, "The Story of Russian America," in *Crossroads of Continents,* ed. William W. Fitzhugh and Aron Crowell (Washington, D.C.: Smithsonian Institution Press, 1988), 70–82.

16. The formulation of a bicultural Alutiiq identity has been most forcefully argued by Father Michael Oleksa, a Russian Orthodox archpriest who served the village of Old Harbor on Kodiak Island. See his *Alaskan Mission Spirituality* (Mahwah, N.J.: Paulist Press, 1987); and Oleksa, "The Creoles and their Contribution." For an overview of education, language, and cultural development in Russian America, see Richard Dauenhauer, "Education in Russian America," 155–63, Michael E. Krauss, "Alaska Native Languages in Russian

America," 205–13, and Barbara Sweetland Smith, "Russia's Cultural Legacy in America: The Orthodox Mission," 245–53, in *Russian America: The Forgotten Frontier,* ed. Smith and Barnett.

17. While the likelihood of harsh reprisals against women for either their assertions or the actual practice of Native healing today is not strong, the elders' memory of punishment for speaking their language and other Native practices remains vital. Further, the historical record of the enslavement of Native people by the Russians is an important and formative part of historical consciousness.

18. According to the specifications of the ANCSA, Native rights to the land were traded for a settlement of nearly a billion dollars and forty-four million acres of land to be administered through thirteen Native corporations. While this historic legislation ended decades of struggle by Native people for a clear definition of land use and policy, it also raised a score of troubling issues. Today, people are questioning the applicability of a corporate structure to Native life and reassessing the future of their land under the current system.

19. A report published by the Alaska Federation of Natives in 1989 cites the rates of suicide and homicide at four times the national average and accidental death at five times the average. In almost all cases, incidents are alcohol-related. See *The AFN Report on the Status of Alaska Natives: A Call for Action* (Anchorage: Alaska Federation of Natives, January 1989).

20. One can reasonably speculate that this slower reawakening of Native pride on Kodiak is the result of more than two centuries of suppression of Native culture. Because of the early contact period (1700s) and the attempts by the Russians and then the Americans to eradicate Native culture, much of what was maintained of Native practices and beliefs was not visible. There has also been a lack of scholarly attention to Kodiak's people partly because the culture is perceived as too permeated by European influences to have survived in any recognizable form. This has changed in the past decade, beginning with a large-scale archaeological project at Karluk on the southern end of the island and the recent attention to cultures of the North Pacific in conferences and exhibits, such as the Smithsonian Institution's "Crossroads of Continents."

21. I learned of Oleanna's work from an Anchorage-based anthropologist, Nancy Yaw Davis, after I had been interviewing women on Kodiak for several years. The response to one of my initial inquiries was characteristic of how Native people guarded their conversations with non-Natives. One villager replied, "Oh, she used to do that lancing and all that 'witchdoctor' stuff. Didn't they outlaw that?"

22. The Community Health Aide Program (CHAP) is a village-based health care delivery system formally initiated by congressional legislation in 1968. Administered through the Alaska division of the Indian Health Service, the program trains village women to act as liaisons with Western physicians in providing primary health care to villages all over rural Alaska. The roles of the

CHAs provide striking parallels to those of the traditional midwives, a historical connection that has been obscured in the written historical record. Despite this historical continuity, the CHAs work within a Western biomedical system and administer the current policy regarding Native healing and mandatory hospital births.

23. See the twentieth anniversary edition of *KANA KASITAQ: The Newsletter of the Kodiak Area Native Association*, 1966–86.

"We're More than a Novelty, Boys": Strategies of Female Rappers in the Rap Music Tradition

CHERYL L. KEYES

... 'Cause they see a woman standing up on her own two
Sloppy slouching is something I won't do

Some think that we can't flow [rap]. . . .
Stereotypes they got to go, got to go![1]

Rap music evolved among African-American inner city youth of New York City during the 1970s. It is described as a quasi-song with rhyme and rhythmic speech, which draws on Black street language and is recited over an instrumental sound track. During the later 1970s, rap music began attracting the attention of music entrepreneurs, who were enchanted with its rhyme, rhythm, and commercial potential. By the mid-1980s, this musical genre had become the most vital of the new popular music forms in the music industry.

As rap music gained popularity in the mainstream, its image was associated with Black males. This image, however, is drastically changing. By the mid-1980s, the rap music industry had expanded to include a growing number of Black female artists. Like their male counterparts, women rap about aspects of inner city life and their desire to be "number one"; unlike male rappers, they shed light on everyday realities from a woman's perspective.

Although women artists are becoming more visible in the rap music arena, they are often misrepresented by both the music industry and critics. Critics fail to recognize the significance of women rap artists, perceiving them as merely incidental to the rap music tradition. Since the rap music industry is predominantly male, female rap artists are consistently stereotyped as inferior to men in their abilities to create or perform. Women find it difficult to compete in the rap music industry on their own terms. As female rapper Princesa stated, "Only when I led them [rap male producers] to believe that a man had written or produced my stuff did they show interest [in recording me]."[2] To achieve success as rap music artists, women of rap are given little choice except to comply with male standards.

This essay examines the strategies employed by women in gaining equal access and recognition in the rap music industry. Women artists appropriate male performance behavior and use performance as a vehicle to express their responses to stereotypes and male standards, while simultaneously achieving recognition and success in the male-dominated tradition.

The Sources of the Rap Music Tradition

The roots of rap music can be traced all the way from the African epic bardic tradition to rural southern-based expressions of African Americans—toasts, folktales, sermons, blues, children's game songs—all of which are recited in a chanted rhyme or poetic fashion. Except for the sermon, these expressions are mainly performed in secular settings, from the front porch to the local juke joint.

Southern traditions were transported by African Americans during massive migrations to northern urban centers between the 1920s and 1950s. African-American southern cultural traditions were transformed and modified in the new milieu, generating expressions reflecting urban life. Most of the southern rural gathering places where one could hear verbal and musical entertainment were re-created by the new migrants in urban contexts, from concrete ball courts to street corner taverns. Such gathering places, remote from the family home and religious centers, constitute what is referred to by African Americans as the "streets." The street context fostered a new way of speaking known as "rappin" (formerly called "jive talk"), characterized by its personalized style and urban-derived vocabulary.[3]

This style of speaking was not confined solely to the streets. By the 1930s, Black jazz musicians occasionally interspersed the rappin style (quasi-sung, rhymed narrative sections) into their performances. Artists Cab Calloway, Louis Jordan, and the Ink Spots are just a few of the many who utilized the rappin style. The art of rappin to music (in rhyme) on the airwaves was introduced in the 1940s and 1950s by Black radio disc jockeys. Al Benson and Holmes "Daddy" Daylie of Chicago were pioneers in this art.[4] Continuing in the same fashion were Black comedians, who incorporated a rappin style in their comic acts: Pigmeat Markham, Jackie "Moms" Mabley, and Rudy Ray Moore, the man known for popularizing toasts like "Dolemite" and "The Signifying Monkey" in audio recordings. By the mid-1960s, the rappin style was employed in political rhetoric by various Black nationalists, including The Last Poets, a Harlem-based group that often rhymed in rhythm to an African percussion accompaniment. For this reason, The Last Poets are recognized by rap artists as "the first or original style rappers."[5]

In the late 1960s and the 1970s, rappin emerged among Black music artists as two distinct song styles: the love rap and the funk-style rap. The love rap, a rappin monologue celebrating the feats and woes of love, was popularized by Isaac Hayes and further developed by Barry White and Millie Jackson. The funk-style raps were rappin monologues on topics about partying. Funk music artist George Clinton and his group Parliament are considered popularizers of this style of rappin. Unlike rappin performed by the early entertainers, the love and funk-style raps were not in rhyme but were loosely chanted over a repetitive instrumental accompaniment.

By the early 1970s, rap evolved as a musical genre. It is simply a composite of the aforementioned expressive forms, in which rhyme and street talk are recited in rhythm over an instrumental sound track.

Foresisters of Rap

Though some perceive the rise of female rappers in the mid-1980s as commercial hype or as an idea spawned by the music industry, a few women, such as comedienne Jackie "Moms" Mabley and singer Millie Jackson, performed in the rappin style during the early years. Jackson, in particular, revolutionized the idea of women rappin over a musical accompaniment.

Millie Jackson began her career as a blues ballad singer. In her rendition of the blues ballad "If Loving You Is Wrong, I Don't Want to Be Right" (1974),[6] however, Jackson inserted a rappin monologue about the pros and cons of dating a married man. This recording contributed to her current popularity as a rappin singer.

Most of Millie Jackson's rappin monologues are about the dos and don'ts or the feats and woes of love from both a female and male perspective. In addition, she is famous for her ability to create rappin monologues extemporaneously in live performances. For this reason, Millie Jackson is extolled by her fans as the "Queen of Rap." As Millie states, "I'm queen. I'm queen. I don't rhyme when I rap. My rap is not rap rap [rap music style]. It's talk rap."[7] The following song, "Love is a Dangerous Game," illustrates a typical Millie Jackson rap monologue:

... Uh, uh, yep! It's me [Millie Jackson]. I'm back and this time I want to talk to all you people who have a little something on the side. You know who you are, 'cause they've been runnin' around talkin' about what this one don't know won't hurt 'em. But sooner or later, everyone's gonna know and everyone's gonna be hurtin' because what's done in the dark will come to the light. That's why I let my little light shine. I know you're saying "love is so good when you're stealing it" [she sings]. But too much love will give you gas 'cause if the two of you were sleeping around before when you get together on a full time basis, you're gonna think he's doin' the same thing to you and vice-versa. So immediately no trust. No trust, no relationship. Now there are some of you who would like to keep this game going. The big payback: "I can get even." Now that's stupid. How can you pay back something that you haven't borrowed. So I say, "Don't get even, get out!"[8]

Millie Jackson's contemporaries Roxanne Shante and Sparky Dee admit that her style influenced their style of rappin:

SPARKY DEE: And that's where I learned my rap, from talkin' and listenin' to your records, Millie. "Love of Life" and "Search for Tomorrow."

ROXANNE SHANTE: I mocked [imitated] her [Millie Jackson] once or twice.[9]

In general, "females were always into rap, had their little crews [the Mercedes Ladies, for example] and were known for rocking parties, schoolyards, whatever it was; and females rocked just as hard as males [but] the male was just first to be put on wax [record]."[10] Rap artist The Real Roxanne reminisces about how she began her career as a rapper: "People used to do jams outside [in the schoolyard or handball court]. Someone used to bring their two turntables out and plug it into the lamp post outside and that's how they got their [electrical] power. People would listen to their music out in the street and then we would have a few people who would come in front of the turn-tables and start rappin."[11]

There were even a few renowned female rap music disc jockeys during the early 1970s. Music promoter Dennis Shaw recalls a rappin female disc jockey by the name of Lady J, whom he credits as "a forerunner of lady deejays." She was considered an excellent mixer and was "adept to picking popular music that people liked."[12]

By the late 1970s, business entrepreneurs began recognizing the commercial potential of rap music. Among the first promoters to receive national exposure were Sylvia and Joe Robinson, cofounders of Sugar Hill Records in 1979. During that year, the Robinsons produced a New Jersey–based rap group, Sugarhill Gang, whose rap recording "Rapper's Delight" contributed to popularizing rap music.[13]

A year later, Tec, a Philadelphia-based record company, recorded the first solo twelve-inch disc rap song popularized by a female artist, "To the Beat Y'all" by Lady B. This recording was released in the following year by Sugar Hill Records. Lady B professes to her listeners and competitors in such lines as

> I've got eighteen years of experience . . .
> I've got a style that's all my own.
> You've got Lady B on the microphone.[14]

In 1981, Sugar Hill Records recorded a female rap group/crew, Sequence, whose members consisted of Angie B., Cheryl the Pearl, and Blondie. In their most popular hit, "Funk You Up," Sequence boasts about their physical attributes, tantalizing male listeners with such phrases as "I've got such sexy bedroom eyes" and "the heavy hips to make your nature rise."[15] Succeeding "Funk You Up" was another rap by Sequence entitled "Simon Says." In this rap, Sequence reveals their concern about and warning to men who carelessly indulge in sex "but refuse to take responsibility for the babies they help to make."[16] This rap is one of the earliest female commercial rap recordings with a feminist tone. Other female rap artists who were successful during the early stages of rap music include Sha Rock of The Funky Four Plus One, Shelia Spencer, Lisa Lee, and Sula.

The recording careers of many of these female rappers ended rather abruptly, though. Bill Coleman of *Billboard* states two primary reasons why the early female rappers' recording careers were short-lived: "In the past . . . female rappers . . . lost any possible long-term impact because of their sexy, glamorous, and somewhat frivolous image. Others lost their edge by not following initial singles with additional recordings."[17] Disc jockey Grandmaster Flash claims that the early female rappers abandoned rap music because "the [rap music] scene got too competitive and the young women gave up."[18] Many women rappers, however, temporarily left the rap music arena because of such domestic matters as marriage or maternal responsibilities. In spite of these responsibilities, women are returning to the rap scene. They feel that family life provides them with the extra incentive to continue their careers as artists. Roxanne Shante says, "It [family life] makes your job; it makes you strive that much harder, to know that you have to succeed so they [male rappers] won't say, 'See, I told you she was just a girl, she got pregnant, she had a baby and it's over.' "[19]

Contemporary Women of Rap

Female rappers continue to compete against the odds and encounter those who regard them merely as sex symbols, novelties, or performers without longevity. Women rappers of the mid-1980s consciously disproved these stereotypes in various ways. For example, some female rappers have contended they prefer to be regarded as "women" rather than "ladies." To them, *lady* implies being "soft," fragile, or weak, "that image which contributed to the acclaimed demise of the early female rappers."[20] As Sparky Dee says, "You have to come hard [aggressive]. . . . If you come soft, you get booed off the stage; and you can't smile [because smiling indicates vulnerability]."[21] Roxanne Shante points out that the lady "soft" image can be communicated by certain attire: "If I was to get up there in a pair of shoes and a dress, I'd be over."[22]

Although contemporary women rappers do not wear male attire or wish to be male, they modify the male dress style to suit a woman. Male rappers dress in traditional hip-hop attire, such as black leather jacket and pants; female rappers wear leather outfits as well—skirts, jackets, and pants—but designed and tailored specifically for women. Male rappers are also known for wearing big, heavy necklaces made of gold. Although female rappers wear gold necklaces, they place more emphasis on big, heavy-seeming gold earrings. Female rappers wear other stylish attire (now considered unisex) that was once popularized by male rappers, including name-brand sweat suits and sneakers (Gucci, Troop, Fila, and the like), jeans, brass name buckles, and cutout leather gloves.

The wearing of male-derived attire suggests contemporary female rap artists wish to be recognized as equal competitors in both the rap music tradition and commercial industry. More important to their image and success, however, is the way female rappers appropriate stylized male street attitude and behavior in their performances.

Appropriation involves women's adaptation of items, customs, and behavior traditionally associated with male culture.[23] Women rappers often appropriate male behavior and may deny, as Sweet Tee does here, that rap carries any gender characteristics: "I'm trying to do exactly what male rappers are doing. The only difference is that I'm a girl. I'm not trying to do a 'girl's version' of rap. There is none. It's either good rap or bad rap."[24] This statement itself, like the male behavior in Sweet Tee's raps, functions to distract listeners from the underlying feminist messages in her art.[25] In fact, female rappers have recognized they will gain an audience for their raps only by adopting the male aesthetic.

Although many female rappers do not explicitly acknowledge they are "trying to do exactly what male rappers are doing," their appropriation of a male-derived aesthetic is apparent in their performance behavior. Adopting a male dress aesthetic also allows women to express a female message in performance. It is the use of appropriation that marks a major difference between the foresisters of rap and their contemporaries.

Contemporary women of rap appropriate a vocal timbre and stylized speech behavior similar to hardcore male rappers. *Hardcore* refers to tough and aggressive behavior conveyed through the use of expletives, heightened speech, exaggeration, and "dissin'"—the verbal act of *dis*respecting or downplaying someone else's attributes while praising one's self. In rap music, boasting about one's self and insulting an opponent is not at all new, but the extensive use of dissin is a trademark of hardcore-style male rappers.

It is not typical for male rappers to dis female rappers about their rappin skills, for they perceive this as less challenging than dissin another male. When dissin is employed by male rappers, insults are specifically geared toward other male opponents, as illustrated by L. L. Cool J. in the following lines:

> No rapper can rap quite like I can.
> I'll take a muscle bound man and put his face in the sand. . . .
>
> If you think you can outrhyme me, ya' boy I'll bet,
> cuz I ain't met a muthafucka who can do that yet.
>
> Trendsetter, I'm better. My rhymes are good.
> I got a gold made plate that says, "I wish you would." . . .
>
> I couldn't, shouldn't and it'll stay that way.
> The best rapper you've heard is L. L. Cool J. . . .
>
> I'm the pinnacle, that means I reign supreme
> and I'm notorious. I'll crush you like a jellybean.
>
> I'm Bad![26]

As males dis one another, female rappers also dis other females. To reign as a respectable equal in this business, however, female rappers must also challenge and verbally dis their male counterparts, while simultaneously giving them "a taste of their own medicine in hardcore style."[27] Females exploit dissin as an emphatic marker—a way to get a point across to a listener. As Ice Cream Tee states, "When I write and talk about something dangerous . . . I feel like I have to rap it hard."[28] Dissin is therefore consciously executed in an aggressive and boastful manner similar to that of the males. Unlike male rappers, when females rap about their abilities as artists, they do not employ dissin toward males explicitly, as L. L. Cool J.'s rap does: "I'll take a muscle bound *man* and put his face in the sand." Instead, they occasionally make use of the pronoun *you,* which strategically serves to distract from gender or sex. The following excerpts are examples of dissin showing exaggeration and boasting performed by female rappers Sparky Dee and MC Lyte, respectively.

> . . . Who even dare try to battle [challenge] me
> is your worst nightmare.
>
> I'm never moving slow. I'm always fast.
> Think I'll lose a battle, don't make me laugh.
>
> I can beat you and write you and also erase you.
> Whoever want to battle I would love to face you.
>
> This is something for what it's worth.
> It's Sparky Dee's world now I'm runnin the earth.[29]

> I am woman hear me roar.
> Comin' out fresh and fly than I did before.
>
> That's right I'm well respected.
> Don't get stupid, I'm well pretected [protected].
>
> If you want to battle, I'm well prepared.
> Me and K–Rock [MC Lyte's disc jockey] are far from scared.[30]

When boasting and exaggerated language escalates, dissin advances into ritual insults and indirection or signifyin'. Ritual insults are rendered among African Americans in two common forms, known as "the dozens" and "sounding." William Labov has defined *the dozens* as the "oldest term for the game of exchanging insults."[31] This game, which is played primarily by Black adolescents, involves interplay or a verbal duel between opponents in which one makes a *direct* statement about a member of someone's family, especially the mama (mother), in rhymed couplets like the following:

> I saw yo' mama yesterday on the welfare line
> lookin' like she done drank some turpentine.[32]

Though most research on the dozens has been collected among Black males, 1960s Black nationalist H. Hubert 'Rap' Brown once commented that "some of the best dozen players were girls."[33]

Male rappers in general use sounding more than the dozens in their performances.[34] Unlike the dozens, sounding avoids derogatory remarks about the addressee's ancestors but instead incorporates insults about the addressee.[35] In general, insults in sounding are untrue and humorous, for instance:

> Incredible Hulk doesn't compare
> with his funky and dingy hair.
>
> His thick muscle showing all over the place
> and it's too bad that it's a waste.
>
> His private part he never washes
> 'cause it's no bigger than a Vienna sausage.[36]

When male rappers perform sounding, they often ridicule their opponents' incompetence in sexual or physical performance (as in the above example) or in rappin and disc jockey skills. To male rappers, deficiencies in these areas indicate unmanliness.

Although male rappers do not usually sound or dis females about their rappin skills, they directly insult them as women by depicting them as "buffoons, nags, teases, or sluts."[37] In "Girls Ain't Nothing but Trouble" by D. J. Jazzy Jeff and The Fresh Prince, a woman is portrayed as pernicious. The Fresh Prince states:

> Just last week when I was walking down the street,
> I observe this lovely lady that I wanted to meet.
>
> . . . I said, "Hello!"
> She said, "You're kind of cute." I said, "Yes, I know.
>
> By the way sweetheart what's your name?"
> She said, "My friends call me Exotica Lane."
>
> . . . I popped some trash [trivial talk] in a little bit of time.
> I showed some cash then the girl was mine.
>
> I took her on the town . . . wine and dined her . . .
>
> All of a sudden, she jumped out her seat.
> Snatch me up by my wrist and took me out in the street.
>
> She started grabbin' all over me, kissin' and huggin'
> so I . . . said, "You better stop buggin."
>
> She got mad, looked me dead in the face.
> Threw her hands in the air and yelled, "Rape!"
>
> . . . Now I'm in prison charged with aggravated assault.
> But I didn't do nothing, it was the dumb broad's fault.

Chorus:

But nevertheless don't mean to bust your bubble
but girls of the world ain't nothing but trouble.

So the next time a girl gives you a play,
just remember my rhymes and get the hell away.[38]

Contemporary female rappers respond to these depictions by writing follow-up raps to the male versions, thereby creating a dialogue between the sexes.[39] "You don't take it personally," Sweet Tee says, because as Peaches points out, "We got rhymes talkin' about guys."[40] For example, female rapper Ice Cream Tee (I.C.T.) replies to "Girls Ain't Nothing but Trouble" with "Guys Ain't Nothing but Trouble." Her response to The Fresh Prince (F.P.) goes as follows:

I.C.T.: . . . But I'm kind of upset
because I heard a little something that I could not forget.

F.P.: "What's that?"

I.C.T.: I heard you say that girls ain't nothing but trouble.
And now I'm taking the time to bust your bubble. . . .

Guys think they own their girlfriends.
Females aren't possessions we are humans.

We like to be wined and dined by candlelights.
Not being cooped up in the house tryin' to be held uptight.

So Jazzy Jeff and Fresh Prince don't mean to bust your bubble.
But guys of the world ain't nothing but trouble.

Homegirls, the next time a guy give you a play,
just turn your head and cold dis 'em and walk away.[41]

Sounding is more commonly employed by male rappers than females because *direction,* insulting one in a straightforward and unobscured manner, is highly regarded. Women rappers, on the other hand, prefer to dis through indirection or signifyin. Signifyin is employed in verbal dueling with "*indirect* intent or metaphorical reference";[42] the meaning of the statement is allusive and often ambiguous. Female rappers strategically use signifyin in their performances as a subtle way to dis their male opponents, mainly through allusive speech. Through signifyin, women display their distinct prowess as rap artists or "powerful persons of words."[43] The following rap music excerpts illustrate the allusive manner in which female rappers signify on their male counterparts. In the first example, the female rap duo Finesse and Synquis avoid using the word *male* in direct reference to their male competitors. Instead they use the words *punk* and *wet dream* to indicate they are speaking specifically about men:

> I deserve an encore.
> I'm bustin' hardcore.
>
> Don't try to dis me *punk*.
> I'm bringin' hard for you, your crew, posse[44] or soloist.
> MC Finesse the best female vocalist of all time. . . .
>
> Most rappers think they're getting busy.
> To me they sound dizzy.
>
> Once they see Synquis is on the mike, the crowd say,
> "Is she a human or machine?"
>
> I'm a rhyme fiend.
> Don't never think about battling me, cuz that's a *wet dream*.[45]

In the next example, female rappers Salt-N-Pepa exult that their disc jockey, Spinderella, is not a "fella" but a girl d j. Salt-N-Pepa challenge those they call "mix masters," "cut masters," "grand masters," and "jam masters" in asserting that Spinderella is equal to or superior to them. Adherents of rap music recognize these names as famous male disc jockeys, for example, Jam Master Jay of the rap group Run D.M.C. or the renowned mix innovator Grandmaster Flash. Salt-N-Pepa intentionally omit the last names of these disc jockeys but nevertheless make the point that Spinderella is equal to or even better than her male disc jockey counterparts:

> Like a fever she'll heat up,
> burn and beat up.
>
> If you can't put up,
> then shut the hell up.
>
> For you *mix masters* and *cut masters*,
> true *grand masters*, even *jam masters*,
>
> Listen to what I'm saying on the mike.
> She's hard as a man.[46]

The use of "hardcore" and "hard as a man" by Finesse and Synquis and Salt-N-Pepa, respectively, further suggests their appropriation of Black male street behavior. When the elements of appropriation and dissin have been effectively accomplished in their performances, women rappers are lauded by their fans as uncontested persons of rap.

Henceforth, these women enter the rap music arena for their verbal ingenuity rather than (as in the past) for their physical attributes.

Vocal timbre—that distinctive quality peculiar to a voice—further enhances the performances of contemporary female rappers. Timbre, as employed by rappers, encompasses articulation and tonal aspects, ranging from legato, velvety, and mellow to harsh, percussive, and boisterous. The vocal timbre of female rappers corresponds to the image they wish to portray. Among such earlier female rappers as Sequence, Sha Rock, and Lady B, the smooth, velvety, and mellow quality predominated, which was consistent with their "sexy, glamorous" image. This vocal quality was typical among early style rappers—both men and women—and defines the old school/style of rap. Rap music promoters Lumumba Carson and Dennis Shaw trace the legato, mellow quality to the "sexy" male radio jockey style of talking: "What was selling the people is he [the old-school rapper] had this enormous great voice and I think if I can equate it with some things, early Frankie Crocker and early Gary Byrd [prominent Black radio disc jockey personalities of New York City]. . . these guys used to put emphasis on their voice . . . it was almost sexy to the women."[47]

Hardcore male rappers have departed from the sexy style by incorporating a harsher, raspy, boisterous, and percussive style of delivery. Contemporary female rappers have extended the hardcore timbre in their rappin style as well. For example, female rapper Shocky Shay is described as having a "street-style, slightly raspy sound"[48] that mesmerizes her audience. While some women artists use the hardcore timbre merely as a stylistic device, others employ this style as a means of distancing themselves from the expected lady "soft" image. As Sparky Dee states, "I don't sound soft at all. I'm hard. I wake up and I go, [hard] hello. . . . "[49] The hardcore timbre expresses the image contemporary women of rap wish to portray—intimidating, challenging, and aggressive—thus transcending the sexual stereotypes and limitations that inhibited the success of early female rappers.

Through the process of appropriation, women encode their intimate feelings regarding relationships with men. The manner by which they choose to convey their feelings is described by some critics as "a gender-switching, macho approach to romance"[50] that shows men how it feels when the shoe is on the other foot. Shocky Shay is credited for exploiting a macho-like approach to romance in her raps, as expressed to her male lover in the following:

> . . . I have to rough you up and cut you up and treat you like cattle
> You should have been good, boy, we wouldn't have to battle.

So now you just listen with your hands in a cup
and don't say [a] word, you know my right is enough

. . . ['cause] You got no rights![51]

Other women utilize the rap medium as a dialogue with their audiences about exploitative male relationships from a feminist perspective. For example, in "Paper Thin," MC Lyte addresses her rap to a fictitious male character, Sam, whom she identifies as her boyfriend. Sam undoubtedly is flirting with another woman but thinks MC Lyte is unaware of his infidelity. Lyte, however, tells Sam she is completely aware that he is trying to take her for a fool, which is why she states:

When you say you love me, it doesn't matter.
It goes into my head as just chit chatter.

You may think it's egotistical or just worry free.
What you say I take none of it seriously

and even if I did I wouldn't tell you so.
I'll let you pretend to read me and then you'll know

'cuz I hate when one attempts to analyze.
Fact I despise those who even try

to look into my eyes to see what I am thinking.
The dream is over, your yacht is sinking.[52]

MC Lyte further incorporates in this rap the "gender-switching, macho approach" by taunting her man, Sam:

You ain't got the bait that it takes to hook this,
ha! ha! ha! ha! ha! ha! Sucker you missed. . . .

I treat all of you like I treat all of them.
What you say to me is still paper thin.[53]

Lyte's public acknowledgment that Sam's expressions of love were paper thin is not a source of embarrassment for her but a means of empowerment.[54] Furthermore, the gender-switching, macho approach is just another way female rappers prove to their male counterparts that women can exert full authority and control over those men who simply take them for granted.

Conclusion

Women rap artists continue to encounter the notion that "you got to prove yourself double."[55] Some feel that "it's hard on girls when it comes to record companies. You've got to prove yourself first before the record company be one hundred percent behind you, before you record."[56] The increased flow of recordings from those women who pick up the mike has brought an entirely new perspective to rap music, however.[57] Salt-N-Pepa, whose debut album, *Hot, Cool & Vicious,* achieved platinum success, have successfully paved the way "for a new generation of female rappers in what has long been a male-dominated form."[58]

Success for female rap artists is predicated on their ability to overcome such barriers as sexual stereotypes about themselves as women. Unlike their foresisters, contemporary women of rap have become more than a tantalizing whim. Although they appropriated a male aesthetic in their performances—dissin in hardcore style as well as unique attire—women rappers are nonetheless moving beyond the shadows of their male counterparts and acquiring a voice within this tradition. As one female artist observed, "Before we used to be treated like little sisters; now we're seen as peers."[59]

There still exists among women of rap a conscious need to maintain a sense of womanliness and "female respectability that is the ideal of feminine face"[60] in this male-dominated tradition. Some have chosen to utilize the term *ladies* without having to justify their doing so, as in Queen Latifah's rap "Ladies First," while others, like Yo-Yo, have started such organizations as the Intelligent Black Women's Coalition (I.B.W.C.) in response to the rap industry's ongoing sexism, including misogynist lyrics. In general, women express through the rap medium their personal feelings about female and male relationships, but more important, they speak for the empowerment of women. Although acceptance and recognition are crucial to contemporary women of rap, they want to be regarded as more than just a novelty.

Notes

I would like to thank disc jockeys Ill Will and J.C. of Downstairs Records in New York City for their invaluable assistance. Special thanks goes to Eileen Hayes, Phyllis May-Machunda, and Joan Radner, without whose encouragement and persistent support this essay could not have been envisioned.

1. Queen Latifah, "Ladies First," *All Hail the Queen* (Tommy Boy Records TBC 1022, 1989). © 1989 T-Boy Music Publishing, Inc. (ASCAP) c/o Lipservices. International Copyrights Secured. All Rights Reserved. Used by kind permission.

2. Carol Cooper, "Girls Ain't Nothin' but Trouble?" *Essence* 19, no. 12 (1988): 80.

3. Among the rappers, the term *rapping* is spelled *rappin*, without the apostrophe. It is acceptable among Black English speakers to drop the *g* of *ing* endings. I will therefore use this spelling throughout this essay and will later also spell *dissin* and *signifyin* without the *g* to reflect their pronunciations. For further reading on rappin as a conversation genre, see Roger Abrahams, "Rapping and Capping: Black Talk as Art," in *Black America*, ed. John Szwed (New York: Basic Books, 1970), 132–42; William Labov, *Language in the Inner City: Studies in the Black Vernacular* (Philadelphia: University of Pennsylvania Press, 1972); Cheryl L. Keyes, "Verbal Art Performance in Rap Music: The Conversation of the 80s," *Folklore Forum* 17, no. 2 (1984): 141–51; Geneva Smitherman, "The Power of the Rap: The Black Idiom and the New Black Poetry," *Twentieth Century Literature* 19, no. 4 (1973): 259–74; Geneva Smitherman, *Talkin and Testifyin* (reprint, Detroit: Wayne State University Press, 1986); and Clyde Taylor, "The Language of Hip: From Africa to What's Happening Now," *First World* 1, no. 1 (1977): 25–32.

4. See Norman W. Spaulding, "History of Black-Oriented Radio in Chicago, 1929–1963" (Ph.D. dissertation, University of Illinois at Urbana-Champaign, 1981); and Gilbert A. Williams, "The Black Disc Jockey as a Cultural Hero," *Popular Music and Society* 10, no. 3 (1983): 79–90.

5. Afrika Bambaataa, personal interview, June 10, 1986.

6. Millie Jackson, "If Loving You Is Wrong, I Don't Want to Be Right," *Caught Up* (Spring Records, distributed by Polydor SPR 6703, 1974).

7. Millie Jackson, quoted in Jill Pearlman, "Girls Rappin' Round Table," *Paper* (Summer 1988): 26.

8. Millie Jackson, "Love Is a Dangerous Game," *Millie Jackson: An Imitation of Love* (Jive Records, distributed by RCA 1016-4-J [cassette], 1986). Used by permission of Zomba Enterprises, Inc., and Willesden Music.

9. Ibid.

10. Ms. Melodie, quoted by Jill Pearlman, "Girls Rappin'," 25. The term *crew* refers to a group of people associated with a particular rapper. The crew in many ways parallels the amen corner or responsorial sayers found in the Black church; but unlike the amen-sayers, the crew's responses are rehearsed prior to each public performance and recording. Crews provide an essential part of the performance a rapper wishes his or her audience to respond to. The more members in a rapper's crew, the greater his or her power, status, and merit as a performer.

11. Personal interview, July 30, 1986.

12. Personal interview, July 12, 1986.

13. Sugarhill Gang is credited with recording the first commercial rap, "Rapper's Delight." Members of the rap music community claimed that Sugarhill Gang used rhymes initially created by New York rappers. As a result, New York City rappers do not recognize "Rapper's Delight" as the first rap recording. Instead, they credit "King Tim III," by a New York–based funk group, the Fatback Band, as the first authentic rap recording. This recording preceded "Rapper's Delight" in the same year. "Rapper's Delight"

remains, however, one of the longest commercial raps recorded, fifteen minutes.

14. Lady B, "To the Beat Y'all," *Greatest Rap Hits* (Sugar Hill Records SH 246A, 1980).

15. Sequence, "Funk You Up," *Funky Sound—Tear the Roof Off* (Sugar Hill Records SH 561, 1981).

16. David Toop, *Rap Attack* (Boston: South End Press, 1984), 122.

17. Bill Coleman, "Female Rappers Give Males Run for The Money," *Billboard* 100, no. 21 (1988): 29.

18. Reebee Garofalo, "Hip Hop for High School," *Radical America* 18, no. 6 (1984): 33.

19. Roxanne Shante, quoted in Pearlman, "Girls Rappin'," 26.

20. The Real Roxanne, personal interview, July 30, 1986.

21. Sparky Dee, quoted in Pearlman, "Girls Rappin'," 27.

22. Roxanne Shante, ibid.

23. Joan N. Radner and Susan S. Lanser, "Strategies of Coding in Women's Cultures," herein.

24. Sweet Tee, quoted in Coleman, "Female Rappers Give Males Run for the Money," 29.

25. Joan N. Radner and Susan S. Lanser use the term *distraction* to describe strategies that drown out or draw attention away from an underlying message ("Strategies of Coding," herein).

26. L. L. Cool J., "I'm Bad," *Bigger and Deffer* (Def Jam Records, distributed by CBS Records CT40793 [cassette], 1987). "I'm Bad," by J. T. Smith, R. Ervin, and D. Simone, copyright 1988 Def Jam Music, Inc. / LL Cool J Publishing (ASCAP). Used by permission.

27. The Real Roxanne, personal interview, July 30, 1986.

28. "New on the Charts," *Billboard* 101, no. 40 (1989): 32.

29. Sparky Dee, *Don't Make Me Laugh* (New Plateau Records NP 50039 [12″ LP], 1986). Reprinted with permission (p) © 1986 STM Music, Inc. / Sypdo Music.

30. MC Lyte, "I Am Woman," *Lyte as a Rock* (First Priority Music, distributed by Atlantic Records 90905-1, 1988). Reprinted with the permission of First Priority Music.

31. William Labov, "Rules for Ritual Insults," in *Rappin' and Stylin' Out*, ed. Thomas Kochman (Urbana: University of Illinois Press, 1972), 274.

32. From Cheryl L. Keyes's personal collection (unpublished, n.d.).

33. H. Rap Brown, "Street Talk," in *Rappin' and Stylin' Out*, ed. Kochman, 206; reprinted from Hubert Rap Brown, *Die Nigger Die* (New York: Dial Press, 1969).

34. The rap group Wuf Ticket recorded a rap called "Ya Mama," which used the dozens (Prelude Records PRL D644 [12″ LP], 1982). This rap remains the only dozens rap commercial recording.

35. Claudia Mitchell-Kernan, "Signifying, Loud-Talking, and Marking," in *Rappin' and Stylin' Out*, ed. Kochman, 317.

36. Blowfly (Clarence Reid), "Rap Dirty" (T. K. Disco Records 438, 1980).

37. Janine C. McAdams, "The Rap against Rap: Sexist Images Put Down Women on Road to Big Sales," *Billboard* 101, no. 24 (1989): B-14. Such depictions of women appear in such rap recordings as "Dump Girl," by Run D.M.C.; "Dear Yvette," by L. L. Cool J.; "Latoya," by Just-Ice; "Girls, Let's Get Butt Naked and Fuck," by Ice-T; "Give the Drummer Some," by M.C. Kool Keith; and "Girls Ain't Nothing but Trouble," by D. J. Jazzy Jeff and The Fresh Prince.

38. D. J. Jazzy Jeff and Fresh Prince, *Girls Ain't Nothing but Trouble* (Word-Up Records WD-001 [12″ LP], 1986). Used by permission of Zomba Enterprises, Inc.

39. Female raps that follow up male versions include "The Real Roxanne," by Roxanne; "Roxanne Revenge," by Roxanne Shante (versus "Roxanne, Roxanne" by U.T.F.O.); and "A Fly Guy," by Pebblee-Poo (versus "A Fly Girl," by the Boogie Boys). See *The Answer Album—Rap vs. Rap* (Priority Records 4XL 9506 [cassette], 1987).

40. Sweet Tee and Peaches, quoted by Jill Pearlman, "Girls Rappin'," 26.

41. Ice Cream Tee, *Guys Ain't Nothing but Trouble* (Word-Up Records WD-002 [12″ LP], 1988). Used by permission of Zomba Enterprises, Inc.

42. Mitchell Kernan, "Signifying, Loud-Talking and Marking," 326. See also Thomas Kochman, "Strategic Ambiguity in Black Speech Genres: Cross-Cultural Interference in Participant-Observation Research," *Text* 6, no. 2 (1986): 153–70.

43. The Real Roxanne, personal interview, July 30, 1986.

44. A *posse* is a group of rappers from the same locale, borough, or city.

45. Finesse and Synquis, "I Can Do Better," *Soul Sisters* (Uptown Records, distributed by MCA Records MCA 42177, 1988). "I Can Do Better," by Cedric Miller and Don Taylor, © 1988 EMI April Music, Inc., Across 110th Street Publishing, Songwriters Association, and Ultramagnetic Music. All Rights controlled and administered by EMI April Music, Inc. All Rights Reserved. International Copyright Secured. Used by permission.

46. Salt-N-Pepa, "Spinderella's Not a Fella (But a Girl D.J.)," *A Salt with a Deadly Pepa* (New Plateau Records STM 1011 [cassette], 1988). Reprinted with permission (p) © 1988 Next Plateau Music, Inc. / Sons of K-Oss Music.

47. Dennis Shaw, personal interview, July 12, 1986.

48. Janine McAdams, "Female Rappers Step into the Spotlight," *Billboard* 101, no. 37 (1989): 79.

49. Sparky Dee, quoted by Jill Pearlman, "Girls Rappin'," 27.

50. Ibid.

51. Shocky Shay, "You Got No Rights," *Shocky Shay No Joke* (Orpheus D4-75608, 1989). "You Got No Rights," words and music by Charlene B. Simmons and Donald Bowden, © Copyright 1989 by MCA Music Publishing, A Division of MCA Inc., Bush Burnin' Music Inc. Used by permission.

52. MC Lyte, "Paper Thin," *Lyte As a Rock* (First Priority Music, distributed by Atlantic Records 90905-1, 1988). Reprinted with the permission of First Priority Music.

53. Ibid.

54. Tricia Rose, "Never Trust a Big Butt and a Smile," *Camera Obscura* 23 (May 1990): 119.

55. Millie Jackson, quoted in Pearlman, "Girls Rappin'," 25.

56. Ibid.

57. Coleman, "Female Rappers Give Males Run for the Money," 25.

58. Ibid., 1. Other talented contemporary women of rap who are becoming nationally prominent include MC Lyte, Sparky Dee, Queen Latifah, The Real Roxanne, Roxanne Shante, Princess Ivori, Monie Love, Ice Cream Tee, Ms. Melodie, Nikki D., Isis, Princesa, MC Trouble, Shocky Shay, Shazzy, Harmony, Yo-Yo, Peaches, Antoinette, 2 Much, Finesse and Synquis, L'Trimm, J. J. Fad, Cookie Crew, Oaktown's 3-5-7, and Non-Stop, a female rap quartet.

59. Roxanne Shante, quoted in Ben Mapp, "Women Rappers Break New Ground," *Billboard Spotlight Issue: State of Rap* 103, no. 47 (1991): R-21.

60. Roger Abrahams, "Negotiating Respect: Patterns of Presentation among Black Women," in *Women and Folklore: Images and Genres,* ed. Claire R. Farrer (Prospect Heights, Ill.: Waveland Press, 1975), 67.

"At Home, No Womens Are Storytellers": Potteries, Stories, and Politics in Cochiti Pueblo

BARBARA A. BABCOCK

The primitive woman has no choice, and, given the duties that go with marriage, is therefore seldom able to take much part in public life. But if she can be regarded as being at a disadvantage in this respect from our point of view, she does not regard herself as being at a disadvantage, and she does not envy her menfolk what we describe as their privileges. She does not desire, in this respect, things to be other than they are. . . .

—E. E. Evans-Pritchard, *The Position of Women in Primitive Societies*

The world man actually lives in, in the sense of his inescapable necessities and the inevitable conditions of life, always bulks very small in relation to the world he makes for himself.

—Ruth Benedict, "Magic"

In the last twenty years, Helen Cordero, a Cochiti Pueblo woman who learned to make pottery at the age of forty-five, has changed the shape of Pueblo ceramics (see Figure 1). When Helen modeled the first *Storyteller* doll in 1964, she made one of the oldest forms of Native American self-portraiture her own, reinvented a longstanding but moribund Cochiti tradition of figurative pottery, and engendered a revolution in Pueblo ceramics comparable to those begun by Nampeyo of Hopi and Maria of San Ildefonso—a revolution that has reshaped her life as well as that of her family and her pueblo, not to mention the fortunes of innumerable other Pueblo potters (see Figure 2).[1] She is not, however, without ambivalence about the consequences of her creativity: *See. I just don't know. I guess I really started something. I guess I'm a big Indian artist. But,* she will hasten to add, *I don't like to be called*

Figure 1: Helen Cordero shaping a *Storyteller* at a Pecos National Monument demonstration in 1974. (Courtesy of Pecos National Monument; photograph by Tom Giles)

famous. My name is Helen Cordero. It's my grandfather, he's giving me these. [2] But, like it or not, Helen, like her grandfather, Santiago Quintana, who was Ruth Benedict's favorite teller of Cochiti tales, is one of those "gifted individuals who have bent the culture in the direction of their own capacities" (see Figure 3).[3]

I first met this indefatigable woman who is always in a hurry on a June afternoon in 1978. Fascinated by the *Storyteller* dolls then becoming popular, I had finally screwed up my courage and driven to Cochiti Pueblo to talk with the inventor herself. That particular day Helen was having a new hardwood floor laid in her pottery room, so we sat outside under a cottonwood tree. After we had talked for over an hour about her *potteries,* her patrons, and her grandfather, she asked me why I was asking her all these questions. I replied that I was thinking about writing an article about *Storyteller* dolls, and without hesitation she responded, *There are three books about Maria* [the famous potter of San Ildefonso Pueblo] *and none about me.* Thus began a complicated and important relationship that has redefined my life and

Figure 2: The first *Storyteller,* eight inches high, shaped by Helen Cordero in 1964. (Courtesy of the Museum of International Folk Art, Museum of New Mexico; photograph by Glenn Short)

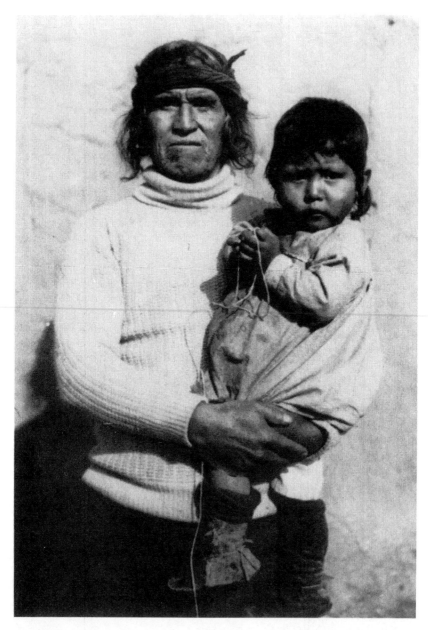

Figure 3: Santiago Quintana with one of his many grandchildren, Cochiti Pueblo, circa 1906. (Photograph courtesy of the National Anthropological Archives, Smithsonian Institution)

my work. The difficulties as well as delights that Helen and I have had *gathering all these words and pictures together into a big book* about her art and experience have convinced me that re-presenting another woman is not an unproblematic enterprise. Betwixt and between Cochiti Pueblo, museum archives, and the world of dealers and collectors who traffic in Indian art, I have been forced to rethink and revise many assumptions about women's art and creativity, about feminism and cross-cultural inquiry, about biography, autobiography, and life history, and about the meaning of things.

When I turned from talking with Helen and many other Pueblo potters who have imitated her invention to reading scholars in an attempt to understand the dynamics of this revolution in contemporary ceramics, I discovered that for the most part, discussions of innovation in ethnic and tribal arts have followed an art historical approach, examining the creativity of the artist or performer in relation to the tradition he or she has inherited and the subsequent changes his or her work has wrought in the aesthetic system.[4] In contrast to modern Western art, primitive and folk art is generally regarded as subservient to tradition and community values, and the assumption that such "art forms reinforce the bonds of the community rather than make manifest and challenge the oppositions within it" is rarely questioned or examined.[5] Less frequently and more recently, innovation has been interpreted from a psycho- or sociobiographical perspective—that is, in relation to the life history and motivations of the innovator and the ways in which he or she is already "marginal," "deviant," etc.[6] Unfortunately, this necessary corrective to the myth of anonymous, collective, tradition-bound creativity tends toward a romantic reification of the alienated genius, which says a great deal more about how "we" regard the creative person than about how "they" do. That is beginning to change as scholars move beyond or behind these extremes to examine the dialectic of creativeness and constraints, the sociocultural consequences of as well as conditions for creativity, and the politics as well as the poetics of innovation.[7] In insisting on the inseparability of the poetic and the political, of artistic innovation and social innovation, I am indebted to Ruth Benedict and Victor Turner, who opposed the separation of the social and the symbolic and the related separation of science and humanism in anthropological analyses. They instead insisted on culture as creative process and on the ways in which performers and performances, be they verbal, dramatic, or artifactual, not only follow but also revise and revitalize accepted rules, acting out and challenging aesthetic conventions and social values.[8]

More than simply reflecting or expressing social structure and worldview, any significant new form reconstructs cultural reality, causing a dislocation in the economy of cultural representations: "A work of art does not substitute, but institutes an original awareness of existence, on the whole; it does not so much reproduce and represent as produce and present a total experience."9 The *Storyteller* doll as conceived and realized by Helen Cordero not only "materializes a way of experiencing" and "brings a particular cast of mind out into the world of objects, where men can look at it" but also comments on and expands the premises of Pueblo existence.10 When Helen Cordero re-created her grandfather in clay, it was one of those "fecund moments" when an artist discovers a structure for her sensibility and experience that "makes it manageable" for herself and "at the same time accessible to others."11 It is, therefore, "in the tenor of its setting," in the discourse surrounding it, that I have looked for both the sources and the consequences of the powerful generative image that she created, asking, to paraphrase Roy Wagner, how Helen Cordero's invention is related to a Cochiti woman's perception of herself and her world.12

All innovation involves a dialectic between convention and invention, and when Helen Cordero began making *little people* over twenty years ago, she continued, with a difference, a centuries-old ceramic tradition. For over a thousand years, Puebloan potters have shaped the clay of the Southwest into representative human and animal forms as well as utility ware. The majority of prehistoric anthropomorphic figurines are female, and on the basis of contextual archaeological evidence as well as ethnographic data from the past century, archaeologists have conjectured that the Pueblo figurine complex was associated with reproductive ritual—both agricultural fertility cults and rites of human increase.13 Historic figures, such as the mother and child effigy made at Cochiti over one hundred years ago, would seem to confirm these connections (see Figure 4). Her dress is painted front and back with corn-plant designs, and here, as throughout Pueblo ritual and religion, the combination of painted and modeled design makes explicit the relationship between human reproduction and other life-giving forms of generation, especially corn.14 The most sacred of all ritual objects is a perfect ear of corn (*i'ariko* at Cochiti), decorated with beads and feathers and addressed as "Our Mother."15

As the Anglo presence increased with the coming of the railroads to New Mexico in the 1880s, the production of such figures as this markedly decreased. Pueblo potters did not, however, hesitate to capitalize on the growing tourist market, and in addition to bowls and jars, Cochiti women made an abundance of small desacralized human

Figure 4: *Mother and Child Effigy,* artist unknown, Cochiti Pueblo, 1875–80. This seven-inch-high polychrome figure, collected by Rev. Sheldon Jackson in the late 1870s, is the earliest known Cochiti *Singing Mother.* (Courtesy of the Princeton University Museum of Natural History; photograph by J. Bradley Babcock)

and animal figures for sale. Anglos bought and sold countless "curiosities," "idols," or "monos" but did not regard them highly or, except Santa Fe dealer Jake Gold, encourage their production. In the first half of this century, pottery production at Cochiti, as in many other pueblos, declined. As Helen Cordero has said, *for a long time pottery was silent in the pueblo.* Nonetheless, this ancient tradition endured, and among those few figurative forms that continued to be made, the image of a woman holding or carrying a child or a water jar or a bowl of bread was the most popular. In the decade before Helen Cordero *started up on little people,* at least three Cochiti potters were still making these *singing ladies, singing mothers, or madonnas* (see Figure 5).

By the late 1950s, the six children that Helen had raised were grown, and like other Cochiti women, she began doing bead and leatherwork to make a little extra money. Unfortunately, most of the profits went for buying more materials, and one day Fred Cordero's aunt, Grandma Juana, said, *Why don't you girls go back to potteries? You don't have to buy anything; Mother Earth gives it all to you.* And so, Helen *started on pottery* with her kinswoman Juanita Arquero, who had learned to make pottery as a child, and *spent six months under her.* Her bowls and jars were *all crooked,* and she despaired of ever *getting it right.* Juanita suggested that she *try figures instead and it was like a flower blooming.* She began with little animals but was soon shaping countless small standing and seated figures, many of them continuing the Cochiti tradition of pottery mothers and children (see Figure 6). One of the first times Helen *showed them out* at a Santo Domingo feast day, folk art collector Alexander Girard bought all that she had and asked her to make more and larger figures and bring them to his home in Sante Fe. The first *Storyteller* (see Figure 2) was made in response to his request for a larger seated mother with more children. Helen recalls that *when I went home and thought about it, I kept seeing my grandfather. That one, he was a really good storyteller and there were always lots of us grandchildrens around him.*

In addition to telling stories to his many grandchildren and being esteemed in the pueblo as a gifted storyteller, the leader of one of the clown societies, a *mucho sabio,* and the most powerful of the *principales* (the tribal council), Santiago Quintana (see Figure 3) was the valued friend and collaborator of several generations of anthropologists and observers of Cochiti life: Adolph Bandelier, Frederick Starr, Charles Saunders, Edward Curtis, and lastly Ruth Benedict, who collected many of the *Tales of the Cochiti Indians* from him and wrote warmly of her "old man" in letters from the field.[16] When Helen Cordero remembered her grandfather's voice and shaped that first image of

Figure 5: Cochiti *Singing Ladies,* 1955–60. Shaped by, *left to right,* Damacia Cordero, Teresita Romero, and Laurencita Herrera. Made by three of Cochiti's well-known figurative potters, these Pueblo women with a baby on a cradleboard, five-and-a-half inches high; a bowl of bread, seven-and-a-quarter inches high; and a water jar, six-inches high, exemplify the type of figures produced at Cochiti in the decade preceding Helen's invention of the *Storyteller.* (Courtesy of, *left to right,* the Laboratory of Anthropology, Museum of New Mexico, and Ruth Weber Collection, Santa Fe; drawing by Trudy Griffin-Pierce)

him telling stories to five grandchildren, she made two significant modifications in the *singing mother* tradition: she made the primary figure male rather than female, and she placed more than a realistic number of children on him. In addition to embodying this dialogic relationship between convention and invention, *Storytellers* are obviously "about" relationships—between generations, between past and future, and between stories and *potteries* (see Figure 7).[17] Less obviously, Helen's figures in particular are about the relationship between male and female creativity and the reproduction of the cultural order, for her reinvention of this important mode of cultural production and tradition of representation—pottery making—controlled by women transformed an image of natural reproduction into a figure of an important mode of cultural reproduction—storytelling—that is controlled by men and that both embodies and expresses generativity.

From the body of the *Storyteller* sprout countless children and grandchildren, and from his open mouth emerges "life for the people"

Figure 6: *Singing Mother,* by Helen Cordero, Cochiti Pueblo, 1960–61. This five-and-a-half-inch figure is characteristic of many small figures made by Helen Cordero between 1959 and 1963 and is very similar to those made by other Cochiti potters between 1920 and 1960. (Courtesy of the Marjorie Lambert Collection, Santa Fe; photograph by Glenn Short)

Figure 7: *Storyteller,* by Helen Cordero, Cochiti Pueblo, 1971. This twelve-and-a-half-inch *Storyteller* with seventeen children took first prize at the 1971 Santa Fe Indian Market. In 1976, it was featured on a poster printed by the collectors for Helen's one-woman show at the Heard Museum in Phoenix, and in 1982, it appeared on the cover of National Geographic Magazine. (Courtesy of the Collection of The Hand and the Spirit Crafts Gallery, Scottsdale, Arizona; photograph by Glenn Short)

in the shape of stories, testifying yet again to Pueblo culture's instinct for survival and its capacity to revitalize itself.[18] Whether one looks at the Pueblo worldview and its dynamics of cultural survival from the perspective of religion, kinship, pottery making, or narrative traditions, one finds that Pueblo identity and individual and social integration are conceived in terms of fertility and regeneration: "one story is only the beginning of many stories";[19] clay images of domestic animals are blessed and buried in the corral "so that there will be more of them";[20] and corn, "the seed of seeds," multiplies itself many times from a single grain.[21] The history of the *Storyteller* is itself an expression of this reproductive dynamic, for that first *Storyteller* was the beginning of countless *little people.* Helen herself has made more *Storytellers* and won more prizes than she can or will count—*it's like breads, we don't count* (see Figure 7). By 1973, when the "What is Folk Art?" exhibit was mounted at the Museum of International Folk Art in Santa Fe, the success and popularity of the *Storyteller* was such that at least six other Cochiti potters had imitated her invention (see Figure 8). A decade later, no less than fifty other Cochiti potters and over a hundred potters throughout the New Mexico Pueblos were shaping *Storytellers* and related figurative forms. Many of these imitations are female figures, and as far as Helen is concerned, they are emphatically *not really Storytellers.* They may call them *Storytellers, but they don't know what it means. They don't know it's after my grandfather. At home, no womens are storytellers!*[22]

In the six years that I have known Helen, I have repeatedly heard her insist on both the ancestral and the masculine attributes of her figures. Given the fact that she and her mother (who was Esther Goldfrank's principal informant) tell stories and that half of Ruth Benedict's narrators were most assuredly female, why this assertion that appears to contradict observed "fact"? And, why, I have asked much more recently, given the obvious economic benefit to the pueblo, did one of its officers try to persuade the tribal council to forbid the well-known Cochiti *Storyteller* potters—all of whom are women—from having exhibits of their work and from giving pottery-making demonstrations at museums and national parks? What I would like to suggest is that these two questions are not unrelated and that answers to them provide clues as to the local significance of Helen Cordero's creativity and to the generative and transformative and dangerously liminal power of the image she invented. It seemed very strange indeed that the all-male tribal council would have debated whether or not women potters should demonstrate the making of *Storytellers* to Anglo tourists when extra income is sorely needed to

Figure 8: Cochiti *Storytellers* in the "What is Folk Art?" exhibit at the Museum of International Folk Art, Santa Fe, 1973. *Left to right*: Helen Cordero, Felipa Trujillo, Aurelia Suina, Juanita Arquero, Frances Suina, Seferina Ortiz, and Damacia Cordero. This is one of very few *Storytellers* produced by Helen's teacher, Juanita Arquero, whose artistry is primarily expressed in the finest of contemporary Cochiti bowls and jars. (Courtesy of the Museum of New Mexico; photograph by Arthur Taylor)

support summer ceremonials and when Pueblo pottery has been made for an Anglo market for over a century. The more I considered this "social drama" that occurred in the summer of 1982, the more entangled I became in a complicated situation involving the politics of reproduction and issues of discourse and authority—of who has the right to represent what to whom. Crises initiate reflexivity, and this one forced me to realize that I had naively assumed—as have other scholars of Pueblo ceramics—that pottery and politics have nothing to do with each other. As I contemplated conflict and clay, I began to see that *Storytellers* as conceived and invented by Helen Cordero were *not just pretty things made for money* in terms of personal identification (*All my potteries come from my heart. They're my little people*), but in terms of the degree to which they resist and revise discursive constraints.[23]

When Helen Cordero insists on the ancestral and masculine attributes of her *Storyteller,* she is doing much more than emphasizing the difference and uniqueness of her *potteries.* She is both explicitly and implicitly "authorizing" her creation. Explicitly, by invoking ancestral authority and power: *It's my grandfather, he's giving me these. He was a really wise man. He had lots of stories and lots of grandchildrens, and we're all in there, in the clay.* [24] Implicitly, by insisting on the masculinity of her composite figure, she identifies her pottery with a sacred, masculine activity—a tradition that is both patriarchal and genealogical. Women do tell stories at Cochiti, but they do not tell the stories—the master fictions—by which the people live. As Parsons and many other Pueblo scholars have pointed out, men and women have differential access to sacred discourse.[25] Origin myths and legends as well as songs and drums and kachinas and kivas and all the other aspects of sacred discourse, including the ceremonial Keresan in which it is spoken, are controlled by men. As Helen's uncle, Joe Trujillo, remarked several decades ago, "Our kivas are like—how you say in English? Yes, like men's clubs. The women are only admitted for certain ceremonies, but most of the time we men are there alone. Religion is man's business with Indians."[26]

If women are practically peripheral, they are symbolically central to this "man's business," which involves, among other things, a transcendental appropriation of the female principle. Pueblo religion is elaborated around the idea of fertility and is indigenously described as a vast, interconnected symbolic web at the center of which sits Spider Woman, Thought Woman, the "mother of all."[27] Not surprisingly, the practice of religion involves both comic and serious female impersonation. The cacique, or religious leader of the pueblo, whose chief functions concern rain and fertility and the well-being of his "children," is not only regarded as the representative of Iyatiku, the Corn Mother; he is, after he is installed in office, symbolically viewed as a woman and referred to in female terms.[28] The cacique is responsible for the spiritual and physical welfare of the pueblo, and he "takes care of his people by looking after 'his children' just as the Mother (Iyatiku) whom he represents looked after the images in her basket."[29] In Keresan emergence narratives, Spider Woman sends Iyatiku ("bringing to life") and her sister Nao'tsiti ("more of everything in the basket") up into the light, to this earth, with baskets crammed full of seeds and little clay images and sacred cornmeal, with which they create and pray into being all forms of life.[30] The continued association of clay figures with the creation, maintenance, and reproduction of Pueblo life is this practice of collectively representing Keresan townspeople in male and female clay images that are kept and cared for by the cacique.

If Iyatiku's clay figures are regarded as the embodiment of "life for the people," so too are the stories about Iyatiku that are kept and told by men, such as Helen's grandfather. Both sacred and secular stories were and are one of the primary modes in which the family, the clan, and the community regenerates itself, for such narratives both describe and create "chains" linking generation to generation and back again, and they involve what Silko describes as the vital dynamic of "bringing and keeping the people together."[31] In the words of contemporary Keresan storytellers Leslie Silko and Simon Ortiz, "you don't have anything if you don't have the stories"[32] and "the only way to continue is to tell a story and there is no other way."[33] What is remarkable about these stories, past and present, oral and written, is that the idea of fertility and the model of reproduction is re-presented again and again in the language of and about the stories, in their content, and in the embedded style in which they are structured and told. Nowhere is this more manifest than in the images of a grandfather storyteller, his belly full of "life for the people," giving birth to both children and stories that Leslie Silko and Helen Cordero have created in words and in clay.[34]

Both cosmologically and socially, the Keres world is constructed of a series of oppositions, of which male versus female is primary.[35] Given the fact that woman is ideologically and symbolically central, that clans are matrilineal, and that residence was traditionally matrilocal at Cochiti, it has been fashionable if not doctrinaire to describe the distribution of power as complementary and to ascribe to women much more "real" power than they in fact have.[36] Once upon a time, Cochiti children received their social identity and physical place from their mother.[37] But times have changed, and while children are still of their mother's clan and clans still fulfill a nurturant function, Cochiti clans and "clan mothers" are far less important and powerful than they once were.[38] Wage labor, increased prosperity, and government housing have virtually abolished matrilocal residence—a man who wants his own house, builds it. If one's livelihood does not depend on one's fields, the fact that one's wife "owns" them matters little. With Catholicism in the Rio Grande Pueblos came absolute monogamy, greatly increasing a man's status in the household and his power over his wife.[39] At the same time, the two kiva organizations or moieties— Turquoise and Pumpkin—are larger and more powerful than ever, and they are patrilineal. Upon marriage, women become members of their husbands' kivas and assume the role of "helpers"; children take their father's surname and belong to his kiva. Today, kiva membership is a much more significant determinant of Cochiti social identity than clan affiliation.

Man's business at Cochiti is political as well as religious, for the Pueblo government is a theocracy. Supreme power resides with the cacique and the heads of the three medicine societies who annually choose the six major secular officers—governor and lieutenant governor, war captain and lieutenant war captain, and "fiscale" and "lieutenant fiscale"—who are equally divided between the two kivas and become members of the tribal council for life. While the governor controls secular affairs and the fiscale manages the Catholic church, the war captains, who represent the mythic twin war gods, are the "ceremonial police," whose principal duties are preserving traditions and secrets and leading the fight against tribal enemies.[40]

In sacred discourse and religious practice, in social and political organization, and in domestic and family situations, the relationship between the sexes is a classic example of female power and male dominance.[41] For all their ascribed symbolic significance, Cochiti women are, in Edwin Ardener's terms, a "muted" rather than an "articulate group," excluded from "the dominant communicative system of the society—expressed as it must be through ideology and that 'mode of production' which is articulated with it."[42] *We don't have any say about that* is a phrase I have heard from women at Cochiti more times than I can count. However, as Ardener and others have pointed out, in a world in which discourse is controlled by men, women's ideas or models of the world about them finds expression in forms other than direct speech. But, as Ardener also notes, far too few ethnographers have talked to women or deemed their modes of expression worthy of investigation. This is true even in Pueblo studies, where despite the fact that a larger than usual amount of ethnography has been done by women, the overwhelming focus has been on male-dominated discourse.

Frank Cushing, who was an iconoclast, and Ruth Bunzel, who was a woman influenced by Franz Boas's insistence on the importance of art, were exceptions to this male bias in their recognition that for generation upon generation of Pueblo women, pottery making has been a primary and privileged mode of expression.[43] In Pueblo life, *potteries* are one of the few forms of "objective culture" that have been identified with and created almost exclusively by women.[44] Traditionally, men were associated with this mode of production but excluded from the transformative activities of shaping and firing clay. "In the beginning, Itc'tinaku [Spider Woman] considered how the people should live" and sent her mother and father down to them as "Clay Old Woman and Clay Old Man." Clay Old Woman "began to coil a pot with her clay, and Clay Old Man danced beside her singing while she worked."[45] "He" has continued to dance and sing, and "she" has continued to shape the flesh of Mother Earth into ceremonial, utilitarian, and commercial forms, *talking to and thanking Grandma Clay* at every stage of the creative process.

As archaeologists have demonstrated, as Cushing so finely described in "Zuni Breadstuff," and as the Cochiti story about the origin of pottery I have just quoted reflects, settled Pueblo existence as it developed in the southwestern United States over two thousand years ago and was lived until the latter part of the nineteenth century was inconceivable without rain, without the cultivation of corn, and without pottery to store water and grain. Clay not only was essential to life but in traditional Pueblo belief was regarded as a living substance as well. A pottery vessel was not thought of as an inert object but as a "made being," acquiring a kind of conscious and personal existence as it was being made. "As a receptacle for water and food, it held, and was in turn, a source of life,"[46] and the designs with which it was painted had "one dominant theme, a prayer for rain for the maturing crops."[47] Moreover, in the Keresan origin myths I have already cited, innumerable forms of life originate as clay images. In addition to the descendants of these clay people that the cacique takes care of, human and animal ceramic figurines are associated, both historically and prehistorically, with the idea of fertility, with agricultural fertility cults, and with rites of human increase.[48] In this worldview, not only are baby making and culture making not incompatible, but they are inseparable; with both their bodies and their hands, women reproduce the cultural order.

If Pueblo ceramics were once a primary mode of production, they were also and still are symbolic forms, containers of cultural value and models of and for reproduction and regeneration.[49] Their *potteries*, like their stories, their rituals, and their kinship system, connect the reproductive aspect of generation with the cultural basis of thought, transmission, and "in a different voice," clay sings. With the encroachment of an Anglo world and the expansion of an Anglo market for Indian objects, pottery making has become increasingly important as a mode of cultural survival and as a cultural voice, a statement of ethnic identity. *Potteries* are, in Bourdieu's apt phrase, "symbolic capital," for "in a very real way, the survival of the craft symbolizes the survival of the people."[50] Although ceramic scholars have not talked about it in these terms, precisely because it is "symbolic capital," Pueblo pottery making is also an institutionalized mechanism for consolidating and preserving female power.[51]

While women produce these necessary and symbolic vessels, men have nonetheless traditionally controlled their distribution and marketing, along with other forms of communication with the outside world. This, too, is reflected in the Cochiti story about the origin of pottery as well as in subsequent ethnographic accounts: after Clay Old Woman shaped the clay, "the old man took the pot and gave a piece of it to everybody in the village."[52] Since at least the fifteenth century, "the exchange of pottery has played a considerable economic role in Rio Grande Pueblo culture," and this trading has been the business of men.[53] Matilda Coxe Stevenson recorded the following situation at Zia Pueblo in the late 1880s: "The Sia women labor industriously at the ceramic art as soon as their grain supply becomes reduced, and the men carry the wares to their unfriendly neighbors for trade in exchange for wheat and corn. As long as the Sia can induce the traders through the country to take their pottery they refrain from barter with their Indian neighbors. The women usually dispose of the articles to the traders, but they never venture on expeditions to the Santa Ana and the Jemez."[54]

After 1880, the railroads and the influx of Anglos to the territory created both an expanding "tourist" market for Pueblo pottery and wage-earning jobs for men, and women took increasing responsibility for marketing the products of their labor. Predictably, there was resistance, and as late as 1925, when Kenneth Chapman, Odd Halseth, and others at the Museum of New Mexico were encouraging pottery "revivals," they discovered that the Santo Domingo Pueblo council did not want Santo Domingo women to take their pottery to the newly instituted Indian Fair in Sante Fe. Acculturation, automobiles, and the advent of an Anglo "art" market that names and wants to know its Indian artists has changed all that. Women still dominate the manufacture of pottery—of approximately two hundred figurative potters in 1984, only twenty were men—but they have also assumed control of its distribution and have entered into a cash economy and the business of communicating with the outside world—activities that were once their husbands' prerogatives. While Pueblo pottery has continued to be an important vehicle of identity maintenance, it has also become a means of identity change and a crucial variable in the transition from a subsistence to a cash economy.[55] Both the fortunes of this ancient craft in this century and the recent "social drama" centering on pottery at Cochiti support the argument of several students of material culture that the objectual aspects of a culture are more conservative, more innovative, and more readily diffused than its behavioral and ideological aspects.[56]

In the remarkable revival of figurative pottery that Helen Cordero's *Storyteller* has engendered in the last twenty years, women potters have done much more than reshape their traditional roles in terms of economics, mobility, and communication.[57] By creating not only *Storytellers* but also *Nightcriers, Drummers, Turtles,* and other ceremonial and mythic figures and by exhibiting and demonstrating their art, they have assumed the right to re-present and interpret to the outside world at least some of the aspects of the very discourse in which they are displaced. Both endorsing and challenging men's ideological hegemony, a clay *Storyteller* is a woman's visual re-creation of a man's verbal and symbolic representations of a woman's biological experience. It is her reappropriation of her own symbolic power and his right to articulate it. The very gender ambiguity of *Storytellers*—both presentational and perceptual—is a statement of competing interests in the terrain of symbolic production. *At home, no womens are storytellers,* but women are potters, and with the transformative power of their hands, they have contrived to tell stories about storytelling, to subvert masculine discursive control, and to disturb the distribution of power profoundly. In this case, the struggle between the powerless and the powerful has been displaced quite literally onto the surface of things. It would seem, in terms of Zygmunt Bauman's reformulation of the distinction between static and dynamic cultures, that the sociocultural system at Cochiti—and probably in other pueblos as well—is changing from a static one "in which rights to signs are derivative from social position" to a dynamic one "in which social position is derivative from the possession of signs."[58]

Helen Cordero and her sisters are manipulating considerably more than clay. They are reproducing "with a difference," and they are figuratively as well as literally playing with fire. Helen teases me a lot, and on one recent occasion, I could not resist the temptation to give her a hard time about her fancy new Frigidaire Harvest Gold ice-dispensing refrigerator. She stopped making tortillas, turned from the stove—which she had also just replaced with a new Magic Chef—because the old one with its self-cleaning oven had ruined the *potteries* that she was preheating before firing them outside *in the old way, the right way*—and said quite seriously, *I'm getting me what I always wanted.* She has empowered three generations of other Pueblo women to do the same, to reshape their lives and the roles traditionally allotted to them.

Clearly, Edward Evans-Pritchard talked to "primitive women" very different from the ones that I have—if he talked to them at all—and just as clearly, the tribal official's attempt to silence them reflects the highly authoritarian nature of Pueblo society and bespeaks a recognition that continuity over time is a political as well as a biological and cultural problem.[59] Although that official's motives were reportedly baser, in acting as he did, he was reasserting the traditional Pueblo male right to mediate with the outside world and protect what he deems sacred discourse as well as attempting to reinvoke an ancient male prerogative to appropriate and control female generativity and creativity. It was, you can almost hear him saying, one thing for old Santiago Quintana to travel to California or to share his culture and its stories with Bandelier and Benedict; it is quite another for his grand-daughter to hop a plane in Albuquerque and to make *Storytellers* and talk about her grandfather and his stories in Denver. Times have changed, and this time he lost his case against the "womens," but that's another story.[60]

Notes

This essay was originally published in *Journal of the Southwest* 30, no. 3 (1988): 357–89. Used by permission of the publisher.

1. For discussion and documentation of the *Storyteller* revolution, see Barbara A. Babcock, "Clay Changes: Helen Cordero and the Pueblo Storyteller," *American Indian Art* 8 (1983): 30–39; Barbara A. Babcock and Guy and Doris Monthan, *The Pueblo Storyteller: Development of a Figurative Ceramic Tradition* (Tucson: University of Arizona Press, 1986).

2. This statement and those that follow in italics were made by Helen Cordero in conversations between 1978 and 1984. When we began to work on the story of her life and art, she insisted that she would not *spill the beans,* and I have not discussed sacred discourse or social and ceremonial organization with her or any other *Cochitis.* The information about these matters

contained in this essay was obtained from already published accounts by various observers of Cochiti and Keresan life in the past century and from conversations with anthropologists who lived and worked at Cochiti under very different constraints in previous decades.

3. Ruth Benedict, "Configurations of Culture in North America," *American Anthropologist* 34, no. 6 (1932): 26.

4. See Daniel Biebuyck, ed., *Tradition and Creativity in Tribal Art* (Berkeley: University of California Press, 1969).

5. Raymond Firth, "The Social Framework of Primitive Art," *Elements of Social Organization* (Boston: Beacon, 1966), 167.

6. See Warren L. d'Azevedo, ed., *The Traditional Artist in African Society* (Bloomington: Indiana University Press, 1973).

7. For a general theory of the nature of innovation and the consequences of as well as conditions for the appearance of novel ideas, see Homer Barnett, *Innovation: The Basis of Cultural Change* (New York: McGraw-Hill, 1953).

8. Many of these points are made by Judith Modell in her discussion of Zuni mythology in *Ruth Benedict: Patterns of a Life* (Philadelphia: University of Pennsylvania Press, 1983). She argues that Benedict's achievement in this and "other folklore pieces, was to incorporate a notion of imaginativeness into the study of culture" (243).

9. Fritz Kaufmann, "Art and Phenomenology," in *Essays in Phenomenology,* ed. W. Natanson (The Hague: Martinus Nijhoff, 1969), 147.

10. Clifford Geertz, "Art as a Cultural System," *Modern Language Notes* 91 (1976): 1478.

11. Maurice Merleau-Ponty, "Indirect Language and the Voices of Silence," in *Signs* (Evanston: Northwestern University Press, 1964), 169.

12. Much of my argument, in addition to this statement, is indebted to Roy Wagner's stimulating meditation on culture as creativity, as invention, in *The Invention of Culture* (Chicago: University of Chicago Press, 1981).

13. For further discussion of both prehistoric and historic Pueblo figurative pottery traditions, see Babcock and Monthan, *Pueblo Storyteller.*

14. For an encyclopedic inventory of Pueblo religion, see Elsie Clews Parsons, *Pueblo Indian Religion* (Chicago: University of Chicago Press, 1939). For discussions of fertility as the root metaphor or master trope of Pueblo culture, see especially H. K. Haeberlin, *The Idea of Fertilization in the Culture of the Pueblo Indians,* Memoirs of the American Anthropological Association, vol. 3, no. 13–16 (Lancaster, Pa.: American Anthropological Association, 1916); Frank Hamilton Cushing, "Zuni Breadstuff," in *Indian Notes and Monographs,* vol. 8 (New York: Museum of the American Indian, 1920); and Ruth Benedict, *Patterns of Culture* (Boston: Houghton Mifflin, 1934). See also Mary Black, "Maidens and Mothers: An Analysis of Hopi Corn Metaphors," *Ethnology* 23, no. 4 (1984): 279–88, for an analysis of Hopi corn metaphors.

15. Parsons, *Pueblo Indian Religion,* 182, 319–23.

16. For descriptions of Santiago Quintana, see Ruth Benedict, *Tales of the*

Cochiti Indians (Albuquerque: University of New Mexico Press, 1931), xi; and her September 5, 1925, letter to Margaret Mead, in Margaret Mead, *An Anthropologist at Work: Writings of Ruth Benedict* (New York: Equinox Books, 1973), 300.

17. Gregory Bateson argues that it is probably an error to think of art as being about any one matter other than relationship, in his important essay "Style, Grace, and Information in Primitive Art," in *Primitive Art and Society,* ed. Anthony Forge (London: Oxford University Press, 1973), 254–55.

18. For discussion of the Pueblo capacity for revitalization, the dynamics of cultural survival, and the importance of art therein, see Alfonso Ortiz, "The Dynamics of Pueblo Cultural Survival," paper presented at the American Anthropological Association meetings, Washington, D.C., 1976; J. J. Brody, "The Creative Consumer: Survival, Revival, and Invention in Southwest Indian Arts," in *Ethnic and Tourist Arts,* ed. Nelson Graburn (Berkeley: University of California Press, 1976), 70–84; and Brody, "Pueblo Fine Arts," in *Handbook of North American Indians,* vol. 9, ed. Alfonso Ortiz (Washington, D.C.: Smithsonian Institution Press, 1979), 603–8. The description of stories as "life for the people" is from the title poem of Leslie Marmon Silko's novel *Ceremony* (New York: Viking, 1977), 2.

19. Leslie Marmon Silko, "Language and Literature from a Pueblo Indian Perspective," in *English Literature: Opening Up the Canon,* ed. Leslie A. Fiedler and Houston A. Baker, Jr. (Baltimore: Johns Hopkins University Press, 1981), 56.

20. Elsie Clews Parsons, "Increase by Magic: A Zuni Pattern," *American Anthropologist* 21, no. 3 (1919): 279.

21. Cushing, "Zuni Breadstuff," 54.

22. The image of a large composite figure covered with smaller versions of itself universally connotes reproduction and, by implication, femaleness. Not surprisingly, Helen's *Storytellers* have been perceived as female both by Anglo consumers and by Pueblo potters who have imitated her invention. In his suggestive essay "Levels of Communication and Taboo in the Appreciation of Primitive Art" (in Forge, *Primitive Art and Society*), Edmund Leach argues that punning, particularly sexual ambiguity, is very common in art forms: "My general proposition is that all true artists tend to devote their principal efforts to themes which contain elements of sensory ambiguity and are subject to taboo.... When we examine the products of exotic cultures the confusions which first fascinate us are those which have a physiological base, they are the confusions between male and female, between food and not food, between symbols of dominance and symbols of submission" (230, 234).

23. For discussion of Helen's *potteries* as autobiographical statements, as shaping and shaped from personal experience, see Barbara A. Babcock, "Modeled Selves: Helen Cordero's 'Little People,'" in *The Anthropology of Experience,* ed. Victor W. Turner and Edward M. Bruner (Urbana: University

of Illinois Press, 1985), 316–43. See also Victor Turner, "Social Dramas and Stories about Them," *Critical Inquiry* 7, no. 1 (1980): 141–68.

24. In *Cochiti: A New Mexico Pueblo, Past and Present* (Carbondale: Southern Illinois University Press, 1968), Charles H. Lange has this to say about ancestral power: "A fundamental belief in the religious orientation of the Cochiti is that supernatural power is believed to be held by certain individuals at specific times because these powers have been transmitted to cultural predecessors from supernatural beings during various eras of the past. The specific powers vary in accordance with the person's official capacity, or status, and also to the extent to which he is worthy of that status" (232).

25. Parsons, *Pueblo Indian Religion*, 40.

26. Edith Hart Mason, "Enemy Bear," *The Masterkey* 22, no. 3 (1948): 85.

27. Parsons, *Pueblo Indian Religion*, 192–93.

28. See especially Robin Fox's discussion of the term *yaya* (*mother*), which is used for both the cacique and his stone fetish, in *The Keresan Bridge* (New York: Humanities Press, 1967), 143.

29. Parsons, *Pueblo Indian Religion*, 336.

30. For transcriptions, summaries, and interpretations of Keresan emergence narratives, see Benedict, *Tales of the Cochiti;* Franz Boas, *Keresan Texts,* Publications of the American Ethnological Society, no. 8 (1928); Fr. Noel Dumarest, *Notes on Cochiti, New Mexico,* Memoirs of the American Anthropological Association, vol. 6, no. 3 (Lancaster, Pa.: American Anthropological Association, 1918), 135–236; C. Daryll Forde, "A Creation Myth from Acoma," *Folk-Lore* 41 (1930): 370–87; Parsons, *Pueblo Indian Religion;* Lucien Sebag, *L'invention du monde chez les indiens pueblos* (Paris: François Maspero, 1971); Matilda Coxe Stevenson, "The Sia," *Eleventh Annual Report of the Bureau of American Ethnology* (Washington, D.C.: Smithsonian Institution, 1894); Matthew Stirling, "The Origin Myth of Acoma and Other Records," *Bureau of American Ethnology Bulletin,* no. 135 (1942); Leslie A. White, "The Acoma Indians," in *Forty-Seventh Annual Report of the Bureau of American Ethnology* (Washington, D.C.: Smithsonian Institution, 1932), 17–192; White, *The Pueblo of San Felipe,* Memoirs of the American Anthropological Association, no. 38 (Menasha, Wis.: American Anthropological Association, 1932); White, *The Pueblo of Santo Domingo,* Memoirs of the American Anthropological Association, no. 43 (Menasha, Wis.: American Anthropological Association, 1935); White, *The Pueblo of Santa Ana,* Memoirs of the American Anthropological Association, no. 60 (Menasha, Wis.: American Anthropological Association, 1942); and White, "The Pueblo of Sia," *Bulletin of the Bureau of American Ethnology,* no. 184 (1962). The motif of creation through the molding of meal, dust, or clay is not limited to origin myths but is widely found throughout Pueblo narratives.

31. Silko, "Language and Literature," 59. For a very suggestive Jungian analysis of the importance of "chains" of generations, etc., in creation myths as a way of being linked "with historical continuity, i.e., from the inside, with one's ancestral soul, to be connected with the archetype foundations of the

244 / Barbara A. Babcock

psyche, as counter-magic against dissociation," see Marie-Louise von Franz, *Patterns of Creativity Mirrored in Creation Myths* (Zurich: Spring Publications, 1978), 204.

32. Silko, *Ceremony,* 2.

33. Simon J. Ortiz, *A Good Journey* (Berkeley: Turtle Island, 1977), 9.

34. See, for example, Figure 7 and Silko's title poem in *Ceremony,* 2.

35. Pueblo "world structure," as a "relentlessly connected universal whole" in which "men, animal, plants, and spirits are intertransposable in a seemingly unbroken chain of being," constructed in terms of a series of oppositions, is something of a structuralist's dream according to Alfonso Ortiz, "Ritual Drama and the Pueblo World View," in *New Perspectives on the Pueblo,* ed. A. Ortiz (Albuquerque: University of New Mexico Press, 1972), 143. For a structural analysis of Tewa worldview, see Ortiz, *The Tewa World: Space, Time, Being, and Becoming in a Pueblo Society* (Chicago: University of Chicago Press, 1969); of Keres through their creation myths, see Sebag, *L'invention du monde.*

36. The position one ascribes to women in Pueblo society depends significantly on whether one focuses on ideology or praxis. As Bennett and others have remarked, those interpretations (e.g., Benedict) that center on the former, which Bennett calls "organic," see Pueblo culture and society as integrated and harmonious. Those who focus on the latter (e.g., Goldfrank), which he calls "repressive," emphasize the tension, conflict, and fear of Pueblo life, and the extent to which the individual (male or female) is suppressed and repressed. See John W. Bennett, "The Interpretation of Pueblo Culture: A Question of Values," *Southwestern Journal of Anthropology* 2, no. 4 (1946): 361–74. The truth, I suspect, is somewhere in between, and one must look at the position of women in both ideology and praxis. On the basis of cross-cultural evidence, including Alice Schlegel's Hopi work, Peggy Sanday argues in *Female Power and Male Dominance: On the Origins of Sexual Equality* (Cambridge: Cambridge University Press, 1981) that "female economic and political power is ascribed as a natural right due the female sex when a long-standing magico-religious association between maturity and fertility of the soil associates women with social continuity and the social good" (114). I would respond, not necessarily so, especially not in increasingly acculturated situations that have modified both the social and religious position of women and certainly not among the Keresan Pueblos.

37. For discussion of the "manly/womanly dichotomy" in terms of which the Keres order their world and of the anthropology of Keres identity, see Julius Miller, "The Anthropology of Keres Identity" (Ph.D. dissertation, Rutgers University, 1972). See also Mary Austin, *The Land of Journey's Ending* (1924; Tucson: University of Arizona Press, 1983), for discussion of the relationship between house and kiva.

38. For discussion of Cochiti clans, their curing and nurturant functions, their declining importance, and concomitant changes in Cochiti social organization, see Robin Fox, *Keresan Bridge;* and Fox, *Encounter with Anthropology* (New York: Harcourt Brace, 1973).

39. In discussing Pueblo attitudes toward innovation in 1949, John Collier observed that "with Christianity, in the Rio Grande Pueblos, came the morality and custom of indissoluble marriage. It was a radical innovation, and apparently was welcomed by the males because it increased their status and power: the man no longer dwelt in the kiva, but lived in his children's home as co-head of the establishment. The absolute prohibition of divorce became a custom, guarded as such by the officials and priests of the ancient Pueblo religions" (*Patterns and Ceremonials of the Indians of the Southwest* [New York: E. P. Dutton, 1949], 51). For further, cross-cultural discussion of the decline in indigenous female power with colonialism, see Sanday, *Female Power*, chapter 7.

40. For discussions of Cochiti social and ceremonial organization and changes therein between the early 1920s and the early 1950s, see Esther Goldfrank, *The Social and Ceremonial Organization of Cochiti*, Memoirs of the American Anthropological Association, no. 33 (Menasha, Wis.: American Anthropological Association, 1927); Lange, *Cochiti;* and Fox, *Encounter with Anthropology.*

41. Here and elsewhere, I am following Ernestine Friedl's definition of *male dominance* as "a situation in which men have highly preferential access, although not always exclusive rights, to those activities to which the society accords the greatest value, and the exercise of which permits a measure of control over others" (*Women and Men: An Anthropologist's View* [New York: Holt, Rinehart, and Winston, 1975], 7).

42. Edwin Ardener, "Belief and the Problem of Women and the 'Problem' Revisited," in *Perceiving Women,* ed. Shirley Ardener (London: Malaby, 1975), 22.

43. In particular, see Frank Hamilton Cushing, "A Study of Pueblo Pottery as Illustrative of Zuni Culture Growth," in *Fourth Annual Report of the Bureau of American Ethnology* (Washington, D.C.: Bureau of American Ethnology, 1886), 437–521; Cushing, "Zuni Breadstuff"; and Ruth Bunzel, *The Pueblo Potter: A Study of Creative Imagination in Primitive Art* (1929; New York: Dover Publications, 1972), for discussion of the meanings, uses, and importance of pottery in Pueblo life.

44. Simmel describes *objective culture* as the world of cultural forms and their artifacts that have become independent of individual human existence. Objective culture is the domain of objects that function as instruments for the cultivation of the person or as conditions under which the individual can become a cultural being. He observes that objective culture is overwhelmingly a product of male activity and that, with few exceptions, the artifacts of culture represent the objectification of the male spirit. In his insightful discussion of "Female Culture" and the ways in which female psyche "becomes visible," he notes that "we should expect from women a special interpretation and mode of forming phenomena in the plastic arts." See Georg Simmel, *On Women, Sexuality, and Love,* trans. Guy Oakes (New Haven, Conn.: Yale University Press, 1984), 6–7, 22, 83.

45. Benedict, *Tales of the Cochiti*, 12.

46. Margaret Ann Hardin, *Gifts of Mother Earth: Ceramics in the Zuni Tradition* (Phoenix: Heard Museum, 1983), 33.

47. Kenneth Chapman, *Pueblo Indian Pottery of the Post-Spanish Period* (Santa Fe: School of American Research, 1950), 6.

48. For beliefs and practices associated with rites of increase and the use of clay figures therein, see Elsie Clews Parsons, "Nativity Myth at Laguna and Zuni," *Journal of American Folklore* 31, no. 120 (1918): 256–63; Parsons, "Increase by Magic"; and Parsons, *Pueblo Indian Religion*. For further discussion, see Babcock and Monthan, *Pueblo Storyteller*.

49. Here and elsewhere, I am indebted to Annette Weiner's "model of reproduction," derived in part from Bourdieu, which she has developed in several essays and which is based on the premise "that any society must reproduce and regenerate certain elements of value in order for the society to continue. . . . These elements of value include human beings, social relations, cosmological phenomena such as ancestors, and resources such as land, material objects, names, and body decorations" ("Reproduction: A Replacement for Reciprocity," *American Ethnologist* 7, no. 1 [1980]: 71). See also Weiner, "The Reproductive Model in Trobriand Society," *Mankind* 11, no. 3 (1978): 175–86; Weiner, "Trobriand Kinship from Another View: The Reproductive Power of Women and Men," *Man* 14, no. 2 (1979): 328–48; and Weiner, "Sticks and Stones, Threads and Bones: This Is What Kinship Is Made Of," paper presented at the conference on Feminism and Kinship Theory, Bellagio.

Within this model, Weiner distinguishes between *reproduction*, referring to cultural attention and meaning given to acts of forming, producing, or creating something new, and *regeneration*, referring to the cultural attention and meaning given to the renewal, revival, rebirth, or re-creation of entities previously reproduced. More recently, she has formulated the notion of *elementary cycling*, by which she means "the cultural configuration of the state of affairs that encompass birth, growth, decay, death, and regeneration. . . . The life cycle of individuals, now understood as those processes which attach relations and objects to an ego and detach them at other times for other egos, cannot be separated analytically from the societal configuration wherein the natural phenomena of birth, growth, decay, and death are culturally circumscribed . . . in this way, the configurations of elementary cycling is the basic logical form out of which integration between the individual and society takes place" ("Sticks and Stones," 10).

Whatever else it may be, the *Storyteller* as conceived and created by Helen Cordero is the embodiment of elementary cycling. I am also indebted to Claude Meillassoux's Marxist analysis of precapitalist formation, in "From Reproduction to Production: A Marxist Approach to Economic Anthropology," *Economy and Society* 1, no. 1 (1972), in which he argues that "agricultural self-sustaining formations described here . . . rely less on the control of the means of material production than on the means of human reproduction: subsistence and women. Their end is reproduction of life as a precondition to production. Their primary concern is to 'grow and multiply' in the biblical sense. . . . the relations of production are established between 'those who come before' and 'those who come after'" (100–102).

50. Brody, "Creative Consumer," 76.

51. For further cross-cultural discussion of institutionalized mechanisms "for consolidating and conserving female power during colonialization," see Sanday, *Female Power*, 37 and passim.

52. Benedict, *Tales of the Cochiti*, 22.

53. David H. Snow, "Some Economic Considerations of Historic Rio Grande Pueblo Pottery," in *The Changing Ways of Southwestern Indians: A Historic Perspective*, ed. A. Schroeder (Glorieta: Rio Grande Press), 55.

54. Stevenson, "The Sia," 11–12.

55. For further discussion of the value of Pueblo pottery in the transition from a subsistence to a cash economy and the importance of the Acoma pottery-making tradition for women's economic survival, see Terry R. Reynolds, "Women, Pottery, and Economics at Acoma Pueblo," in *New Mexico Women: Intercultural Perspectives*, ed. Joan M. Jensen and Darlis A. Miller (Albuquerque: University of New Mexico Press, 1986), 279–300.

56. See, in particular, Barnett, *Innovation;* Nelson H. H. Graburn, *Ethnic and Tourist Arts* (Berkeley: University of California Press, 1976); and Lawrence E. Dawson, Vera-Mae Frederickson, and Nelson H. H. Graburn, *Traditions in Transition: Culture Contact and Material Change* (Berkeley: Lowie Museum of Anthropology, 1974).

57. For further discussion of the *Storyteller* revolution and the development and diffusion of this new genre of Pueblo pottery, see Babcock, "Clay Changes"; and Babcock and Monthan, *Pueblo Storyteller*.

58. Zygmunt Bauman, "Semiotics and the Function of Culture," in *Essays in Semiotics*, ed. Julia Kristeva, J. Rey-Debove, and Donna Jean Umiker (The Hague: Mouton, 1971), 287.

59. In addition to Weiner's "Reproductive Model," "Trobriand Kinship," and "Reproduction," see Mary O'Brien, *The Politics of Reproduction* (London: Routledge and Kegan Paul, 1981); Karen Ericksen Paige and Jeffrey M. Paige, *The Politics of Reproductive Ritual* (Berkeley: University of California Press, 1981); and Elizabeth S. Zelman, "Reproductive Ritual and Power," *American Ethnologist* 4, no. 4 (1977): 714–33, for further discussion of the "politics" of reproduction. There is abundant evidence and discussion of the highly authoritarian nature of Pueblo society and the power exerted by the religious hierarchy, but see especially Esther Goldfrank, "Socialization, Personality, and the Structure of Pueblo Society," *American Anthropologist* 47, no. 4 (1945): 516–39; Florence Hawley Ellis, "Authoritative Control and the Society System in Jemez Pueblo," *Southwestern Journal of Anthropology* 9, no. 4 (1953): 385–94; Edward P. Dozier, "Rio Grande Pueblos," in *Perspectives in American Indian Cultural Change*, ed. Edward H. Spicer (Chicago: University

of Chicago Press, 1961), 94–186; and Fox, *Encounter with Anthropology*. See also Meillassoux, "Reproduction to Production," for a Marxist perspective on the politics of reproduction. He argues that in "agricultural self-sustaining formations [which Pueblo society once was] concern for reproduction becomes paramount . . . [and] reproduction of the unit, both biologically and structurally, is assured through the control of women . . . [and] the shift from production for self-sustenance and self-perpetuation to production for an external market, must necessarily bring a radical transformation, if not the social destruction of the communities" (100–102).

60. In conclusion, my thanks to Helen Cordero, who has shared her life and her work with me and changed my life in the process, and to Susan Aiken, with whom I have shared the experience and the interpretation of muteness. Cochiti Pueblo is not a place where the politics of reproduction are discussed as such, and feminist anthropologists have been rightly cautioned both against projecting our own political concerns and theoretical models onto our analyses of the position of women in other cultures and against using data about women there to buttress arguments about women here. Nonetheless, if we are not attuned to gender dynamics and the politics of discourse in the cultures we are studying as well as in our own, we will perpetrate such idealistic and projective distortions as the ideas that simpler societies are not contaminated by sexual politics and that potteries and politics have nothing to do with each other. Finally, my apologies for being unable and unwilling to give a more detailed account of what transpired at the tribal council.

PART FOUR

Women Interpreting the Stories They Tell

Throughout this book, feminist folklorists have interpreted the creations of other women; here, in a reflexive concluding section meant to open outward into discussion rather than to close the (unclosable) subject of coding, two women write about their own creative performances. Aware of the issues of women's self-expression around which this book revolves, Susan Gordon and Kay F. Stone, professional storytellers who perform and re-create traditional tales, talk about their own self-expression through their stories. They discuss why they choose to tell these stories, how their audiences have responded, how they have reshaped their tales according to what they have learned from listeners, and what the process of developing the stories has taught them about their own experience. As they build their accounts, they image the feminist project of uniting the personal with the professional and scholarly.

Each teller presents her own version of a single narrative. Susan Gordon writes about "The Handless Maiden" (AT 706), a tale of suffering and recovery, pain and healing, which has become central to her repertoire as a teller in therapeutic settings; Kay F. Stone discusses the evolution of her own story "The Curious Girl" out of "Frau Trude" (AT 363), a tale in which a disobedient little girl is changed to firewood and burned by a witch.[1] Both tellers have chosen to work with tales from the Grimms' *Kinder und Hausmärchen*, a collection from another time and continent, but still a staple in North America despite major criticism from feminists in recent decades.[2] It is striking that both women have chosen tales that seem to promote a markedly antifeminist image of female passivity, obedience, and dependence. "The Handless Maiden" shows a young girl submitting first to mutilation by her father and later to banishment from her husband's domain, suffering in the wilderness for fourteen years until she finally comes to a secure position in the world—as wife and mother. "Frau Trude" had its origin in a cautionary nursery rhyme, warning little girls to obey their parents and not to yield to the dangers of curiosity. Gordon and Stone believe, however, that they have found in the core of these tales images of female strength, not weakness. Their versions—powerful metaphors for the developmental truths the tellers perceive—recuperate for modern North American listeners the stories of another culture and present women's messages through them.

It is important to notice that although Gordon and Stone have come in retrospect to complex realizations about the messages their tales carry, they did not set out to create their versions of the stories with such explicit goals in mind. They have written these essays after the fact, discovering and for the first time trying to articulate what they have achieved. Writings by contemporary theorists and therapists have helped Gordon interpret her telling of "The Handless Maiden," but scholarship had no major shaping influence on the development of her version. For Gordon, as well as Stone, the listeners' responses were crucial for the creative process, because these qualified and sharpened their own growing understanding of the tale.

These essays—studies, as Stone puts it, of "transformation"—thus offer insights into the interrelationships of performance and creation and of self and art. To readers interested in the strategies of women's coding, they also offer detailed images of the process that Susan Lanser and I have termed "appropriation," by which women adapt the materials of patriarchal culture to feminist purposes. They show this process in all its drama as a positive, creative discovery of self and meaning. They show the imaginative energy coding can sometimes release, the celebratory energy that may help impel oppressed people—not only women—across the threshold from resistance into an autonomous relationship with the world. They show us the power of finding, shaping, and telling our own stories.

Notes

1. The AT number refers to numbering in Antti Aarne and Stith Thompson, *The Types of the Folktale: A Classification and Bibliography,* Folklore Fellows Communications No. 184 (Helsinki: Academia Scientiarum Fennica, 1973).

2. For a summary of feminist fairy tale scholarship, see Kay F. Stone, "Feminist Approaches to the Interpretation of Fairy Tales," in *Fairy Tales and Society: Illusion, Allusion, and Paradigm,* ed. Ruth B. Bottigheimer (Philadelphia: University of Pennsylvania Press, 1986), 229–36.

The Powers of the Handless Maiden

SUSAN GORDON

Feminist folklore scholars have rightly criticized the Grimms' *Märchen* for presenting helpless, passive female protagonists as the prototype of the ideal woman. "The Handless Maiden" certainly seems to collude in this image of female passivity; she puts out her hands to be cut off by her father, is depicted as needing angelic aid at every crucial transition in her life, and returns home only when she is found by her husband. As Kay Stone points out, however, the images of women in *Märchen* are often much more complex than a first reading might suggest.[1] When I first read "The Handless Maiden," as a beginning teller, I found an inner, coded story, which said that we can lose our hands through no fault of our own and that even handless we are not powerless.

In my eight years of developing and telling this story, I have found that my original response to it has been sustained. My work with "The Handless Maiden" has helped me recognize that each of us may be wounded and need a place of healing where we can become whole again. The Maiden showed me that the recovery of oneself is an internal and lengthy process that is linked to one's ability to care for oneself and for another. The story said that the Maiden would need to leave home not once but twice to regain her hands. The first leaving is leaving one's parents and becoming an adult without refusing one's familial legacy. The second leaving requires a person to leave behind a conventional and prescribed image of himself or herself and to become the self he or she most needs and desires to be.

As a professional storyteller, I tell to entertain; I also tell in educational and religious settings and, increasingly, in therapeutic settings with children, adolescents, and adults. "The Handless Maiden" is a central story in my repertory for any group of people who come together to reflect on their lives and their choices. The responses of listeners from all these settings have been included in this essay.

I describe in the essay how this story has helped both the listeners and me to examine our lives, our roles, and our possibilities in life. I also discuss my development of the tale from the Grimms' telling to the version you will read. The creation of this tale, as I tell it, has largely been an intuitive and artistic process. My understanding of the events in the Grimms' tale and listeners' responses to my telling have shaped the tale and helped me appreciate what it offers. I am not a systematic scholar but a storyteller eager to explore other avenues of understanding my art. It was only after my telling reached its current form that I began to read the scholarship of folklorists, psychologists, human development and women's studies theorists and found in their writing an articulation of the intuitive learning I had gained by telling the tale for myself and my listeners. I have tried to include some of their thoughts in this essay.

The core of my telling comes from the Grimms' version of "The Girl Without Hands," as Marie-Louise von Franz retells it in *Problems of the Feminine in Fairy Tales.*[2] Von Franz's commentary on the story informed my understanding and my telling of "The Handless Maiden."[3] There are no major plot differences between my telling and the Grimms' version, except for the addition of the Russian motif in which the Queen recovers her hands while rescuing her child.[4]

I have written out my telling of "The Handless Maiden" as it sounds to my ears when I tell it. The breaks at the end of each line indicate the rhythm of the telling. The sound of my voice, the emphases, pauses, and silences, are shown by the placement of the words on the page and the use of space. Readers may want to read the story once silently for the events and the movement and then aloud to discover in themselves the voices of the characters.

The Handless Maiden

There was once a miller
who was poor by his own doing.

He was out walking in the woods one day
when a little old man LEAPED out at him
and said, "What are you doin'
and where are you goin'?"

The miller said, "I'm out here choppin' wood.
Any fool can see that."

And the little old man said,
"Well, you need never do that again.
If you'll give me what's standing in your back yard,
I'll give you all the gold you've ever desired."

And the miller said, "Gold?—
I've never had enough gold
and there's nothing in my back yard
but an old apple tree.
Done," he said.

And the little old man said,
"In three years,
I'll be back to get what's mine."

And he vanished.
The miller turned and he went home.

When he got there,
he found his wife waiting for him.
"Where have you been
and what have you been doing?" she asked.

"Why?" he wanted to know.

"Because," she said,
"There is gold coming through the roof,
it's pouring in through the windows,
it's coming through the paddles of the mill,
and I know you well enough
to know you've had a hand in this."

"It worked," he said, "It worked!"

"What worked?" she asked.

"Well," he said,
"I met this little old man in the woods
and he told me that if I'd give him
what was standing in my back yard,
—ain't nothing but an old apple tree—
that he'd give me all the gold I've ever desired."

His wife looked at him.
"You fool," she said, "you fool.
What you met was no little old man
but the evil one.

And what you gave him was not our apple tree,
but our *daughter* who was standing out back."

The miller looked at her and said,
"Well, what's he going to want her for?"

His wife just shook her head
and walked away in disgust.

For the next three years,
that girl lived in fear.

But on the day the Devil came for her,
she washed her hair,
and braided it down.
She buttoned on her best dress,
and she stood out in that back yard
and drew a circle of chalk around herself.

And she was so clean,
the Devil couldn't lay his hands upon her.

He turned
and he raved to the father,
"She's mine! She's mine!
You sold her to me, have you forgotten?"

"No," said the miller,
"I didn't forget,
but I didn't draw that circle of chalk,
didn't put that dress on her neither.
Ain't nothin' I can do about it."

"Oh, yes, there is," said the Devil.
"You let her stand there.
Don't you give her a bite of food;
don't you give her a sip of water;
and in the evening when the wind rises,
she'll be covered with dust
and then she'll be mine."

The Devil left.
The father left
his daughter standing in the yard.
He didn't give her a bite of food.
He didn't give her a sip of water.

And in the evening,
when the wind rose,
she was covered with dust.

She was just as dirty as the Devil could hope for.
But about midnight, she began to cry
and she cried so long and so hard
that she cried herself clean.

And so the next morning,
when the Devil came
he couldn't lay his hands upon her.
And he turned and he raged at the father,
"She's mine, she's mine!
You sold her to me.
Have you forgotten?"

"No," said the miller, "I didn't forget,
but I didn't cry those tears;
I didn't get her clean neither.
Ain't nothin' I can do about it."

"Oh, yes, there is," said the Devil.
"Go get your ax."

And the miller said, "My ax?
What do you want me to get my ax for?"

" 'Cause you're going to cut your daughter's hands off
and then she'll be mine."

And the miller said,
"But that's my daughter standing there.
How can you ask me to do such a thing?"

"It's easy," said the Devil.
"You either cut your daughter's hands off
or *you* come with me right now."

"Oh," said the miller,
"I guess it's easier than I thought."
And he went and he got his ax.

He walked toward his daughter, saying
"Now, you heard the man. I ain't got no choice.
I ain't got no choice."

She looked at him.

"No choice?   No choice?
    Oh, my God.
I would give almost anything in the world
not to be your daughter,
but I am.   *I am.*
So you do with me what you will."

    She held out her hands.

Without a moment's hesitation,
he brought his ax down through them.

The Devil, he left satisfied.
The miller—left his daughter
standing in the yard.

And now she cried.
She cried in her pain;
she cried in her misery.
She cried all day long;
She cried all night long.
She cried so long and so hard that,
                              by morning,
        she had washed *even the stumps*
    where her hands had been
                                   clean.

And so,
the next morning,
when the Devil came for her,
he was obliged to leave without her.

And the miller turned to his daughter
and he said, "Stay with us.
We owe all of our good fortune to you.
Stay with us
and we will take care of you the rest of our days."

She looked at him.
"Stay with you? No.
If I stayed with you,
I would become just like you.
I will not. I will not."

"I will go out in the world," she said,
"and I will seek the care of compassionate men."

Her mother bound her arms behind her back
and she set out.

She wandered all of that day.
She wandered until it was evening.
At last, she came to a village
and when she entered it,
she found, in the center of the village,
    a castle,
but around the castle,
there was a wall
and around the wall,
a moat.

But, over the castle wall,
she could see a pear tree
and on it, all of the pears were numbered,
shining gold and silver in the moonlight.

And she called out, "My God, I am so hungry!
Give me some of that fruit."

And the tree bent to her.
The wall broke.
The moat parted,
and that girl walked in.

She stood beneath the pear tree.
She rose to meet it
but it bent to meet her.
And she ate a single pear.

Now, there was a gardener there
and he had seen all that she had done.
And it was his job
to see that no one touched the King's fruit.
But he did not touch her.

Instead, he went to the King and he said,
"Look, there's somebody or something in your garden
and I don't know who she is or what she is,
but I'm not the man to mess with her.
When she calls out,
walls break,
moats part,

trees bend.
She doesn't have any hands.
She's covered in *light*.
Besides that,
she's the most beautiful thing I've ever seen."

And the King said,
"Beautiful is she?
Well, then I'll see her for myself."

And the next night,
he kept watch,
and when it was dark,
the girl rose from the place
where she had hidden all day
and, once again,
she stood beneath the pear tree
and, once again,
it bent to her.

She ate, from it, a single pear.

And the King called out,
"Are you a maiden or are you some kind of spirit?"

She looked at him and said,
"I'm no spirit. I'm just a girl,
but I've been forsaken by all."

"Oh, no, you haven't,"
said the King,
"because no one as beautiful as you
is forsaken by me."
And he led her into his palace
and he had a salve made
and when it was spread upon her wounds,
they healed.

He watched that girl
and he could find no fault in her.
He fell in love with her
and they were married.

He had made for her
a pair of silver hands
and when she slipped them on,

first one and then the other,
she could button her own dress,
comb her own hair,
even reach down and scratch
that hound dog pup
that the King had given her.
And that puppy would wiggle all over
to feel her touch
   even if she couldn't feel him.

All went well for nearly a year.
But just before the young Queen
was to give birth to their first child,
the King was called away to war.

He went to his mother and he said,
"Watch out for my wife.
See that no harm comes to her
and send me news when the child is born."

And his mother promised that she would.

And the King saddled his horse
                and rode away to war.

And this,
this
was *just* the moment
that the Devil had been waiting for.
He sat himself down
beneath an apple tree
halfway between the palace
and the battlefield
             and he didn't have to wait long.

For when the mother of the king
sent word to her son,
saying
   "Your wife is well
   and you have a new born son!"
             the Devil put sleep upon the messenger.

And he took that letter
and he sent one in its place
that said

"Your wife is a witch
and your son is a changeling."

When the King received that letter,
he didn't know what to make of it,
but, at last,
he wrote back, saying,
    "Take care of my wife;
    see that no harm comes to my son."

But that letter never arrived.
For the Devil just took it
and he sent one in its place that said,
    "I have no wife and I have no son.
    So, whoever's in their place,
    kill them and be done with it."

When the King's mother saw that letter
she thought
that her son had gone mad
                with the war
and she wrote back,
saying,   I'll do no such thing."

But that letter never arrived.
The Devil took it
and he sent one back
to the mother, saying,
    "You will do as I have commanded you.
    So that I know that it's done,
    cut out the eyes and the tongue of my wife
    and put them in a silver jar
    where I may see them upon my return."

And now, it was the mother
    who no longer knew what to do.
At last,
she called the young Queen to her.
She showed her the letters and said,
    "Why?   Why has my son asked me to do such things?"

The young Queen read the letters.
She looked once at her silver hands
and then she looked up.

"I do not know," she said.
"For I have done nothing to deserve this.
No harm will come to me
and no harm will come to our son.
I will not stay here."

The mother said, "I will not harm you.
It is a calf that I will kill
and it's its eyes and tongue
that my son will see upon his return.
But you are right, you had best not stay."

And she bound the baby upon the young Queen's back
and, once again, she set out,
and, once again, she wandered.

But this time, she had not wandered far
    before she came to a green and growing woods
        and when she did, she knew she was welcome there.

She made her way into the woods,
and in the center of it,
she found a small cottage.

She pushed open the door
and there was a table, laden with food.
She sat
and she ate her fill
and when she was done,
she nursed her young son.

Days passed into weeks and weeks into months.

One day, the young Queen was out walking
with her son in a sling about her waist.
It was hot and she was thirsty.
She came to a pool of water
and bent down to get a drink
and, as she did, her son
twisted in the sling,
saw his reflection in the water,
kicked free
and fell into the water
and out of her sight.

"No!"
And reaching

with hands that could not feel
for a child she could not see
she plunged into the water.

She felt her hands close about him
and she brought him up crying, wet, cold.
She held him close.
And as she began to wipe the water from his face,
she realized that she was holding him with her own hands.
That her own hands had grown back!

She turned
and she looked
and there in the water
were her silver hands.
She bent down and picked them up
and put them in her pocket.

In the months and years to follow,
she took her young son into the woods
and she would say,
"See, that's wild rampion.
Pick it and you can eat.
Those, those are mushrooms.
You mustn't touch those.
Those are poisonous,
but these you can eat."
She showed him how to snare a rabbit
and where he should lie
and wait for the deer.

Seven years passed.
And the King came home from war.
And the first words out of his mouth were,
    "My wife, my son."

His mother looked at him.
  "Your wife, your son?
  What makes you ask?"
And she went
and got the letters
and the silver jar.

He read the letters
and then he opened the silver jar.

And when he did, he began to weep.
He wept as if his heart had broken.
He wept as if he would never stop.

At last, his mother took pity on him,
  "Hush," she said, "hush.
    She's not dead."

"Then where is she?" asked the King.

His mother said, "I do not know.
She left and said she would not live here any more."

The King said, "Then I will find her
and I will not return home
until I can come home with my wife and my son."

And that very day, he saddled a fresh horse
and he rode out.

He rode high into the mountains
and she wasn't there.
He rode down along the seacoast
and she wasn't there.
He rode into the villages
and he asked the wise old women,
  "My wife, my son?"
But no one had seen them.

Seven more years passed and, then,
  almost by chance,
he rode into the same green and growing woods.
And when he did,
    he knew she was near.

He dismounted from his horse
and he lay upon the grass.
For the first time, he truly slept.

Now, his son was out hunting
and he came upon this man,
lying all wild and ragged in the grass,
and he hardly knew what to make of him.
  But he went and he got his mother and he said,
"There is somebody or something in our woods
and I don't know who he is

and I don't know what he is,
but, oh Mother, I think he belongs to us."

His mother came and she said,
"It's your father; it's your father!
He has come at last."

The boy bent down to wake him.

But the Queen said,
"No, let him sleep.
He needs the sleep."

But it was almost as if
the King had heard their words in his sleep,
for he turned and he stirred and he woke.
And there, standing before him,
was his wife
and that tall boy
must be his son!

Then he looked again
   No, that wasn't his wife
      for his wife had had silver hands.

But the Queen knew what it was
that he thought
and she said to her son,

   "Sorrowful, go and fetch my silver hands
   so that your father will know that it is truly I."

And the boy went
and he got the silver hands
and he brought them
and gave them to his father.

And then the King recognized her.

He picked her up
and he swung her high into the air.
He held her close
and then he set her upon his horse.

The Queen gathered up the reins.
And, with her husband walking on one side
and her son on the other,
she rode home.

Invitation

"[The] common concern of the story is the actual life of the hearer."

—John Shea, *Stories of God*

When we hear a story, we receive an invitation: we are called to identify with the main character in the tale. This identification comes about quite differently for different people, because we hear out of the experiences in our own lives.

I was sitting in a car, on a February evening, waiting for my daughter, when I first read "The Handless Maiden" in *Problems of the Feminine in Fairy Tales*. I had heard folktales and family tales told six months before at a storytelling festival. That event was the first time in my adult life that I had been in the presence of a language that touched all of me, excluded nothing, that encompassed all of the pain, joy, humor, and terror of being human, of failing and succeeding. A look around the tent, at everyone laughing and crying, let me see that these stories had encompassed and held us all. I came home and began telling the stories I had heard to my children and their classmates at school. At the same time, I began writing and researching a paper on how stories naturally invite us to examine our own lives and choices and then to grow beyond them.

I was thumbing through von Franz's book, in preparation for the paper, reading idly, taking notes, when I happened upon this tale. By the time I finished the story and von Franz's discussion of it, I was crying. "The Handless Maiden" had worked as stories are meant to. Because the description of the miller and his wife had made me aware of my felt inadequacies as a parent, I left the story expecting to identify with them. Instead, I had identified with the Maiden and her plight. Stories both acknowledge and cut beneath our images of ourselves; they "invite us out of our destructiveness"[5] and ask us to envision new possibilities. The Maiden's loss of her hands invited me to understand the origins of my handlessness, and her healing to see that despite the way we feel, and sometimes behave, each of us can sustain losses and yet be generative, caring, and competent.

I doubt that I would have identified this story as my own or learned to tell it as I have if it had not been followed by Marie-Louise von Franz's commentary. She wrote about the miller who was looking for the quick fix, who did not understand that when you let go of a living thing—tree, child, or self—something has been given away that cannot easily be recovered. She wrote about mothers who had to stay distant from their children and about men and women who function as automatons, working and living without feeling. The story, embedded in descriptions of her own clients and ruminations about the characters, invited me to begin to examine the conceptions upon which I had built my life and to move beyond them.

I did not understand this invitation in a way that I could put in words. What I did understand was that the woods, a place where I felt the Queen was welcome, was a place of healing. My worldview had expanded. I was seeing in the woods, in the Maiden's tears, in the way the healing occurred, other ways of being and functioning than I normally understood to be possible. I saw there was a way to acknowledge our losses and grow through them.

This story became a prism through which I began to look, to understand myself and the world around me. When I first read "The Handless Maiden," I did not understand that every person carries secret hurts, childhood anxieties, which are difficult to face, but if avoided, often create handless adults who act out or deny their fears, to the detriment of themselves and others with whom they live and work. Neither did I know that my image of motherhood was essentially an impossible, isolated perfection based on societal expectations and gender definitions that leave women unable to nurture with their whole selves. I did not understand how deeply the cultural expectation that men will work and women nurture limits and estranges men and women, leaving them both far less capable than they really are to nurture each other, the children, and the world they have in common.

Though both my telling and the Grimms' documents the maiming of a child and through that act, the estrangement, violence, woundedness, and incompetence that characterize our world and our relationships, the Grimms' tale reinforces and validates the limitations placed on women by leaving the Maiden passive, pious, and dependent on her husband at the end of the tale. My telling of the Maiden reads through the coded text of the tale and makes explicit the clear and active choices the Maiden and later the King make. It recovers this tale as a healing story. That it takes seven years for the Queen to regain her hands and seven more for the King to find her documents the severity of our personal and societal wounds and helps the listeners recognize the time it takes to heal.

"The Handless Maiden," as I tell it, is a story of human development. Listeners of every age and both genders have discovered that they have been handless like the Maiden. I believe it is especially a story of women's development from powerlessness to self-assertion, because in the choices of its characters it describes the need for a woman to separate and recover her whole self, in a way that is not dictated by the existing hierarchy, in order to live with all the fullness of which she is capable.

Poverty and Estrangement

"Only a relatively 'whole' society can vouchsafe . . . the infant."
—Erik Erikson, *Identity: Youth and Crisis*

The story of "The Handless Maiden," in both the Grimms' tale and mine, shows an impoverished world in which something living is sold for gold. The father does not understand the implications of his own act; the mother understands the actual nature of his bargain but fails to make herself understood. A child becomes handless when her parents refuse successive opportunities to intervene on her behalf.

Although I have made only one alteration in the plot at the beginning of "The Handless Maiden," I have made significant tonal and relational changes. When I first found and learned to tell this tale, I saw the cutting off of the Maiden's hands as a graphic and undeniable image of the ways children can leave home, hurting and uncertain. Once I recognized that children can become handless as a result of their parents' actions, I also realized that the parents' abandonment of their daughter was an indication that something was very wrong within and between the miller and his wife. So I portray the miller and his wife as angry, needy, embittered, suspicious, and estranged from one another, behaving as men and women often do when they feel unempowered, misunderstood, and unsupported. My tonal and relational changes in the story also create an image of how people feel and act when they have not understood or accepted the developmental choices before them.

Listeners respond to the voices I have given the characters. Children who draw the miller's house after hearing my telling draw it and describe it as "trashed." The house is often unpainted. If there are any curtains in the windows, they are torn, and the ground in front of the house is muddy and bare. The house is never described as cluttered or dirty in the telling, and so it seems that the children are drawing the spiritual and emotional poverty of the place. This is the home that the miller and his wife have created between them. It is important to understand who they are and how their roles and decisions have contributed to their poverty and the subsequent maiming of their daughter.

I had been telling the story for two years when Shelby (not her real name) identified herself as an incest survivor following her participation in a storytelling class that I taught. She felt the story of "The Handless Maiden" was the story of her life. The most painful parts of the story for her were the father's unawareness that his daughter was behind the house, the cutting off of the Maiden's hands by her father, and the binding of them by her mother. "It's like incest," Shelby said, "first the abuse happens and then you have to hide it and put it behind you."[6] When Shelby and other abuse and incest survivors claimed this story as their own, they radically deepened my awareness of what depraved choices parents can make, how emotionally and physically maimed children can be. They also made explicit, once again, the incestuous intentions of the original Grimms' miller.[7]

Although these listeners showed me that the story is a story of extreme abuse, I felt it was also a story of less visible woundings that occur almost as a part of our normal developmental process. The split between the miller and his wife, in which the miller does not recognize the worth of his daughter, the wife stands silent, and a child loses her hands, is not just an aberration that occurs in violent and abusive families. It reveals the different ways of functioning that many social theorists see running throughout familial interactions in Western cultures.[8] The story makes visible two imbalances in which power is frequently abused: one, between men and women; the other, between adults and children. Although I have created characters who speak and act like abusers and their spouses, I believe they also embody, in an extreme form, the feelings and characteristics of men and women throughout our society.[9]

At the beginning of "The Handless Maiden," the miller is alone in the woods, a place that symbolizes both lostness and the opportunity for regrowth. His mill has failed—an image suggesting that the choices he has made have not sustained him—and he is out chopping wood. When an old man accosts him, offering gold for what is behind his house, the miller in my telling is curt and impolite. He seems bitter over his lot, primed to take gold as the quickest way to alleviate his poverty, a decision that von Franz suggests reflects his poor judgment and a very limited understanding of his actual needs.[10]

While the miller may represent any of us when we are profoundly disconnected from our deepest needs, he is a male character, and so I believe his poverty also has its roots in societal expectations of men. Jack Bradt, a therapist skilled in men's issues, spoke of the attrition of feelings in men from the time they are little boys.[11] Many theorists link the male's diminishing ability to feel with the demands of male development. They suggest that boys, in defining themselves as masculine, separate from their mothers in an emphatic and defensive way. Because the separation is so traumatic, it fuels the male's sense of rage and loss. It is from this sense of deprivation and anger that Carol Gilligan, Erik Erikson, and Nancy Chodorow see the male creating our primarily hierarchical, positional, and patriarchal world, in which feelings, attachment, and intimacy are dangerous needs that remind a man of his desire for nurture and will compromise his ability to be the self-sufficient provider he feels he is supposed to be.[12] It is this image of male development that seems most congruent with my understanding and depiction of the miller. I believe the miller's failure fuels his sense of desperation and inadequacy. He sounds so angry, he may represent the male who deeply resents having to provide for a family when his own unrecognized needs seem unmet.

When the miller returns home, his wife angrily asks where he has been and what he has been doing, as if he is an incompetent fool who has sold them out before. None of the women writers on female development and psychology says that women are innately better nurturers than men; it is only that women have been raised to be aware of the connectedness between us all.[13] This is the position of the miller's wife. She is at home, where she is able to see their daughter in the yard, so it is she who communicates to her husband the true nature of the bargain he has made.

In the Grimms' tale he never even acknowledges her words; in mine he ridicules her: "What's he going to want her for?" I believe the information the wife gives the miller threatens his already tenuous hold on himself. If he acknowledges the harm he can do to his daughter, he will also have to recognize that he has reached a crisis point in his own life and face his own unaddressed needs and vulnerability.

When the miller ridicules his wife, she just turns and walks away in disgust. In the Grimms' tale, she slips away so silently that the reader never even remembers her momentary presence. Even von Franz, who is so perceptive in her discussion of the miller, fails to notice the wife. I believe the wife's disappearance signifies the rejection of her knowledge by the patriarchal world; the loss of the Maiden's hands shows how crucially it was needed. In my telling, the wife's rage makes her visible, and listeners question her absence and wonder why she did not do more.

Women have traditionally been kept from exercising their power; they have been expected to nurture both children and men, whether or not they feel capable of the task or desire to do it. Because women have been restricted to this nurturing role and continue, even in this time of changing work definitions, to fulfill it, they tend to view the world as a series of connected relationships that must be maintained at all cost. I believe this awareness, though a strength, binds a woman until she learns to know and care for herself as a separate person.[14]

The miller's wife has little sense of her own identity. She speaks once on behalf of her daughter and never again on behalf of either her child or herself. I believe the wife sounds so angry because she feels limited and compromised in her life choices. I think she may be aware of her husband's neediness, but because she feels captive to and limited by male expectations, she has no generosity toward him. Her anger is effective only in enforcing their differences and does nothing to protect the child.

Beneath the anger, her actions reveal deeper conflicting needs that she seems to have lost sight of. A supervising therapist suggested that since women, and not men, have been given permission to explore the feeling, relational world, the miller's wife is probably deeply aware of the need for nurture in the world and in her own life. When her knowledge is refused and ridiculed, however, she loses her own sense of what is important and fails to attend to what she knows. If the miller seems oblique and dense, unable to acknowledge pain, the wife seems aware of their impoverishment but completely immobilized by her conflicting emotions. Even if she is furious with the miller, the idea of severing any of the relationships around her fills her with confusion, doubt, and guilt.[15] Although many writers make the point that men have traditionally silenced women,[16] I believe the miller's wife is caught between her need to maintain connections and her need to free herself, a conflict that has kept women paralyzed and silenced as effectively as any level of overt male intimidation.

In addition, when a woman has been raised to nurture and not to provision the family, she feels dependent on the man. As one listener said, "She didn't want to be cast out herself. She didn't want the hard road. She didn't have any place to go." A third grader said of the miller's wife, "She should have divorced that man instead of letting him cut off the girl's hands." Another option was open: the miller's wife did not realize that if she had acted on her knowledge, she would have maintained connections, taken the first step in creating an equitable and functional marriage, saved her daughter, and found herself. But when a woman doubts her self-worth, her vision of the world, and her own capacities, "moral obligation, rather than expanding to include the self, is rejected completely . . . and survival, however 'selfish' or 'immoral' returns as the paramount concern."[17]

When the miller says, "What's he going to want her for?" and his wife walks away in disgust, they leave their daughter standing out in the yard long before the devil returns. I believe the devil's reappearance signifies their continual inability to acknowledge their impoverishment. I learned firsthand how trapped we, men and women, are within our roles. Two years ago I told this story to a group of adolescent boys, who gasped and cried out at the cutting off of the Maiden's hands. But when they discussed the miller, they said, "Well, he didn't have any choice. The Devil would have taken him to hell." Both the miller and the boys seem to have a pragmatic attitude that overrides their sensibilities. In essence, they are saying, "Well, it's just her hands, we still have our fortune, she's not dead, we'll come out ahead." What I, as a woman, noted was my inability to reply, my own silence, and confusion, no different from the miller's wife. Weeks later I remembered what the boys and I had known all along: the miller and his wife were already living in hell.

In the Grimms' version of the tale, the miller is afraid when the Devil appears, but I have made him cocky. In my experience, people are often belligerent and defensive when they are facing a crisis. When the miller says, "Didn't put that dress on her; didn't draw that circle of chalk, ain't nothing I can do about it," he is not only absolving himself of all responsibility for his daughter's welfare but also inviting the Devil to direct his rage at his daughter rather than at himself. The miller obeys every one of the Devil's commands without question or even the hint of concern, until the Devil tells him to cut off his daughter's hands. Like many of us, the miller only acknowledges the crisis he is in when the enormity of the situation will not allow him to deny it any longer. Yet when he is given the choice either to cut off his daughter's hands or to go with the Devil himself, he cuts off her hands without even thinking twice.

The miller's response to the Devil's choice reveals the depth of his spiritual and emotional impoverishment. Beneath the bravado, callousness, and cruelty is a person who has no belief in his ability to meet the challenge at hand, a person so isolated and distrustful that he asks no one for help. Whether the miller begs his daughter's forgiveness or excuses himself by saying, "Now you heard the man, I ain't got no choice," he makes apparent his conviction that he is a powerless victim who is regulated by external powers beyond his control.[18]

Cutting off the daughter's hands is a vivid image of the physical and sexual violence that occurs in families. It is also a portrait of the societal limitations placed on women. A male therapist said he left a telling of the Maiden convulsed with guilt, because the story had made apparent for him all the ways men, himself included, had limited women. Finally, the loss of the hands also depicts the subtle and not so subtle emotional maiming that occurs to most children because we, their parents, are often limited, maimed, ignorant, and fearful ourselves. All children need to find the world a place they can trust; they need to believe in their capacity to do good and their ability to solve the dilemmas they will face. But none of us reaches adulthood unscathed, certain of the beneficence of the world or the goodness and power within us.

Alice Miller has written with great clarity about the way all adults are without sympathy for the children they once were.[19] When we are without sympathy for the child we were, when we forget what it was like to grow up male or female in our society, we are also unable to empathize with and provide for the children we bring into the world. I believe the miller and his wife are symbols for the impoverished, angry children within us all. Their unacknowledged and refused needs account for the choices they make. While I tell "The Handless Maiden" for listeners whose lives have been filled, like Shelby's, with betrayals as extreme as the Maiden's, I have found it equally important to tell the story to those who think they have the world by the tail and only incidentally notice their own depression, self-alienation, and feelings of worthlessness.[20] I have learned that while the story provides the most betrayed in our society the opportunity to name wounds and envision recovery, it also offers and even insists on this process for all of us.

In my telling of "The Maiden," the miller's wife reappears in the story after the Devil is gone and her daughter is handless. Her appearance reminds the listener that she has been there all along, has seen everything. The mother binds her daughter's wounds. This image was an especially strong one for Shelby. She said, "I can see it; it's all done in white gauze and"—she paused—"it looks like care, but it isn't; it's restraint." A therapist commented that the story "made her really angry": angry at the ways men have limited women, angry at the mother because she "did nothing" to stop the father and then "bandaged" the Maiden. She felt this was "a message, woman to woman, that the mother would acknowledge her daughter's pain, but not challenge the patriarchy."

This story does arouse anger—anger that has clarified and shaped the tale. When I learned "The Handless Maiden" in January of 1983, I was also learning a Brer Rabbit tale. I found myself singing, dancing, stomping out the song in that story, "Ti Hi Tunga He, I like 'em pea, I pick 'em pea. It grow on the ground; it grow so free. Ti Hi Tunga

He."[21] I needed that encoded slave tale to speak out my rage about the wrongs in "The Handless Maiden," to break out of my sense of bondage to prescribed gender roles. The Brer Rabbit story about stealing what is "owned" by someone else allowed me to acknowledge my need to define myself as a woman. "The Handless Maiden" illustrates the abuses of power between men and women, between adults and children. It makes visible the ways we are vulnerable and connected in our lives; the miller and his wife show us how this knowledge can be refused and the poverty that ensues. Shelby said, "[The story] makes me angry! Anger is a trigger that protects me. [It] says, if you feel angry about this, something is definitely wrong." It was after the Brer Rabbit tale had freed my rage and forced my awareness that I began to tell the miller and his wife as the embittered, estranged, limited, and needy people I believed them to be.

Recovery: Innocence, Acceptance and Decision

When I first told "The Handless Maiden" to children in a therapeutic setting, the supervising therapist said, "Telling that story . . . was a test of whether we adults were going to be straight with kids about the evil we know exists, about acknowledging that there is this level of pain, anguish, and suffering in the world, this kind of not knowing [whether hands can be regrown] and waiting in the world."

Abused children have had extreme responses to this story. A girl drew the house of the miller and his wife. She crayoned blood and blood and more blood pouring down a storm drain in a street, as if all the blood the Maiden had shed, and all the pain she had felt, had been wasted. An eleven-year-old boy, who had been repeatedly abused, also identified with the Maiden. He drew himself shot and bleeding on a bridge. He said he was not certain that he could pull himself up and get away, that he could keep himself from being shot again. The story of the Maiden allowed these children and those who worked with them to recognize how severely they had been wounded.

The tale also outlines a path of recovery so that, perhaps, with assistance and care these children would see that they could heal and that they did not have to repeat what had occurred to them.[22] Our wounds do not have to be so extreme for us to have the same depth of response, the same need to recover. It was a fifth-grade boy in a normal educational setting who flew up out of his chair after a telling of "The Maiden," saying, "I don't have to be a drunk like my Daddy!" As a storyteller, I knew from the beginning that I could tell "The Handless Maiden" only because I was certain the recovery process outlined in the story, as well as the description of how handlessness comes about, could be trusted.

When I first decided to tell "The Handless Maiden," the only character whose voice I had was the Devil. But as this demonic voice asserted itself and told the story with evil glee, I was redefining the angels that surrounded the Maiden and making my first conscious and substantial changes to the tale. The Grimms' tale is filled with angels. They accompany the Maiden when she arrives at the King's castle and when she enters the woods, and they act as an intermediary between her and her husband when he arrives in the woods. I knew I could not tell angels, so I tried to see the Maiden as she appeared to me when she approached the King's castle, and I realized she was covered in light. That, for me, took the place of angels. It communicated what I felt about her, that she was *protected from within* and stood "in beneficent contact with the mighty powers of the universe."[23]

When I made this change, I discovered what Gilligan repeatedly documents: when women let their voices be heard, the world itself can be transformed.[24] The Grimms' tale has been described as "patriarchal" because it depicts the Maiden as a "passive victim, saved by her own patient faith in God, and saved by God and other authoritative male figures."[25] When I described the Maiden as covered in light, I undid this vision of her. Her spiritual force appears as a light within her, an image that suggests not only her empowerment but ours as well.

Some questions trouble nearly every listener. Barbara (pseudonym), a skilled therapist who heard the story several times, asked: "Why did the Maiden put out her hands? Why didn't she fight back or run away?" I had to work out these questions for myself before I could tell the tale. I was telling "The Handless Maiden" to my mother one evening and she said, "It doesn't sound to me as if you like this story very well." "I don't," I said. "I hate the girl; she's such a wimp. She just stands there and lets her hands be cut off." My mother was silent for a moment, and then she said, "But she had strength enough to cry." Her words helped me see strength in the Maiden, where I had seen only passivity. From this point on, the story flowed, unstopped, and the dialogue developed between the characters. It was only later, in the process of examining the Maiden's development, that I understood the gift my mother had given me: by absolving the Maiden of responsibility for her parents' actions, she had freed her to continue on her journey and me, as her teller, on mine.

In the Grimms' text, the Maiden says, "Dear Father, do with me what you will. I am your daughter." I have come to understand that these words are not a passive concession to her father's brutality. They simply acknowledge that in the adult-child relationship the power of choice always belongs to the adult and that, as a child, the Maiden could not control the choices her parents made or deny the circumstances in which she lived.[26] Handlessness occurs when we are too young to prevent it. Children have an unerring ability to assimilate and reflect the true state of their parents' impoverishment or health. They automatically assume the blame for the parents' deficiencies because they have an "inborn proclivity for feeling powerless, deserted, ashamed and guilty in relation to those on whom [they] depend."[27]

In a school for emotionally impaired children, a ten-year-old black child drew the calf from the story, calling it a "sacrificial lamb." A year later, he chose to play the role of the Maiden in an improvised drama of this story. As the Maiden, he said the father did not have any choice except to cut off his hands. This boy had identified the role his parents were asking him to play (the sacrificial lamb) instead of risking change themselves. As a child, however, he could not shift the responsibility back to them.

The Maiden places the responsibility with the adults. She shows us in many ways that the child is not responsible for the parents' actions. She cleans herself, draws a circle of chalk around herself, and cries herself clean. The recovery of our innocence is essential. Without it, we cannot risk; we will be so full of doubt and self-hatred that we will not be able to move beyond the limited images of ourselves to the unforeseen possibilities that lie before us.

After the miller cuts off his daughter's hands, she cries "in her pain and in her misery." This ability to be aware and responsive to oneself, aware of the situation one is in, and not separated from it, means that we may be handless, but we are not helpless. Out of the Maiden's acknowledgment of pain and betrayal comes her ability to make choices. This is her strength. The Maiden's decision is to leave. Her father asks her to stay, saying that "we will care for you," but she does not stay, because she knows that she truly needs care and that there is none where she is. This is an almost impossibly difficult admission for any child to make, and it allows the listener to see it is often only in adolescence and adulthood that we recognize our own handlessness, can accept it, and begin to make our own choices.

I do not believe the Maiden leaves home with any thought of recovering her hands. Instead, she has begun the process of changing the one thing over which she has control: her own life. She has, however, recognized the need to forge a new identity as a woman and to discover how care comes about. After wandering, hungry, a day and a night, the Maiden arrives at the castle of the King.

Over the castle wall she sees a pear tree. It seems that the luxuriant tree awakes in the Maiden some sense of her own generativeness, grace, and connectedness to the earth. Only the King may eat its fruit; but when the Maiden calls out, never questioning whether she is worthy of food and care, the walls break and the tree bends to her. In that one image, I see two very important developmental pieces. First, we must believe ourselves worthy of sustenance and care. Second, if we attend to our needs and speak them, the walls between people can crumble.[28]

The pear tree is one of the two or three most frequently drawn images from the story. But many women listeners, despite their attraction to the pear tree, do not welcome the King or the marriage. As Shelby said about the Maiden, "I wish she could have said to her parents, 'I have an apartment. I have a job. I have a car. I'm going out on my own now.'" Barbara, a therapist I interviewed, put it more strongly: "The King rescues her, marries her because she's beautiful, goes off and leaves her after giving her silver hands. The King giving her silver hands is a commentary on the way women have always tried to get their healing and their power, from men. First you get some power from a man who is okay enough to acknowledge you and then you become like him."[29]

When I first began to tell the tale, I hated the Maiden's silver hands. I saw them as cold, clunky, and unmanageable, not as a gift but as a representation of a largely patriarchal system into which the girl had to fit. Then Steve Gorn, an artist and musician who was listening to my telling, said, "But they were given to her in love."[30] Steve's words and my recognition of the truth in them changed an entire section of the story.

The change looked like this:

Grimms:	*Gordon:*
"He took her into his royal palace, and as she was so beautiful and good, he loved her with all his heart, had silver hands made for her, and took her to wife."	"And he had made for her a pair of silver hands. And when she put them on, first one and then the other, she could button her own dress again, comb her own hair, and even scratch the hound dog pup the King had given her. And that puppy would wiggle all over to feel her touch, even if she couldn't feel him."

When I spoke out my feelings and Steve replied, I developed a solution that was "contextual and narrative,"[31] containing both our experiences and illuminating the heart of the Maiden's difficulty: doing with feeling.

Marriage, Childbirth, and Individuation

The Maiden and the King are wed, and she is a young queen, pregnant, and with silver hands when the King is called away to war. The birth of their child is "just the moment" the Devil has been waiting for. In every fairy tale, there is always one person, the protagonist, capable of change and growth. From this point on in "The Handless Maiden," however, there are two people, the Queen and the King, who will choose, grow, and mature.

If we understand the King and Queen to be symbolic figures representing the developmental journey of both men and women, we see that the King represents the person who has "little attunement to his own internal world . . . or capacity to 'hang in' when [a] relationship becomes conflicted and stressful,"[32] as it can when a child is born. Men who have responded to this part of the story have shed a different light on it, illustrating the burden to provide that they often feel. One man said, "But, when my wife had a baby, I worked harder; I was gone all the time, because I thought that was what I had to do."[33] And so the King is gone, on his own journey. The young Queen is left with the child and the task of caring for another when she has not been cared for herself. The story follows uncannily the developmental process outlined for both men and women by many feminist development theorists and psychologists.[34] The man must decide if he truly wants this intimacy he has tasted, and the woman must find a way to listen to herself and care for herself, if she is to care for another and live out her belief that human beings are connected and interdependent, which her own experience of handlessness tells her is true.

Such changes do not happen without pain and doubt. The Devil confounds the messages announcing the birth of the royal child. The Queen is called a "witch" and her son a "changeling," a child who is not real and feels no pain, which is the way abusive parents often view their children.[35] I see these messages as symbolically depicting the Queen's doubts about herself and the doubts of those around her.[36] The messages end with a demand for the death of the mother and the child and are highly descriptive of the losses we fear if we change.[37]

While the miller and his wife see themselves without choices, the King, Queen, and mother-in-law understand they can choose, and they do. The King asks for the safety of his wife and child, the mother-in-law refuses to carry out orders to kill them both, and the young Queen leaves.

After this point in the story, at the cusp between her innocence as a child and her decisions as an adult, the Queen becomes stronger, her actions clear and resolute. Although I have made no plot changes here, I have systematically strengthened the Queen as a woman protagonist, through story details that were both conscious and unconscious on my part.

Separation and Homecoming

In every other version of the story, the Queen leaves the King's castle in tears, but in my story she says to her mother-in-law, "No harm will come to me, and none to our son. I will leave." In many versions, the mother-in-law is depicted as the Evil One, causing the Queen to be cast out a second time. The Grimms' version, however, depicts her as caring. I found the mother-in-law's caring integral to the telling of my story. Her strength *as a woman* set the stage for the changes in the story and the adult strength of the Queen. I think I understood that the Queen needed to have a strong woman role model to provide her a glimpse of her own power and possibility.

The Queen must discover who she is for herself, though. Barbara said, "Sometimes I wonder why she [the young Queen] didn't just leave. And leave the kid with the Queen Mother. She would have been an adequate parent." Then she answered her own question: "But then, her [the Queen's] way of healing was to teach her kid new things"—and, I would add, to learn new things for herself. "And not just say, well, 'cause your Dad's not here, I can't teach you how to snare a rabbit." Frank Pittman, in his lecture on parenting and therapy, says that adults often grow up only when they accept the responsibility of being a child's parent, because then it becomes clear what issues must be addressed, what work must still be done in their lives.[38]

With her son bound on her back, the Queen wanders, but it seems to me she does not have to travel far to find "the green and growing woods," because except for her son, she is alone and is not searching beyond herself or asking another for strength. The woods were the story's most lasting image for me. They seemed proper medicine for her wounds. The Queen is no longer in a cultivated garden, where she is expected to live within another's conception of what it means to be a woman, but she is in a woods, where she is connected to the earth, aware of the bounty, and no longer estranged from herself. The discoveries she makes here are her own.[39] In the center of the woods the young Queen finds a cottage and in it a table laden with food. To Shelby, "She sat and ate her fill and then she nursed her son" was the most meaningful line in the story. Shelby returned to it again and again; she said, "She has to eat first. You can't give what you don't have.... If you're struggling to breathe, you can't help your child."

In the Grimms' tale, the Queen's hands grew while she was living in the woods. The story stressed that the cottage in the woods is a place where "everyone [may] live freely," and so I felt the growth of her hands was occurring in relation to her slow, deep recovery of herself.

My listeners, however, often objected to the fact that "her hands just grew" through no action of her own, and in 1986, the Russian motif of recovering her hands while rescuing her child from drowning appeared in the story while I was telling it before a group of battered women.[40]

Gilligan writes that "crisis reveals character" and that it also "creates character."[41] An important ingredient in psychological recovery is the ability to relive the most difficult family experiences successfully.[42] Although the Queen seems physically incapable of the task, I have her plunge her silver hands in the water, feeling with hands that do not feel for a child she can no longer see. It is not until she has brought the child up, crying, wet, and cold, and is holding him in her arms, wiping the water from his face, that she realizes her hands and her feelings have returned through her need to use them.[43] The Queen's refusal to allow her child to drown is also linked to the recovery of her identity as a woman. We can hear the Queen loudly, clearly, firmly saying: *No!*—and it is this woman, who knows herself and her own desires, who rescues the child.

When the King comes home from war, the first words out of his mouth are "My wife, my son." The King represents a person who is suddenly recognizing his connectedness with others, his need for intimacy.[44] His response stands in sharp contrast to the miller's belief that he needed no one and nothing, except gold, to relieve his impoverishment, just as the Maiden's clear and active choices contrast to her mother's earlier paralysis. In my work with sexual offenders, I have come to believe that the King's response and developmental process depict the actions and the internal changes that an abusive parent must accomplish before regaining readmittance to his or her home. Once again, however, we see in extreme conditions the path of normal development. The journey of a person who desires intimacy is not different in kind, only in degree, from that of the offender. Both have their roots in a fear of vulnerability and connectedness.

When the King reads the letters and sees the eyes and tongue in the silver jar, he begins to weep "as if his heart had broken, as if he would never stop." This is grief of the deepest kind, not unlike the Maiden's when she loses her hands and recognizes the poverty of her parents' existence. But grief, alone, is not sufficient. The man must act on his recognition; the King desires reunification with his wife and son enough to search unceasingly for them. Intimacy with another begins with intimacy with oneself; it means to become self-conscious, aware of and responsive to one's deepest needs. It includes becoming aware of the part one has had in creating the world that exists. When we do not recognize the need for relationships and we hurt another, we, like the miller and his wife, forfeit our own being.[45] I believe the King's need for another, instead of reducing him to a frightening "infantile helplessness,"[46] defines him as a person with a deep sense of purpose and a journey to complete.

Welcome

When the King comes into the woods, he knows his family is near. He dismounts from his horse, lies on the grass, and "truly sleeps." After his son comes upon him, lying all wild and ragged in the grass, he finds his mother and tells her, "I don't know who he is or what he is, but oh, mother, I think he belongs to us." These words carry the child's need for reunification, his longing to accept and love both parents, both parts of himself, without rejecting either.

Just as the child has the desire and need to love both parents, his parents must find ways to be present for the child. Mary Catherine Bateson, anthropologist and author, speaking to a meeting of family therapists in Washington, D.C., in 1985, said that the nations of this earth have only one solution: "They must view the world as their child and each other as divorced parents, who, even though they hate and distrust each other, are committed to trying to raise the child, the world, to adulthood." Her remark struck me very deeply, because it acknowledged the presence of distrust, bitterness, estrangement, and pain within and between us and also the steps we must take "to vouchsafe the infant."[47]

Often such a reunification does not come easily. Many times it does not come from the parents themselves,[48] but there can be many models for it. Following my telling of "The Handless Maiden" to a group that included sexual offenders, their spouses, and women who had been molested as children, Thomas Berg, a therapist who worked with the group, commented on the process, "The hostility raised by the story remained for weeks. But the emotional vent that had been opened actually helped to resolve the problems. One abused woman said she hated to be in the same room with the offenders, but through the course of that session, she began to develop a dialogue with the men. 'It wasn't a friendly dialogue at first,' but the men began to understand from her story what they had done to their own daughters and she began to see 'that not all men were like her father, and these men, who were in part like her father, were trying to change their lives.' "

This same sense of distrust and hostility can be seen as a normal developmental process. Many women listeners are angered by the King's return and the Queen's acceptance of him. Sometimes they mishear the story and believe that he, rather than the Devil, demanded the death of his wife and his son; often they are furious with the King for not knowing the Queen without her silver hands. They are angriest because the story says to them that the Queen needed to be rescued and married to have a full life. My response to the anger of one woman was to strengthen the end of the story. I had the Queen take up the reins of the horse, because it was my way of acknowledging that the Queen was intact and was making the choices that suited her, from her own sovereignty.

When I compare my ending with the Grimms', I realize the effect of the slowly culminating differences in our tellings. In the Grimms' version, after regaining her hands, the Queen does no work but lives a quiet and extraordinarily passive existence until her husband finds her. There seems to be no passion on her part at their reunion, only on his, suggesting that a passive, helpless, asexual, and submissive existence for women is the ideal. In my story, I see a woman who warmly welcomes the King, a Queen who is alive with grace, passion, and dignity.

I have always loved the person of the Queen at the end of the story. I am caught up short by the grace and perception I see in her when the King does not know her without her silver hands. Out of her knowledge and compassion, she is willing to give him the sign he needs to recognize her. I do not see her ever wearing the silver hands again or becoming less than she is, competent and caring, but she has kept them as a token of his care and perhaps of her own wounding and healing.

Marie-Louise von Franz and Frank Pittman say that a person does not lose a sense of woundedness but instead transforms it and keeps it as an awareness of the continuing need to develop the self and of how human beings both hurt and heal.[49] I believe the Queen may accept the King because her own suffering allows her to recognize the suffering the King has also undergone.

In the story the Queen says, "It's your father. It's your father and he has come at last." For years I told this part of the story almost by rote, with little ability to welcome the King, but one day while teaching a workshop to therapists, I began to cry while telling the last part of the story. I had worked intensively that year with sexual offenders and had discussed that work in the workshop. My listeners said, "You're crying because this ending isn't possible for the offenders." "No," I said, "I'm crying because it is." My tears expressed my sudden awareness of that possibility and my first real welcome of the King. While I was telling the listeners that offenders could make this incredibly difficult journey of reunification, I was also realizing that some parts in me that had been estranged from each other had come together.

This is the secret to the Queen's ability to welcome. It is only a whole person who can truly welcome another. As a listener said, "She didn't just sit at home, spinning, waiting for the King; she set out, protected herself, learned to hunt and care for herself and her son." But while she was discovering ways of being that exceeded patriarchal gender definitions, she could not provide the same internal and emotional growth for her husband. She could not force the King to value her and her sense of their interconnectedness. She could only value it in herself; he must seek her out. That he has come, that he has made his own journey, fills her with joy and ignites her welcome.

Barbara asked repeatedly how the Maiden made these choices of maturation and development. She said, "She's too good. It's as if cutting off her hands didn't stop her from doing what she needed to do. I wonder what source she drew her strength from when all she had was silver hands?" I had to ask the same question of myself when I understood how I had strengthened the Maiden/Queen.

Barbara answered her own question. She spoke about her most lasting image from the story, the pear tree, which she saw as bountiful, and how that image connected with her own life. She spoke of a time when she had felt abandoned and handless. She said she had gotten silver hands too, but "in a less receptive way." She had gotten them on her own, because she "didn't want anyone to see her bleeding stumps." She said her "hell bent for leather way [of reconstructing her life] has not been as healing as the story says healing can be." Then she said, "I think, *I know!* Her source, her healing is ultimately connected with her soul. What was never severed from her was her own soul. Healing is about receiving and nurturing. There is a bounty and it is necessary to ask for it."

"The Handless Maiden" is an extraordinary story because it begins by documenting violence and estrangement in our lives and the ways gender definitions exacerbate this wounding; it accepts these realities as given and shows the losses that occur if we cannot move beyond them. The story depicts with amazing accuracy the developmental journey every feminist theorist I read believes men and women in American culture need to make. It shows the male having to choose relationships and the woman needing to separate to live out her sense of connectedness in a generative way.

When the journeys of the King and Queen are brought together, an image of a single journey emerges that, I believe, must be made by all of us if we are to become capable, caring adults. Although the King does no harm in the story, he carries within his person the awareness of our human propensity to hurt one another. He models the ability to recognize and evaluate one's actions. He feels remorse and demonstrates the steps one takes to correct wrongs done. The Maiden/Queen serves as a constant reminder that we become handless through no fault of our own and that even handless we are capable of the choices of maturation and development. All human beings need to recognize and sort through their harmful tendencies while coming to recognize their essential goodness.

When listeners recognize the developmental process occurring in this story, they begin to realize that a single tale can offer a listener a vision for his or her life. The accomplishment of the developmental tasks that occur in "The Handless Maiden" may take a lifetime and many other stories, though. The Maiden never expresses certain common feelings and behaviors in the story, such as rage, humor, or trickery, and yet, for her to be the assured, purposeful, competent, and caring person she is, they must have been felt, faced, and integrated within her.[50] So I always follow the telling of "The Handless Maiden" with my adaptation of an Appalachian Jack Tale called "Big Jack, Little Jack,"[51] in which anger and the desire for revenge is acknowledged and played out. The story depicts the conversion of self-destructive anger into a series of creative decisions that reminds the listeners of the healthy desire to win and the delights of outwitting an enemy joyfully.[52]

Although these feelings are never addressed directly by the Maiden, I have included and implied them, in my version, by the Queen's ability to teach her son how to hunt. I believe her ability to hunt successfully but not wantonly and to share these skills with her son indicates the reclaiming and using of the hostile and aggressive side of herself, which we all have, and which she, given her experiences, had much reason to fear in herself.

Although, at times, it is difficult to be optimistic about growth within and between us, as men and women, I believe the way "The Handless Maiden" story developed offers a model for such change. When I began to tell "The Handless Maiden," the only thing I knew was that the story had touched me deeply and was pushing me to recover my own history as a woman, wife, and mother. I learned to tell the story because it was personally true for me. But it is only telling each of our stories in the presence of others that allows our person and our story to develop. As listeners responded to the telling, my worldview and my vision of what was possible deepened and expanded. I was involved in a process of discernment, and each of the listeners' contributions that seemed "true" to me became a part of the story. I believe this interactive and reciprocal process, centered around the awareness of the Maiden's basic goodness, parallels and illustrates the process by which all actual change occurs.

Although I believe "The Handless Maiden" as I tell it is in its final form, I know, in some ways, it is still restrictive. It defines the family as man, woman, and child. The man is still distant, only the woman nurtures; it does not contain images of all the meaningful ways we can construct our lives. And so I hope that you will hold "The Maiden" against the fabric of your experience, as I held the Grimms' tale against mine, and note where the story informs your life, and where your life informs the story, and create it anew.

Notes

1. Kay F. Stone, "Feminist Approaches to the Interpretation of Fairy Tales," in *Fairy Tales and Society: Illusion, Allusion, and Paradigm*, ed. Ruth B. Bottigheimer (Philadelphia: University of Pennsylvania Press, 1986), 229–36.

2. Marie-Louise von Franz, *Problems of the Feminine in Fairytales* (Dallas: Spring Publications, 1972), 70–74. I am also especially familiar with the following versions: Aleksandr Afanas'ev, "The Armless Maiden," in *Russian Fairy Tales* (New York: Pantheon Books, 1983), 294–99; Italo Calvino, "Olive," in *Italian Folktales* (New York: Pantheon Books, 1980), 255–61; and Jakob and Wilhelm Grimm, "The Girl Without Hands," in *The Complete Grimms Tales* (New York: Pantheon Books, 1972), 160–66.

3. Von Franz, *Problems*, 74–93.

4. Afanas'ev, *Russian Fairy Tales*, 279.

5. John Shea, *Stories of God* (Chicago: Thomas More, 1978), 24.

6. Interview with "Shelby," January 16, 1988.

7. Maria Tatar, *The Hard Facts of the Grimms' Fairy Tales* (Princeton, N.J.: Princeton University Press, 1987), 9–10, 80.

8. Carol Gilligan, *In a Different Voice* (Cambridge, Mass.: Harvard Univer-

sity Press, 1982), 7; Nancy Chodorow, *The Reproduction of Mothering* (Berkeley: University of California Press, 1978), 190, 211–19; Deborah Anna Luepnitz, *The Family Interpreted: Feminist Theory in Clinical Practice* (New York: Basic Books, 1988), 220–25; Erik Erikson, *Identity: Youth and Crisis* (New York: Norton, 1968), 261–65; Nancy Chodorow, "Family Structure and Feminine Personality," in *Women, Culture, and Society,* ed. Michelle Z. Rosaldo and Louise Lamphere (Stanford, Calif.: Stanford University Press, 1974), 43–44.

9. Alan Dundes, "Projection in Folklore: A Plea for Psychoanalytic Semiotics," in *Interpreting Folklore* (Bloomington: Indiana University Press, 1980), 41, 52–53. Dundes's interpretation of "The Handless Maiden" makes the case that girls can become handless out of a love of and desire for their fathers. While this idea was not a part of my conscious reconstruction of the tale, in my experience, girls can become less functional as a result of loving their fathers, especially when the father is perceived to represent a larger, freer world, and the girl's mother is viewed as constrained, limited, angry, and disapproving. Linda Leonard, *The Wounded Woman* (Boston: Shambhala Publications, 1983), and Judith Arcana, *Our Mothers' Daughters* (Berkeley: Shameless Hussy Press, 1979), discuss in detail some of the relational variations considered normal in this society that contribute to the creation of unempowered women.

10. Von Franz, *Problems,* 75–76.

11. Phone conversation with Dr. Jack O. Bradt, Mt. Horeb, Wisconsin, April 1990.

12. Gilligan, *In a Different Voice,* 7–8, 46; Chodorow, *Reproduction of Mothering,* 167–69; Erikson, *Identity,* 262–64.

13. Chodorow, *Reproduction of Mothering,* 167–69; Gilligan, *In a Different Voice,* 7–8.

14. Gilligan, *In a Different Voice,* 7–8; Chodorow, *Reproduction of Mothering,* 166–70; Monica McGoldrick, John K. Pearce, Joseph Giordana, eds., *Ethnicity and Family Therapy* (New York: Guilford, 1983), 42. Gilligan and Chodorow discuss the ways women see the world as a series of connected relationships. Gilligan discusses how this way of seeing, though a strength, initially limits a woman. McGoldrick points out that women are still maintaining relationships even while working outside the home.

15. Gilligan, *In a Different Voice,* 18, 78–81, 87; Dana Crowley Jack, *Silencing the Self: Women and Depression* (Cambridge, Mass.: Harvard University Press, 1991), 48–53.

16. For cogent and literate exploration of the many ways women have been silenced, see Mary Field Belenky, Blythe McVicker Clinchy, Nancy Rule Goldberger, and Jill Mattuck Tarule, *Women's Ways of Knowing: The Development of Self, Voice and Mind* (New York: Basic Books, 1986), 22–33. See also Adrienne Rich, *Of Woman Born: Motherhood as Experience and Institution* (New York: Norton, 1986), 68–73; Luepnitz, *The Family Interpreted,* 59–63; Erikson, *Identity,* 262–64; and Jack, *Silencing the Self.*

17. Gilligan, *In a Different Voice,* 87.

18. M. Scott Peck, *The Road Less Traveled* (New York: Touchstone Books, 1979), 43.

19. Alice Miller, *The Drama of the Gifted Child: The Search for the True Self* (New York: Basic Books, 1981), 6. Miller describes with precision and feeling the ways angry and abusive behavior is deeply embedded in our culture and makes itself felt even in the best families. She discusses how adults from these families cannot account for their feelings of alienation, depression, and distrust, because they feel as if their lives were surrounded with the best of care.

20. Ibid., 5–7.

21. Joel Chandler Harris, "Mr. Rabbit and Mr. Bear," in *Uncle Remus* (New York: Schocken Books, 1965), 111–15.

22. Michael Enright, "Sex Abuse: Stolen Innocence," *Frederick Post,* February 18, 1988, 1, 8.

23. John Niles, "Translator's Preface," in Max Lüthi, *The European Folktale* (Bloomington: Indiana University Press, 1982), xviii.

24. Gilligan, *In a Different Voice,* 62–63, 149–50, 173–74.

25. Joan Radner, introduction to a presentation on "The Powers of the Handless Maiden," Annual Meeting of the American Folklore Society, Albuquerque, New Mexico, October 22, 1987.

26. Erikson, *Identity,* 82, 117; Miller, *Drama of the Gifted Child.*

27. Kim Chernin, *The Hungry Self* (New York: Times Books, 1985), 122–23; Erikson, *Identity,* 75–76.

28. Gilligan, *In a Different Voice,* 173–74.

29. Interview with "Barbara," March 1988.

30. Steve Gorn was coleading a week-long storytelling residency with the storyteller and teacher Laura Simms in August 1982. His comments were made to me during a practice telling of "The Handless Maiden."

31. Gilligan, *In a Different Voice,* 19.

32. Harriet Goldhor Lerner, *The Dance of Anger: A Woman's Guide to the Changing Patterns of Intimate Relationships* (New York: Harper and Row, 1986), 50.

33. Tape recording of a men's group discussion of my telling of "The Handless Maiden," led by Dr. Jack Bradt, Mt. Horeb, Wisconsin, April 1990.

34. Gilligan, *In a Different Voice;* Chodorow, *Reproduction of Mothering;* Harriet Goldhor Lerner, *The Dance of Intimacy: A Woman's Guide to Courageous Acts of Change in Key Relationships* (New York: Harper and Row, 1989).

35. Frank Putnam, *Diagnosis and Treatment of Multiple Personality Disorder* (New York: Guilford, 1989), 49, 265; Marie Borland, ed., *Violence in the Family* (New Jersey: Humanities, 1976), 6; Alice Miller, *Thou Shalt Not Be Aware: Society's Betrayal of the Child* (New York: New American Library, 1986), 6, 157–58, 316–17; Ellen Bass and Laura Davis, *The Courage to Heal: A Guide for Women Survivors of Child Sexual Abuse* (New York: Harper and Row, 1988), 105, 135, 298; Janet Langlois, personal communication, February 2, 1988.

36. Lerner, *Dance of Anger,* 34–40.

37. Ibid., 34–40.

38. Frank Pittman, "Parenting and Therapy," a lecture given at The Family Networker Conference, Washington, D.C., March 1988.

39. Belenky et al., *Women's Ways of Knowing,* 161.

40. Von Franz, *Problems,* 87; Afanas'ev, *Russian Fairy Tales,* 297. Von Franz describes the rescue of the child from water in her commentary on "The Handless Maiden" and refers the reader to the Russian variant of the story as the source.

41. Gilligan, *In a Different Voice,* 126.

42. Irvin Yolem, *The Theory and Practice of Group Psychotherapy,* 3d. ed. (New York: Basic Books, 1985), 3, 16–17.

43. Von Franz, *Problems,* 87.

44. Gilligan, *In a Different Voice,* 163–64, 165.

45. Rollo May, Ernest Angel, and Henri F. Ellenberger, eds., *Existence: A New Dimension in Psychiatry and Psychology* (New York: Clarion Books, 1958), 52–54.

46. Gilligan, *In a Different Voice,* 46.

47. Erikson, *Identity,* 82.

48. Putnam, *Diagnosis and Treatment,* 317; Bass and Davis, *The Courage to Heal.*

49. Pittman, "Parenting and Therapy"; von Franz, *Problems,* 89.

50. May, Angel, and Ellenberger, *Existence,* 49.

51. Richard Chase, *The Jack Tales* (New York: Houghton Mifflin, 1943), 67–75. I have also heard Ray Hicks, a teller from Banner Elk, North Carolina, tell this story as "Lucky and UnLucky Jack." The tale has been passed down in his family; his father, Roby Hicks, was one of Chase's informants.

52. Bruno Bettelheim, *The Uses of Enchantment: The Meaning and Importance of Fairy Tales* (New York: Vintage Books, 1977), 10.

Burning Brightly: New Light from an Old Tale

KAY F. STONE

In an old Grimm tale, a girl is warned by her parents not to visit a witch who lives in a strange house in the center of the forest; she disobeys them, seeks out the crone in the heart of darkness, and is turned into a log for her efforts. This short tale that I came upon while doing research for my doctoral dissertation has become an unexpected focus for my work as a folklorist as well as a performing storyteller.

Looking at what I have written over the past sixteen years, I see that my academic creations have expressed a microcosmic view of the world I see as a whole, a world in which human beings are endlessly curious and creative and imaginative even against all odds. But how often do we deny our own creativity while extolling that of others or claim our own lives are not very interesting in comparison with those of others? The girl in the story thinks it is the crone who is interesting and curious, and thus she denies the value of her own story, with unhappy results.

I write about this story because I sense that the metaphor it offers might be of use, since it deals with the dangers and rewards of the deep and abiding curiosity that has led us to the varied places we now occupy in our own lives. Our inquisitiveness has led us into dangers, guided us to trees of knowledge where we have met our serpents, carried us to witches ready to challenge and respond. Transformation is inevitable.

It is transformation that I speak of here—not only that of the curious girl but also the transformation of myself as an academic writer and a storyteller—with the hope that you might recognize some part of your own story as well.

One of my own pleasantly impossible tasks has been an exploration of how and why stories come into being. Though I did not know it at the time, this task was hidden in my very first academic explorations of folktale heroines, begun in the early 1970s and developed through-out the 1980s.[1] Initially, I was interested in finding out how heroines were portrayed in both traditional and popularized tales and, more specifically, how these portrayals were received by contemporary readers and listeners. During a series of interviews, I discovered that girls and women remembered the fairy tales they had read as children, while boys and men generally did not—though they did recall reading many of the same stories.[2]

My interest in stories continued to grow over the next few years, but it began to take unexpected turns. I found it was not enough to examine folktales and to question others about them; I had to tell them as well—first as part of my lectures, where a summary of a tale was merely an illustration of a point I made, but then as a separate thing, as a "performance" in which tales were told merely for the sake of telling them. As I took part in professional storytelling events and observed other tellers, I was able to see firsthand and over an extended time how tellers, tales, and listeners interact in the living process of verbal artistry. Of course my curiosity was expressed in writing, because that is how I learned to tell academic stories.[3] Personal curiosity is not enough, though. Helpers are needed all along the way. It is simply not true, as we have been taught, that we stand on our own two feet armed and ready to move through our lives as if we were in constant battle with opposing forces. The girl in the story does set out on her own, but her transformation depends on meeting the woman who will test and challenge her. I cannot fail to mention, then, that all of my curiosity would be empty without the patient attentions of Linda Dégh, whose own deep curiosity about the whys and hows of people and the tales they tell has inspired her to write widely about folktales as serious forms of literary expression.[4] In a recent article, she com-ments on storytelling in modern society, noting that "it is society which maintains the need for stories and provides occasions for telling them," and wonders what it is in our contemporary urban existence that continues to draw us to old stories.[5]

I, too, wonder what holds the attention of four hundred junior high school students and their teachers sitting for forty-five minutes in a school gymnasium listening to an old tale about a crone and a girl who is too curious. I have no clear answers, but the quest for them has led me on.

The words I offer here are my first attempt to express in print what I have learned as a scholar of tales *as well as* a teller of tales. I describe the evolution of one particular story, "Frau Trude" (AT 334, Grimm 43), from its beginning as the single text I read in 1973 to its most recent telling as of the writing of this essay.[6] It may sound like a simple task to report how "Frau Trude" became "The Curious Girl," but it has been the most difficult writing I have yet done, since I have had to be both the academic and the performer, both the curious girl and the crone. As a folklorist, I ask myself how and why the story was learned and told and how it developed in the oral context. As a storyteller, I ask myself how the various performances shaped the tale as it was told and retold to listeners who consciously and unconsciously influenced the movement of the story.

Coming to terms with Frau Trude was a different challenge from what I was used to meeting in my academic writing: her story demanded unraveling its patterns of significance from the inside out instead of interpreting from the outside in. Like the girl in the second text of the tale, I had to discover the unknown story. So you will be able to follow what I am saying more fluidly, I print both texts in full here, one as I read it in a translation of the Grimm tales and the other a single written text of my oral variant developed over four years of performance.[7]

My task is to describe how the first text evolved into the second; to discuss the influences of my own interpretations *and* audience responses and influences; and to examine the metaphoric relationship to actual everyday life on a small scale. And I intend to have fun while doing so.

I first met Frau Trude while reading traditional tales as part of my dissertation research. I spent three years sitting on those tiny little chairs in the children's section of dozens of libraries reading through the folktale collections. When I met Frau Trude, she did not offer pleasant company. Her story enraged me because it seemed to be viciously and precisely aimed right at me. I *was* that overly curious and disobedient girl, and I did not like the fact that she was eventually overwhelmed and destroyed by the witch. It was an ugly story, but it was part of what I was studying. I cited it, put it into my dissertation statistics, and classified it according to the neat four-part scheme I used for describing folktale heroines. After that, I occasionally used it as a negative example when I was conducting interviews, but I did not find it useful in any other way. I *never* would have judged it suitable for performances.

But Frau Trude did not wish to be forgotten. Her story returned most unexpectedly, ten years after I had first read it, when I was trying to resolve another story that I had been working on. I carefully reread "Mistress Trudy" to see if I had missed something. Here is the text as I found it in 1973 and reread it again ten years later, the whole story told in two brief paragraphs.[8]

Mistress Trudy

Once upon a time there was a girl who was stubborn and inquisitive, and whenever her parents told her to do something, she'd never obey. How could she get along well? One day she said to her parents, "I've heard so much about Mistress Trudy; I'll call on her sometime. People say that her house looks queer and that there are many strange things in it. I've become quite curious." The parents strictly forbade her going there and said, "Mistress Trudy is a wicked woman, given to evil things, and if you go there, we'll disown you."

The girl paid no attention, however, to her parents' orders and went to Mistress Trudy's just the same. When she got there, Mistress Trudy asked her, "Why are you so pale?" "Oh," she answered, shaking all over, "I'm so frightened at what I've seen." "What have you seen?" "I saw a black man on your stairs." "That was a charcoal burner." "Then I saw a green man." "That was a huntsman." "Then I saw a blood-red man." "That was a butcher." "Oh, Mistress Trudy, I shuddered; I looked through the window and I didn't see you but I did see the devil with his fiery head." "Is that so!" she said. "Then you saw the witch in her proper garb. I've been waiting for you for a long time now and have longed for you. Now you shall furnish me with light." Thereupon she transformed the girl into a log and threw it in the fire, and when it was all aglow, she sat down beside it and, warming herself at it, said, "That really does give a bright light."

Not surprisingly, this unpromising story did not become part of my repertoire when I began to perform folktales in the mid-1970s. However, a few years ago when I was playing around with a story of my own that refused to resolve itself, "Frau Trude" returned unexpectedly to mind. I turned aside this intrusion, but the story refused to go away. As stubborn as the curious girl, I resisted until curiosity nudged me into rereading the Grimm text to see if there was some hidden potential I had missed.

I found nothing at first, but I decided to try retelling it as close to the text as possible to free whatever had caught my unwitting attention. Only after several tellings did I sense something in the girl's transformation by fire that had been missed in that first reading: *She gave a bright light.* I also heard Mistress Trudy's words with new ears: "I've been waiting for you for a long time now and have longed for you." With these equivocal words, the story began to develop new configurations, and after five years of retelling, it transformed itself into something quite different from the cautionary tale I had first read.

Once the story was on its new path, it continued to flow, with the theme of transformation rather than destruction as its central motivation. Frau Trude lost none of her properly menacing cronishness; she continued to be as threatening as she was in the Grimm text, but she was also willing to accept and reward the girl's curiosity and persistence instead of simply annihilating her for improper behavior.

Here is the text of my retelling as of June 18, 1990. This is a written re-creation composed specifically for this essay. I have told the tale often enough that this is an accurate artistic re-creation, if not an objective scientific rendering. It will serve our purposes in this form. This one text is representative of the many that have moved the story toward its present shape, one that has been relatively stable for the last two years. It remains, in my one mind, multitextual.

The Curious Girl

Once there was a girl who was stubborn and curious, and always disobedient to her parents. Whenever they told her to do one thing she'd do another.

Now how could a girl like that *not* get into trouble? And she did.

One day she said to her parents, "I think I'll visit Frau Trude one day. They say she lives in an interesting house full of strange things, and I'm ever so curious to see her."

Her parents protested. They said, "Frau Trude is a godless woman who does evil things, and if you go there you will be our child no longer!"

But she did not listen.

Without telling her parents, she set off through the woods one day. Soon she crossed a small stream, and when she stepped onto the other shore the woods around her seemed darker and more dismal.

As she walked along she suddenly heard a sound like thunder coming from behind her and she turned to look—and saw a dark rider on a dark horse who came roaring toward her.

She leapt aside.

When they had passed, deep darkness fell all around her and she could no longer see her way. But she continued on, following the path beneath her feet.

Soon after she heard a raging sound behind her and turned again and saw a glowing red rider on a red horse speeding toward her and she leapt aside. When they had passed the sky above became blood red.

Now she was frightened, but she continued on her way.

After some time she heard a deafening sound behind her and turned again, this time to see a brilliant white rider on a white horse flashing toward her. She threw herself out of their path. When they had passed by, bright day shone all around her and she found herself in a clearing at the very heart of the dark forest.

And there indeed was a strange house, and around it was a fence made of human bones. The curious girl was terrified, but she crept up to the house and looked in the window. There she saw the figure of a woman, all in flames but not consumed.

The girl heard a voice call her name and then bid her to enter. She stepped up to the door and slowly opened it.

When she was inside she saw only an old woman sitting beside the fireplace. This was Frau Trude, who spoke to her politely:

"Why are you so pale and shaking, my dear?" she asked.

"Because I've seen such strange things!"

"Oh? What have you seen?"

"As I was walking I saw a dark rider on a dark horse."

"That was only my Dark Night."

"Then I saw a red rider on a red horse."

"That was my Red Morning."

"But then there was a white rider on a white horse."

"Yes, that was my Bright Day. And what else did you see, my dear?"

"Oh, then I looked in your window, Frau Trude, but I didn't see you at all—I saw a woman all in flames."

"Did you, now! Then you have seen the witch in her true form. I have been waiting for you and longing for you. You will burn brightly for me."

And so saying, Frau Trude turned the girl into a log and threw the log on her fire. As the fire blazed up she sat down next to it to warm herself and said, "Indeed, it *does* burn brightly."

Suddenly a shower of sparks leapt out of the fire and into the air. Frau Trude leapt up, and changed the sparks into a fiery bird, and then she caught that bird.

"Clever girl! But you'll never get away from me! You will remain a bird forever and my servant to all eternity—unless you can fulfill my bargain: If you can tell me one story that I've never heard before, I'll let you go. If you cannot, you will be in my power forever."

"That's not fair," replied the girl who was now a bird. "You know many more stories than I do."

"That is true," said the old woman. "So I'll give you all the time you need to learn more. Return to me when you're ready. I will be waiting for you."

The girl flew away in the shape of a bird. She thought of all the languages she could speak now, knowing that the birds understand the speech of all living things. And so she began to wander in the world, flying everywhere.

She went to the east and to the west, north and south, and everywhere she learned more stories. She spoke to the trees and to all green growing things, to the birds and all others who could fly, and to all creatures who could creep, walk, leap, or swim. And she wandered to villages and towns and cities, learning stories from everyone who lived there.

A long time had passed and the girl had become a woman, still wandering in the shape of a bird.

One day Frau Trude heard a strange song outside her house in the heart of the dark forest. She went out to see, and found a fiery bird singing from the tree nearest her window.

"Ah, it's you," she said. "I've been waiting. Have you brought me a story?"

"Yes, I'm ready now," the woman who was a bird said boldly. "I have all the stories in the world to tell you!"

"Good," Frau Trude answered. "I haven't heard a fine tale for a long time. Begin."

And so she told Frau Trude all the stories she'd learned from all of creation. Some were short and some long, some were plain and others fancy, but they all carried the truth in them.

When she finished, Frau Trude gazed at her warmly and exclaimed, "Excellent stories, and well told too . . . But I knew every one of them long before you were born!"

The woman who was a bird stood speechless. She had no more stories. None at all. But when she opened her mouth to cry out, words came out on their own, first one at a time and then running together like a small river:

"Once there was a girl who was stubborn and curious, and always disobedient to her parents. Whenever they told her to do one thing she'd do another. . . . "

On the surface of the text alone, the two stories seem quite the opposite in their resolution. "Frau Trude" is a stark cautionary tale that warns of the dangers of disobedience and curiosity for girls, but "The Curious Girl" rewards these same risks. Not only does the girl survive and mature, but she becomes empowered as well. How could these two stories be related in meaning at all? There must have been something I was missing.[9]

I reread the story as I had first encountered it to check on the wording and to see its relative situation in the Grimm collection. The surrounding stories are similar and might have colored my initial reading. "Mistress Trudy" is placed between "The Godfather" and "Godfather Death." Their similarities were as fascinating to me as if they had been musical variations on a theme. In all three tales, the protagonists must confront an overwhelming force that threatens their existence.

In the first story, "The Godfather," a father sets out to find a godfather for his child and meets a stranger who gives him a bottle of magical water that cures death. For no particular reason, the man decides to visit the stranger and meets objects on the way up that he does not understand and that the godfather later lies about. When the man insists that he *has* seen the godfather through the keyhole, wearing horns, he is yelled at and runs away in fear.

This dissatisfying story is a badly garbled variant of "Godfather Death," which comes right after "Mistress Trudy." While "The God-father" lacks clear motivation and certain resolution, "Godfather Death" is strong in each of these: a son is promised as a godchild to Death, who, when the child has become a man, gives him water that cures any illness. The godchild misuses the water twice: first, when he cures a poor man out of compassion and is warned by Death, and second, when he cures for more selfish reasons and is carried off by Death.

"Frau Trude," or "Mistress Trudy," presents yet another variation on the theme of supernatural relationships. The girl is not promised to anyone by her parents—in fact, they try to warn her against unholy alliances. She goes out of her own curiosity. She does not receive any magical objects either, which is appropriate given her more tenuous relationship: she's an intruder, not a godchild. In contrast to the first man, she knows what she is doing and is definitely more adventurous:

"I think I'll go and see her one of these days," she tells her parents. The man in "The Godfather" simply muddles through with no plans. Frau Trude is also a much more formidable opponent than is the silly godfather, who lies about the objects on the stairs and who yells at the man, "Damn you, that's not true," but allows him to escape. Frau Trude's answers are deceptively more gentle and patient than his—and her quarry does not get away.

In the more forceful "Godfather Death," the deadly godfather, unlike Frau Trude, is initially a mentor who teaches his godchild how to cure illnesses. This motif revealed new possibilities for the crone in "Mistress Trudy." It is another negative example of what happens when one challenges the mentor before being ready to do so. The silly man in the first story gets away because the godfather is even sillier. The other two are not so lucky. They both meet death in the form of fire because of their arrogant disobedience. She is turned into a log and thrown on the fire, while he is taken to a dark cave where he watches as his candle of life is extinguished.

In this trio of stories, all three of the characters are disobedient, but the first is so incompetent he does not even know where he is going or why, while the last one is too calculating and ambitious. By contrast, the girl is self-motivated but not greedy, and she does not run away. Nor does she have her flame extinguished. Quite the opposite—the fire blazes up.

What caught my unconscious attention was the fiery nature of this girl. Unlike the two men, she single-mindedly seeks out her antagonist against the advice of her cautious parents. She is disobedient, and she is looking for trouble. But then other folktale heroines are also disobedient. Snow White can not resist her witch either, nor does Sleeping Beauty evade the spindle. Cinderella sneaks off to the ball three times and returns home, where she *lies* cleverly to protect herself. It is not difficult to find all sorts of heroines who are disobedient; therefore, I reasoned, it must be the girl's particular form of defiance that dooms her in the Grimm text, since disobedience is so widespread. She is, after all, stubbornly set on visiting "a godless woman who does evil things"—a crone, a witch, an old woman who is too intriguing to miss.

I remember that the "witch" in our neighborhood lived right across the street. She wore strange clothing and kept a "jungle" in her yard that she watered at dawn and at midnight (or so my sister and I believed). My mother told us to leave her alone. Once we sneaked into her "garden" when she was away to see if there were any curious things there, but we escaped safely before she returned and so avoided

298 / Kay F. Stone

being turned into logs. We never went there on Halloween, nor did any of our friends. I have since discovered that most of my students have had at least one witch in their neighborhood. Most of us have. One year a student went back to interview the kids on the block where she had grown up and discovered that *their* witch was her own mother. These women were fascinating, even if they were pitiful. They excited my curiosity when I fell into the field of folklore. Witches have never been like anyone else we know. They might even live "in an interesting house full of strange things," as did the woman across the street from me. Frau Trude lives.

One reason she lives is to warn that curiosity is just as dangerous as our mothers tried to tell us. If we take her warning as a challenge, we might learn something. Maybe.

It is easy to be distracted by the negative "noise" about the dangers of curiosity in "Mistress Trudy" and to read it as the cautionary tale it was meant to be. What came through to me between the lines was something else, though. Even when my conscious mind furiously rejected the apparent destruction of the curious girl, something of her determined inquisitiveness remained in my mind for several years. Certainly, it was related to my own mulish insistence on disobeying my mother whenever she said (with some frequency) "Girls don't do that," whatever "that" happened to be at the moment.[10] The angry child in me recognized the girl in the story who did not allow her parents to subdue her curiosity, even though they threatened her with abandonment.

But she, unlike me, did not sneak into the witch's domain unseen. She arrived at Frau Trude's strange house in broad daylight after a harrowing night journey, pale and shaking but still able to open the door, enter, and respond to Frau Trude's questions. Frau Trude's ironic words, "I've been waiting for you a long time now and have longed for you," herald her violent transformation by fire. She is told she will burn brightly, and indeed she does. That caught my attention.

In fact, it was the girl's enchantment into a block of wood that sparked my interest when I reread the tale. I was able to see her test by fire as an elemental encounter, and once my mind was open to this more positive possibility, the other elements began to present themselves as I began to reexperience the story and eventually to try retelling it. As the story evolved, the curious girl passed through fire as a log and then a shower of sparks, through air as a bird, through earth as a wild hare, and through water as a fish. Through these metamorphoses, she experienced the sacrifice of her ego-self, which in the end gave her even greater power—freedom over herself as a fuller human being. In finding the unknown story—her own—she connects herself with all of the other stories she has brought back for Frau Trude, her teacher.

In this new light, the Grimm tale seemed to me not so much disagreeable as unfinished, open-ended. Storytellers usually understand the open-ended nature of traditional tales as well as folklorists do, because such flexibility keeps any individual story alive by giving the teller enough room between the lines to convert old into new.

The conversion of the story did not happen all at once. Frau Trude was not an easy woman to live with, and I did not want to risk her ire by mistelling her story. I was very cautious when I related it publicly for the first time, opening with the Grimm text word-for-word (it was short enough for me to memorize easily) and then re-forming the story into my version of "Curious Girl." My intention was to emphasize the negative contrast of the two stories, one which I viewed as "bad" and the other as "good." I continued to recount the stories in this way to many different audiences, listening for their responses. Gradually the story began to change.

It was (and still is) a surprise to me that my senses of the two seemingly opposite tales started to grow toward each other, until they became two sides of a coin rather than two separate coins. Variations on a theme. Eventually, they united into a single text, so that the beginning of "Curious Girl" came to be phrased in words echoing from "Frau Trude." In this form the story of "Curious Girl" continues to unfold.

What continued to push the story into new growth was my own curiosity. I wanted to know what happened to the girl after she was thrown into the fire. How did she survive, and why? I knew there was something about to happen next, but I did not know what it would be. Every time I told "The Curious Girl," I learned at least one thing that I had not noticed before, and each thing that I learned gave its energy to my next telling. In this way, the story grew on its own, and it became easier and easier to tell as I myself became more willing to enter through Frau Trude's door.

When I first began using it in Winnipeg schools, the girl went through various transformations that represented fire, air, water, and earth. This got to be very elaborate. After her fiery rebirth, she was turned into a fire-bird by Frau Trude, and as she tried to escape in water, she became a fish, and finally she was a rabbit burrowing into warm earth. She was offered her own shape back if she could tell a story that Frau Trude had never heard. This challenge has become the center of the story for me and for many of my listeners, and gradually it allowed a clear focus that burned away extraneous material. Four particular audiences have had a direct impact on the continued unfolding of the story.

Here is the first. I spent a week in late September of 1987 in Quebec visiting a friend and her nine-year-old daughter. One night she invited the neighbors and their children, and we had a warm candlelit evening where *everyone* told a story. Some told stories they had read, some reported stories they had experienced directly, and I told "The Curious Girl." When I had finished, my friend's daughter said, "Why does that girl have to turn into all those animals?" As I pondered her question, it became clear that the transformations into the four elements were indeed unwieldy and unnecessary. It seemed I was becoming a fundamentalist: "Now get all four of those elements in there or this won't work."

So I stopped telling "Curious Girl" for a while and let my bird fly to a new place and learn fresh stories. I sat in my thinking chair with a beer and a cigarette for several weeks, pondering the nine-year-old's question, which I rephrased: "Why do you [adults] make your lives so complicated?" Eventually, I came to understand that the elements of the girl's transformation did not all have to be expressed explicitly. I began to try out other connections, until only the fiery sparks and the fire-bird remained explicit. Water and earth were implied when she stepped over the stream to enter the forest, and earth manifested itself in the trembling that preceded the coming of the three riders. The story had begun to simplify itself, to become more lucid and transparent.

The second experience came in May of 1988. I was attending the annual meeting of the Folklore Studies Association of Canada, and I was also doing one performance for an audience largely of adults in Windsor, Ontario.[11] I stood in front of fifty-odd strangers in a church basement, where they had spent the last hour and a half listening to folk music. They were all scattered about on those unpleasant folding metal chairs that clank when shifted. I chose to tell them "The Curious Girl" because the story was ready to go again, primed for further transformation. As I aimed the words at that particular group of listeners that night, a few new phrases came into the story, but the most memorable change came at the end, when they applauded spontaneously *before* I had spoken Frau Trude's final words in which she acknowledges the unknown story and frees the bird. They responded at the point when the curious girl says the first words of her own story, which repeat the opening lines of the text. At first I was surprised and a bit concerned, wondering if they were anxious to get me off stage. Then I understood the open-ended potential of such a conclusion and its powerful circular movement. The oral version now ends here,[12] bringing readers/hearers more directly into the act of creation by leaving the full resolution in their hands. The creative ambivalence matches that of the Grimm tale and leaves room for further re-creation. Recreation is play, and playing is both wonderfully serious and imaginative.

In October of 1988, I told the story as part of an American Folklore Society panel, "Women and Power." My function on the panel was to provide a direct example of what we had all been talking about, and "The Curious Girl" seemed an ideal choice since both the girl and the crone were powerful women. Five of us sat at the table in the front of the room offering our varied presentations on women in life and in literature to an attentive audience composed largely of women. They were alert. Since I was the last speaker, the discussion that followed our panel began with responses to the story. Many centered their remarks on the girl's belated recognition of the power of her own life history, a topic that was related to the contributions of other panel members as well. Participants also acknowledged that telling one's own tale is only the beginning and that true freedom comes when one's own stories connect with all those from others. It was also suggested that any who fail to go beyond ego-identity would remain in service to the inner crone instead of growing into equality with her. This could be rephrased in elegant Jungian terms, but little would be added.

The contributions of this audience deepened my own perception of the story instead of effecting more explicit changes. For example, we talked about the story as an academic metaphor; academics have been trained to look into the window and describe what is seen. Often our academic vision is as limited as that of the curious girl: what is observed through the window is only one aspect of what is there potentially and actually. In this case, it is a woman surrounded by flames but not consumed by them. This image has strengthened itself in my mind as a result of telling the tale to this particular audience. I have also *become,* on occasion, the woman in flames.

Later that year in Winnipeg, "The Curious Girl" was told back to me by a ten-year-old boy at an informal gathering of Winnipeg storytellers. The dozen of us were sitting around in a casual circle in a corner of the pleasant lobby of Lion's Place, where we meet twice a month and share stories informally. A few of the adults occasionally bring older children, who participate fully. David had heard "The Curious Girl" told once by me and another time by his mother. At this time (1988) in the story's life history, the girl was given her own shape back before she went off to learn the stories of the world. When David came to that point in the story, he had her retain the bird shape as she learned her stories and transformed her only when she returned and succeeded in telling her final story. This simple alteration was much more powerful in motivation and so spontaneous that both he and his mother were certain I had told it that way. I do now. Only by telling her story can she become fully herself again, find her own true shape. No more crash diets.

This story has grown as I have told it to these audiences and others, but it has also evolved in response to my own changing personal context, my own ripening perspectives as I have aged and grown. I am the mother of a very curious daughter myself, and I understand that mothers have every right to fear for their adventurous daughters and even to threaten them with all sorts of frightening things out of love, however misguided. This understanding softens the mother's warning in my telling of the tale. She cautions her daughter about dangerous curiosity, but she does not threaten her with abandonment.

I also know fully well that one cannot be a mother without also being a witch at times, as I know from having become both mother and crone in the years since my first encounter with Frau Trude. The mother's warning *and* Frau Trude's challenging of the girl contribute to her unexpected transformations. What was, to me, implicit in the Grimm cautionary tale comes into full bloom in the retold one. The "good" and "bad" mothers become one, both protecting *and* testing the girl who wants to find out about the world outside.

I have also learned that change always brings trouble of one sort or another. It is very tempting for us as women to remember how we have been cautioned in the past and to turn away from our challenges—the unknown forest, the strange riders who cause the earth to tremble, the questioning old woman—as we meet them metaphorically in our own experiences.

It is easier, too, to accept the dualistic perceptions we have been surrounded with for years and years and to sort people and experiences into positive and negative, good and bad, white and black. In this scenario, Frau Trude is truly a "godless woman who does evil things," and the girl is tragically disobedient. As I said earlier, when I first began to tell the story, I split it into "good" and "bad" versions with the intention of contrasting the two. As my own perceptions moved away from dualism, however, I found I no longer needed to split the stories. They became one for me as I came to accept the girl's treatment in *both* versions as challenge rather than as punishment, as transformation rather than as defeat. In this way the girl's path to her enlightenment burns brightly before her. Even in the Grimm tale, the potential for transformation is obvious.

It is *not* obvious, then, that "Frau Trude" can be seen only as a cautionary tale. This wisdom came to me from telling the tale rather than thinking about it and from listening to what others had to say rather than struggling through intellectual analysis. I am *not* suggesting that analysis is not useful, but thinking by itself did not solve the mystery of the woman in flames who throws the girl into the fire. I had to experience her much more directly to feel the fire. This story more than any other I have told has taught me to risk losing my shape (in this case my shape as an academic) to find out what is beyond the fire. I *am* curious.

In the spring of 1990, I finished this essay yet again and sent it off to Jo Radner for her editorial response, and when I read the concluding words of her letter, they seemed to capture my intent so clearly that I include them here: "Tellers can go all over the world learning other people's stories and they can tell them well; but the story they *need* to tell (to themselves at least, if not the public) is the only one they have: their own. That is the base from which we really learn to understand the languages/lives of other creatures; the way we save our lives from the strangers who would consume us for their own purposes."

While writing and rewriting this essay over the past three years, I have sensed an unspoken, continuing dialogue between the curious girl and the crone as they retell their stories to one another. Because it *has* been a dialogue rather than two monologues, the story of the story has grown, and I have been drawn into the fire. Relevant parts of my own story have presented themselves as part of the dialogue in ways that are illuminating rather than self-indulgent (ah yes, a very fine tightrope to walk).

This essay has frustrated me more than any other I have written. I understand the power of *telling* stories all too well, which has made me uncomfortable with putting them down in print for an unknown audience. I sit here at my modern writing machine on a rainy night in June imagining the curious girl typing out all the stories she had learned and preparing to send them off to Frau Trude in the morning mail. If she had done that, mailed them off instead of telling them, that girl would still be a bird to this very day. As a writer, I find that a sobering thought.

On the positive side, my attempt to set down this story's story coherently in print has compelled me to look at the tale from very different angles and to sketch the different shapes it has taken as it has moved along. In doing so, I have become more aware of the essences of character and action and motivation that have moved *me* along: the dynamic union of negative and positive forces that bring about metamorphoses; the dangers and the ecstasies of deep curiosity; the punishments and rewards of freedom-seeking; the absolute necessity of listening to the stories of others as well the necessity of telling our own as part of the ocean of stories. And I wonder: Is it possible to ignite oneself without being consumed?

Notes

This writing, as all others, has had many transformations from conception to birth. It would never have come into being without the responses of Jo Radner, Joan Walter, Wendy Porter, Carolyn Hample, Rubena Sinha, Cathryn Wellner, and Marvyne Jenoff. I owe the title to Keith Louise Fulton, head of the women's studies program at the University of Winnipeg.

1. See, for example (in chronological order), "Things Walt Disney Never Told Us," in *Women and Folklore,* ed. Claire R. Farrer (Austin: University of Texas Press, 1975), 42–50; "Fairytales for Adults," in *Folklore on Two Continents: Essays in Honor of Linda Dégh,* ed. Nikolai Burlakoff and Carl Lindahl (Bloomington, Ind.: Trickster Press, 1980), 40–67; "Misuses of Enchantment," in *Women's Folklore, Women's Culture,* ed. Rosan A. Jordan and Susan J. Kalčik (Philadelphia: University of Pennsylvania Press, 1985), 125–45; and "Three Transformations of Snow White," in *The Brothers Grimm and the Folktale,* ed. J. McGlathery (Urbana: University of Illinois Press, 1988), 52–65.

2. Most of those I talked to were females, since it was difficult to find males who remembered specific "fairy tales," if they could recall reading them at all. Transcripts of these interviews with individuals from ages eleven to sixty-eight and with small groups (three to five girls) from ages eleven to seventeen are in my *Romantic Heroines in Anglo-American Folk and Popular Literature* (Ph.D. dissertation, Indiana University, 1975), appendix X. I continue to ask because I am still curious: What stories do *you* recall, and why do they continue to haunt you?

3. See, for example (in chronological order), "To Ease the Heart: Traditional Storytelling," *National Storytelling Journal* (Winter 1984): 3–6; "Macht mit mir, was ihr wollt" [Do with Me What You Will], *Die Frau in Märchen,* ed. Sigrid Früh and Rainer Wehse (Kassel: Röth, 1985), 164–73; "I Never Told This Story to Anyone Before," *National Storytelling Journal* (Fall 1985): 3–7; and "Oral Narration in Contemporary North America," in *Fairy Tales and Society: Illusion, Allusion, and Paradigm,* ed. Ruth Bottigheimer (Philadelphia: University of Pennsylvania Press, 1986), 13–31.

4. She is most deservedly well known for her classic study of Hungarian traditional narrators in *Folktales and Society,* rev. ed. (Bloomington: Indiana University Press, 1989). She has continued to write challenging articles on

the märchen genre as well as on most other narrative forms, such as legends and jokes, and is particularly interested in the continuing power of traditional materials in contemporary urban culture.

5. Linda Dégh, "The Variant and the Folklorization Process in Märchen and Legend," *D'un conte . . . à l'autre* (Paris: Editions du CNRS, 1990), 169.

6. AT 334 is the classification for the tale type called "Household of the Witch" in Antti Aarne and Stith Thompson, *The Types of the Folktale: A Classification and Bibliography*, Folklore Fellows Communications No. 184 (Helsinki: Academia Scientiarum Fennica, 1973). Grimm 43 identifies this as the 43rd story in the full Grimm collection of 210 tales. See note 8 for translations.

7. While I am familiar with current attempts to transcribe oral texts from taped retellings using careful ethnopoetic style, I have chosen not to try any of these methods meant to re-create an "authentic" oral voice, since I am recomposing a printed form of the told story. Every time I tell it, I respond to the unique context of the audience. Since this audience—you—will be reading it rather than hearing it, I put it down with this in mind.

8. I first read "Frau Trude" ("Mistress Trudy," "Dame Trudy," or "Mother Trudy" in other translations) in *The Grimms' German Folk Tales,* trans. Francis P. Magoun, Jr., and Alexander H. Krappe (Carbondale: Southern Illinois University Press, 1960), 157; the text is reprinted here by permission of Southern Illinois University Press. I prefer the more flowing words of two translations that appeared after my dissertation was completed: Ralph Mannheim, *Grimms' Tales for Young and Old: The Complete Stories* (New York: Doubleday, 1977), 151–52; and Jack Zipes, trans. *The Complete Fairy Tales of the Brothers Grimm,* 2 vols. (New York: Bantam Books, 1988), 173–74.

9. The suggestions of Susan Gordon and Jo Radner were most helpful in guiding me back to possible influences. I carefully reread Jo's commentary on decoding in Joan N. Radner and Susan S. Lanser, "The Feminist Voice: Strategies of Coding in Folklore and Literature," *Journal of American Folklore* 100, no. 398 (1987): 412–25. Decoding in these terms does not apply to "Frau Trude," which is a male-translated text of a male-collected tale based on a male-written poem. Still, it was useful to review my own conscious and unconscious retellings in light of decoding feminist messages.

10. My mother's memories of my childhood are quite different and perhaps even more accurate than mine, if such things can be measured. She recalls *encouraging* me to be adventurous, while I recall making her the witch in my dreams.

11. My performance was for the Old Sandwich Song Circle in Windsor, Ontario, on May 28, 1988.

12. It seemed to me that this conclusion was less effective in the written version, and I had initially put Frau Trude's words back in, but Jo Radner felt that the coda was not needed.

Notes on the Contributors

Barbara A. Babcock is a professor of English and of comparative cultural and literary studies at the University of Arizona. She has also taught at the University of Texas and Brown University, where she was director of the Pembroke Center for Teaching and Research on Women. Trained in compara tive literature and anthropology at the University of Chicago, Babcock has published widely in folklore, symbolic anthropology, literary criticism, and feminist studies. In addition to critical and feminist theory, her principle research interests are modes of reflexivity and inversion, ethnoaesthetics and folk art (in particular the art and experience of Pueblo potter Helen Cordero), and the work of women anthropologists in the Native American Southwest. Her publications include *The Reversible World: Essays in Symbolic Inversion* (1978), *Signs about Signs: The Semiotics of Self-Reference* (1980), *The Pueblo Storyteller: Development of a Figurative Ceramic Tradition* (1986), *Daughters of the Desert: Women Anthropologists and the Native American Southwest, 1880–1980* (1988); and *Pueblo Mothers and Children: Essays by Elsie Clews Parsons, 1915–1924* (1991).

Angela Bourke is a visiting professor (1992–93) at Harvard University's Department of Celtic Languages and Literatures, on leave from the Department of Modern Irish, University College Dublin, Ireland, where she also directs the M.Phil. in Irish Studies Program. She has been a visiting professor at the University of Minnesota at Minneapolis St. Paul, a visiting research associate at Oberlin College, and the associate director of the Yeats International Summer School, Sligo, Ireland. Bourke has lectured widely in Europe and the United States on Irish tradition and women's verbal art. She is the author of articles and short stories in Irish and English and (as Angela Partridge) of *Caoineadh na dTrí Muire: Téama na Páise i bhFilíocht Bhéil na Gaeilge* (The Lament of the Three Marys: The Crucifixion in Irish Oral Poetry).

Susan Gordon is a professional storyteller from Ijamsville, Maryland, who does much of her work in therapeutic settings. She has designed programs of storytelling and related activities for such groups as women jail inmates, the elderly, emotionally handicapped children, adolescent boys in residential treatment, and survivors and perpetrators of sexual abuse. She also performs as a member of Voices in the Glen, a Washington, D.C., storytelling group, and teaches storytelling.

Cheryl L. Keyes is an ethnomusicologist and folklorist. She is assistant professor of folk studies in the Department of Modern Languages and Intercultural Studies at Western Kentucky University, where she teaches courses on African-American folklife and music, American traditional song, folklore genres, urban folklore, and world folk music. She has conducted research in Mali, West Africa, on traditional music and verbal art. She has also done research in New York City and Detroit on African-American urban music and is currently working on a manuscript on rap music.

Janet L. Langlois is an associate professor in the English Department and the director of the Folklore Archive at Wayne State University. She has published *Belle Gunness, the Lady Bluebeard* (1985) and articles in *Contemporary Legend, Canadian Folklore Canadien, Journal of American Folklore, Journal of Folklore Research,* and *Signs.* She is currently working on projects concerning urban theory and folk narrative.

Susan S. Lanser is a professor of English, comparative literature, and women's studies at the University of Maryland. She has written two books, *The Narrative Act: Point of View in Prose Fiction* (1981) and *Fictions of Authority: Women Writers and Narrative Voice* (1992), as well as essays on feminist criticism, women writers, women's studies, and literary theory. She is currently engaged in two projects, one studying the relationship between eighteenth-century women's literary theories and their social politics, the other exploring romantic friendship and lesbian identity from 1740 to 1820.

Joanne B. Mulcahy is affiliated with the Northwest Writing Institute at Lewis and Clark College in Portland, Oregon, where she teaches folklore, anthropology, and gender studies. Before going to Oregon to serve as director of the Oregon Folk Arts Program, she worked in Alaska as an anthropologist and an advocate for women. While working as program coordinator for the Kodiak Women's Resource Center from 1979–81, she wrote a series of articles about women's lives and the arts and ethnic identity of Kodiak's Native people. She is currently writing a life history of Mary Petersen, a Native Alutiiq traditional healer.

Linda Pershing is an assistant professor in women's studies and the Human Diversity Program at the State University of New York at Albany. Her principal areas of interest are feminist folklore theory; the intersection of gender, race, and class as they are expressed through folklore performance;

and material culture. She is co-editor of *Feminist Theory and the Study of Folklore* and is working on a book about the Peace Ribbon that was tied around the Pentagon in 1985, examining the ways in which women's fabric arts became a vehicle for participants' social and political critique of the nuclear arms race.

Joan N. Radner teaches folklore, storytelling, Celtic studies, and English and Anglo-Irish literature as a professor at the American University in Washington, D.C. Her publications include *Fragmentary Annals of Ireland* (1978), *Irish Drama 1900–1980* (1989), and articles on early Irish and Welsh history and literature, modern Irish folklore, the folklore of the deaf community, and women's folklore.

Polly Stewart has been teaching folklore, world mythology, and Chaucer at Salisbury (Maryland) State University since 1973. She directed or co-directed the Eastern Shore Folklife Festival (1976), the Maryland Folklife Festival (1978), and the Delmarva Folklife Festival (1983) and conducted fieldwork for festivals in Utah and Idaho (1979, 1980, and 1981). Beyond public-sector folklife programming, her folklore research interests include folksong, verbal style in folk narrative, and relations of regionalism to local history.

Kay F. Stone has taught classes in folklore, mythology, and storytelling since 1972 at the University of Winnipeg in Manitoba, Canada. She has been a performing storyteller for almost that long, having been tricked into it by a teacher who attended a workshop on folktales. She has written several articles on women and folktales, folktales as transformational literature, and storytelling as a continuing art form with powerful potential.

Margaret R. Yocom is an associate professor of English at George Mason University, where she teaches folklore and American studies. Her fieldwork has taken her home to her Pennsylvania German family, away to the Inuit of northwestern Alaska, and then to New England. Her publications on feminist and family folklore have appeared in *Western Folklore* and *Southern Folklore* and in several books of essays. She is the assistant editor of *Ugiuvangmiut Quliapyuit*, a collection of King Island Inuit folktales, and is currently writing about the folk art of the Richard family of Rangeley, Maine.

UNIVERSITY OF ILLINOIS PRESS
1325 SOUTH OAK STREET
CHAMPAIGN, ILLINOIS 61820-6903
WWW.PRESS.UILLINOIS.EDU